Policy Sciences and Population

Policy Sciences and Population

Edited by

Warren F. Ilchman
Harvard University

Harold D. Lasswell
Yale University

John D. Montgomery
Harvard University

Myron Weiner
Massachusetts Institute
of Technology

Lexington Books
D.C. Heath and Company
Lexington, Massachusetts
Toronto   London

Library of Congress Cataloging in Publication Data

Main entry under title:

Policy sciences and population.

    1. Population policy—Addresses, essays, lectures. 2. Policy sciences—Addresses, essays, lectures. 3. Underdeveloped areas—Population—Addresses, essays, lectures. I. Ilchman, Warren Frederick.
HB871.P625   301.31   75-1586
ISBN 0-669-99358-1

Copyright © 1975 by D.C. Heath and Company.

All rights reserved. No part of this publication may be reproduced or transmitted in any form or by any means, electronic or mechanical, including photocopy, recording, or any information storage or retrieval system, without permission in writing from the publisher.

Published simultaneously in Canada.

Printed in the United States of America.

International Standard Book Number: 0-669-99358-1

Library of Congress Catalog Card Number: 75-1586

Contents

Part I	General Papers	
	Introduction to Part I *Roger Revelle*	3
Chapter 1	**Population Knowledge and Fertility Policies** *Warren F. Ilchman*	15
Chapter 2	**Internal Migration Policies: Purposes, Interests, Instruments, Effects** *Myron Weiner*	65
Chapter 3	**Planning to Cope: Administrative Consequences of Rapid Population Growth** *John D. Montgomery*	95
Chapter 4	**Population Change and Policy Sciences: Proposed Workshops on Reciprocal Impact Analysis** *Harold D. Lasswell*	117
Part II	Country Studies	
	Introduction to Part II: The Importance of Context in Population Policy Analysis *David C. Korten*	139
Chapter 5	**Growth Centers and Primacy in Kenya** *Clay G. Wescott*	149
Chapter 6	**Government Policies and Interests in Nigerian Migration** *Paulina Kofoworola Makinwa*	171
Chapter 7	**Migration Policies and the Shaping of Sudanese Society** *G.A. Balamoan*	193

Chapter 8	Migration and Fertility in Indonesia *Mayling Oey*	217
Chapter 9	Relations of Production and Fertility Levels: The Case of Northeast Brazil *Maria Helena T. Henriques Lerda*	241
Chapter 10	Incentives for Family Limitations and Sterilization in India *Devendra K. Kothari*	253
Chapter 11	Structure and Decisions in the American Family Planning Program *Korbin Liu*	269
Chapter 12	Organizing for Population Change in Malaysia *Zakaria Haji Ahmad and Siew-Nyat Chin*	281
	Index	299
	About the Contributors	307
	About the Editors	309

Policy Sciences and Population

Part I:
General Papers

Introduction to Part I

Roger Revelle

No man can foretell the future: prophetic ability is a gift from heaven that does not come to ordinary human beings. But the essence of public policy is that it is a step into the future—an attempt to attain desired goals by influencing what will happen. The thesis of this book is that a better approximation to a desired future will be achieved if the formation and carrying out of public policies can be illuminated through scientific understanding.

Our focus is on population policies—the policies of government that are intended to influence or respond to changes in the size, geographical distribution or demographic characteristics of a nation's population. We are mainly concerned with two kinds of population-influencing policies—those intended to affect the people's fertility behavior, that is, the number of births, and those affecting migration within the country or across its borders.

Policies may be intended to influence population variables either directly or indirectly. Providing family planning services or legalizing abortion may have direct effects on the number of births. Decreasing tax exemptions or restricting government housing to families with a small number of children may have indirect effects. Other policies with non-population-related objectives such as inheritance laws, social security pensions, and minimum wage laws for urban workers may have unintended effects on fertility or migration. Population-responsive policies, such as increased appropriations for education and health services to meet the needs of rapidly growing numbers of children, may, under the right conditions, result in changes of fertility behavior, and thus can be population-influencing as well as population-responsive.

This book is the first outcome of a continuing faculty-graduate student seminar on "The Policy Sciences and Population" sponsored by the Harvard Center for Population Studies beginning in the academic year 1973-74.

The first four chapters represent the contributions of faculty members to the creation of a framework of application of the policy sciences to problems of population policy. In the following eight chapters, graduate students from different countries examine available data on past or present population policies of their countries in the light of this framework. Both the faculty and student contributions are intended to illuminate the needs for the development of criteria for data gathering and of methods for obtaining and using data for future policy purposes. These will be given special emphasis as the seminar continues in future years.

Harold Lasswell has defined five scientific tasks for the guidance and analysis of public policy. What are the value goals to which a policy is addressed? What are the past and present trends towards the realization of these goals? What social conditions and processes account for the direction and intensity of these trends? What projections of the most probable future developments can be made? And what policy alternatives are likely to achieve most in reaching the desired goals? In approaching these questions, the scientist's task is to assist in attaining the objectives of public policy through the control rather than the forecasting of future events. The policy scientist can help in designing strategies by which goals can be realized. Even more important, he can help in the modification and strengthening of public policies through the systematic analysis of new information as the future unfolds.

Lasswell has drawn a conceptual map of the social processes in which policies are embedded, in terms of *participants*, who are seeking *values* and preferred *policy outcomes* through *institutions* and the use of *resources*. In other words, who does what to whom, for what purposes, by what means, and with what effects? He believes that the fundamental object of policy should be to improve the quality of life by attainment of a higher level and wider distribution of certain basic human values: power (political participation), enlightenment (knowledge and interpretation), wealth (economic goods), well-being (safety, health, and comfort), skill (education and training), affection (intimacy and loyalty), respect (recognition and status) and rectitude (freedom and justice).

Vital public policies, like other living organisms, have a life cycle, which Lasswell divides into seven stages, called "policy outcomes":

1. Intelligence: the gathering, processing, and dissemination of information as a basis for public policy decision and private choice.
2. Promotion: the use of persuasion and other means to sharpen the perceptions and to affect the opinions of the public and of policymakers.
3. Prescription: the articulation of authoritative norms and sanctions through legislative statutes, executive decrees or administrative regulations.
4. Invocation: the initial acts of implementing a prescription through establishment of administrative structures and allocation of funds, manpower and facilities.
5. Application: the continuing processes of carrying out a policy through specific action programs.
6. Termination: the ending of a particular prescription and its application, and the adjustment of residual claims. This may occur because the policy has been ineffective, its objectives have been attained, it is no longer needed in the light of changed circumstances, or a new policy, with the same or similar objectives but which is expected to be more effective, is substituted for the old one.
7. Appraisal: the evaluation of the intended and unintended effects of a policy and the allocation of praise or blame. The stage of appraisal of one policy is often the beginning of the intelligence stage for a new one.

It is evident that our metaphor of the life cycle of a policy is only partly valid. For a population-influencing policy, information needs to be continually gathered and analyzed to guide the application of the policy throughout its lifetime; administrative organizations, the adequacy of resource allocations, and the impact of the policy on behavior patterns should be frequently appraised; and the promotion of policy objectives and programs by political leaders and opinionmakers, at all levels from the head of government to the village "influential man," should be carried out as often as possible.

Public policies in the real world have a hierarchical structure. One of the fundamental policies of most developed countries is economic growth, which is sought through a variety of secondary policies, including development of the agricultural, industrial, transportation, and other economic sectors, and also population policy intended to lower fertility and thereby to reduce dependency burdens and future labor force pressures. An overall policy to lower fertility may lead to a series of subordinate policies: family planning; more female education and improvements in the status of women; "population education" in the schools; provision of incentives for small families and disincentives for large ones; or laws regulating the age of marriage of women. A family planning policy in turn can be carried out through several specific measures: e.g., legitimation of abortion, provision of contraceptives through commercial channels, establishment of health and family planning clinics throughout the countryside, or promotion of family planning by midwives or "lady health visitors." As we descend in the policy hierarchy, policies become more specific, detailed, and experimental, and policy goals and measures become less distinguishable. Near the top of the hierarchy, a policy may be a statement of long-term intentions and goals, to be sought through different measures in the light of changing circumstances.

A similar hierarchy of "target groups"—the group of people within a society who are the object of intervention in a public policy—is suggested by Warren Ilchman. The members of each potential target group make choices based on the balance between their preferences and their resources. One task of the policymaker is to aggregate a number of these groups into a "target population" for which his limited policy resources can be most effectively used. Economies of scale may be maximized in a policy for fertility reduction if the behavioral motivations of the target population are sufficiently specific and particular to be affected by the limited resources that can be allocated to the policy. At higher levels of aggregation, broader levels of generalization about behavior may be made, but policy interventions to take account of these broader regularities may be too expensive, too time consuming, and too problematic. It may be more useful, for example, to select as the level of aggregation for a target population all married couples in a particular city, in which the wives are of reproductive age and have six or more years of education, rather than a larger group of couples in the city or the state, without regard to the wives' level of education.

A second strategy for selecting target groups is also suggested by Ilchman. These are groups "at the margin" of family size distributions or other characteristics of fertility behavior, instead of the much larger groups near the mode or the mean. In making these suggestions for limiting the size and composition of target groups, Ilchman emphasizes that population policies: to intervene in expected behavior in order to secure behavioral changes, represent the use of scarce public resources. These resources include both economic and administrative resources and the policy resources of information, authority, status and coercion. Policymakers need the kinds of knowledge about fertility behavior that will enable them to make better choices among alternative policy interventions within the limitations of their resources: Who might be the objects of intervention? What degree of change might be achieved? How much and what kind of resources can be used? What differences in the method of intervention will effect differences in the outcome? What are the costs to the objects of intervention, and the benefits to those who provide the resources for intervening?

When population policies require a trade-off between economic and political resources, the choices among policies often lie on a curve or "frontier" of economic productivity versus political feasibility. The task of the policymaker is to choose the point on this curve that is optimal at a particular time, depending upon the relative weights that must be assigned to economic and political factors.

Ilchman concludes that the best source of knowledge needed to improve decisions in fertility control policies is the record of past and present public interventions and the implications for knowledge of future ones. He believes most can be learned from tracking the policy inputs, transformations, and outcomes of policies that have been marked by conspicuous success or failure; e.g., control over access to services in Singapore on the one hand and family allowances for inducing higher natality in an Eastern European country on the other. But the myriad policies of all countries that are explicitly either pro- or anti-natalist, or that affect indirectly the calculus of parents in deciding whether to have more children, can also be profitably studied. The effects of direct and indirect policies on the economic and social determinants of fertility, on the intervening social technologies and biological determinants, and on the dependent variables of intercourse and fertility, all need to be examined. Public experiments providing incentives for lower fertility should be especially revealing. But all population policies can become a source of natural experiments in the social sciences, providing the dimensions of "how much, of what, for whom, in relation to what previous and subsequent behavior" can be measured. Collaboration between social scientists and policymakers might also be enhanced by the use of game simulation in population policy studies.

Problems of policy administration are discussed in the chapters by John D. Montgomery and David C. Korten, but from two opposite points of view,

Korten focuses on the administration of population-influencing policies, for fertility control, while Montgomery is concerned with the needs and the demands for administrative services produced by the interactions of rapid population change with other social changes, and with the responses of administrative systems to changing demands. These responses depend upon the political conversion of the needs created by rapid population change into demands, and on the potential of the administrative system to mobilize resources and to increase the services it can provide. Montgomery discusses three kinds of interactions between rapid population change and other economic and social variables: changes in the age structure of populations in urban and rural areas; comparative development or stagnation in agriculture and industry as these relate to urban and rural population change; and equal or unequal opportunities for these groups.

Montgomery shows that the administrative responses to rapid population change will be structurally different in large or small areas of high or low population density. The responses will also vary for different kinds of services. "Client-oriented" services, such as urban transportation, water supplies and sanitation, or educational systems, are more vulnerable than "area-based" services, such as radio and television broadcasting and weather forecasting. In client-based services it will often be necessary to reorganize the administrative system or to introduce new technologies in order to avoid administrative breakdown.

Montgomery suggests that in order to be able to cope with rapid population change, nations establish population analysis units to examine and analyze the need for population-responsive policies and the unintended consequences for population change of existing or contemplated policies having non-population-related objectives, such as tax and inheritance laws or investments in urban infrastructures. A central population agency is also advocated by Korten, but with the primary responsibility of programming, promoting, and coordinating a nation's population-influencing policies, particularly those aimed at lowering fertility. One function of such an agency would be to examine all government policies from the standpoint of their actual or potential effect on fertility behavior. Another would be to work with private family planning associations and commercial firms in the development of experimental programs for family planning services, and new marketing and distribution techniques for contraceptives. The agency should also call on the ministries of education, community development, industry, labor, and social welfare to establish a variety of community- and organization-based educational and distributional services. The need for a wide range of activities under the cognizance of an independent population agency may become particularly critical because of the rapidly progressing integration, in most developing countries, of family planning services with other health services within the ministries of health, and the resultant loss of concern by these ministries for separate broadly-based population responsibilities.

Underlying all the other tasks of an independent population agency is the promotion, support, and direction of population research, and its translation into knowledge that can be used both as a basis for decision by policymakers and as a guide to managers and administrators responsible for carrying out policy measures and programs.

Rapid population growth in the poor countries is among the most serious problems ever faced by human beings, because of the apparently slow but seemingly inexorable character of its consequences. As Korten says, the challenge is:

how, for the first time in human history, to bring about a planned worldwide change in a specific set of highly personal human behaviors for the long-term benefit of mankind. This is a bold undertaking, to say the least, and ... (it) is the cutting edge of social change. If the challenge is to be met it must also be at the cutting edge of the effective application of management skill and social science research.

Although the only feasible long-run solution to the problems of rapid population growth is a lowering of fertility, some of the more visible short-run costs of growth can be reduced by policies of population dispersal, aimed at holding back rural to urban migration and distributing migrants among smaller cities and towns. In discussing the political justifications of these policies, Myron Weiner points out that "it is easier to attribute many of the ills of rapidly growing cities to the daily influx of migrants than to the daily births of babies," even though, in many cases natural population increase accounts for a larger fraction of urban growth than migration. He shows that an equally powerful motive for migration-control policies, particularly at the level of local governments, is to preserve the social class and ethnic composition of a community by keeping out migrants who differ in class or ethnic background from the majority of the present inhabitants. National governments also adopt internal migration policies, designed to settle parts of their population in sparsely peopled territories and border regions, in order to consolidate or extend the government's control.

Weiner describes seven policy instruments used by governments to affect internal migration: (1) the disposition of public services in both urban and rural areas, (2) income policies in the urban areas, (3) administrative decentralization, (4) industrial location and regional development, (5) pass laws and other controls on potential migrants, (6) preferential interventions to benefit local people as against migrants, and (7) the effect of immigration policies on internal migration. He points out that governments often describe their migration policies as having other objectives, such as protection of the environment, avoiding overcrowding, reducing pollution, or minimizing hazards to the health and safety of the community. Zoning regulations by the municipal governments in the United States are a notorious example of the divergence between publicly stated and real objectives of a migration policy.

As Weiner also demonstrates, many policies that affect the distribution of populations are not intended to do so, but are chosen for other reasons. In the less developed countries, these are commonly economic development policies, designed to bring about a rapid rate of industrial growth, and they are supported by powerful interest groups that will benefit—chiefly the urban middle classes and unionized labor.

Paulina K. Makinwa has appraised the effects of policies of this kind in Nigeria since World War II. The lion's share of federal and regional governmental investments was allocated to urban areas, while only meager attention was paid to rural development. Rural incomes were drained off by the government marketing boards, which buy export crops from the farmers at prices much below their selling prices on world markets. The profits made at the expense of the farmers were mainly used for industrial investments, either directly or through grants to regional development and finance corporations, and for construction of urban infrastructures. Minimum wage laws increased the differential between rural and urban incomes for those who were employed.

These policies satisfied the interests of a powerful coalition of professionals, labor unions, and businessmen. The farmers, who form the majority of the population, were placated by introduction of free primary education throughout the rural areas. The political outcome was to keep the incumbent political parties in power. The demographic result was a vast increase in rural-to-urban migration, particularly of young male primary-school leavers, migrating to four relatively small areas: metropolitan Lagos, Port Harcourt and nearby cities in the southeast, Benin in the midwestern state, and Kano and Kaduna in the north.

The constantly swelling tide of incoming migrants has overwhelmed the urban infrastructure of Lagos, and unemployment and underemployment in all these cities has become a nightmarish problem. This is still true even today, when Nigeria, as one of the OPEC nations, is obtaining large windfall revenues from the fourfold increase in world oil prices.

Perhaps because Nigeria has such a large population, it is not dominated by one or two primate cities. A different situation prevails in Kenya, where Nairobi and Mombasa have received the brunt of rural-urban migration and have skimmed off young men from the rest of the country. Clay Wescott shows that without vigorous governmental intervention, the proportion of the country's entire urban population in these two cities will continue to increase. The primacy of Nairobi has retarded development of a large part of the country. Three-quarters of the national area has been said to be "functionally not part of the Kenya nation ... the imprint of the central government seems weak and ineffective."

To attack this problem, the government of Kenya is planning the development of a hierarchy of rural growth centers, small towns, and intermediate cities.

The latter are planned for populations of 100,000 to 200,000 by the year 2000. Even if these plans were implemented, Nairobi and Mombasa would still have three million and two million inhabitants, respectively, or nearly 20 percent of the projected population of the country. According to Wescott, stronger policies are needed, including location policies for new industries, reallocation of expenditures on urban infrastructure to smaller cities and towns, improved transport throughout the country, and administrative actions to reduce price and wage differentials between Nairobi and Mombasa and the rural areas and smaller cities. Whether these measures can be formulated and carried out will depend on what Myron Weiner calls the "hard realities of politics," that is, on the perceived needs of the coalition of interest groups that control the government and for which it is the spokesman. Some groups would benefit and others would lose from these policies, and the outcome will be determined by the division of political resources among them.

Unlike internal migration policies, which have developed only recently in response to the rapid growth of large or primate cities in many countries, policies to influence or control migration across national boundaries have a long history. G.A. Balamoan has studied the impact of these policies on the formation of population and society in the Sudan. He shows that about 70 percent of the approximately twenty million present inhabitants of the Sudan immigrated into the country during this century, or are the children of such migrants. Prior to the formation of the Republic of the Sudan in 1956, British and French colonial policies were of critical importance in promoting this migration and in shaping its composition and direction. Similar pro-immigration policies have been continued by all the successive national governments of the Republic of the Sudan since independence. Balamoan estimates that between 1910 and 1920 the net annual increase of population in the Sudan was around six percent, corresponding to a doubling of population size in less than twelve years. The rate of increase declined after 1920, to between 3 and 4 percent a year from 1950 to 1960. The population has probably again grown more rapidly in the past few years owing to immigration from the Niger-Senegal regions of the Sahel.

The long tradition of encouraging immigration into the Sudan may have begun with the sharp decline of population during the Mahdist regime (1880-1898), when the country lost perhaps as much as 80 percent of its people. The tradition still persists that the Sudan is underpopulated, and there has been no policy aimed at human fertility control, although, since 1970, some official support has been given to family planning activities, for reasons of maternal and child welfare.

Balamoan has focused on the purposes of colonial and Sudanese migration policies, the interests supporting and opposing them, the types of policy instruments employed, and the effectiveness of the policies in inducing migration of different ethnic groups. He discusses also the economic and social consequences of the enormous influx of populations from sub-Saharan and tropical Africa, including the problems of ethnic conflict and mixing, and of employment and economic development. Ethnic conflicts have persisted in spite of the "melting pot" policy which has been followed in an attempt to dissolve barriers and the problems of development have been worsened by the difficulties of assimilating large numbers of unskilled and illiterate immigrants. Ethnic disharmonies have been important in shaping the present Sudanese government's views of population problems, particularly the apparent belief that the country is still underpopulated and hence that there is little need for programs of fertility control.

Just as patterns of internal migration are often a result of the interactions among countervailing government policies, so migration policies can interact with other kinds of population policy. For example, in Indonesia, according to Mayling Oey, Javanese who have been resettled in Sumatra under the impact of the government's "transmigration" policies have a considerably higher fertility than the Javanese remaining in Java. The government induced migration of young married couples, 91 percent of whom were landless laborers, by providing them with two hectares of cultivatable land in Sumatra. The resulting prosperity created a labor shortage which induced further migration.

Oey believes the higher fertility of the settlers is at least partly related to the fact that educational and health services in the resettlement areas have lagged behind those in Java. Infant and child mortality are much higher than in Java and educational levels are significantly lower.

The stated objective of the transmigration policy is to foster the economic development of regions of low population density in Indonesia, yet the unbalanced age structure resulting from high fertility in these regions is likely to retard development. If fertility is to be reduced, the government will need to pay much more attention to improving the social infrastructure, and will need to establish vigorous family planning programs.

The northeastern quarter of Brazil has been historically a region of poverty and underdevelopment, which has been made worse by infertile soil, frequent devastating droughts, and in recent years, rapid population growth, even though much of the excess population has been drained off by migration to the more productive and prosperous regions of the country. Population densities are low, and calculated fertility rates indicate that the populations exercise a degree of control over their own fertility, yet living conditions for the great majority are near the level of bare subsistence.

Maria Lerda has described the relations between ecological situations and human fertility in the northeast. She shows that in areas of relatively high agricultural productivity (but still low in absolute terms), where land is available for peasant cultivation, fertility rates are 10 to 20 percent higher than in the most backward and poverty-stricken areas. This would appear to be a classical example of a population caught in a "Malthusian Trap." The Brazilian government is encouraging migration and resettlement of northeasterners in the frontier areas of the Amazon Basin. Unless this migration policy is supplemented by policies to reduce fertility among the resettled populations, the next generation may be worse off than the present one.

The formulation and implementation of policies for fertility reduction in Peninsular Malaysia are described by Zakaria Haji Ahmad and Siew-Nyat Chin. The path of organizing for population change in Malaysia largely followed the sequence of "policy outcomes" described by Harold Lasswell. Prior to 1964, there had been private efforts and organizations devoted to the provision of family planning services, but the government's attitude toward these activities was "at best tolerant, at worst hostile." In 1964, however, the Minister of Agriculture publicly stated that Malaysia could not achieve self-sufficiency in food production without reducing its rate of population growth. Shortly afterwards a Cabinet subcommittee on family planning was formed and baseline research was initiated. Sample surveys of "knowledge, attitudes, and practices" of contraception were conducted, and a study was undertaken on the impact of changes in rates of population growth on per capita economic indices.

A National Family Planning Board was established in 1966 and a target was set for reduction of the rate of population growth to 2 percent by 1985, corresponding to birth and death rates of approximately twenty-six and six per thousand, respectively. When accomplishments lagged behind the intermediate targets, efforts were made to increase the demand for family planning by incentive schemes. Responsibility for review of all government policies that might influence population change was placed within the government's planning unit. In recent years, the quality of data collection and analysis has been upgraded, and greater emphasis has been placed on review and evaluation of agency and program performance. In view of the actual and potential ethnic conflicts in Malaysia, the organization and administration of population-influencing policies has been remarkably successful.

India was among the first countries to begin a family planning program, in the early 1950s, and the Indian government has spent more money on family planning than any other country in the world, with the possible exception of China. Yet the Indian birthrate is still more than twice the death rate, and the population is growing at more than 2 percent a year, doubling in thirty years. It is easy to say that the government of India should have spent more money on the family planning program, commensurate with the enormous size of the task, or that the program was inefficiently organized and managed, or that it was not given enough moral support by top Indian political leaders. It is more likely that the difficulty lies elsewhere.

The middle and upper classes in India ordinarily have only two or three children, while poor families in the countryside, the landless laborers and the small farmers, often have six or more. Nowadays most of these poor people have heard about family planning and approve of its use—but only after they have several children, especially sons, who will survive and be able to take care of them in their old age, and who in the meantime will be able to help out with the work on the farm, or to supplement the family income in other ways. Less than one out of five rural women can read or write; bearing and rearing children is the principal way in which they can find meaning in their lives.

Davendra K. Kothari has examined one of the major aspects of India's Family Planning Program—the program of vasectomies and incentives to acceptors. By the end of 1972 over thirteen million men had been sterilized, about 10 percent of the reproductive age group; with wide variations in this proportion among the different states. The average age of the wives of the acceptors was 32.8 years, and their average number of living children was 4.5, compared to a median completed fertility for Indian women of 5.5. Thus the impact on fertility reduction has been small.

Kothari makes several suggestions for more effective fertility reduction policies, including: (1) a change in policy concept from family planning to "population planning," in which emphasis would be placed on the interests of the community and the advantages to the individual in discharging an obligation to society; (2) establishment of a separate Ministry of Population headed by a powerful political leader; (3) greater authority for the central government vis-à-vis the states; (4) more careful selection of the target population; (5) introduction of population education in post-primary education; (6) a "cafeteria approach" to birth control, in which all methods are utilized; (7) more realistic target-setting and selection of target groups, and more frequent evaluation. To these possible changes in implementation of established policy, I would add major efforts to increase female literacy and educational levels, to provide opportunities for women outside the home, to improve maternal and child health, and to achieve a more equitable distribution of incomes.

From 1965 to 1973, the United States government supported a national family planning program, designed primarily to help low income women who were thought to be in need of subsidized family planning services. A new agency, the National Center for Family Planning Services, was created for this purpose in 1969 and "phased out" in 1973. Korbin Liu has analyzed this experience, using as a framework Lasswell's sequence of policy outcomes and Ilchman's categories of factors that determine policy effectiveness (resource accumulation, resource combinations in a policy production function, decision rules, administrative infrastructures, and target group construction) with special attention to changes in these factors and in their relationships over time.

He shows that knowledge about unwanted fertility among American couples, resulting from lack of access to reliable means for avoiding or terminating pregnancy, was effectively utilized in the initial stages of policy formation and implementation, but the translation of this knowledge into selection of a "target population" was defective, and evaluation of the impact of the program on unwanted fertility was too late to be useful.

Financial, administrative, and manpower resources for the program were not coordinated, with the result that a considerable portion of those resources was ineffectively used. Some "decision rules" hampered the program; for example, the opposition of certain interest groups which resulted in the decision to prohibit the use of federal funds to pay for abortions; the opposition of private physicians to provision of free contraceptive services; and the formula basis for allocating funds to different regions, based on estimated size of the target populations. Conflicts over jurisdiction among different federal agencies, and the placement of regional and headquarters staffs of the National Center for Family Planning simultaneously under two different lines of authority within the Department of Health, Education and Welfare, seriously weakened the administrative infrastructure of the program.

Several general lessons can be learned from these country studies. One is that a single policy cannot exist in isolation. Policies with different objectives interact to produce both intended and unintended results. Another is that governments need vastly better models of the specifications for policy design and application and of the impact of single policies and policy clusters. Despite their long history, the policy sciences are still at the stage of description and classification. If they are to be useful to policymakers, they must progress to the next step of understanding the dynamics and forces involved. We have suggested that, like other sciences, this next step can be approached through a combination of theoretical construction and the testing of hypotheses by social "experiments," that is the careful analysis of quantitative data and qualitative observations gained through experience with different policies.

1

Population Knowledge and Fertility Policies

Warren F. Ilchman

Policy Knowledge and Scholarly Knowledge

The knowledge that is needed by policymakers in making their choices is not necessarily the same knowledge professors discover in their research, store in their journals, or teach to their students. This truism is more believed by policymakers in the breach than in the ordinary course of granting research contracts or seeking advice from scholars. From most of these encounters, policymakers come away discouraged by the seeming incapacity of scholars to understand their requirements, while scholars despair of the insensitivity of policymakers to the scholarly process. Neither judgment need be so. The requirements for knowledge by policymakers can provide for scholars the most fruitful opportunity to test and discover hypotheses about public behavior; the demand by scholars that knowledge for policy-making purposes include the context in which choice is to occur and the long-term likely outcome of events provides policymakers their most fruitful opportunity to improve these outcomes and to conserve resources. Such a conviction is not simply born of optimism but of an understanding of the scholarly and policy processes as compatible enterprises.

Population Knowledge

A case in point is the subject of the social and economic correlates of fertility. From the policymakers' point of view, this subject has been relatively unimportant and unconsulted. Until now, the issue has been primarily to provide services to meet an existing and, to a degree, cumulating demand, not to induce a demand where none or little existed. This required knowledge of marketing, training, and improvements in contraception. For purposes of estimating the demand, Knowledge-Attitudes-Practices (KAP) studies were useful, especially in the political context of proving to regimes that demand for family planning programs did exist and that there was less public opposition than many had suspected or feared.[1] The surveys were also helpful in providing information about preferences for different contraceptives and gaps in the knowledge of potential users. The surveys potentially could have been used to identify target groups, but their construction as questionnaires and the realities of family planning politics and administration diminished their utility for this purpose. Finally, the political knowledge needed to transform small elite private programs into larger public programs, and the administrative knowledge to articulate these usually with existing public medical systems, seemed not to exceed what the supporters of these programs and their occasional foreign advisers had at their disposal.[2]

But the issue has changed. To the continuing and important task of filling existing demand for family limitation has been added the task of shaping and accelerating that demand, and of constructing public policies to induce more families to accept family limitation as a goal and to accept it sooner. This decision comes as it becomes apparent to many that present programs rapidly attain and remain at a plateau, that net acceptors begin to decline in number, and that supply of contraceptives cannot create its own demand.[3] To undertake the new task, the task of fashioning policies of incentives and sanctions to encourage the desired behavior, requires that policymakers consider the "policy worthiness" of findings from the scholarly study of the social and economic correlates of fertility.

Policy Knowledge

What is it that such knowledge should provide? Policies provide for the use of scarce public resources to intervene into expected behavior to secure more or less of that behavior from more or less of those presently or potentially so behaving. To be useful to policymakers, the knowledge of the correlates of fertility should instruct those who must make choices, with or without such guidance, about their policy interventions: who might be the objects of intervention, what degree of change might be achieved by how much and what kind of resources, what methods of intervening make what difference to the outcome, how long the intervention should last until the behavior is self-sustaining in enough people, what are the costs of intervention from the point of view of those who are the objects of intervention and the benefits to those who provide the means for intervening, whether enough resources are available publicly to achieve the purpose, and whether too many or not enough resources are available to the objects of the intervention so that the desired behavior might not be forthcoming. Knowledge of previous public interventions of the same general sort in the same or similar settings is always preferable; if this is not available, what would then be of value would be knowledge of what correlates with desired behavior in the absence of significant public intervention and the imputations about interventions that might be inferred from those correlates.

Modesty of Policy. Answers to these questions, which might then serve to instruct the choices to be made by policymakers, must also take into account three features of the policy process. First, the knowledge must be tailorable to the varying degrees of commitment and purpose policymakers have for fertility control; the objective function, as it were, of policy. An explanation of what would bring down the birthrate if vast quantities of regimes resources were applied and there was no limit on time may be of little use if only a fraction of those resources were available and results had to be achieved in a few years. Despite the idiom that is often used in public campaigns, such as "wars on poverty," "stamping out illiteracy," the policy realities in terms of resources and time horizons are frequently more modest, usually to bring behavior within an acceptable range, not to transform a population.[4] This is partly because there are not enough resources for such a purpose and too many competing objectives, partly because the phenomenon to be acted upon is embedded in other phenomena that are to be left alone, partly because what it might take to "solve" the problem would contravene other values, and partly because the social technologies are not as yet invented. A regime committed to take ten points off the birth rate is not committed to ZPG (zero population growth); a regime intervening to reduce the birth rate may settle for one less child in families of over five children. A scholar incapable of thinking of different explanations for different degrees of purpose, or degrees of intervention for degrees of modified behavior, is incapable of being of much assistance in devising population policies.

Grossness of Policy. Another reality that must be accommodated by scholars is that policies are usually relatively gross attempts to bring about change. They are "gross" in that they are attempts by regimes to influence the behavior of large numbers of people through the use of rather limited repertoires of interventions.[5] The objects of intervention are usually quite diverse in all but one or a few respects. It is assumed that these common features allow groups to be treated as if they would respond similarly, that the common features are the actuating ones that will trigger the appropriate response to a set of interventions which must be relatively inflexible and formula-istic if large numbers are to be affected. If enough people behaved as a regime would like them to behave—both in numbers and degree—regarding a particular value, then a "policy" would be unnecessary; likewise, if there were enough resources so that every case could be treated as a special case, there again would be no policy as such; no grossness of aggregation, no formula-istic intervention. An example might be the much-debated 5.3 million women in the United States family planning program.[6] The issue here is not whether there are 1.2 million or 8 million women who are going to be provided a limited range of contraceptive methods within a limited range of delivery systems. The issue is that a large number of women who have in common that they are in childbearing years and have less than a certain income, but who are utterly diverse in all other characteristics, are treated as if at least a high proportion of them will respond appropriately and commonly to a limited set of interventions. Differences in parity, married status, residence, region, race, and financial supportive networks are all deemphasized as actuating or significantly affecting variables.[7] Similar examples obtain in other policies. To assist those with public responsibilities requires of scholars the skill of considering groups in populations as building blocks for policies, to construct or discover common denominators that permit the "optimal grossness."

The Political Economy of Policy. Finally, a scholar must recognize that policies take place in a political and administrative context in which all choices have costs. Public choice as policy occurs within a context of scarce resources, competition for alternative uses of those same resources, and often against the will and use of their resources of those who are the objects of policies.[8] To assist in devising population policies scholars must begin by assuming that population events have differential impact on different sectors and differentially affect the attainment by members of these sectors or groups of their values. Changes in size of groups, rate of their growth, their distribution in space and changing composition by age, sex, or qualitative characteristics, such as education, all have differential consequences and benefits. It is not, in most instances, the increasing birthrate that is as provocative of policy as it is a question of "whose" birthrate.[9] Moreover, it is likely that population policies are not necessarily in the interest, as they perceive it, of the objects of policies; others, at least in the short run, are perceived as the beneficiaries. While the idiom of population scientists is universalistic—"the tragedy of the commons"—the results of these population events are particularistic and particularistically understood. And it is in this particularistic context, where groups are differentially endowed to shape, support, or oppose public action, that policies are chosen or not, implemented or not, encouraged to flourish or to wither away. By having knowledge about the limits and opportunities inherent in the political and administrative context, of what is feasible, maximal, and optimal, a scholar could propose modifications in policies or in their sequencing. To propound explanations of fertility and how public interventions might accelerate the choosing of low fertility values, and to do so innocent of the cost and benefits of alternatives in political and administrative choices, opens a scholar to the charge of reading like any other utopian writer.

In other words, scholarly knowledge is useful insofar as it provides a guide to public choice in the context of scarce public resources, a guide as to which choice should be taken among many that might be taken, a guide to which subsequent choices should be taken in light of the initial decision. Scholarly knowledge is useful in policymaking insofar as it improves, if acted upon, the likelihood of desired outcomes occurring and conserves on resources used in the intervention. If a population scholar wishes to be of assistance to those presently or soon to be responsible for population policies, he must be able to understand what it is a policymaker would like or ought to like to know: the relationship between the resources obtainable and transformable and the purposes at issue.

The scholar should also have the skill and the ethical sensibility to be able to say to those in authority "you can't get there from here."

A Hypothetical Example:
Abortion vs. Education of Girls

This could perhaps be better seen by taking some hypothetical examples. There is considerable evidence that the availability of cheap, safe, and legal abortions reduces the fertility rate; there is also overwhelming (though not causally documented) evidence that education for girls, especially for at least four years, is conducive to lower fertility as well. Let's assume that abortion is technically (and I will use, somewhat incorrectly, the terms "technical" and "economic" as the same) more likely to have a cheaper and faster impact on fertility than is increased access to education; the latter, after all, is long term, and is provided to those who, as potential childbearers, might be sterile, celibate, or would successfully contracept anyway. On the other hand, extending educational opportunity has some impact and is almost universally a politically valuable policy for a regime to do and to be identified with. That can hardly be said about expanding and legalizing abortion services. As a policy for improving the status of women, however, there could be a combination of providing abortion facilities and increased schooling that could be both technically and politically viable.

Let us say for every combination of programs in our policy on the status of women there are two aspects: there is (1) a division of funds between abortion and schooling and (2) a level of funding for the two activities together. Let us also say that each level of funding/distribution combination can be judged simultaneously on technical and political grounds and that there are several combinations which we would describe as technically productive (that is, high output relative to input), technically feasible (costs and results are more or less equal), and technically unfeasible (compared with costs, the output is too small).[10] Let us also say, for purposes of illustration, that for each technically productive choice, one is politically productive (that is, the political resources to choose and implement it are much less than the political return the choice provides), another is politically feasible, and a third is politically unfeasible. Mirabile dictu, this provides a nine-cell matrix with each combination cross evaluated by both criteria (Figure 1-1).

The archetypal political scientist advising on population policies would be often at (in!) cell G—all schools and no abortion; the archetypal family planning specialist at cell C. The policy scientist, hopefully, would be where the policymaker usually is: considering options in A, B, D, and E; minimally with B and D and ideally with A. Now conceivably choice A, which best combines political and technical criteria, could be less politically profitable than D and less

	Politically Productive I < 0	Politically Feasible I = 0	Politically Unfeasible I > 0
Technically (Economically) Productive I < 0	A	B	C
Technically (Economically) Feasible I = 0	D	E	F
Technically Unfeasible I > 0	G	H	I

Figure 1-1. Political Economy Matrix for Comparison of Choices

technically effective than B, but combines the mutual productivities of technical and political resources best. The matrix should also be looked at over time. What is chosen as the A combination at one period may make possible at another time an even more effective cell A, one which might have previously resided in cell C.

This could also be shown on a graph (Figure 1-2). The points in the matrix are transposed on to the graph and our interest is where to locate A. The urge to split the difference has to be resisted. Needless to say, how one values abortion and schooling as tradeoffs depends on how one feels about each in relation to the other. In times of considerable political difficulty and a "cope-able" birth rate, A might be closer to D; in times of greater regime stability and a more pressing burden of births, A might be closer to B, or more correctly seen in Figure 1-3. Such graphs are simplex and perhaps misleading for the literal minded; the lines do not reveal preferences, they only describe them. Moreover, a real policy choice has many other elements. But the example, defective though it might be in many respects, reminds us that we cannot have technical judgments in the absence of political judgments and vice versa.[11]

A Real Example: Migration within Indonesia

One example of such fruitful collaboration comes from the field of formal demography. Since Dutch times, there has been a policy to encourage migration from densely populated Java to other, less densely populated islands, especially Sumatra. Over the years this policy has been modified so that primarily young married couples are encouraged to migrate, thus affecting the rate of increase of

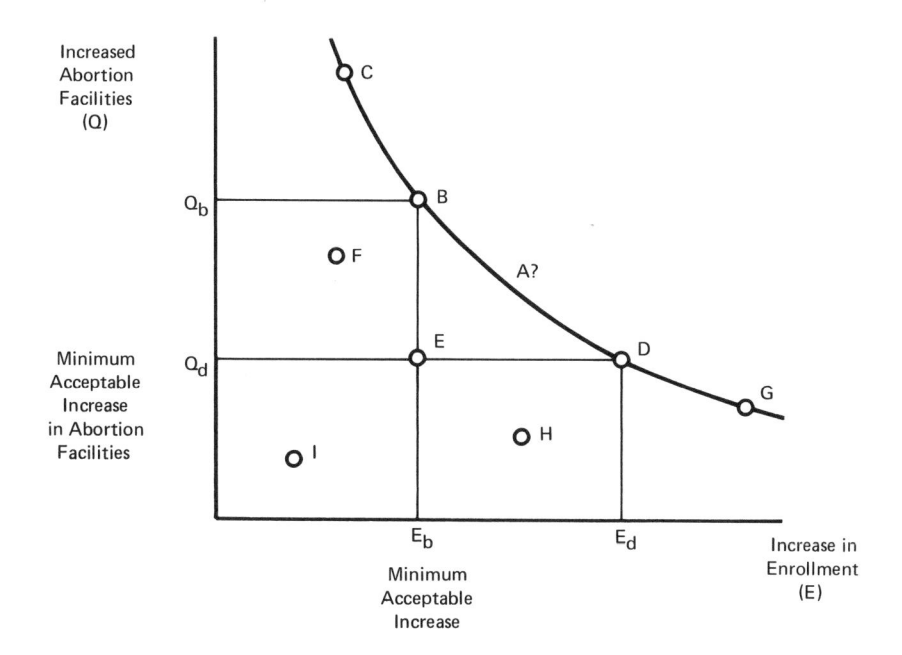

Figure 1-2. Political Economy Alternatives in Choice

population as well as the population size. The policy question has been, how large a program of migration must there be to reduce the rate of population increase and even to keep the population of Java stationary, and how might this compare with alternative policies? Using demographic theory and extrapolations from the impact of emigration on Barbados and Mauritius, Nathan Keyfitz demonstrates for the Indonesian policymakers:

Thus to bring about a drop from the actual increase of 30.54 per thousand to one of 20.00 per thousand the departure of 41.7% of each cohort would be required if they leave at age 25, and of 27.9% if they leave at age 20. The poor returns on emigration as a means of population control are suggested by the fact that if 30 to 40% of each cohort were to leave this would only hold the population down to 2% annual increase, or a doubling every 35 years.[1,2]

Compared with alternative uses of capital, the migration policy is costly and with negligible results. Keyfitz concludes, "Migration to the other islands can realistically aim at the development of those islands, but hardly at the solution of Java's population problem."[1,3]

This standard is in contrast to what ordinarily prevails. More frequently, scholars are found standing guard at the outermost limits of the feasibility

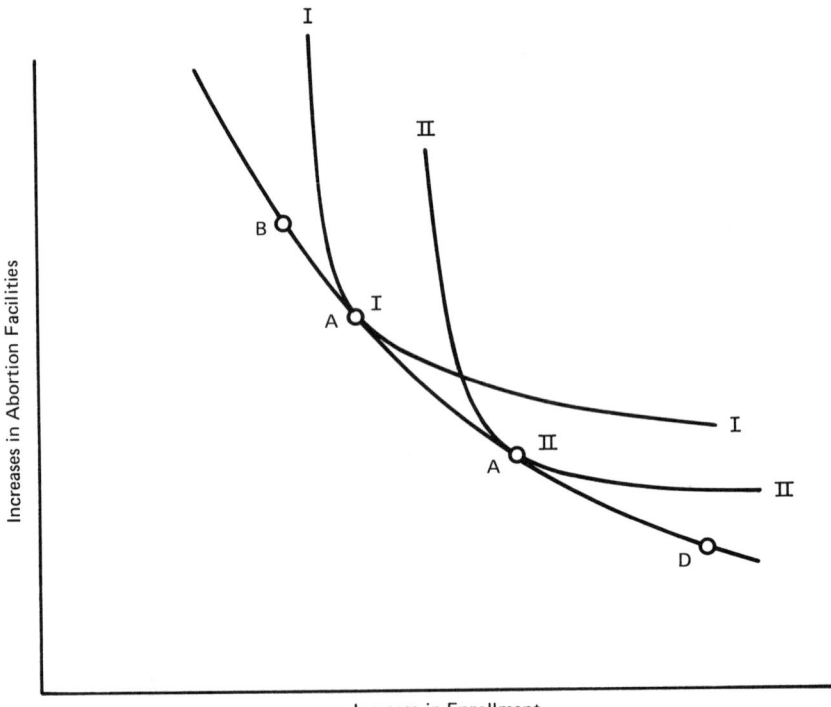

Figure 1-3.

frontier; their chief counter to any proposal for public action is a warning that there will be unintended consequences.[14] A policymaker is left uninstructed and uninformed by those with a claim to systematic and more leisurely obtained knowledge. It also deprives the scholar of the best source of new and test of existing hypotheses where real behavior is altered or not by measurable interventions over demonstrable periods of time. Whether this also characterizes scholars in the subject of social and economic correlates of fertility is a problem to which we now turn.

Population Hypotheses and Their Applicability to Policy

There are four theories or hypotheses about fertility that inspire empirical research and potentially yield knowledge that is valuable for policymaking: the demographic transition theory, the threshold hypothesis, the differential fertility hypothesis, and the distributive justice hypothesis. They overlap and are not necessarily distinct in all respects, though they may be differentiated by the level of generalization at which they are pitched, the kind of research their proponents undertake, and how detailed their policy recommendations are. While a summary review will not do justice to them as scholarly achievements, such a review may demonstrate where it is likely that guides for policy choice may be found.

The Theory of the Demographic Transition

More than any other organizing idea, the theory of the demographic transition dominates the population sciences. Like the "market" and the "laws" of supply and demand in economics, the reciprocal relationship between births and deaths and the assumption that there will be a long-run balance between them are part of the basic paradigm most population scientists carry in their heads. In brief, the demographic transition argues that the demographic history of the world (assuming it follows the demographic history of Europe) is marked by the usual three phases; in the first phase, the birth and death rates are high; in the second the death rate falls more quickly than the birth rate; in the final phase, birth rates decline and over time roughly equal death rates. The argument is that the forces holding up death rates are weaker and those maintaining high fertility stronger. In addition, the intermediate variables that restrain fertility from attaining its biological limits are not strong enough to adjust in the short run the birth rate to the death rate, but do so as conception is increasingly deemed a question of choice, as the utility of children declines, and as the means of effective contraception increase.[15]

The parallel with classical economics is very apt. If births are thought of as "supply," deaths as "demand," and viable life the equivalent of "price," the theory of demographic transition has a homeostatic mechanism much akin to the market. In the multitudinous maximizations of family units (the domesticized Economic Man), the demographic unseen hand operates over time to restore the long-term balance, a balance disturbed by man initially by interference with the birth-death process through measures of nutrition, sanitation, health, and civil order, an interference especially virulent in the world's poor countries, and a balance restored through a complex mechanism of urbanization, industrialization, growth of the nuclear family, and extrafamilial employment for women. Like those who believe in market economics, the advocates of the demographic transition seem impervious to impressive evidence that births are not reciprocally determined by deaths, that the birthrate operates quite independently of the death rate, that the socioeconomic variables are not acting primarily to restore the balance between the two, and that some of the characteristics of the completed transition, such as the nuclear family, behave contrarily in the midst of the transition.[16] Indeed, it is about as likely that one can find a "pure transition" as one can find a "pure market," though like market economists, the advocates of the demographic transition as a way of explanation ask to be judged on what occurs "in the long run" and on their results as predictors. Even one who has done much to show the inadequacy of the theory contends:

> Looking backward at the history of the most highly modernized countries, the demographic transition correctly tells us that in all such countries fertility and mortality were much higher in the pre-modernized state; looking forward to the future of countries that in 1945 still had high fertility and mortality, it correctly predicted that mortality would decline before fertility, producing rapid growth. In neither instance does it specify in terms that can be translated into quantitative measures the circumstances under which the decline of fertility begins.[17]

Unless a mechanism is isolated and amenable to acceleration by the concentration of efforts through public interventions, without some specificity about "how," the policy value of the transition theory is limited. In keeping with the analogy to classical economics and the population equivalent to laissez-faire, some transition theorists and researchers see their role as advocating the need for better information and better contraceptive means; others content themselves with musings on the equivalent of the purely competitive market in population, the theory of stable population.[18] There is even the variant of the "trickle down" theory of development that might make a policymaker, impelled by theory to serve the more advantaged "pioneers," totally ignore the Taiwanese peasant farmer who is especially keen on forms of contraception better than the folk variety.[19] Those scholars who operate within transition theory and try to evaluate the impact of external interventions, such as in the Khanna project in India, are surprised when the birth-death reciprocity seems less important, at least in the short run, than social and economic changes going on about them.[20] For some who work within this paradigm, the result is inevitable only a question of time. Donald Bogue confidently predicts:

> From 1965 onward, therefore, the rate of world population growth may be expected to slacken at such a pace that it will be zero or near zero at about the year 2000, so that population growth will not be regarded as a major social problem except in isolated and more "retarded" areas.[21]

And he has been contributing his efforts to perfecting the "market." For others who operate within the theory, such as Kingsley Davis, the need for restoring balance is so urgent and the traditional methods of the pretransition era so inadequate that a massive intervention to restructure sex roles is mandatory.[22] Some have even recommended as a policy measure the withholding of food or medical supplies in case of famine or epidemic so as to accelerate the long-term balance. More than guides to policy, theorists of the demographic transition often become spokesmen and legions for the varying forces in the population debate.

The policymaker choosing amidst scarce resources might be persuaded by the transition theory, but its advice either does not transcend what might be done under any circumstance, i.e., provide improved and accessible contraception, or it would bankrupt the regime faster than the political consequences of increasing and changing densities. The issues of how, for whom, when, what, how much, and for how long, are not in any way answered. Sequences of choices, their costs, and priorities are all eclipsed in the sweep of the demographic transition. Of course, it can be helpful to be told that balances are eventually self-correcting and that emphasis should be placed on better information and contraception; resources can be saved from actions to shape more dramatically the demand for curtailed fertility and used elsewhere. But if one does not believe that the demographic transition theory is correct or applicable to a particular regime, one can hardly rest assured with the policy advice that comes from its proponents.

The Threshold Hypothesis of Fertility Decline

More substantial for policy purposes is the threshold hypothesis of fertility decline. While it was developed within the theory of the demographic transition, it does not depend on holding the long-term reciprocity of births and deaths as the key determinant. Moreover, it is not correct to refer to the hypothesis as "the" hypothesis; there are many variations and the "official" U.N. version is used here only for the sake of illustration.[23] The problem they all share, however, is to explain what factors account for the decline in fertility experienced by most industrialized countries and to work from that point to what high fertility countries might do to follow suit.

The hypothesis ultimately divides the world into those nations which are marked by low fertility (GRR < 2.0) and those with relatively high fertility (GRR > 2.0); the two groups show a substantial difference on indicators of income per capita, energy consumption, urbanization, non-agricultural activities, hospital beds, life expectancy at birth, infant mortality, early marriage, female literacy, newspaper circulation, radio receivers, and cinema attendance. At the same time, within each group, there is a great range on the values. This led the writers of the document to state:

...in a developing country where fertility is initially high, improving economic and social conditions are likely to have little if any effect on fertility until a certain economic and social level is reached; but once that level is achieved, fertility is likely to enter a decided decline and to continue downward until it is again stabilized on a much lower plane.[24]

Subsequent analysis narrowed the more telling indicators to income per capita, newspaper circulation, radio receivers, and female literacy, and these were christened "indicator values in the 'reduced' threshold zones...".[25]

Since the U.N. study there have been many attempts to find what value or group of values can be associated with a large number of a nation's population reducing their fertility. The correlations are always disappointing; the subsequent rationalizations are always convoluted.[26] A recent study referring to Latin America finds high and low fertility nations at very unpredictable places in terms of the values, leading the author to state that "there are no clearly defined threshold values."[27]

Whether the metaphor of "threshold" is helpful or not, there is still the undeniable fact that low fertility countries in the sample all scored high on certain values. Surely, it is not farfetched to say that the activities expressed in those values have fertility consequences and low fertility values have consequences for those activities. On close inspection, these activities have in common or are the result of a high investment per capita, a substantial capital intensiveness, whether one is talking about non-agricultural employment, education, health, the media, services, and so forth. Such a setting is one that is also marked for parents by a diminishing marginal utility of children or the wish to increase the "quality" of their children. On the other side of the sample, the high fertility nations are characterized by values indicating a much lower per capita investment and a frequent high marginal utility for children. What is seldom conjectured is that, rather than a threshold obtaining which implies movement in a single direction, only at different paces, the difference between the two groups is mutually caused and will remain. The high capital intensiveness and low marginal utility of children in rich countries (and among the rich in poor countries) is related to the low capital intensiveness and the high marginal utility of children in poor countries. In other words, the incentives for high fertility in the rural countryside, an incentive since the "transition" began and unrelated to mortality rates, are still there and they are part of the world demand for cheap primary products and fueled by the price instability and terms of trade between industrialized and poor nations.[28]

Perhaps the threshold hypothesis is true and it is only a question of methodology and improved data before coefficients of compelling persuasiveness are obtained. When that happens, may it be assumed regimes will know where to look for policy changes in order to accelerate a decline in fertility? Probably not. In the first place, while policymakers might be led to areas where the correlation is strong, they will not know what caused what or whether a third factor "caused" both, or whether the two phenomena are mutually exclusive in potential target groups. Nor will they know from the record, even if causality could be demonstrated, how much of what achieves what degree of what is wished. Moreover, as these correlations are macro and system-wide, policymakers will not know how the factors impinge on the lives of target groups or even who target groups ought to be: those who are closest or most distant from the requisite values. Even if they do, they will know nothing about the content of "education" and the "media"; presumably they could be pro-natalist as easily as anti-natalist. Nor will they know, if a cluster of factors is indicated, which of them or how much of each is sufficient and which or how much is necessary. There could be no instruction on what might occur if only part of the cluster can be acted upon in policy terms. How does one know that interfering with the utility of children will not leave poor families even more impoverished? Finally, policymakers learn nothing from the hypothesis about the political and administrative costs and requirements—who will bear the costs, who will reap the benefits, what is the time horizon, etc.—to implement policies to achieve higher scores on the values; what kinds of coalitions will be required to achieve these ends, including the end of restructuring world trade relations.

The Differential Fertility Hypothesis

Undiscriminating, profligate of scarce political resources, hardly a guide for choices that policymakers might feel confident to make, the threshold hypothesis does not even lead to whom population policies should be oriented. On the other hand, a sensitivity to target groups has been the purported contribution of the differential fertility hypothesis. Again, to refer to "the" hypothesis in the singular is misleading: the hypothesis is really a residual category for the findings of the vast number of population scientists who have been searching for explanations of fertility by looking at the attributes of real live people who have had or might have children.[29] This work, however, will be described as if it emerged from an overarching notion of the determinants of fertility.

The assumption of the hypothesis is sensible enough: people's choices are affected by their life experience and circumstances. No macro "investment in media" or "cinema attendance" here, the differential fertility hypothesizers seek differences in people regarding their real fertility. Once these differences are known, then perhaps policies can be fashioned to strengthen what seems to strengthen what behavior policymakers want. Perhaps a specific example will be helpful and the CELADE study of several Latin American cities could represent the field.[30] From that study, we learn:

1. that marital status is not always a good predictor of fertility;
2. that urban-born women have fewer children than rural-born women now in cities;
3. that there is a lineal relationship between amount of education of the mother and the number of live births;
4. usually, that the higher the occupational status of the father the lower the fertility of the wife;
5. that working women have fewer children than those who do not work;
6. that religiosity does not seem to determine fertility levels and certainly does not seem to affect the eventual use of contraception.

One might object to the formal methodology: the respondents are all urban women, the concern is with the factors that reduce fertility (because of the KAP-bias) and not with what keeps it high, the questions are more appropriate for Indianapolis than for Bogota, the multivariate cross-hatching of attributes is not explored.[31] But even if these criticisms were corrected in subsequent surveys, the policy value would still remain limited, though real. If fertility reduction is taken as the objective and the need to shape demand for this as the policy problem, then policymakers really *only know who constitutes that demand in the absence of public intervention.* Nor can policymakers guess from the approach the intensity of either demand or opposition. Moreover, in each category, as they deal with averages, there are those who are deviant. A more helpful analysis might explore the deviant cases, looking, for instance, at the attributes of rural-born women with low parity or high school graduates with high parity. What is not the "norm" may be easier to influence by policy measures. There is also the implication that each factor, each attribute, has equal influence on each birth for the same woman. That is uncommonsensical, as work, residence, income, religiosity vary over life and might play a role in one birth choice and not another. Nor does the methodology give policy notions about how much of what attribute might be varied with what outcome, partly because fertility level determines the attribute just as often as the other way around. Similarly, many of the attributes are probably beyond touching, and for those that are liable for intervention the political economy of doing so must be interpolated.

Attributes as Categories or Concepts. A final criticism must be registered against the approach from a policy-making point of view. There is a mistake perpetuated in the differential fertility hypothesis that treats an attribute, whether it is income, residence, or religiosity, as if it were the same wherever it is found, the population equivalent of lung tar and cancer. Recent, otherwise helpful summaries of the literature on the social and economic correlates of fertility, conclude in most instances that the findings of the differential fertility hypothesis are weak because they are often contradictory.[32] One would hope so. "Income" at the same nominal level means different things in different settings and to different groups within the same setting; "religiosity" means one thing in a highly secularized setting and another in one marked by widespread and publicly endorsed religious activity. Consensual unions, functional inclusiveness of families, extra-familial labor of women, and so on, are categories under which to group diverse but similar activities or phenomena. They may be relevant in one setting and not in another; had other activities not been present, they might have made a "difference" in a third setting. These categories are not concepts that can be measured by a universal scale of the possession of determining attributes or of intensity of independent existence. When one tries to treat them in this fashion—to get international differentials, without which a scholar feels he is stuck with a paltry case study— is to play havoc in providing instruction for those who must choose publicly in relation to a specific setting and specific constituencies.

The Difference "Education" Makes. A particular case in point is education. Education, like income, is not a thing; it is a category under which a variety of activities are included. These differ by content, relationship to life circumstance, duration, cost to parents, outcome in employment, etc. Fertility does not "vary with education." Fertility possibly varies with the varied activities that are summarized by the noun education. These are in different combinations in the life experience of different persons, and the combinations are relevant to policy.

The work on the effects of "education" on fertility, however, should not be so quickly dismissed. While there is a penchant for scholars to prescribe education for any social ailment, and their findings might be thought to be a trifle self-serving, it is certainly true that more evidence about differential fertility has been accumulated for education than for any other factor. Most of it suggests a negative influence on fertility. More than that, educational activities are perhaps the most amenable to serve as policy tools, so that the findings of scholars have the potential here of assisting policymakers. Educational activities are at a level where there can be experimentation; they can be made sector and time specific; their costs and benefits, politically and administratively, can be assessed as easily as they can be for other policy areas. In other words, the tailorable and aggregative knowledge required for public choice can be discovered by scholars and it can be used in future choices by policymakers. Potentially, the repeatable recipes, which are the objective of a truly applied social science, might be found.

To what extent have the findings on education in the Third World led in this direction? From Table 1-1, it should be apparent that the literature is contradictory and based on very diverse samples.[33] In many instances, proof of the difference that "education" makes is comparisons between family sizes of college graduates and illiterates. Social status, employment, and income are not checked in relation to education and fertility. Few studies are standardized for age or duration of sexual union; thus younger and better educated women at an earlier point in childbearing are compared with older and, for reasons of availability of education, less educated women with completed fertility. That "education" makes a difference is hardly surprising. Except for those few studies that deal with willingness of respondents to accept contraception, there is no specification in these studies about what in education inclines a former student to regulate his or her fertility. Content of education is apparently held constant. Presumably, one could argue that physical incarceration of the young might be as effective as schooling, except that one is restrained by a deep-seated belief that the content of education may have something to do with the choices later made by the educated. Even then, there is no universally observed relationship

Table 1-1
Findings on Education and Fertility

Researcher	Country	Sample	Date	Adjusted[1]	Educational[2]	Percentage[3]	Difference	Content[4]
Driver 1963	India	2,589 households rural	1958	Age	Husband's none, primary, middle, high, matric., col.	78%	inversely related, though high school graduates less than matric.	None
Dow 1971	Sierra Leone	5,952 women 15-49 Freetown, villages, urban areas	1969-70	Age	Literacy Literate/illiterate Education one or more years/none	125% approve of contraception	Literacy – not totally inverse; literates in towns have higher fert. Education – same; higher ideal size for illiterates	None
Moore 1952	Mexico	600 women in 2 factories	1948-49	No	grades 1-6	NP	Qualifiedly inverse	None
Morsa 1966	Tunisia	2,175 married women in 12 centers	1961	Age	Husband: none, traditional, primary, higher Wife: none/some	NP	Inverse for contraception approval and use	None
Miro 1966	Colombia, Arg., Ven., Brazil, Pan., Costa Rica	c. 2,300 women in 7 cities	1963-64	Age	Husband: none, traditional, primary, higher Wife 9 gradations	NP	"Strongly inverse" – entire sample suggest no difference for wanted fertility	None
Iutaka et al. 1971	Brazil	1,280 married males in 6 cities	1970	No	Primary and less/secondary and more	95%	slightly inverse	None

Paydarfar/ Sarram 1970	Iran	641 married women in Shiraz	1968-69	Age Duration	Husbands: none, elementary, high school, univ.	40%	inverse	None
Miro/Mertens 1968	Latin America	seven city; rural and small urban areas women	1960s	No	Urban: none, some primary; pri, some secondary, secondary, some univerity Rural: none, some primary, primary, secondary, complete secondary	NP	inverse; twice as much use of contraception, though as high as 45.4% and 25% for uneducated, urban and rural respectively	None
Andorka 1969	Hungary	census 191 areas near towns	1960	No (?)	over 8 years/ primary education	?	education with variables of agriculture, earning women and urbanization, less than half the variation	None
Yaukey 1962	Lebanon	900 women towns and villages	1959	No	illiterate/literate	NP	Moslem educated have same or higher fert. than uneducated; inverse for Christians	None
Tabah/Samuels 1962	Chile	2,000 women 20-50 urban	1970	Age Duration	Not discriminated	NP	More dependent on economic than on educational level; little difference between ideal and real	None

Table 1-1 (cont.)

Researcher	Country	Sample	Date	Adjusted[1]	Educational[2]	Percentage[3]	Difference	Content[4]
Gendell 1967	Brazil	Censuii 1940-1960	1940-1960	NR			strong correlation via economic activity of women	None
Kripalani et al. 1971	India	76 couples slum dwellers	1969	No	illiterate, primary, secondary husband and wife combinations	NP	Contraception acceptance higher if both are educated; little education more valuable than a lot.	None
Hong/Joong 1962	Korea	119 males close to Seoul	1961	age parity	none, primary, middle school plus	NP	Demographic characteristics more important than education, but education important for contraception; still 55.1% of not educated accepted contraception; more educated would like larger families.	None
Maroufi-Bozargi 1967	Iran	779 women in family planning clinic; urban	1964-65	No	read and write or completed any education/illiterate	78%	Lower survival rate for illiterates'; ultimate fertility about the same.	None
Liu 1965	Taiwan	census; registration urban/rural macro	1961	No	Percentage of females over 12 as primary school graduates	84%	Female education more important than male; all have high fertility.	None

Rele 1963	India	2,380 couples rural	1956		Duration not available	literate/illiterate	Husbands 102.8%	Hardly sig.; wives more than husbands	None
Morrison 1956	India	124 males rural	1954	No	0-4, 5-7, 8 plus grades	NP	Least sig. variable	None
Olusanya 1969	Nigeria	5,029 married women, urban and rural	1966	No	literate/ illiterate	NP	Not apparent	None
Minkler 1970	India	70 teachers 70 unskilled workers	?	No	educated = 13.7 years uneducated = 1.7 years wives 2.8 husbands	NP	virtually same ideal family: same on contraception	None
Freedman et al. 1964-65	Taiwan	2,432 women 20-39 urban	1962-63	No	none, primary, primary, grad., secondary, sec. grad., graduate plus	63.1%	inversely related, though abortion 9x's greater among those without education	None
Ahmed and Ahmed 1965	E. Pakistan Bangladesh	195 males urban	1963	No	illit., primary non-matric., undergrad., grad.	NP	limited: realized family size largest among grads.	None

Table 1-1 (cont.)

Researcher	Country	Sample	Date	Adjusted[1]	Educational[2]	Percentage[3]	Difference	Content[4]
Khan/Choldin 1965	E. Pak. Bangladesh	607 women, 13-49 in 5 villages	1963	No	husband: literate/illit.	NP	little difference; higher adoption of contraception by illits.	None
Hatt 1952	Puerto Rico	13,272 women	1947-48	NR	None, 1-3, 4-5, 6-8, 9-12, 13 plus	NP	inverse for age of marriage, union, and ideal family size	None
El Badry 1965	Egypt	census	1960	Age Duration	0, 1-2, 3, 4-5, 6	NP	Illiterates less fertile	None
Jain 1969	Taiwan	2,443 women urban	1962			NP	Fecundability increases with education	None
Rosen/Simons 1971	Brazil	726 mated women in 5 communities	1963-65	NR	NR	NP	low influence	None
Abu-Lughod 1965	Egypt	census	1960	Yes	illiterate, barely reads, reads and writes, primary, intermediate, went beyond	NP	inverse	None
Stoeckel/ Choudbury 1969	E. Pak. Bangladesh	2,078 couples rural	1967	Yes	Husbands'—none 1-3, 4-6, 7 plus	89.8%	small difference 7.73 for illit. and 6.89 for 7 plus TFR	None

Timur 1971	Turkey	64,000 acceptors in family planning	1966-67	No	literate/ illiterate	NP	young acceptors more literate; old acceptors less literate	None
Klinger/ Szabady 1969	Hungary	8,800 women 15-49	1960	No	0, 1-4, 5-8, 9-12, 13 plus	40%	3-5 times more likely to use contraception if university and secondary educated	None
Prachuabmoh 1967	Thailand	1,207 women near Bangkok	1964	Age	no formal/some formal	158%	positive association	None
Taeuber 1960	Japan	Fertility of Japan Survey	1950	Yes	0-6, 7-9, 10 plus husbands only	77%	Decline was across the board; though fertility inverse	None
CELADE 1965	Chile	70 women 25 km from Santiago	1964	Yes	ten discriminations	60%	inverse	None

NP Not possible because of methodology or particular construction of data.
NR Not Relevant

[1] Adjusted refers to whether data are adjusted to age and duration of sexual union.
[2] Educational refers to number of level discrimination; unless otherwise stated, the reference is to women's education.
[3] Percentage of fertility of highest educated to lowest educated level.
[4] Content refers to whether the researcher asked questions and/or speculated on content of education as a factor in fertility behavior of the educated. General statements about changing roles and employability of educated are not considered as substantive comments.

between education (whether it is literacy, specific grades or levels) and declining fertility. A discouraging conclusion a policy-minded scholar might take from the studies listed in Table 1-1 is that it would be better from a fertility point of view to have women remain illiterate than for them to have less than four to six years of formal education.

The episodic character of research on this subject should not permit the judgment that the confidence scholars feel about the demonstrated effect of schooling on fertility is misplaced. The individual cases might have relevance to policymakers in those same settings. Nor should the appraised record on the differential fertility of the educated signal approval of a massive, standardized World Fertility Study. Unless educational activities are thought of in a more disaggregated and causal way with a view towards altering educational policies, then even this "bevatron" of standardized definitions and massive samples will make little difference.

The Distributive Justice Hypothesis

The final hypothesis is the distributive justice hypothesis for fertility decline. Treating it last is appropriate because it is the most recent. It is an "externality" of the present discussions regarding the relationship between growth and development, a discussion marked by the increasing conviction by some Third World regimes and international and bilateral aid-givers that equity may enhance and not impede growth.[34] Like those who are making the wider argument on distribution and development, the proponents of the distributive justice hypothesis for fertility decline contend that the dominant hypothesis, the threshold hypothesis, separated wrongly the questions of population growth and increased welfare.[35] The threshold hypothesis, the capital-biased version of the explanation of fertility decline, assumes that population increases and welfare via savings and investment are contradictory; unless there is a reduction in population growth, savings and investment will be jeopardized and increased welfare postponed. As more and more couples participate in the fruits of modern investment, they will voluntarily accept family limitation; investment eventually solves the problem of fertility. Until then, concentrate on family planning and on savings. To this the distributive justice hypothesis poses the thesis that the best way to bring about lowered fertility and increased savings and investment is through increased welfare, through a more equitable distribution of goods and services and opportunity.[36] Moreover, contrary to the growing apprehension that only the Chinese-derived cultures can succeed in family limitation, those who hold this hypothesis to be true claim that family limitation occurs when welfare is substantially increased, regardless of cultural setting.[37]

The evidence mustered for the hypothesis points to a relationship between wider distribution of goods and services and income *and* a decline in fertility.

Labor intensiveness in industry, land reform, paramedical health services widely spread, access to education, all combine, according to the hypothesis, to create the condition for fertility decline. When the range of interpersonal comparisons and the opportunity for conspicuous inequality are narrowed, when the ability of some to exploit heavily others is reduced, couples begin to question the necessity for large families; diminishing marginal utility of children and a desire to increase their quality set in. Regimes comparable in all other ways but these distributive measures are regimes that also differ in birth rates, lower rates being achieved by those with greater equity.[38]

This hypothesis is the most congenial to the purpose of this chapter. All the redistributive measures mentioned by people who have written on this hypothesis are potential policies. They are experimental and their results may be tailorable to different situations. At the same time, the findings so far do not give a picture of how much (and of what) distribution makes what difference in fertility. One does not know how much and what is necessary and what is sufficient. Is the hypothesis a "Big Push" hypothesis in which nothing much will occur unless everything "is in place"?[39] Can measures taken in isolation be defeating? Might not increased wage income or distributed land raise fertility as well as to lower it? Are certain measures especially catalytic? Moreover, because policies are potential does not mean that they are politically or administratively possible. The distribution of opportunities in a regime is not the product of chance; it is always the outcome of contending forces. Changing distribution requires engaging these forces. Some regimes may have to pay the price of high fertility simply because the alternative of greater distribution is not theirs to choose or to want to choose. Indeed, it may well be that the distributive justice hypothesis is a populist version of the threshold hypothesis.[40] Finally, there are no population policies as such deriving from the hypothesis, no guides for the deliberate population-influencing choices that will shape a demand in relevant publics for lower fertility.

An Improved Population Knowledge for Population Policy

One should probably distrust any evaluation as sweeping and abstract as was the preceding analysis of the leading population hypotheses. Many valuable insights were, doubtless, ignored and achievements left unappreciated. As these scholars did not undertake their studies with the intention of providing the kind and quality of knowledge necessary for public policies, they perhaps should not be criticized for failing to do so. Moreover, it might be argued that these scholars share with others in the social sciences a reluctance to study public interventions into expected behavior, but to study instead expected behavior in a "more natural" social state, and to resist allowing their definitions of problems and standards of research to be influenced by anyone but academic peers. The result, however, is that there is little that seems helpful as guides to public choice. The expected behavior presented as the human reproductive record in various settings occurs in the context of unspecified interventions from all quarters. From two hypotheses, there are some implications for government action ("modernization" and "distributive justice"), but the derivative research does not suggest for whom, how much of what, for what period, and at what costs. Another hypothesis and its derivative research can suggest for whom intervention is less necessary or unnecessary, but not what public intervention for others over what period and at what cost. While many of the scholars would argue that their work has inspired much applied family planning research and action and it would certainly qualify by the utilitarian calculus used here, it should also be pointed out that such research presumes a demand and is less appropriate when one is trying publicly to induce a demand for family limitation.

Knowledge of Policy Intervention

If one's goal is knowledge to improve public choices, then the best source of that knowledge is the record of past and present public interventions and the implications for knowledge of scenarios for future ones. This is because many of what are termed today's social and economic determinants of fertility are, in origin, yesterday's public policies. Indeed, a "determinant" may be behavior that public resources need no longer be used to produce. Moreover, future demographic profiles will partly be the product of the public policies chosen and implemented by regimes in the next decade. The word "partly" is used in recognition that there will be other factors. It may well be, however, that the only knowledge of which there can be any certainty is the knowledge of the outcome of public policies, for in public interventions there is the possibility of experimentation and of measuring the intensity, quantity, and duration of the intervention and the previous and subsequent behavior of the objects of intervention.

It should be recalled the standard for knowledge that is being sought. The ultimate evaluation is whether a person charged with making public choices can act on the knowledge with success, whether the knowledge increases the likelihood of desired outcomes or reduces the cost of choice. It is a knowledge that incorporates the wider political and administrative costs as well; a flexible knowledge that can be tailored to different degrees of purpose, time horizons, and resources available; a knowledge that is sensitive to the potential modesty as well as to the varied grossness of public policies. In use, the knowledge would approximate a repeatable recipe in human affairs, spelling out generally the resource composition and deployments that are involved in variable outcomes of public intervention.

Conspicuous National Population Policies. There are five areas where such knowledge might be found. The first is tracking the policy inputs, transformations, outputs, and outcomes for existing population policies marked by conspicuous success or failure. From these extremes, especially the extreme where the odds entirely favored those who failed or disfavored those who succeeded, there is potentially more to learn than what is yielded from relatively routine situations. Extraordinary policy achievements or failures produce "recipes"; routine policy situations produce "tips." Candidates for the former are: control over access to services in Singapore, social security and delayed marriage incentives in Mauritius, paramedical health services and infant survival in Ceylon, family allowances for inducing higher natality in a regime in Eastern Europe, and transforming the abortion system in India from an illegal and unsafe one to a legal and safe one. As analysis, these studies should focus on the choice options in policy selection and implementation so that persons responsible at later periods for choosing among policies, implementing them, and evaluating results can use this research as a point of reference.

Routine Population Policies. But the more routine situations and their policies deserve research as well, not simply because they may have been mischaracterized, but also, as the source of monographic and case literature, to serve at the country level as a point of evaluation. All regimes have many policies which are explicitly pro- or anti-natalist in objective, though not necessarily in the outcome of their enforcement. These include policies relating directly as incentives or sanctions to parenthood, to illegitimacy, and to the provision and access to contraception, sterilization, and abortion. There are also myriad policies that affect the context in which fertility choices are made or not made, and that as public interventions affect for parents the calculation of costs and benefits of further children or affect the accessibility of a mate for procreation. If these are not always polity-wide, they are often at other levels of government or deal with special categories, such as public servants.

The policies are summarized under column A in Table 1-2 (directly fertility related) and Table 1-3 (indirectly fertility related). Though listed in no special order, the economic and social factors in fertility are in columns B and C, the intervening variables under D and E, and the dependent variables of intercourse and fertility under F and G. Preponderantly the greatest attention has been paid to the items under B and C and their influence on F and G; a more sophisticated literature looks at the same factors on their intervening mediations through the social technologies for fertility (D) and biological factors (E).[41] Despite a lengthy bibliography on "population policies" and a section on the subject in each issue of the *Population Index*, there has been little work on population policies, those public actions that appear under column A in the two tables.[42] The policies there catalogued operate directly on individuals and couples making fertility choices (A → F and G or A → D → F and G) or they operate on what is

Table 1-2
Fertility Related Public Policies

Independent Variables₁	IV₂	IV₃	Intervening Variables₁	Intervening Variables₂	DV₁	DV₂
Public Policies—use of public resources to reinforce or change B-E and thus affect F and G A	Economic Determinants B	Social Determinants C	Social Technologies D	Biological Determinants E	Intercourse Variables Exposure to Risk F	Fertility G

Fertility Related
1. Incentives and sanctions
  a. Family allowances
  b. Dependent deductions
  c. Access to services
  d. Bonus schemes
2. Contraception and other methods
  a. Prohibition of manufacture, import and information
	Growth GNP Wealth PCI
	
	Distribution of income
	
	Investment
	
	Wages
		Marriage Norms
		
		Family Norms
		
		Ethnic, group class mobility
			Age at marriage
			
			Abstinence
			
			Celibacy
				Puberty
				
				Ovulation
				
				Lactation
					Age at entry into sexual union
					
					Reproductive time between and after sexual union
						Conception

Political and Administrative Variables for policy selection and implementation

41

Political and Administrative Variables for policy selection and implementation

	Employment	Sex roles	Divorce	Genetic-make-up	Coital frequency	Gestation
b. Prohibition of contraception information	Housing	Education as source of norms	Contraception Chemical Mechanical Other			Infant survival
c. Public provision without cost	Land tenure					
d. Public provision with cost	Services					
e. Public authorization without subsidy	Inheritance		Sterilization	General Health		
f. Public authorization for private provision with subsidy	Education as a source of employment		Abortion			
3. Pre-natal and post-natal medical care and role assistance	Resources		Infanticide	Nutrition		
	Energy		Prostitution			
4. Adoption and illegitimacy	Waste		Homosexuality			
	Infrastructure					

Table 1-3
Indirectly Fertility Related Public Policies

Independent Variables₁	IV₂	IV₃	Intervening Variables₁	Intervening Variables₂	DV₁	DV₂
Public Policies—use of public resources to reinforce or change B-E and thus affect F and G	Economic Determinants	Social Determinants	Social Technologies	Biological Determinants	Intercourse Variables Exposure to Risk	Fertility
A	B	C	D	E	F	G
Indirectly Fertility Related						
1. Costs of raising children	Growth GNP	Marriage	Age of marriage	Puberty	Age at entry into sexual union	Conception
a. Housing	Distribution of income	Family Norms	Abstinence	Ovulation		
b. Education	Investment	Ethnic, group class mobility	Celibacy	Lactation	Reproductive time between and after sexual union	Gestation
c. Retirement benefits	Wages					
d. Food allowances						
e. Day care						
f. Extra-familial opportunities for women	Employment	Sex roles	Divorce	Genetic-make-up	Coital frequency	
2. Presence or absence of mate	Housing	Education as source of norms	Contraception Chemical Mechanical Other			
a. Conscription	Land tenure					
b. War						
c. National non-military service						
d. Migration regulation						
e. Public works employment						

Political and Administrative Variables for policy selection and implementation

f. Extra-familial opportunities for women
3. Rules governing making and dissolving of marital unions
   a. Marriage age
   b. Dowry-bride price
   c. Divorce
   d. Re-marriage after dissolution
   e. Inheritance
   f. Marital status as qualification or disqualification for other services
   g. Marriage loans
   h. Disabilities for non-marriage
4. Programs affecting morbidity and general health and nutrition

Political and Administrative Variables for policy selection and implementation

Services

Inheritance

Education as source of employment

Resources

Energy

Waste

Infrastructure

Sterilization Abortion

Infanticide

Prostitution

Homosexuality

General Health

Nutrition

Infant survival

included under B and C.[43] Indeed, many of the so-called "social and economic determinants" are policy effects on the contexts in which fertility and migration choices are made. This prose jumble of letters and code words might be summarized as shown in Figure 1-4.

Listing policies and making explicit by the use of arrows and letters what depends on what in an explanation is about as helpful as compiling compendia of public statutes on population. Those who do the latter in the "Law and Population" approach give the impression that it is enough to know a law is enacted and that variable compliance to it is related to the original legislation and not to the more valuable knowledge of the measures taken to translate law into concrete acts regarding peoples' fertility choices.[44]

It is the knowledge of the variable outcome of these actions, these uses of public resources to intervene in expected behavior, that will be useful. And it must be collected in a systematic and cumulative way with an eye towards discovering a "repeatable recipe" mentioned earlier. Short of that is anecdotage. These recipes would spell out the resource costs, broadly construed, and the time requirements that were mixed to achieve a difference in expected behavior. These recipes are developed not simply to provide authoritative evidence in the public debate over values but to take the next step and suggest what actions will translate that purpose into measurable results.

Experiments with Incentives. The third approach to finding policy-relevant knowledge is the research now arising from the experiments in providing incentives for low fertility—the tea estates in India, rubber estates in Malaysia, and educational bonds in Taiwan.[45] In almost every respect, the orientation of this research is aimed in the right direction: the incentives are resource interventions into expected behavior, the results can be compared with the previous behavior of the participants in the program and with natural control groups, and the mode is experimental. From this research, there will come not

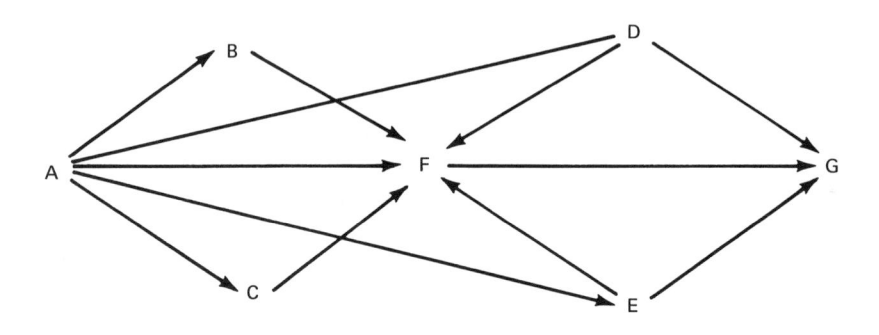

Figure 1-4.

only answers to the major question "will it work," but also to the more instrumental questions of the size of various incentives, their redemption characteristics, and the length of time possible to sustain involvement, etc. Indeed, from the point of view of providing knowledge that will economize on choice, this research may be as fruitful as any yet considered. At the same time, the particular setting of the experiments, especially the context of control over employment in a plantation by the agency providing the incentive, may limit their generalizability.

Public Policies as Experiments. The fourth approach to research for improved policy is as much an attitude as a subject matter. The world in which population events occur must be looked at more experimentally; indeed, policy interventions must be conceived of as the sources of experimental evidence for future choice. What has been ignored is that collectivities of human beings are units which are continuously producing experimental evidence in regard to the outcomes of external interventions into their expected behavior. The problem is to find a social unit of apposite size, benchmarks for the distribution of previous behavior, *an intervention into expected behaviors that is measurable by extent, degree, and duration*, and a measure of the distribution of subsequent behaviors.[46]

Most social science that is recommended for its utility for policy neglects two of these features: apposite size of unit and the measurable degree of intervention. Owing to the ease and economy for scholars of using data collected by national governments, the national unit is all too frequently the referent for evidence. The national unit is not appropriate in most instances: the data are usually collected for other purposes than those of the policy researcher; too much that is critical for policies in a national unit (whether it is Chad or China) gets swallowed by averages, and a national unit contains too many unisolatable intervening and possibly interdependent variables. Moreover the dimension of "how much of what for whom in relation to what differences in previous and subsequent behaviors" is absent. Land tenure systems do not intervene as such; nor does "functional inclusiveness" of the family or the host of other disembodied and ultimately unmeasurable forces that supposedly bombard fertility behavior.

Public policies, then, become a chief source of natural experiments in the social sciences: a potentially observed alteration in expected outcomes by the introduction of a new factor. The variable application of public policies (in one area before another), their variable implementation (x degree, extent, duration in Year 1 and y quantities in Year 2) and the variable participation in policies as beneficiaries and deprivatees (certain categories of individuals before or to the exclusion of others) create experimental situations with natural control groups. The results of the intervention will allow, to a greater degree than at present, a quantification of more elements in the equation. Moreover, the objects of the intervention can be questioned to provide a more finely-tuned analysis of the extent to which the intervention affected an existing disposition to act.

The problems that plague other forms of social science have their effects here as well: quality-quantity problems, numbers of potentially "empty" cells, focus of attention problems, etc.—but they are certainly fewer than otherwise obtain and certainly less destructive of the objective of providing better knowledge for the achievement of public purposes. Indeed, the chief deficiency in using public policies as the source of experimental evidence is that the treatment can seldom be withdrawn to see if a different behavior ensues, or, in the case of fertility, the behavior is often irrevocable if the treatment were withdrawn.

What might be done for a particular regime is to take three public policies: e.g., provision of secondary education for girls and boys (not necessarily in the same school); the provision of irrigation, and the distribution or redistribution of farm land so as to increase size of holdings. These experimental situations would furnish second order effects data and indicate if alternative methods might be less consequential demographically, and would test these hypotheses:

a. Increased education for both sexes has a positive effect on migration and a negative effect on fertility.
b. Increased income through the provision of irrigation water for double cropping and more lucrative crops has a positive effect on fertility and a negative effect on migration.
c. Increased holdings of agricultural land, within a range, has a positive effect on fertility and a negative effect on migration.

Population Policy Simulation. Finally, as the best guides to choice do not always emerge from the record, a vigorous social scientist-policymaker collaboration would be enhanced by the adaptation of game simulation to population policies. For population questions, there are presently "micro" games that heuristically depict the choice situation in families for numbers of children, spacing, and means of contraception.[47] But little has been done in the admittedly difficult area of policy choice and fertility interventions. Apart from national security games, the results in policy areas have not been encouraging.[48] But there seems to be no better alternative to discover policy options open to a regime, the stratagems in bureaucratic bargaining during implementation, and tactical relationships between the responsible agency and target groups. The adaptation of game simulation to population might result in a "experimental" situation to suggest policy research and provide a demonstrated educational experience for educating future population specialists. Three games should be created and perhaps later be adopted to computor playing as well:

1. Simulation of the political process, involving the regime, major political and administrative forces, and the media, in which a variety of fertility policy

options are tested for the necessary coalitions, compromises, and tactical possibilities.
2. Simulation of the implementation process, involving not only the responsible agency for implementing the policy but all other competing and relevant agencies as well.
3. Simulation of responsible agency, support and target group interactions, in which alternative tactics, decision rules, resource combinations, and organizational arrangements are explored.

*Knowledge of Resource Accumulation
and Deployment*

Whether in game simulation or analysis of the record of conspicuous national policies to shape demand for family limitation, the central problem is how public resources are obtained and used in interventions into expected behavior. No analysis which purports to be of value to policymaking can escape this problem; it is the crux of optimizing outcomes and minimizing costs. As a problem, however, it breaks down into five separate points of focus: resource accumulation, the policy production function, administrative infrastructure, decision rules, and target group construction. The first four can only be briefly described. The fifth, target group construction, will be discussed in greater detail, as it is as task more akin to what is conventionally done by scholars of the social and economic correlates of fertility.

Resource Accumulation. Obtaining and sustaining resources for the purposes of policy is the first area for which there can be technical knowledge of consequence. It should be recalled that, while policy is often a means to alter behavior on the cheap, of getting a major effect with minimum resources, policies cost. To get the resources to use in policy, both in general and in particular, costs the regime in alternatives foregone (and their costs and benefits) and in rewards to those who provided the political capital. Moreover, policy resources once accumulated need to be replenished; policies are more or less continuous interventions. Those who provide the resources may feel sufficiently rewarded, if the objects of policy comply with it, that a future supply is likely or that the origins of the resources used in policy are sufficiently vague that high or low compliance are irrelevant to their continued flow. On the other hand, there are direct costs in resources for policy and costs to neutralize opposition. It should also be recalled that most objects of policies do not necessarily consider the policies in their interests, though they may find noncompliance too expensive, and they and their allies can use their resources to divert the policy. Unwitting or witting allies can often be found in the regime itself in terms of resources flowing from other policies.

Knowledge of resource accumulation for public policy is normally the purview of political scientists. Their contribution to improving the knowledge base for public policy has been more promised than real.[49] In the field of population policies, some political scientists have discovered that there are interests to be served in various policies and that there can be opposition to population policies, especially those induced by external aid agencies.[50] They have not moved to the level of a technical political knowledge that can be mixed with other technical judgments to find out what policy choices might enhance the flow of resources and what coalitions might neutralize opposition. In addition, there is little speculation on the costs of alternative policies that might be used for the same ends.

Policy Production Function. The policy production function is the second focus for developing knowledge for the better utilization of resources. The issue of sufficiency of economic resources is, of course, obvious. It should surprise no one that most fertility limitation programs are rather unproductive; at their level of support in relation to the task, the need for infrastructure and the needed economies of scale, their attained productivity may be nothing short of miraculous. On the other hand, policies can fail to achieve a level of compliance with monetary resources that all observers would agree would be adequate. The reason for the latter is that the policy production function is more than a decision about economic resources; it includes the other policy resources of authority, information, status, and coercion.[51] As all policies are combinations of resources and it is the combination that affects variable compliance, one can immediately be on the outlook for resource shortages or shortfalls in combinations. For instance, high economic funding and little authority to spend is no better than the reverse. A policy with too little information or status for its operatives can be equally unproductive. Recent work in other fields suggests that the more authority is delegated to user groups, the better the information flowing to those who are responsible, the higher their status in the eyes of the objects of policy, and the higher the rate of compliance.[52] Timing is equally important in many instances. When authority to spend exists for only a few months out of the fiscal year because of a complex system of approvals, resources are diminished in their productivity if not in their nominal value. The timely converging of resources can be as valuable as absolute amounts of any one. When scholars compare population policies, one source of "repeatable recipes" is the analysis of policy production functions.

Decision Rules. A third focus is decision rules for the implementation of policies. It is perhaps commonplace to assert that policies are not self-enforcing, but there has been, astonishingly enough, little systematic work on policy implementation. One cannot stop with analyzing resource accumulation or the policy production function; one must also analyze the decision rules that were used or could be used to translate policy purposes into concrete public acts. These guides to choices about resources are mini-social science hypotheses that are or could be tested daily by administrative action. Once the policy production function is determined, the decision rules translate that purpose into the who, what, when, how much, how long, and by what criteria, that constitute the substance of administrative choice.[53]

Some decision rules are required by the constitution or laws of the regime (e.g., employment preferences for certain groups); others are the amalgam of political necessity, administrative convenience, ignorance, and sheer common sense. There are decision rules about allocations between objects of interventions, about divisions of resources and procedures in implementation, and about evaluation of performances. When all budgets of public programs are cut 10 percent, regardless of the fact that some budgets should be doubled and others wiped out altogether, what is observed is the workings of the decision *rule of equity*—all units receive the same treatment. When a family planning program concentrates on central cities, one of the decision rules is that funds should be concentrated where health services are concentrated—the decision *rule of advantage*. The point here is, regardless of their sources, decision rules are hypotheses about the results various choices will bring, and while decision rules that are used may bring a degree of the results sought, they may waste potential as well. As most policy analysts move from policy intervention to targets fulfilled, detouring only to identify political or bureaucratic saboteurs, they miss the point at which political wherewithal often gets lost.

Let me illustrate decision rules in three areas. First, there are decision rules about which units are to receive what resources. These are allocational decision rules. Policies are seldom detailed enough to spell out this issue and it is often left to hunches about "payoff" in political and policy terms. Often the allocational decision rule can alter the whole intention of the policy.[54] The decision rule of equity states that each unit receives the same amount. When it is applied to a population policy, it means that every political unit receives the same size of allocation, thus loosing the productivities that would accrue if units were treated unequally and received differential amounts of resources. If these units were treated equally, there would be some where demand would go unfulfilled and others where resources would go abegging. *Per contra*, another decision rule, such as a rule which rewards backward areas or disadvantaged people, might result in increasing the incidence of backwardness. Whatever their theoretical and resource feasibility, it is clear that population policies must be formulated and analyzed in this dimension as well.

The same may be said about evaluational and implementational decision rules. In the former, the hypotheses that get transformed into criteria to evaluate performances are hunches about what constitutes performance. Input decision rules for evaluation (e.g., cost per participant), transput decision rules (e.g., delay, size of inventory), output decision rules (e.g., percentage of target reached, births averted, etc.), and outcome rules (e.g., cost/benefits), all yield different answers and the unit flagged for high performance by one decision rule may go unnoticed by another. While we need guides to choice for future allocations, some decision rules may perpetuate less productive units, and their outcome must always be considered experimentally.

Implementational decision rules are those guides to choice which instruct those using resources from the point of allocation to the actual intervention into the expected behavior of the target group. Each instruction is an hypothesis, results of which may serve to commend this decision rule again and in a different setting. There are decision rules about which level in the hierarchy will initiate an intervention, what size and kind of intervention, and what responses from target groups constitute the range of accepted altered behavior. A flavor of this can be found in the rules listed in Table 1-4, where, shorn of their social science jargon, these rules guide those who might be making implementative decisions regarding incentives in fertility programs.[55] Ultimately, the decision rules read a bit like folk wisdom. A similar digest could be performed for Everett Rogers' hypotheses in *Communication Strategies for Family Planning*.[56] While many would seem trivial and self-evident, they are potentially part of the choice process in transforming purpose into action. They are also variably productive.

Table 1-4
Decision Rules for Incentive Systems

1. Larger incentives will produce more . . . than smaller incentives "within some limits."
2. Incentives tied to family size will be more difficult to administer and will produce more political objections.
3. Incentives are more effective than control schemes using no incentives.
4. The larger the incentive the more likely the "incented" will be attracted by the incentive and less by the object of the incentive.
5. The more attractive the incentive the greater the fraud and corruption.
6. Cash and material incentives are more sought than bonds or other forms of deferred payment.
7. The more plural the objectives the less effective is the incentive.
8. Incentives offering opportunities for existing children will be politically more acceptable (and hence less costly) than those for foregoing birth alone.
9. Positive incentives are more effective among the poor; blocked sanctions are more successful for higher income families.
10. Incentives made available only to the poorest groups in areas where the poorest are largely of a different race, religion, caste, or other grouping will be criticized as prejudicial.
11. Where birth records are poor, incentives for sterilization are more corruption-proof than no-birth incentives.
12. As demand is present, incentives for non-birth or sterilization should be made smaller at outset than later. Incentives to doctors and canvassers more effective at outset.

Source: Adapted from E.J. Pohlman, *Incentives and Compensations in Population Programs* (Carolina Population Center, 1971), *passim*.

Their potential for losing resources or increasing product is ignored by population scholars at their peril, though not necessarily to their intellectual stimulation.

Administrative Infrastructure. The fourth focus is administrative infrastructure. A policymaker may have done all the right things: assured a supply of resources, devised a policy production function appropriate to his purposes, resources, and time horizon, and thought through the implications of the decision rules chosen. But all the resources saved and potentially fruitfully deployed could be lost if there were inadequate administrative infrastructure. By that term is meant those fundamental investments in personnel, procedures, capital equipment, and physical space that ultimately economize on administrative action, that facilitate higher compliance with a policy's purpose. While the relationship is hardly linear, to a point it can be argued that the more effective investment the less adequate need be the decision rules, production function, etc. Infrastructure, like its "economic counterpart," reduces the costs of production, allows administrative decisions to be more predictable; but it is also costly, often marked by indivisibilities, and long in gestation.[57]

A scholar wishing to evaluate or to advise on a population policy would be concerned, in quantitative terms, with the extensiveness and intensiveness of the infrastructure: how much of the country was covered with a network and how substantial and continuous was any one aspect. A family planning program might have infrastructure that covers an entire regime, but a mobile van that can be visited by a participant in the program only once in three months is not intensive enough to allow a judgment on other grounds of a program. Qualitatively, the concern should be with the predictability or dependability of transactions with the unit from the target group's point of view.[58] A long-term consideration involves losses in resources that arise from "conflicts" by those who are the infrastructure, that is the use of resources for other than policy purposes. Here one need not only mean the private appropriation of policy resources. Just as profligate in terms of lost resources and services are the conflicts between professionals and non-professionals, conflicts between competing agencies in cognate area, conflicts between headquarters and field imperatives, conflicts between role definitions and role occupants, and conflicts between perceived organizational needs and policy needs.[59]

Target Group Construction

The final focus is target group construction. A chief consideration for policymaking and for policy research is how—in fact and not in the language of a statute—the target group is determined. For a resource intervention to involve a difference in behavior, it must affect the choice budgets of the target groups.

Some in the target group will respond regardless of the substance of the intervention on the basis of a generalized deference to official requirements; a few in the target group will resist the desired behavior whatever the resources used in the policy. As long as the latter group is relatively small and unconvincing to those potentially on the margin, regimes may tolerate a degree of noncompliance. Indeed, they may have no choice.

Choice Budgets. A policymaker has some notion of target groups and their choice budgets in the formulation of policies. A choice budget is the ever shifting priorities for personal action by members of potential target groups based on the relationship between their preferences and their resources. In this case, the resources are construed broadly and include legitimacy, economic goods and services (money), status, information, and violence.[60] These resources are held in different amounts and with different individual and combined values by members of different sectors. It is often by the resources held and sought and the kinds of preferences pursued that political leaders and policymakers can create coherent groupings for political and policy purposes. The resources are used by individuals to move towards what they prefer, to get more resources for that purpose, or to resist those whose actions contravene their objectives. By means of policy interventions, to enhance resource holdings or their value (or to block their reduction) or to reduce them (or to keep them from being increased), varying degrees of behavior may be achieved. Or changes may not occur because the resource intervention was not significant enough in size or composition, the transfers from allies and even other public programs were too great, and the margin on which the target group's action depended was not enhanced or diminished by a particular intervention. Whatever is sought by that target group, including higher fertility, can still be accomplished regardless of the resource loss or contribution.

Construction by Aggregation. However, knowing about choice budgets and thinking in those terms is only half the skill; the other half is knowing whose choice budgets to bring together for policy purposes, the ability to aggregate sufficiently large numbers of sectors so that the limited repertoire of interventions that inevitably marks any policy can be more effective. Two methods, both seemingly unknown to scholars, are (1) to aggregate by ascending degrees of generalization and (2) to disaggregate by examining the marginal cases. The first appears methodologically more complex, though it is ultimately commonsensical. The objective here is to achieve a level of aggregating sectors that provides maximum economies of scale. By that one means seeking the level of "optimal ignorance" in explanation, the point of knowing that a higher level of explanation might dictate other policy interventions, but that for the policy situation at hand a lower level of explanation and generalization will do. Perhaps the more appropriate phrase is "ignore-ance," for the issue is what may be safely ignored, even though it may be true.

This calculus is contrary to the inclination, well reinforced and rewarded, of scholars. As "true" knowledge and not necessarily applicable knowledge is sought, there is the urge to seek exhaustive explanations to be guides, if necessary, for policymakers. Exhaustive explanations are those levels of generalization about behavior that admit of fewest exceptions, the latter usually being given a statistically deviant status. The rewards for exhaustive explanations spur the inventive mind to ever higher and higher general theories like "*the* economic theory of fertility decline," tempting the scholar to commit the fallacy of methodological individualism. Unfortunately, exhaustive explanations exhaust. To be instructive of policy, these generalizations would take too long to be enacted, cost too much, have too many intervening variables that would have to be tended to by other policies, and require too many other demands on government to go unanswered. Above all, the outcome is probably too problematic.[61]

By using the calculus of optimal ignorance and seeking explanations of fertility behavior more tailored to policy requirements, the potential policy adviser arranges possible objects of intervention from the most particular to the most general. The explanation of what motivates each level of aggregation is not simply cumulative, a lower level of aggregation might become mostly exceptions at a higher level of aggregation. This perhaps can be seen more easily in Table 1-5. Chandra and Sita Arora appear in all levels. Depending on the level of explanation, their behavior might be considered average or deviant. For policy purposes in City X, one level of explanation might offer various economies of aggregation; a more inclusive unit might require a more inclusive explanation and resulting resource allocations. The level is determined by purposes to be achieved, resources, and time available for policies.

Table 1-5
Levels of Explanation

1	Chandra Arora, Hindu male	Sita Arora, Hindu female
2	All educated Hindu males in City X	All educated Hindu females in City X
3	All educated Hindu couples in City X	
4	All Hindu couples in City X	
5	All educated Hindu males in State Y	All educated Hindu females in State Y
6	All Hindus in cities = "the urban personality"	
7	All Hindus = "the Hindu personality"	
8	All educated couples in poor countries "the modernizing elite"	
9	Males in poor countries "machismo"	Females in poor countries "the cake of custom"
10	Couples in poor countries—"the traditional marriage"	
11	Men—"the male mind"	Women—"the female mind"
12	All couples = "marriage mentality"	

Construction by Disaggregation: Marginalism. The second method is more disaggregative. One might begin by looking at a demographic profile of potential target groups—perhaps the size of families—in the relevant political unit both cross-sectionally and, if possible, longitudinally. In the event no census data were available, a reasonably accurate profile could be constructed by a few interviews. Most explanations of fertility are in terms of averages or of modal behavior; the policy problem becomes how to move the central tendency. As the knowledge is in this direction, the policy adviser might first tailor his population policy to try to move those who are characterized as modal or average. A more sensible method, given limited resources and time, would be to look at the tails of the distribution. Fashioning a family allowance system to those with very low and very high parity, assuming that those who are modal are too numerous and too supported by peer group pressure, the policy may shift the average family size, though not the modal distribution. This might be made clearer in Figure 1-5.

This same point about disaggregation might be looked at another way. One of the problems of the differential fertility approach is that its proponents "divide" the explanatory characteristics (religion, income, work, residence, etc.) into completed family size and leave the impression that the "characteristics" were relevant for each increase in parity. Such a view is uncommonsensical. Residence, income, work, and other characteristics change over a fertility span and have a differential impact. In addition, and perhaps more importantly, the learning experiences of previous births are cumulative influences. By looking at fertility choices as ones taken "on the margin," a whole new dimension for

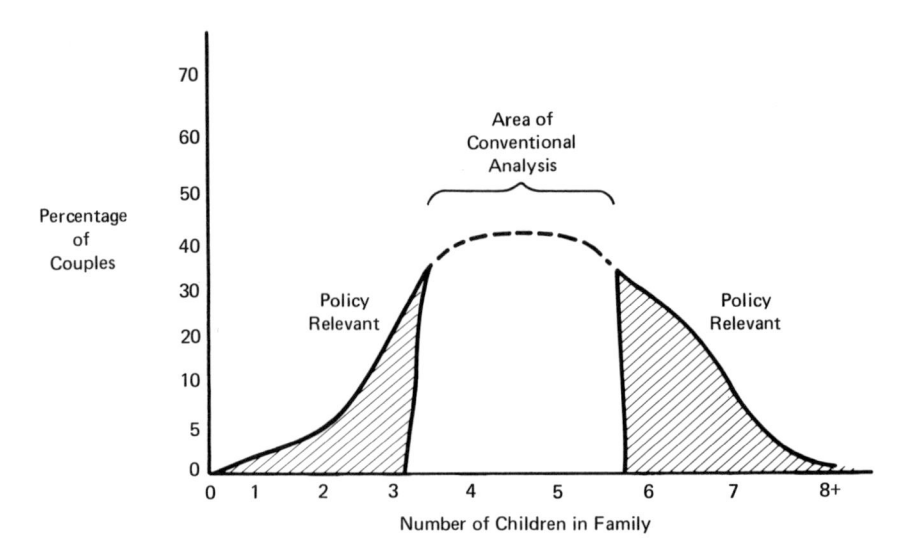

Figure 1-5. Explanations for Policy and for Social Science

research on public intervention is opened up. The suppositious situations that might enter into the marginal calculations for another child can be taken into account.

New Social Science Technologies. Adopting these perspectives on target groups for population policies requires inventing new social science technologies. The new technologies must produce knowledge that is predictive for shorter time periods, for different resource budgets, and for modulated purposes. What is purported to explain the distribution of all fertility choices may or may not be appropriate knowledge for policies where the intention is to motivate 10 percent of the population (usually a fairly sector specific part of the population) to have one fewer child. Several new methods would be appropriate for this task, such as:

1. Modal family choice budgets for groups salient for policies. This would develop in survey research and in indirect indicators methods of discovering the tradeoffs in choice, the transfers in and out from other groups, and the various "vulnerability" factors that might be incorporated in policies.
2. Marginal choice survey analysis. Survey methods must be devised to (a) take into account the cumulative temporal dimensions of choice and (b) create suppositious situations that reveal what factors affect the "margin."
3. Deviant case analysis. Approaches must be devised that explore the choice budgets of those who do not attain or who exceed the modal behavioral choice. By affecting through policy the "deviant cases," the central tendency might be moved more economically.
4. Tracer analysis. Little is known about what happens to policy interventions once they enter into the choice budgets of the target groups. As they are resources, such as family allowances, methods must be devised to discover the disposition of these resources; otherwise there is no helpful knowledge of the determinative influence of these resource additions or subtractions.
5. Longitudinalizing of cross-sectional analysis. As fertility effects of policies are often very long term, methods must be devised to sample in ways that extend the "temporal reach" of a cross-sectional analysis.

Population Knowledge and Population Policy

If scholars began considering their knowledge as hypotheses that could be tested and validated in the public realm and if policymakers began to insist on a standard of research that would focus on the issue of resources and their impact through public policy on behavior, then both the scholarly process and the policy process would be considerably improved. Seldom in life can a person bring together things held apart by convention: thought and action, theory and application, fact and value, purpose and process. While the task of a union of these natural complements (not opposites) is hardly a frequent occurrence or even easy, the opportunity in the population field is ripe for its achievement.

Notes

I wish to acknowledge the many intellectual contributions of my colleagues in the Population Policies Seminar at the Harvard Center for Population Studies in the Spring of 1974: Harold Lasswell, John D. Montgomery, and Myron Weiner, and the students who took the joint seminar. I also wish to thank the director of the Center, Roger Revelle, and members of the staff and of the library for their assistance. This chapter is a revision of two earlier papers, one given at the Battelle Memorial Institute and the other at the Interdisciplinary Communications Program of the Smithsonian Institution.

1. For examples, see chapters in Bernard Berelson (ed.), *Family Planning and Population Programs: a Review of World Developments* (Chicago: University of Chicago Press, 1966).

2. Aaron Segal, *Politics and Population in the Caribbean* (San Juan: University of Puerto Rico, 1969); Jason L. Finkle, "The Political Environment of Population Control in India and Pakistan," in Richard Clinton (ed.), *Political Science in Population Studies* (Lexington, Mass.: Lexington Books, D.C. Heath and Company, 1972), pp. 101-28; Gayl Ness and H. Ando, "The Politics of Population Planning in Malaysia and the Philippines," *Journal of Comparative Administration* 4 (1971): 296-329.

3. Everett Rogers, *Communication Strategies for Family Planning* (Glencoe and New York: Free Press, pp. 287-301); Dudley Kirk, *The Effectiveness of Family Planning Programs in Less Developed Countries: the Evidence from Survey Data* (Palo Alto: Stanford Food Research Institute, 1971); Jack Reynolds, "Evaluation of Family Planning Program Performance: a Critical Review," *Demography* 9 (1972): 69-86.

4. This point is further elaborated in Warren F. Ilchman and Trilok N. Dhar, "Optimal Ignorance and Excessive Education: Educational Inflation in India," *Asian Survey* 11 (1971): 523-43.

5. This point is developed in Warren F. Ilchman, "Measures for Measure: Administrative Productivity in the Second Development Decade," *Philippines Journal of Public Administration* 17 (1973).

6. Judith Blake, "Population Policy for Americans: Is the Government Being Misled?" *Science* 164 (1969): 522-29; Oscar Harkavy et al., "Family Planning and Public Policy: Who is Misleading Whom?" *Science* 165 (1969): 367-73; Judith Blake and P. Das Gupta, "The Fallacy of Five Million Women," *Demography* 9 (1972): 569-88.

7. Korbin Liu, *An Analysis of the U.S. Family Planning Policy*, Center for Population Studies, Harvard University, 1974 (mimeo).

8. This point is elaborated as a basis for a systematic political economy in Warren F. Ilchman and Norman T. Uphoff, *The Political Economy of Change* (Berkeley: University of California Press, 1969); for applications of policy conflict to population questions, see Herman E. Daly, "The Population Question in Northeast Brazil: Its Economic and Ideological Dimension," *Economic Development and Cultural Change* 18 (1970): 536-74; Aaron Segal, "The Rich, the Poor and Population," in Richard Clinton (ed.), *Population and Politics* (Lexington, Mass.: Lexington Books, D.C. Heath and Company, 1973): 173-88; James T. Fawcett, "Population Policy as a Response to Internal Social Pressures: the Case of Thailand," *Concerned Demography* 2 (1971): 26-29; Ernest Attah, "Racial Aspects of ZPG," *Science* 180 (1973): 1143-51.

9. For attempts to reverse the question and ask what impact on politics do population-*qua*-population events have, see Myron Weiner, "Political Demography: an Inquiry into the Political Consequences of Population Change," in National Academy, *Rapid Population Growth* (Baltimore: Johns Hopkins Press, 1971): 567-617; Nazli Choucri, *Population Dynamics and International Violence: Propositions, Insights, and Evidence* (Cambridge: Center for International Studies, MIT, 1973); Gerry E. Hendershott, "Population Size, Military Power, and Anti-Natal Policy," *Demography* 10 (1973): 517-24.

10. This approach is applied to education in Norman T. Uphoff and Warren F. Ilchman, *The Political Economy of Development* (Berkeley: University of California Press, 1972): 3-6.

11. Warren F. Ilchman and Ravindra C. Bhargava, "Balanced Thought and Economic Growth," *Economic Development and Cultural Change* 14 (1966): 385-99.

12. Nathan Keyfitz, "Migration as a Means of Population Control," *Population Studies* 25 (1971): 70.

13. Ibid., p. 72; see also Nathan Keyfitz, "The Youth Cohort Revisited," in W. Howard Wriggins and James F. Guyot (eds.), *Population, Politics, and the Future of Southern Asia* (New York: Columbia University Press, 1973): 231-58.

14. Exceptions to this are the works of two anthropologists: George M. Foster, *Traditional Societies and Technological Change*, 2nd ed. (New York: Harper and Row, 1973); and Burton Benedict, "Controlling Population Growth in Mauritius," in *Technology and Social Change* (1970), pp. 246-76.

15. For example, see Frank W. Notestein, "Economic Problems of Population Change," *Proceedings of the 8th International Conference of Agricultural Economists* (London: Oxford University Press, 1953); Ansley J. Coale, "Factors Associated with the Development of Low Fertility: an Historic Summary," *World Population Conference* 2 (1965): 205-209; Kingsley Davis, "The Theory of Change and Response in Modern Demographic History," *Population Index* 29 (1963): 345-66. I am indebted to Ms. Maria Lerda for several of the citations and arguments used in this and the following section.

16. For a summary article, see Steven Polgar, "Population History and Population Policies from an Anthropological Perspective," *Current Anthropology* 13 (1972): 203-11, 263-67.

17. Ansley J. Coale, "The Demographic Transition," *International Population Conference, Liege*, IUSSP, 1973, pp. 53-72, 68.

18. Tomas Frejka, *The Future of Population Growth: Alternative Paths to Equilibrium* (New York: Wiley, 1973).

19. Ronald Freedman and John Y. Takeshita, *Family Planning in Taiwan* (Princeton: Princeton University Press, 1969), Chapter 7.

20. John B. Wyon and John E. Gordon, *The Khanna Study, Population Problems in the Rural Punjab* (Cambridge: Harvard University Press, 1971).

21. Donald J. Bogue, "The End of the Population Explosion," *The Public Interest* 7 (1967): 19.

22. Kingsley Davis, "Population Policy: Will Current Programs Succeed?" *Science* 158 (1967): 730-39; Kingsley Davis, *Population Policy and International Change* (Berkeley: University of California, 1973 (mimeo.).

23. Statistical Office of the United Nations, "Conditions and Trends of Fertility in the World," *Population Bulletin of the United Nations—1963, #7* (New York: United Nations, 1965), pp. 134-51; David M. Heer, "Economic Development and Fertility," *Demography* 3 (1966): 423-44; Stanley Friedlander and Morris Silver, "A Quantitative Study of the Determinants of Fertility Behavior," *Demography* 4 (1967): 30-70; Irma Adelman and Cynthia Taft Morris, "A Quantitative Study of Social and Political Determinants of Fertility," *Economic Development and Cultural Change* 14 (1966): 129-57.

24. Statistical Office of the United Nations, *Population Bulletin*, p. 143.

25. Ibid., p. 150.

26. E.G., Heer, "Economic Development and Fertility"; Irma Adelman, "An Econometric Analysis of Population Growth," *American Economic Review* 53 (1963): 314-39.

27. A.M. Conning, "Latin American Fertility Trends and Influencing Factors," *International Population Conference, Liege*, IUSSP, 1973, pp. 125-49.

28. Steven Polgar (ed.), *Culture and Population, a Collection of Current Studies* (Cambridge: Schenkman, 1971), pp. 3-10, 87-105; Mahmood Mamdani, *The Myth of Population Control* (New York: Monthly Review Press, 1972); Jean Mayer, "Toward a Non-Malthusian Population Policy," *Columbia Forum* 12 (1969): 5-13.

29. Karen Mason et al., *Social and Economic Correlates of Family Fertility, a Survey of the Evidence* (North Carolina: Research Triangle Institute, September 1971), and Norman Lowenthal and Abraham S. David, *Social and Economic Correlates of Family Fertility, an Updated Survey of the Evidence* (North Carolina: Research Triangle Institute, June 1972), summarize the literature in this field; in doing so, these otherwise helpful efforts fall into the error of treating categories as if they were concepts. See Uphoff and Ilchman, *Political Economy of Development*, pp. 14-17.

30. Carmen A. Miro, "Some Misconceptions Disproved: a Program of Comparative Fertility Surveys in Latin America," in Berelson, *Family Planning*, pp. 615-34.

31. Maria Helena T. Henriques Lerda, *A Framework to Study Rural Fertility in Latin America*, Center for Population Studies, Harvard University, 1974 (mimeo.); Herman E. Daly, "The Population Question in Northeast Brazil: its Economic and Ideological Dimension," *Economic Development and Cultural Change* 18 (1970); 536-74.

32. Mason, *Social and Economic Correlates*; Lowenthal and David, *Social and Economic Correlates–Updated Survey*.

33. Edwin D. Driver, *Differential Fertility in Central India* (Princeton: Princeton University Press, 1963); Wilbert E. Moore, "Attitudes of Mexican Factory Workers Toward Fertility Control," in Milbank Memorial Fund, *Approaches to Problems of High Fertility in Agrarian Societies*, New York, 1952, pp. 74-101; Jean Morsa, "The Tunisia Survey: a Preliminary Analysis," in Berelson, *Family Planning*, pp. 581-93; Miro, "Some Misconceptions Disproved"; S. Iutaka et al., "Factors Affecting Fertility of Natives and Migrants in Urban Brazil," *Population Studies* 25 (1971): 55-62; Ali Paydarfar and Mahmood Sarram, "Differential Fertility and Socioeconomic Status of Shirazi Women," *Journal of Marriage and the Family* 32 (1970): 692-99; Carmen A. Miro and Walter Mertens, "Influences Affecting Fertility in Urban and Rural Latin America," *Milbank Memorial Fund Quarterly* 46 (1968): 89-117; David Yaukey, "Differential Fertility in Lebanon," in Clyde V. Kiser (ed.), *Research in Family Planning* (Princeton: Princeton University Press, 1962), pp. 125-39; Leon Tabah and Raul Samuel, "Preliminary Findings of a Survey on Fertility and Attitudes Toward Family Formation in Santiago, Chile," in Kiser, *Research in Family Planning*, pp. 263-304; Murray Gendell, "Fertility and Development in Brazil," *Demography* 4 (1967): 143-57; Sung-Bong Hong and Joong-Hi Yoon, "Male Attitudes Toward Family Planning on the Island of Kanguha-Gun, Korea," *Milbank Memorial Fund Quarterly* 40 (1962): 443-52; J.R. Rele, "Fertility Differentials in India: Evidence from a Rural Background," *Milbank Memorial Fund Quarterly* 41 (1963): 183-99; William A. Morrison, "Attitudes of Males Toward Family Planning in a Western Indian Village," *Milbank Memorial Fund Quarterly* 34, pp. 262-86; Meredith Minkler, "Fertility and Female Labor Force in India: a Survey of Workers in Old Delhi Area," *Journal of Family Welfare* 17 (1970): 31-43; Ronald Freedman, John Y. Takeshita, and T.H. Sun, "Fertility and Family Planning in Taiwan: a Case Study of the Demographic Transition," *American Journal of Sociology* 70 (1964-5): 16-27; Mohiuddin Ahmed and Fatema Ahmed, "Male Attitudes Toward Family Limitation in East Pakistan," *Eugenics Quarterly* 12 (1965): 209-26; A. Majeed Khan and Harvey M. Choldin, "New 'Family Planners' in Rural East Pakistan," *Demography* 2 (1965): 1-7; Paul K. Hatt, *Background of Human Fertility: a Sociological Survey* (Princeton: Princeton University Press, 1952); M.A. El Badry, "Trends in the Components of Population Growth in the Arab Countries

of the Middle East: A Survey of Present Information," *Demography* 2 (1965): 140-86; Bernard C. Rosen and A.B. Simmons, "Industrialization, Family and Fertility: a Structural Psychological Analysis of the Brazilian Case," *Demography* 8 (1971): 49-69; Janet Abu-Lughod, "The Emergence of Differential Fertility in Urban Egypt," *Milbank Memorial Fund Quarterly* 43 (1965): 235-53; John Stoeckel and Moqbul A. Choudhury, "Differential Fertility in a Rural Area of East Pakistan," *Milbank Memorial Fund Quarterly* 47 (1969): 189-99; Irene B. Taeuber, "Japanese Demographic Transition Re-examined," *Population Studies* 14 (1960): 28-39; CELADE, "La Fecundidad Rural en Latino-americano," *Demography* 2 (1965): 97-114; Thomas E. Dow, "Fertility and Family Planning in Sierra Leone," *Studies in Family Planning* 2, 8 (1971): 153-66; Rudolf Andorka, "Regression Analysis of the Factors Influencing Regional Fertility Differences in Hungary," *International Population Conference*, London, 1969 vol. 1, pp. 488-93; Gul B. Kripilani et al., "Education and its Relation to Family Planning," *Journal of Family Welfare* 18 (1971): 3-8; Nasser Maroufi-Bozargi, "Some Socio-demographic Characteristics of Women Seeking Contraceptive Advice," *Contributed Papers*, IUSSP, Sydney, 1967, pp. 476-82; Paul K.C. Liu, "Socioeconomic Development and Fertility Levels in Taiwan," *Industry of Free China* (1965), pp. 1-16; P.O. Olusanya, "Rural-Urban Fertility Differentials in Western Nigeria," *Population Studies* 23 (1969): pp. 363-78; Anrundh K. Jain, "Socio-Economic Correlates of Fecundability in a Sample of Taiwanese Women," *Demography* 6 (1969): 75-90; Serim Timur and Nuray Fincancioglu, "Demographic and Socio-Economic Characteristics of Turkish IUD Acceptors," in F.C. Shorter and B. Guvenc (eds.), *Turkish Demography* (Ankara: Hacetteppe University, 1969): 173-218; A. Klinger and E. Szabady, "The Hungarian Fertility and Family Planning Study," *Family Planning and National Development*, Proceedings of the IPPF Conference, Bandung, 1969; Visid Prachuabmoh, "Factors Affecting Desire or Lack of Desire for Additional Progeny in Rural Thailand," in Donald Bogue (ed.), *Sociological Contributions to Family Planning Research* (Chicago: University of Chicago, 1967), pp. 364-409.

34. E.g., Mahbub ul Haq, "Employment in the 1970's: a New Perspective," *International Development Review* 13 (1971): 9-13; Dudley Seers, "New Approaches Suggested by the Colombia Employment Programme," *International Labour Review* 102 (1971): 377-389; International Bank for Reconstruction and Development, *Summary Proceedings*, Washington, D.C., 1972, pp. 16-31. These arguments are summarized in Warren F. Ilchman and Norman T. Uphoff, "Beyond the Economics of Labor-Intensive Development," *Public Policy* 22 (1974): 189-218.

35. William Rich, *Smaller Families Through Social and Economic Progress* (Washington, D.C.: Overseas Development Council, 1973); Roger Revelle, "The Balance Between Aid for Social and Economic Development and Aid for Population Control," *International Journal of Health Services* 3 (1973): 667-74;

James Kocher, *Rural Development, Income Distribution and Fertility Decline* (New York: Population Council, 1973); R.C. Repetto, "The Relationship of the Size Distribution of Income to Fertility and the Implications for Development Policy," *Research Paper Series*, Harvard Center for Population Studies, Cambridge, 1974; Lester R. Brown, *In the Human Interest* (New York: Norton, 1974).

36. Rich, *Smaller Families*, pp. 21-38.

37. Ibid., pp. 18-20.

38. Ibid., pp. 35-8.

39. Ilchman and Bhargava, "Balanced Though and Economic Growth," for a discussion of the self-confirming qualities of similar hypotheses for capital investment.

40. Repetto, "Relationship of Size Distribution."

41. Kingsley Davis and Judith Blake Davis, "Social Structure and Fertility: an Analytic Framework," *Economic Development and Cultural Change* 4 (1956): 211-35.

42. See Edwin Driver, *World Population Policy: an Annotated Bibliography* (Lexington, Mass.: Lexington Books, D.C. Heath and Company, 1972); and Edwin Driver, *Essays on Population Policy* (Lexington, Mass.: Lexington Books, D.C. Heath and Company, 1972); Driver uses a very broad and, for the purposes of policy analysis, an operationally imprecise definition of policy. The inattention to public policy probably comes from two sources: (1) the general, though inadequately researched conclusion that the intewar pro-natalist policies in Europe had no effect and (2) the dominance of the population field in the 1950s and 1960s by those interested in extending and universalizing family planning. Among the latter, however, there was recognition of the importance of reserving some attention for public efforts to shape and accelerate demand for fertility limitation. See Bernard Berelson, "Beyond Family Planning," *Studies in Family Planning* 1, 38 (1969): 1-16; Bernard Berelson, "Population Policy: Personal Notes," *Population Studies* 25 (1971): 173-82; Bernard Berelson, "An Evaluation of the Effects of Population Control Programs," *Studies in Family Planning* 5, 1 (1974): 2-12.

43. Tables 1-2 and 1-3 are the product of exploring the country and subject references in Driver, *World Population Policy*, passim. While these references could be systematized in terms of the tables and our public knowledge in the field, thus, ordered to a degree, the research underlying the conclusions is so incommensurate and of such variable quality on any policy, that the results might be misleading in the extreme. See also, Department of Economic and Social Affairs, United Nations, "Measures, Policies and Programmes Affecting Fertility, with Particular Reference to National Family Planning Programmes," *Population Studies* 51 (1972).

44. See book and monograph series of the Law and Population Programme, Fletcher School of Law and Diplomacy, Tufts University, Medford, Massachusetts.

45. Oliver D. Finnigan and T.H. Sun, "Planning, Starting and Operating an Educational Incentives Project," *Studies in Family Planning* 3 (1973): 1-7; Ronald Ridker, "Synopsis of a Proposal for a Family Planning Bond," *Studies in Family Planning* 43 (1969): 11-16; Ronald Ridker and Robert Muscat, "Incentives for Family Welfare and Fertility Reduction: an Illustration from Malaysia," *Studies in Family Planning* 4 (1973). See general discussion in Everett Rogers, *Communication Strategies*, pp. 152-224 and Edward Pohlman, *Incentives and Compensations in Birth Planning* (Chapel Hill: Carolina Population Center, 1971).

46. See, for example, the work of Donald Campbell; e.g., Donald T. Campbell, "Quasi-Experimental Design," in David Sills (ed.), *International Encyclopedia of the Social Sciences* (New York: Macmillan, 1968), vol. 6; *idem.*, "Reforms as Experiments," *American Psychologist* 24 (1969): 409-29.

47. See, for example, the game by Professor Harold Thomas of the Center for Population Studies, Harvard, entitled "Planafam."

48. Martin Shubik and Garry D. Brewer, *Models, Simulations, and Games—a Survey* (Santa Monica: RAND, 1972).

49. The appropriate standard and methodology for such studies has been set by Harold D. Lasswell, *A Pre-View of the Policy Sciences* (New York: American Elsevier, 1971).

50. For example, see Richard Clinton (ed.), *Political Science in Population Studies* (Lexington, Mass.: Lexington Books, D.C. Heath and Company, 1971), Richard L. Clinton and R. Kenneth Godwin (eds.), *Research in the Politics of Population* (Lexington, Mass.: Lexington Books, D.C. Heath and Company, 1972); Richard L. Clinton (ed.), *Population and Politics* (Lexington, Mass.: Lexington Books, D.C. Heath and Company, 1973); Peter Bachrach and Elihu Bergman, *Power and Choice: the Formulation of American Population Policy* (Lexington, Mass.: Lexington Books, D.C. Heath and Company, 1973); Terry L. McCoy (ed.), *The Dynamics of Population Policy in Latin America* (New York: Ballinger, 1974); W. Howard Wriggins and James Guyot *Population, Politics, and the Future*; David Chaplin (ed.), *Population Policies and Growth in Latin America* (Lexington, Mass.: Lexington Books, D.C. Heath and Company, 1971).

51. Ilchman and Uphoff, *Political Economy of Change*, pp. 136-207; see also Warren F. Ilchman, "Decision Rules and Decision Roles: Some Thoughts on the Explanation of Productivity and Productivity of Explanation," *The African Review* 2 (1972): 219-46. For an example of the reallocation of status and its effects, see Robert C. Repetto, "India: a Case Study of the Madras Vasectomy Program," *Studies in Family Planning* 31 (1968): 8-16; for the productivity of more information, see S.S. Lieberman et al., "The Isfahan Communications Project," *Studies in Family Planning* 4 (1973): 73-90; for a contrasting view on the productivities of varying allocations of authority, see Finkle, "Political Environment of Population Control," and S.J. Burki, "Stages in the Formation of Public Policy: an Analysis of Population Programs," Development Advisory Service, Harvard, Cambridge, February 1974 (mimeo.).

52. For example, see John D. Montgomery, "The Allocation of Authority in Land Reform Programs: a Comparative Study of Administrative Processes and Outputs," *Administrative Science Quarterly* (March 1972), pp. 62-75.

53. For a more extended discussion, see Ilchman, "Measures for Measure"; examples of decision rules can be found in Carl Taylor, "Five Stages in a Practical Population Policy," *International Development Review* 10 (1968): 2-7; J. Mayone Stycos, "A Critique of the Traditional Planned Parenthood Approach," in Kiser *Research in Family Planning*; Joan Mencher, "Family Planning in India," *Family Planning Perspectives* 2 (1970): 235-39; Julian L. Simon, "The Per Capita Income Criterion and Natality Policies in Poor Countries," *Demography* 7 (1970): 369-78; William Seltzer, "Measurements of Accomplishment: The Evaluation of Family Planning Efforts," *Studies in Family Planning* 53, pp. 9-16.

54. The classic study of this phenomenon, though not explicitly recognized by the scholar (!), is Philip Selznick, *TVA and the Grass Roots* (New York: Harper Torchbooks, 1966).

55. Edward Pohlman, *Incentives and Compensations.*

56. Everett Rogers, *Communication Strategies*, pp. 399-404.

57. For a further discussion of infrastructure, see Ilchman and Uphoff, *The Political Economy of Change*, pp. 208-55; see also John D. Montgomery, "A Strategy for Analyzing the Effects of Rapid Population Change on the Administration of Public Services," Harvard Center for Population Studies, March 1974 (mimeo.); Moye W. Freyman, "Organizational Structure in Family Planning Programs," in Berelson, *Family Planning and Population Programs.*

58. For a discussion on the point of predictability and infrastructures, see Uphoff and Ilchman, *Political Economy of Development*, pp. 411-15.

59. For example, see S.J. Burki, "Stages in Formation of Public Policy."

60. Contributions toward the notion of choice budgets in population programs might be found in Gordon W. Perkin, "Monetary Commodity Incentives in Family Planning Programs: a Preliminary Trial," *Studies in Family Planning* 57 (1970): 12-15; Gerald C. Wright, Jr., "Population Attitudes of the Poor in North Carolina: Implications for Family Planning Programs in the South," in Clinton and Godwin *Research in Politics of Population*, pp. 135-52.

61. For an application of this approach, see Warren F. Ilchman and Trilok N. Dhar, "Optimal Ignorance and Excessive Education: Educational Inflation in India," *Asian Survey* 11 (1971): 523-43.

2

Internal Migration Policies: Purposes, Interests, Instruments, Effects

Myron Weiner

Why Internal Migration Policies?

Few governments are willing to freely allow their citizens to travel, work, and settle anywhere within the country, notwithstanding the assertion of most governments that citizenship entitles individuals to live anywhere within the nation's boundaries. Governments may attempt to slow the rate of urban growth, disperse populations into smaller towns, encourage people to move to less densely populated regions, or even forcefully "rusticate" urban youth by sending them to rural areas for employment. Zoning and housing regulations may exclude certain social classes from buying property or building in particular localities by imposing costs that effectively exclude income groups below a specified level, or there may be quite explicit policies—if not by the central government then by local governments—to prevent some social classes or ethnic groups from moving into a locality. Governments may use pass laws to regulate where people live by requiring a work permit as a condition of residence, and there may be a policy of excluding anyone from settling in "protected" regions in which certain tribes reside.

Why are governments concerned with where their citizens live and work? What purposes, what values, are they seeking to maximize by attempting to influence the movement of their population? Whose interests are affected by governmental interventions? What instruments do governments employ to influence or regulate movements? What are the consequences of these interventions? These are the questions to be examined in this chapter.

In the developing countries high rates of population growth have made governments acutely concerned with the internal distribution of their populations. Even governments that reject proposals to influence fertility behavior view population movements and population distribution as variables to be manipulated by policies and programs. There are several reasons why this is so.

One reason is that internal population movements affect the size and density of a community more visibly than do natural population increases. In some cases the appearance is the reality. In several African cities, where growth is from 7 to 10 percent per year, natural population increase may account for 2 to 3 percent, while the remainder results from migration from the countryside and smaller towns. Often the appearance is misleading. Urban growth rates in many developing countries are 4 to 5 percent per year, with natural population increase (at 3 percent) accounting for about two-thirds of the urban growth and migration the remaining third.[a] Nonetheless, it is easier to attribute many of the ills of rapidly growing cities—a deterioration in housing stock, the proliferation of slums, inadequate water supply and health facilities, crowded schools and hospitals, congested traffic, growing unemployment, and high crime rates—to the daily influx of migrants than to the daily birth of babies; in fact, migrants do create more of a strain on some public facilities such as housing and transportation than do babies, although babies (or parents on their behalf) may be more demanding than migrants on other public facilities such as hospitals and schools.

Moreover, many governments believe that some of the problems intensified by rapid population growth can be eased by policies directed at the dispersal of populations—partly because they consider population distribution more easily influenced by government policies than fertility, and partly because they may advocate population increases for the country as a whole and view a redistribution policy as a means of reducing some of the costs.

A second reason is that migrations often affect the social class and ethnic composition of a community. Migrants are rarely occupationally or ethnically stratified in the same proportion as the region or city into which they move. Members of a community generally value the particular class and ethnic makeup of their community. Babies are viewed as long-term replacements of existing stock with no significant effect on existing proportions—although differential fertility rates among classes and ethnic groups may make some difference over time. In contrast, migrants may belong to a lower (or higher) income group, speak different languages, subscribe to different religions, and in other ways differ from a majority of the residents in a community. It would be a rare neighbor who did not express pleasure at the birth of a baby, while the entrance into the community of a migrant is often greeted with anxiety or hostility.

Many migration policies can be understood as measures to preserve the existing social structure of a community: through restrictive covenants, zoning ordinances, tribal reservations, community control of schools, preferential employment for local people, etc. Middle class neighborhoods typically want to prevent the establishment of low income squatter settlements, and a tribal or linguistic community may want to exclude those who are culturally different. Upper income groups may feel threatened by the intrusion of lower income people, while those with lower incomes may feel threatened by the intrusion of those who belong to different ethnic communities.

In the class-cleavage societies of Latin America, and the ethnically (and class) divided societies of many countries of Asia and Africa, population movements often threaten the prevailing social structure and power structure of a local community. The result is that while policies to influence fertility are generally

---

[a]The proportion of urban growth due to migration is actually higher in the United States and Western Europe, where population growth rates are lower than in developing countries.

the concern of the national rather than the local government, the reverse is true with migration policies. It is often local communities—towns, cities, and state governments—that wish to regulate the volume and composition of migration. Indeed, there may be conflicts between local authorities desirous of restricting migrants, and national governments that view the right to move as a right of citizenship.[b] But one hastens to add that national government are not themselves adverse to intervening for the purpose (as they see it) of maximizing some general "public" interest rather than the "special" interests of a particular community.

A third reason why governments may be concerned with where people live is explicitly political: to extend governmental control either over a territory or a population. The movement of people to less densely populated areas and to border regions may be an instrument for consolidating control over a region and to preclude the expansion of others into the terrain. For security reasons, a government may want to move people away from a tense border, or, under some circumstances, may want to encourage population settlements. Israel, Brazil, and the Soviet Union have internal population policies guided by such security considerations. And throughout the nineteenth century the United States explicitly encouraged population movements westward as a means of extending territorial control, under the doctrine of "manifest destiny."

By confining citizens to a given territory government may seek to consolidate its control over a portion of the population. The British in Malaysia and the Americans in Vietnam sought to regulate rural settlements as part of a broader counter-insurgency strategy, and in South Africa, the government explicitly separates racial communities as a means of enforcing control among the Africans.

Although some governments may explicitly declare that the desire to extend or consolidate control may have determined their internal migration policies (e.g., Israel and Brazil),[1] more often governments proclaim that their purposes are to develop a backward and low density region, accelerate the development of a low income ethnic group by confining it to a specified region, and so on. From the government's point of view, to make its policy objectives explicit might subject it to undesirable domestic or international criticism.

More generally, public interventions in the migration process often take disguised forms and hide a variety of values and interests. Zoning regulations, for example, notoriously serve hidden objectives. A suburban government may declare that zoning regulations restricting the construction of housing on land lots below a specified size are intended as an environmental protection measure, but its real intent may be to exclude ethnic minorities or working class migrants by raising the costs of construction. Similarly, municipal authorities may

---

[b]The classical assertions of this right are expressed in the French Rights of Man, which guarantees "le droit de libre sejour et libre circulation," and the French Constitution of 1791, which speaks of "liberte d'aller, de rester, de partir."

bulldoze a squatter settlement on the grounds that squatters are despoiling public lands or creating a health hazard (objections that could also be met through a slum improvement program), when the hidden objection is to the settlement of low income villagers in middle class urban communities. Among those social classes where liberal values prevail, that is where people assert the rights of fellow citizens to live and work without discrimination on the grounds of class, ethnicity or community of origin, interventions may be justified by the assertion of other "universal" values: protecting the environment, avoiding overcrowding, reducing pollution, minimizing hazards to the health and safety of the community, etc.

Types of Migration Policies

Among policies explicitly intended to influence migration, we can distinguish those that affect the composition, the direction, and the rate of migration.

Policies intended to influence the *composition* of migrants may seek to shape the occupation, class, ethnic, sex or age characteristics of migrants. Policies intended to influence the *direction* of migration flows may focus on the places of origin, the places of destination, and their interaction. Policies intended to influence the *rate* of migration may focus on in-migration rates, out-migration rates, and the duration of migration.

We can also distinguish between *migration-influencing* and *migration-responsive* policies. Migration-influencing policies are those intended to affect the flows of migration, while migration-responsive policies are intended to ameliorate the effects of a given pattern of migration.[2] Examples of migration-responsive policies are government decisions to regularize illegal squatter settlements and provide public services or, alternatively, to deny public services to such settlements or physically attempt to eliminate them. Governments may pursue a cultural-linguistic assimilation policy toward migrants and their children or an agglutinative policy which permits a migrant culture to adhere to its social structure with little or no linguistic or cultural change. Through housing and educational policies a government may choose to encourage migrants and local people to mix with one another or to remain separate, depending upon whether social interactions among divergent classes and ethnic groups are valued or feared as conflict-inducing.

Each of these migration-responsive policies can also be migration-influencing policies; that is, how a government responds to a migration flow can itself be a factor in the subsequent rate and composition of that flow.

Who Makes Policies?

Within a single political system different levels of government may be concerned with influencing different variables. Local governments are often more concerned with the composition of their migrants and the numbers who come than where they come from; a regional government may be particularly concerned with the ethnic, class, and skill characteristics of migrants moving into the region; a national government may be concerned with the rate at which the urban centers are growing or the rate at which its smaller towns are declining. Migration policies can be pursued, explicitly or inadvertently, by all levels of government.

Moreover, different levels of government have different policy instruments, for they have different resources and sanctions at their disposal. Control over land use may be in the hands alternatively of the local, regional or national government. So, too, is the authority and resources to construct roads, extend electric power, expand communication, and generally create the infrastructures of regional development. The authority to license industries, and dispense (or withhold) tax concessions may be a local, regional or national authority. The distribution of authority and resources in a political system thus shapes the capacity of each level of government to influence the composition, the direction, and the rate of migration.

Government migration policies are also fragmented by administrative units, each with their own interests, resources, and authority. There are population distribution effects to a wide range of administrative decisions. Decisions by departments of public works, defense, transportation, irrigation and agriculture, industry, and education involving the location of public investments have distributive consequences. Government departments rarely have spatial and demographic objectives in mind in the making of location decisions, but these may have cumulative effects on where people live and work. Even with national planning departments, planning is more likely to be sectorally rather than spatially oriented. Moreover, many government agencies may have an explicit concern for coping with some of the needs and demands that accompany migration, especially in the areas of housing and education, but they may be unaware or unconcerned with the effects of those migration-responsive policies on subsequent population flows.

Nor can migration policies be considered without recognizing the variety of political interests groups that are affected and the politically charged atmosphere within which policy decisions are often made: the removal of squatter settlements and slums, decisions to locate industries, the routing of transportation networks, the passage of zoning ordinances and land use laws—all these interventions arouse intense concerns among tenants, homeowners, tax payers, land developers, contractors, industrial investors, etc. Since each of these interests may have quite different concerns, coalition politics is likely to be a feature of migration policy choices.

Prototypes

The pulling together of various levels of government, relevant administrative agencies, and a variety of politically influential interests to form a coherent national policy to shape the composition, direction or rate of migration for the achievement of explicit objectives is an uncommon occurrence. It is instructive, therefore, to look at a number of efforts to formulate policies so that we can better understand both the determinants and consequences of migration policy interventions, and the problems associated with attempting to create a coherent national policy.

In recent years a number of Third World countries with multi-ethnic populations and regional governments have been concerned with influencing the ethnic composition of those who migrate from one region to another; Nigeria, India, and Malaysia are among the most prominent examples.

Many Third World countries have been concerned with the high rate of urban growth, especially to their largest cities. Thailand, Mexico, Kenya, and South Korea are examples.

Still other governments have been concerned with regional imbalances of population and sought to take steps to bring about a redistribution of population between regions. Indonesia and Brazil are examples.

Though in each case there is a concern for several migration variables, in the first instance the policy focus is primarily on the composition of migration, in the second the focus is on the rate of urban growth, and in the third the focus is primarily on the direction of population movements.

In reviewing these three patterns we shall treat each case as prototypical—that is, no one country necessarily fits any single case perfectly, though there are several countries whose governments have pursued policies that closely fit one of the prototypes described here. Since these are migration models in a descriptive sense, not actual cases, we shall give each of the countries arbitrary names: *Xenos* to indicate that the question of who is a stranger in a preoccupation in the first case, *Primus* to indicate that the rank ordering and size of place is a preoccupation in the second, and *Disequilibria* for the third case to indicate that there is a perceived imbalance of populations as between regions of the country.

Xenos

Xenos is a multi-ethnic country. It has six large groups and innumerable smaller ones, differing from one another in language, culture, and identities. The country has a federal system with six states, in each of which a single ethnic group constitutes a majority, though in the country as a whole no one group is in a majority.

In the small, densely populated southeastern state of Enachia reside the Enach people who for the past hundred years have been migrating into the other five states as teachers, doctors, lawyers, journalists, technicians, clerks, and administrators, both in state governments and private businesses. Many Enachs started their own shops and small businesses and some became large industrialists and financiers. They settled in the towns (though in their own region they are agriculturalists as well as town dwellers) and in several they became a majority.

Three change processes have been at work in Xenos since the country became independent nearly twenty years ago. The first is that a declining death rate has accelerated the country's population growth rate to over 3 percent per year so that half the population is under eighteen. The second is that since independence there has been an enormous expansion in the country's educational system; primary school education is now universal and a very large proportion of the country's young people have gone on to secondary schools and colleges. The result is a major increase in cityward migration as educated rural youth have entered the urban labor market in search of employment. The third development is a growth in industry, especially in the large cities, but the growth in employment has not been large enough to meet the demands of the country's rapidly expanding labor force.

The discontent of the urban youth has been particularly acute in the province of Bhumi, where there is a strong political movement demanding the expulsion of the Enachs. Shops of the Enachs have been burned, slogans "Enachs go home," and "Bhumi for the Bhumis" have been scrawled on the walls, and there have been a number of violent clashes between the youth of the two communities.

The state government has begun to systematically exclude, some would say expel, Enachs. Private employers have been instructed to give employment preferences to Bhumis. Enach shopkeepers, on one pretext or another, have lost their licenses. The government has nationalized the private bus company, the electricity supply, and several other Enach-owned firms. The government has also nationalized the private schools attended by Enach children and passed an ordinance requiring that the language of the Bhumis be the medium of instruction in all schools for all children, irrespective of mother tongue.

A substantial number of Enachs have returned to their "home" province, though many are actually the descendents of migrants who had been born in the province of Bhumi and had never even been to Enachia. In the state government there has been some concern that the exodus of the migrant communities would disrupt internal commerce and services, but the government concluded that this disruption is less important than the need to expand employment opportunities for the local population.

Moreover, the government policy proves to be politically popular. The expanding local Bhumi middle class is pleased by the availability of increased employment opportunities. The small indigenous business community welcomes the elimination of some of their competition, although a few businessmen dependent upon Enach businessmen for contracts are in distress. Those with good government connections, however, anticipate that the government will now provide them with generous loans, subsidies, and contracts. Finally, Bhumi administrators see the departure of the Enach civil servants as providing them with opportunities for personal advancement.

Indeed, there are few Bhumis who do not welcome the exodus, for the Enachs were generally seen as an "exploitative" community, aggressive, arrogant, and above all, socially and culturally exclusive. The Enachs, it is widely said by the Bhumis, did not identify with the language, the culture, and the people of the region; they came as aliens and they leave as aliens.

Primus

In Primus nearly one out of every ten citizens lives in Primus City, the capital of the country. Primus City is already three times larger than the next largest city in the country, and it is growing at nearly 6 percent per year, or about twice that of the country as a whole. In-migration from the countryside and from smaller towns is about equal to the annual natural population increase of the city. One consequence of this rapid growth is that the city is experiencing a substantial deterioration in its housing stock and there has been a proliferation of low-cost squatter settlements. The city's parks, whose gardens were once the pride of the European rulers who governed Primus until fifteen years ago, are now crowded with shacks constructed out of metal from oil drums, wood from packing crates, scraps of sheet metal, and other make-shift materials. Some of the main thoroughfares and the bazaar areas are also now occupied by squatter huts so that in some areas it is difficult for people to walk unintruded on main streets.

Both unemployment and underemployment have grown in Primus City. The informal sector has proliferated: many migrants are street hawkers, rickshaw pullers, shoeshine boys, coolies, pimps and pickpockets, or run small pavement "shops," tea stalls, or find jobs as domestics.

Public services have become greatly congested. Hospitals, infirmaries and schools are overcrowded, garbage removal service has deteriorated, drinking water supply is inadequate, and the public transportation system, especially the buses, regularly breaks down under the strain of rush hour traffic. The city is dirtier than it used to be, gastrointestinal diseases have increased, and now there is some begging, though beggers were rarely seen in the main streets of Primus City a decade ago. Municipal departments report that they do not have the resources to expand public services rapidly enough to meet the rapid population increases.

The central government has concluded that steps should be taken to reduce the strain on the urban system by slowing the influx of migrants into the city and by pursuing forceful measures to move some of the present migrants out of the city.

The government has introduced a law requiring that no one can work in the city without first obtaining a pass from the Employment Office proving that he has a job. The Public Works Department and the police have forcibly demolished some of the squatter settlements and provided land on the outskirts of the city to which migrants can move. There have been a few unpleasant skirmishes between squatters and the police, and with the help of a few bulldozers, some squatters have been evicted.

The local population of the city has generally applauded the government's policy. The middle class views the squatter settlements as eyesores and health hazards; local shopkeepers welcome efforts by the police to eliminate the migrant hawkers; and the departments of education, health, transportation, and other departments concerned with providing public services welcome these policies as a way of easing their administrative load.

The squatters themselves, of course, oppose these policies, and while they lack the political power to reverse the government's policies, they have found various ways of undermining the government's programs. Many migrants rent the land made available to them outside the city by the government, then quietly slip back into the city to build new squatter settlements. Some squatters have organized themselves and sent delegations to the government demanding that their settlements be legalized, and that the government provide them with electricity, drinking water, and sanitation facilities. The government has turned down their pleas on the grounds that to legalize and improve the squatter settlements would only attract other migrants who would build more slums in the city. Still, the squatter settlements persist, partly through the lethargy of the government, partly because the settlements are rebuilt almost as fast as they are torn down, and partly because the police, members of the public works department, and municipal politicians are often bribed by slumlords and by the migrant squatters themselves.

The government's Planning Commission has concluded that neither pass laws nor slum clearance are adequate to rid the city of its migrants. They have prepared a number of proposals to encourage urban growth in smaller towns through subsidizing land for industrial development, and tax credits to businessmen for investing in the small towns. The Planning Commission advocates establishing regional "growth centers" and "rural industrialization," which they see as a means of slowing the growth of Primus City while at the same time encouraging regional development elsewhere in the country.

Disequilibria

Disequilibria is one of the high population growth countries in the world, but its government is more concerned with the unequal distribution of the population than it is with the population growth rate. While some parts of the country are among the most densely populated regions of the world, other parts of the country are only sparsely populated. The government has concluded that they ought to attempt to distribute population more equitably by encouraging migrations from the more to the less densely populated regions. They offer a number of reasons for doing so. One is that the less densely populated regions are underdeveloped, but are potentially rich because of their forests, minerals, and, in the judgment of some members of the government, a high agricultural potential. Should these regions be developed, says the government, the country as a whole would benefit, as well as the migrants. A second reason is that the government believes that many of the problems that now exist in the densely populated areas of the country, particularly the crowding of its cities, the fragmentation of already small agricultural holdings, and the widespread unemployment would be considerably eased if some of the population would emigrate to the less densely populated regions.

The government has launched a major resettlement program to its underdeveloped southwest region. They have invested considerable sums in road construction, forest clearance, electric power, and industrial estates. These investments have been welcomed by road builders, the country's engineers, private contractors, and by some investors who see new opportunities for profitable investment. The program has strong support from the ministries of public works, transportation, power, and the departments in charge of forests and mineral exploitation. There is mixed sentiment within the government's Planning Commission and some opposition within the Ministry of Finance.

With the successful clearance of some of the forest lands, and the establishment of several factories, migrants have moved to the southwest. Many of the migrants complain that housing promised by the government is not ready, that the water supply is inadequate, the electric power does not always work, the equipment needed to cultivate the land is not available in the local market, and that there are not enough jobs in the factories to provide employment for all the migrants. Some of the migrants have returned home, but most have stayed, eventually to find both work and housing. The migration flow continues, but it is not as large as the government had hoped.

Meanwhile, the indigenous population of the southwest, mainly a tribal population, is increasingly hostile to the government's settlement program. A handful of local contractors do well, as do some of the large local tribal landowners who are able to sell land to the government at a handsome profit. But most of the local people feel that they have not gained from the regional development program. They have lost the use of much of the forest lands, where they hunted and collected forest produce. They do not have the education to become lawyers, doctors or administrators for the government. A few of the local people have found employment in the new industries, but most of the tribals find it unpleasant to work indoors and dislike the routines of factory life. Political authority is now wholly in the hands of outsiders. The local population still has its own tribal council, but it has no power over the critical developments that are now so dramatically affecting their lives. The tribals particularly resent the condescending attitudes displayed toward them by the migrants, who see them as a primitive, "jangali" people. The local people increasingly feel that economically, politically, culturally, and socially they have become second class citizens in their own region. In a few locales there have been violent clashes between migrants and the tribal population, but these have been effectively controlled by the central police.

A few economic planners in the central government have raised the question of whether the investment by both the government and private sector might have benefited more people if it had taken place in the more densely populated regions where there were already roads, electricity, and industrial centers. They point out that these large expenditures have provided jobs for only a small number of migrants and that local people have not (or at least feel they have not) substantially benefited. But the government continues to believe that on balance the regional development and resettlement program is worth continuing for its long-range population redistribution effects.

The government of Disequilibria is not very keen on a population limitation policy. They believe that the country's international status and its internal development would benefit from a larger population, for it would provide them with a larger internal market, a more sizable army, and the intangible attention, if not respect, that accompanies size. The government sees its development program in the southwest as a way of relieving some of the existing population pressures that grow worse with the continued high rate of population growth; that is, of having what they perceive as the benefits, but reducing the costs of population growth. Disequilibria's internal redistribution policy, therefore, is in part a substitute for a fertility limitation policy.

Policy Objectives

What objectives are served by the migration policies of Xenos, Primus, and Disequilibria? The internal migration policy of Xenos is intended to increase the employment opportunities for local people, while at the same time restructuring the status-employment nexus that would end the dominant position of the migrant population. The policy to restrict migration is a means of coping with the dual problem of ethnic inequalities and blockages to occupational mobility for the indigenous population. In Primus, government policy is directed at preserving a minimum level of services in the capital city and maintaining what the government considers the modern character of the city by discouraging the migration of lower income groups. The intent is not simply the relocation of the urban poor—though some planners might be content with such an objective—but to provide greater income opportunities for the urban poor through the development of smaller urban centers. And in Disequilibria, government sees its migration policies as serving the dual purpose of relieving the population pressures in one region (on employment and land use) while encouraging the economic growth and settlement of another.

Alternatives

In each of these instances government could plausibly have chosen other policies to maximize the same values without attempting to influence internal migration. In Xenos, for example, the state government might have developed a program to increase employment rather than to expel migrants; but clearly the expulsion policy is, in the short run at least, more efficacious in providing employment opportunities, though if it is followed by a declining rate of investment and declining increases in economic growth, the policy might have long-term consequences for increasing employment. In Primus the government could have chosen to reduce income disparities in the city not by expelling the squatter settlements, but by a program of slum improvement; here, too, the fiscal costs may be high, the improvements may take a long time, and the middle class in the city may remain dissatisfied at the persistence of low income housing (and low income people) in their midst, but if the goal is greater income equality within the society as a whole rather than the appearance of greater equity within the confines of the city, then a slum improvement program may be a preferable policy to slum removal. Finally, in Disequilibria government could choose to invest in the high density region rather than in the less developed region with a rural development program or with an educational program deliberately intended to encourage out-migration to the more advanced regions.

The costs and benefits of the policies pursued by the three governments in our hypothetical cases, and the alternative policies that they might have pursued to achieve some of the same objectives, cannot be weighed without asking, at whose cost and for whose benefit? Much of the debate over whether governments should intervene to influence the migration decisions of individuals often fails to recognize that a variety of interests are served, or disserved, that diverse social classes and ethnic groups gain or lose (or perceived themselves as gaining or losing) and that no single public interest or value is served by such policies. While the policymaker may not make the values or interests underlying his policies explicit—indeed, it may be in his interests not to—it is the task of the policy analyst to do so.

Whose Interests Are Served?

Even a cursory examination of our cases reveals the implicit interests served by government policies which, when made explicit, explains what otherwise would appear to be inconsistencies on the part of policymakers. Take, for example, the exhortations of the government of Primus that peasants should not move into its already crowded capital city. Even though the government provides incentives for business to expand in other urban centers (and disincentives to peasants to migrate to the city), the government continues to provide disproportionately more funds for electricity, water supply, and sanitation to its capital city than it does in the rural areas, or in its smaller towns. Indeed, the attitude of the government of Primus toward the expansion of its own primate city is like that of the automobile commuter who welcomes the expansion of public transportation so that traffic on the highway will diminish, thereby allowing him to commute more rapidly! So long as the government continues to provide funds for the expansion and well-being of its major urban center, the influx of peasants from the countryside is a rational response on the part of peasants who seek a larger share of the country's expanding national income.

Similarly, it should be apparent that the policy of the regional government within Xenos to give employment preferences to its own "people" has in no way increased the amount of employment available in the country as a whole; the policy has simply transferred jobs from one social class to another, and if the displacement of the migrant population has decreased the investment rate, then there may actually be a decrease in the rate at which new employment opportunities are created. The policy is intended—in this instance quite explicitly—to benefit one social class at the expense of another.

Policy Outcomes

In each instance the outcome of the policy interventions is not well understood. For Xenos one would want to know whether restrictions on interregional migrations has actually improved the occupational structure of the local community; that is, whether the occupational structure has become more diversified, there has been an increase in occupational mobility, and a rise in real income. One would want to know, too, what the impact of such policies has been on ethnic relations and on regional and national political coalitions; that is, what political price has been paid both regionally and nationally for a policy intended to benefit one ethnic group as against another.

In Primus one would want to know more precisely what the effect of squatter removal has been on the urban poor, whether they have simply relocated themselves in new urban slums, moved to low income settlements on the outskirts of the city, or shifted to regional growth centers. One would want to know, too, whether the urban poor are better off in the smaller towns than in the larger cities, and what the relative per capita costs are to government of providing public services, including water supply, sanitation, education, medical facilities and urban transport, in the small towns as against the large cities.

Similarly, for Disequilibria a closer look is needed at both the costs and benefits of investment in underdeveloped regions as against the costs and benefits of equivalent expenditures in the more developed regions. Have government "transmigration" policies (to use the Indonesian terms for policies to encourage inter-island migrations) resulted in the relocation of populations at a cost commensurate with what would be gained by development expenditures in the migrants' place of origin? Do relocation policies create new opportunities for acquiring skills, developing new lands, and generally expanding the horizons of a migrant population, or is there merely a transfer of poor subsistence agriculturalists from one locale to another with only marginal improvements in income?

Population movements and the distribution of populations that result from movements are the consequences of many other policy choices that have little to do intentionally with population movements. Attempts to cope with the undesirable consequences of migrations (e.g., squatters, urban congestions, etc.) by policies to reduce the rate of migration, change the direction of migration, or influence the composition of migration may in turn reduce the benefits which the existing migration processes have generated. Any assessment of the effects of policy interventions must, therefore, consider what benefits (as well as what losses) have been reduced. Where the benefits of migration prove to be considerable, policymakers should consider policies to reduce the unwanted effects of migration rather than policies to reduce migration itself.

Since migration policies, like migration itself, have primary, secondary, and tertiary effects, any study of consequences must have a long-time perspective. Generational effects are particularly important, for opportunities for the children of migrants may prove to be quite different from those for the migrants themselves. Under some circumstances a substantial proportion of the children of migrants may move upward in the urban labor market, while under other circumstances both the migrants and their children may find themselves in dead-end jobs with little or no opportunities for upward mobility. An analysis of the structure of the urban labor market into which migrants move is important for assessing some of the generational effects of migration.[3]

The net balance of costs and benefits (a phrase we use to encompass social and political as well as economic consequences) may depend upon our time perspective. Under some conditions the immediate impact of slowing migration may be economically negative—by depriving a particular locale of the labor supply and the skills it needs; we would need to know whether the effect of such a policy is to weaken the competitive position of the industry that depended upon migrants and deprive the local population of the services which migrants provided, or whether some compensatory mechanisms would begin to function. Will industry train local people? Will there be a change in technology to reduce the need for labor? Will local educational institutions emerge (or expand) to prepare local people for jobs that migrants once held? Will wages rise to attract local people to take jobs which were previously considered undesirable? Each of these adaptations have different gestation periods.

Policy interventions assume knowledge concerning expected behavior (and its consequences) in the absence of governmental intervention, and knowledge concerning the likely effects on behavior if government does intervene. We need to know what will happen if government does act and if it does not act. In our studies of migration we know even less about the multiple long-term effects of government migration policies than we do of the consequences of migration in the absence of governmental interventions.

Policy Instruments

If it is the assessment of the consequences of migration that leads policymakers to intervene, it is the assessment of determinants of migration that leads policymakers to choose particular instruments for intervention.

We shall examine what we know of the determinants of migration in an effort to see how such knowledge helps us to choose among alternative instruments for policy interventions. Can existing knowledge be utilized to shape a policy that would, for example, encourage people to move from Java to Sumatra, rural dwellers seeking urban employment to move to small and medium size towns rather than to Bangkok, rural Malays to move into new towns instead of to Chinese-dominated Kuala Lumpur, Brazilians in the crowded northeast to cultivate land in the newly cleared terrain in the Amazon region, and low income, unskilled and hitherto non-mobile residents of the backward region of Appalachia to move to employment opportunities elsewhere in the country?

Migration Theories

Everett Lee and Donald Bogue have each provided comprehensive lists of determinants of migration. According to Lee,[4] the determinants can be categorized as (1) factors in the area of origin, (2) factors in the area of destination, (3) intervening obstacles, and (4) personal factors. Bogue's list includes (1) migration-stimulating situations for individuals (such as marriage, graduation from school, employment opportunities, military service, retirement, death of a spouse, political oppression, community disaster, etc.), (2) a list of factors affecting the choice of destination (e.g., the cost of moving, the presence of friends and relatives, possibility of living with someone until established, the climate of the region, subsidized train or plane fares, etc.), and (3) a list of socioeconomic conditions that underlie individual decisions (such as major capital investments in a community to provide more jobs, the quality of housing in a community, and the degree of ethnic and racial toleration).[5] Charles Tilly also lists three factors: opportunity, information, and cost. "The greater the opportunities elsewhere and the greater the flow of information about opportunities, the greater the migration; the higher the cost of mobility, the less the migration."[6] Tilly goes on to suggest factors affecting individual decisions: "When it comes to the individual, the probability that he will migrate to any particular place (or that he will migrate at all) depends on the fit between his needs or qualifications and the opportunities available in that place, the channels of communication he has with that place, and the ties or investments he has in his present location." Stouffer, in his classic account of the determinants of migration, emphasizes the "number of opportunities" available to potential migrants, and suggests that these opportunities vary depending upon where one is located in the social structure of a society at a given point in time.[7]

Migration theory is a form of disequilibrium theory. An imbalance exists between the skills and preferences of individuals on the one hand, and on the other the availability of opportunities to utilize these skills and maximize these preferences in the areas in which they reside as compared to alternative and accessible locations. Migration theory presumes differentials both in places and persons: differences between places in the type and number of jobs available, the skills they require, the salaries they pay, the quantity or quality of housing, schools, public services, the climate, styles of living, political and religious freedoms, personal security, etc., and differentials among individuals with respect to their capacities (abilities, skills, resources) and desires (values and motivations) to benefit from the differentials in opportunities provided by places.

Which differentials in opportunities influence individual choices to migrate are shaped by what individuals value; that is, what is the preferred quality of life. Lasswell's list of values ("power, enlightenment, wealth, well-being, skill, affection, respect, rectitude") are suggestive for understanding what it is that makes individuals in differing cultures, social classes, and ages responsive to differences between places (see Chapter 4 in this volume). Opportunities for education may shape the decisions of one age group, employment that of another, and climate and environmental factors still that of another. Concern for safety ("well-being, to use Lasswell's terminology) may lead one group to move, employment and income opportunities another ("wealth"), and a desire for religious freedom ("rectitude") or ethnic equality ("recognition") still others.

From a policy perspective, therefore, existing migration theory is often too gross for choosing among alternative policies. It is not sufficient to know that differentials are determinants of individual choice. One must know which determinants should be increased or reduced to change the composition, rate, or direction of migration. One must know what kinds of opportunities are likely to motivate people to move or not to move, and what classes of individuals (age cohorts, sexes, ethnic groups, social classes, skill categories) located in what places are most likely to be influenced by what kinds of policy interventions.

Moreover, since policy choices often involve substantial shifts in the utilization of public resources, one must know which interests are most likely to be effected, whose support should be anticipated and whose opposition overcome, if a given policy is to be chosen and implemented.

A brief review of the instruments thus far utilized by governments to effect internal migration, and of several current theories intended to guide policymakers, calls attention to the limitations of our existing knowledge. We shall look at seven policy instruments: (1) the disposition of public services in both urban and rural areas, (2) income policies in the urban areas, (3) administrative decentralization, (4) industrial location and regional development, (5) pass laws and other controls on potential migrants, (6) preferential interventions to benefit local people as against migrants, and (7) the effect of immigration policies on internal migration.

*The Disposition of Public Services
and Housing*

Does the allocation of public services and housing to urban and to rural areas affect population movements? Two related propositions have been proposed. The first is that the denial of public services and housing to urban migrants will serve as a disincentive to migration,[8] and the second is that the provision of increased public services to rural area will reduce the efflux.

Many governments restrict public welfare assistance to urban migrants; deny migrant squatter settlements access to municipal water supply, sanitation services, electricity, and public sewerage disposal; and give preferences in public housing to residents of long standing rather than to recent migrants. While it is often recognized that these policies tend to worsen conditions for migrants, they are advocated on the belief that the provision of services and amenities to migrants would only increase their flow from the countryside to the city. Wellisz writes that "the availability of low-income housing and urban social overhead facilities acts as a magnet to the population."[9]

If migrants are attracted to cities either because they have found a job or are looking for work, how important are public services as an incentive? For those who have already found employment, the quality of services provided by the city may be a secondary consideration, while for those in search of employment, the network of friends and relatives in the city who can provide short-term accommodations and assist in the search for employment may be more important than the housing supply or the public services provided. The fact is that cities with appalling facilities for migrants continue to have a high influx. Friedmann is probably correct when he notes that we have no empirical evidence that either the quality of housing or housing services provided migrants influences the flow from the countryside to the city.[10] However, while the kinds of housing and educational facilities provided may have only a small, or even a zero effect on whether migrants enter a city in search of employment, the presence or absence of such facilities may influence the decision of migrants to bring their wives and children, and, in turn, have an impact on whether the migrant's sojourn is temporary or permanent.

The corollary of this proposition has also been asserted; differentials between city and countryside can also be reduced by an investment in rural amenities. The term rural "amenities," like the term urban "public services," is often left unspecified; it may include an improvement in schools, health facilities, transportation, communications, drinking water, and sewerage disposal. The assumption is that an improvement in rural living conditions would also make the "bright lights" of the city less attractive.

It can be argued equally plausibly that an improvement in transportation reduces the costs of rural-urban migration, that an improvement in communications makes peasants more aware of the opportunities and attractions of urban life, and that more schooling imparts both higher expectations and greater skills among rural youth, both inducements to migration. While there are many sound policy reasons for improving the facilities of rural areas, should such efforts be viewed as anti-migration policies? As Cornelius has pointed out, we know little about the conditions of rural life that influence decisions to migrate.[11] Land tenure conditions, employment opportunities, wage rates, and increases in agricultural output may on balance be more important determinants than public services. In the absence of more precise and tested knowledge, policy proposals to invest in rural areas as a means of reducing out-migration must be viewed with caution.

Income Policies

John Harris and Michael Todaro, in a much-quoted article, have argued that the persistently high rural-urban migration in developing countries is a result of the ratio of wages in the industrial sector to average rural wages. "Rural-urban migration", they write, "will continue so long as the expected urban real income at the margin exceeds real agricultural product—i.e., prospective rural migrants behave as maximizers of expected utility."[12] So long, then, as the minimum urban wages are substantially higher than agricultural earnings, migration to the city will continue. Todaro and Harris note that the ratio is particularly high in African cities, as compared with South and Southeast Asia. The result is that African cities have substantially higher urban growth rates—as high as 10 percent for Nairobi, for example. If their thesis is correct, a reduction in urban wages in relation to rural income would slow migration to cities.

In an article applying the model to Africa, Todaro explains why high migration persists in spite of the growth or urban unemployment.[13] Todaro argues that the interaction of two variables, the differential in urban-rural income and the probability of securing an urban job determines the rate and magnitude of rural-urban migration. Using Gugler's concept of job hunting in an urban area with high unemployment as a "game of lottery,"[14] Todaro concludes that it is rational for a migrant to play the lottery especially when (a) the rural-urban income disparity is high, say if real urban wages are twice that of rural wages, (b) the waiting period for employment is not too long (the possibilities of finding employment within a year are say 20 percent, or one in five), and (c) the migrant is young so that there is a long time horizon that makes it reasonable for the migrant to weigh the time "lost" through waiting for employment against the long-term increases in income.

An important policy conclusion drawn by Todaro is that an increase in urban employment will increase rural-urban migration if income disparity between urban and rural wages continues; moreover, if migration increases more rapidly than an expansion in employment, an expansion of the employed urban labor force could paradoxically be followed by a growth in urban unemployment! Alternatively, he suggests that "a reduction, or at least a slow growth in urban wages, has a dual beneficial effect in that it tends to reduce the rate of rural-urban migration and increase the demand for labour," thereby reducing urban unemployment.[15]

Todaro concludes that unless there is a forceful policy of wage restraints on urban incomes, or high taxes on urban wages, then urban unemployment will continue to grow. Income equity between urban and rural areas is thus a means of stimulating employment while reducing urban population growth through migration. The Todaro-Harris model thus produces counter-intuitive theory and policy: policies to reduce or prevent an increase in urban wages will increase employment; and increases in urban employment will not necessarily increase rural-urban migration if the wage differential between rural and urban areas is small.

Unfortunately, we do not yet have any major comparative studies demonstrating that rural labor is highly responsive to rural urban-wage differentials. The theory implies that, *ceteris paribus*, rural areas with the lowest wages would provide more migrants than areas with higher wages, and that within any given area those with the lowest wages would be the first to leave, corollaries that are by no means supported by the limited empirical evidence we have. Moreover, if the hypothesis is verified, one would need to take a closer look at the political problems that would arise if a government pursued an urban wage restraint policy. Would governments committed to public sector development be prepared to reverse their position that public sector firms be "models" with regard to wages? Would trade unions impede a wage restraint policy? Could there be wage restraints in industry without similar wage restraints in public service employment?

Administrative Decentralization

Administrative decentralization is another instrument for the redistribution of population. The relocation of administrative offices from one city to another has an immediate population distribution consequence since governmental personnel are transferred and hence must migrate or resign their positions. In India, for example, the creation of new states within its federal system and the creation of new state capitals has had a substantial impact on the pattern of urban growth. Federal systems with provincial capitals are less likely to have primate cities[16] —a factor in the historic development of a dispersed pattern of urban settlement in decentralized Germany as against the primate pattern of centralized France. Similarly, the creation of a new national capital has a distributive effect; on at least two occasions population movement was brought about by the government of Brazil when new capitals were created: in 1933 when the capital was transferred from Salvador to Rio, and 1960 when the capital was shifted to Brasilia. It is not always clear, however, whether the creation of a new capital has actually redistributed urban populations and relieved the congestion of the more densely populated cities or whether a new attraction has been created which accelerates still further rural to urban migration.

The distribution of some government services may have an impact on the settlement patterns in urban areas. Though government services ordinarily tend to be placed in areas of existing population densities, governments have located colleges and universities and law courts away from populated areas. In both instances, those who need the services of these institutions have little choice but to travel to or, in the case of students, reside wherever the services are located.[17]

Since in most countries government is the largest single employer, decisions as to where to locate their personnel have significant multiplier effects. Thus, courts attract lawyers, hospitals attract patients and chemists, universities attract students and book stores, and the field offices of the agricultural extension service attract sellers of farm machinery, fertilizers, and pesticides. The transfer of governmental personnel in numbers is also likely to have an impact on shopkeepers and on the entire service sector.

Unlike many other policy interventions to influence the redistribution of population, the decision to move one or more government offices is easier to enforce than a decision intended to influence the behavior of those outside of government. Nonetheless, it should be recognized that the re-organization of government for population redistribution purposes is likely to encounter strong opposition; government officers are notoriously loathe to move to less attractive urban centers, while land speculators have an intense preference for some sites over others. In any event, the decentralization of government offices and government-supported services should be considered part of the armory of instruments for influencing the distribution of populations.

Industrial Location and Regional Development

A variety of government policies involve efforts to move investments from one locale to another. A number of countries are creating new towns or encouraging "growth centers" among intermediate cities and towns. Other countries are concerned with the growth, economically and demographically, of entire regions. Among the developed countries new towns and growth center policies have been adopted in France, Great Britain, Japan, South Africa, the Soviet Union, Sweden, and the United States, while policies to disperse industries or support more backward regions have been pursued by Argentina, Finland, Great Britain, Ireland, Japan, the Netherlands, South Africa, the Soviet Union, the United States, West Germany, Belgium, Finland, South Africa, and Sweden.[18]

Central to each of these policies is the capacity of government to influence the location of industrial investment.[19] When new industries are in the private sector, a combination of regulations and incentives (including subsidies) may be employed to coerce or encourage investors to move to smaller towns or to less attractive regions. But whether it is the location of public or private investment that concerns government, attention must be given to a variety of infrastructure investments: electric power, transportation, communications, warehouses, water supply, facilities for the disposal of industrial waste, and arrangements that will ensure investors (public or private) sources of raw materials, equipment, spare parts, as well as marketing outlets. Policies to redirect investment away from areas to which investors might otherwise move requires sophisticated economic analysis and planning, the capacity for considerable administrative coordination, and a degree of political support that most governments find difficult to achieve. Reviewing the efforts to relocate populations through such policies in developed countries, Berelson concludes that in spite of these policies "the trend of the urban centers continues—not always to the central city but outward into the metropolitan area—and governments have found it extremely difficult to stop or lessen the flow."[20]

Moreover, it is problematic as to whether regional investment and regional growth necessarily improves the income and well-being of those who live in the region if migrants freely enter. As William Alonso writes, "a project in a backward region which depends for its labor on people brought in from outside the region may raise the per capita income of the region but lower the welfare of the original inhabitants if it introduces shortages or higher wages."[21] Paradoxically, then, a redistribution of population may, under some conditions, equalize income as between regions while having little and even a negative impact on income distribution as between social classes.

Pass Laws

A number of countries have used direct restrictive measures to control the flow of populations through the adoption of pass laws (Indonesia) and internal passports (South Africa). Potential migrants are prohibited from traveling or residing in an area without a work permit. In some countries, food rationing cards may be issued only to those who hold work or residential permits. Unable to find non-coercive policies to slow the rural influx into cities, many urban planners are increasingly attracted to the adoption of such restrictive controls. However, such restrictions are not easily enforced. Migration serves a double function. From the point of view of the economic system, it is a mechamism for expanding labor supply; from the point of view of the individual, it provides an opportunity for social mobility. Arbitrary pass laws that forbid people from entering an area for employment when it is clearly in their economic interest to do so are likely to be evaded: enforcement officers are likely to be bribed, identification papers forged, and exceptions sought as an illegal black market in the labor supply emerges.

To the extent that such restrictions prove to be successful in reducing or halting the efflux from rural areas and the influx into urban areas, there are likely to be other social and political consequences. If the escape hatch from rural areas is forcibly closed, the level of rural political protest may increase. Individuals living under distressful conditions may turn to organized political protest if the option of emigrating is closed by state intervention.[22] The relationship between the growth of political dissidence in the Soviet Union and restrictions on emigration provides a recent illustration of this proposition, although here the policy is one of restrictions on leaving the country. In South Africa there is reason to believe that the Bantus have not accepted restrictions which prohibit their movement into the metropolitan areas.

To impose legal restrictions on internal movements and on emigration may thus imply the need for a far wider range of social controls than are implied by mere pass laws, residence-tied work permits, and internal passports.[23]

The willingness of policymakers to employ, and the readiness with which some policy analysts advocate, the use of compulsory means to prevent the efflux or influx of population suggests both an impoverishment of our knowledge concerning the determinants of migration and a lack of awareness of the possible secondary effects of such restrictions.

Preferential Interventions

Local and regional governments are often extraordinarily inventive in finding policy instruments to give preferences to those belonging to autochthonous populations as against migrants, especially when migrants belong to "alien" ethnic groups.

The Indian states provide a laboratory for examining a wide variety of preferential policies. Outsiders are not permitted to buy land (Kashmir, and the reserved tribal regions of Madhya Pradesh and Bihar). Employers are required to give preferences to the hiring of local people (Maharashtra). Engineering and medical colleges have quota systems limiting the number of places allocated to those who come from other states (Rajasthan, Orissa, Madhya Pradesh). Governments provide more favorables loans for local businessmen than for those who come from other states (Maharashtra and Assam). Finally, there are local political groups that threaten to commit violence against newcomers from other regions or states (Telengana, Maharashtra, and Assam).

In recent years, such instruments have proliferated in a number of multi-ethnic societies including Nigeria and Malaysia, as well as India. These preferential policies are often applied with considerable vigor, almost always receive intense local support, and invariably involve broad local coalitions of mobilized political groups. They tend to be more precisely formulated in law and administration than many other migration policies, for they are targeted for specific places, are designed to keep out specified groups, and provide preferences to particular local groups. There is some evidence—though more in the way of illustrations than any systematic comparative analysis—to suggest that they may be among the most effective migration policy instruments for the achievement of their specific objectives.

Preferential policies, however, are intended to do more than simply slow the rate or change the ethnic composition of migration. They are often intended to increase the employment opportunities and income of the local population in relation to ethnic groups in other regions of the country. The effects of such policies on diversifying the occupational structure of the local population and increasing their employment and income has yet to be researched.

The proliferation of preferential policies suggests that regional development policies do not necessarily benefit those who live within the region in a society that freely permits internal migration, especially when for historical, educational, or cultural reasons ethnic groups have different capacitites to compete in the labor market. In the absence of a regional development program that is particularly suited to meet the existing skills and motivations of the local population, or educational programs that make it possible for local people to compete effectively against outsiders for employment, the kinds of preferential policies described here are likely to be more widely used.

Immigration Policies and Internal Migration

In recent years there has been a growing awareness of the ways in which government's international migration policies may affect internal populations movements. A classic description of the relationship can be found in Brinley Thomas, *Migration and Economic Growth*[24] in which he reports that the lack of movement on the part of American blacks in the period between the Civil War and the First World War was largely influenced by U.S. immigration policies. With the ending of immigration on the eve of World War I, there was a dramatic rise in the migration of blacks from the South to the North, but there was again a decline between 1920 and 1924 when there was an upsurge of migration from Europe. The Immigration Restriction Act of 1924 abruptly ended immigration and a new era of black migration to the North and the West began. The out-migration of blacks from the South opened up new opportunities for blacks in education and employment, and played a significant role in reducing the regional income disparities between the North and the South that had persisted at least since the Civil War. The migration also subsequently transformed the racial composition of American cities, with profound effects on American political and social life. Who, in 1924, would have foreseen the multiple and long-term effects of changing immigration law, effects that would still be felt fifty years later?[25]

Since the Second World War, the countries of Central and Western Europe have followed explicit policies of utilizing labor from the Mediterranean countries to satisfy their manpower requirements. It has been argued that with the drying up of Europe's rural labor supply, the importation of labor from Algeria, Yugoslavia, Greece, Turkey, Portugal, and Spain was a critical factor in Europe's postwar recovery and development.[26]

Had the labor supply not been available through immigration, however, it is likely that a greater number of French, Swiss, and Austrian rural dwellers would have moved into urban industrial employment. The costs of such labor would have been higher, and that, in turn, would have had an impact on such questions as to whether industrial investments should be made at home or abroad, and what kinds of technologies (and at what cost) should be utilized, decisions which, in turn, would have influenced population settlement patterns.

Multiplier Effects

The instruments used by government to carry out migration policies range from exhortation to compulsion, with a variety of intermediary incentives and disincentives. A critical element in the selection of instruments is a consideration of whose choices one is seeking to influence. Unlike fertility behavior where one person's choice has little or no effect upon choices made by others, migration choices have multiplier effects. The decision of the owner of a firm to move his company to another city or suburb affects the decisions of countless employees. The movement of a firm with many small ancillary suppliers is likely to have a greater impact on population redistribution than the movement of the head office of a firm. Similarly, the multiplier effects are greater when the decision to move is made by a married peasant with children than a young unattached peasant. There may also be greater multiplier effects if migrants are in upper income rather than lower income groups. All too often policymakers pay too much attention to choosing policy instruments that might affect the behavior of solitary migrants, and too little attention to instruments that might influence the behavior of individuals whose choices will have multiplier effects on the decisions of others.

Conclusion

Migration policies are generally adopted for a variety of reasons, almost never for exclusively demographic objectives. The purpose may be to ease overcrowding in one or more urban areas of the country, to preserve the social structure and ethnic characteristics of a particular locale, to provide greater employment opportunities for one community as against another, to provide the skilled manpower for the development of a particularly underdeveloped and underpopulated region, to achieve greater income equity as between regions, social classes, and ethnic groups, to extend governmental control over a given population or territory of the country, and so on.

These varied objectives can be and often are pursued by attempting to influence population movements through public interventions. But alongside these explicit and intended policies to influence migration, there are a wide variety of other policies pursued for quite different reasons that may have the opposite effects. Indeed, almost all the instruments of policy discussed here are often utilized for reasons that have little or nothing to do with migration. Moreover, government policies to affect the patterns of industrial and regional development, administrative centralization or decentralization, wages in the advanced industrial sectors, and the delivery of public services and housing may be pursued in ways that run counter to explicit internal migration policies. One reason is that much of what governments and their supporters want—a rapid rate of industrial growth or higher wages in the modern sector, or a rapid expansion of education and employment opportunities for the middle class—often produces unwanted consequences, one of which is the pattern of population movement. If governments are reluctant to take forceful measures to influence population movements, it is because they do not want to give up those objectives and policies whose benefits exceed the losses that result from migration. Rapid urban growth, primacy, population movements to the more rather than the less developed regions—for a variety of reasons governments may desire to change these developments, but at what cost? At the cost of slowing industrial growth? Losing the political support of critical groups? A heavy burden on public resources that might better be used for other objectives? Will the solutions prove to be more costly than allowing the problems to continue?

A central theme of this chapter is that immigration policies can best be understood in the context of the political process. To consider policy choices only in the context of the quest for more accelerated development, a more satisfactory dispersal of population, or greater equity or any one of a number of desirable objectives is to overlook the hard realities of politics. Governmental interventions benefit some groups, deny benefits and impose costs on others. Government itself is no impartial arbitor or disinterested agency choosing to maximize some hypothetical public interest, but it is itself the spokesman for a coalition of interests, some of which are within and some of which are outside of government.

These observations, so commonplace for political scientists, are frequently overlooked in much of the literature on migration theory and migration policies. What we need are studies of governmental policies that indirectly or directly influence internal migration, describe the purposes, values and interests pursued by competing political actors, describe the coalitions that affected the choices of policies and programs, measure the impact of policies (while assessing what changes would have occurred in the absence of policies), and, finally, consider who benefits and who loses through government actions. The empirical study of policy interventions will itself illuminate our theoretical understanding of the migration process, its determinants and its consequences.

Notes

I am grateful to my three Harvard Population Center seminar associates, Harold D. Lasswell, Warren Ilchman, and John D. Montgomery, for their critical comments on an earlier draft of this chapter. I have also profited considerably from suggestions by Wayne A. Cornelius, John R. Harris and other participants in the M.I.T. Migration and Development Workshop.

1. For an examination of the role of considerations of national security and national power in resettlement policies in Brazil see Herman E. Daly, "The Population Question in Northeast Brazil: Its Economic and Ideological Dimension," *Economic Development and Cultural Change* 18 (1970): 536-574.

2. I have borrowed the distinction from *Rapid Population Growth: Consequences and Policy Implications*, prepared by the National Academy of Sciences (Baltimore: Johns Hopkins Press, 1971). The NAS report distinguishes between population-influencing policies that affect or are intended to affect population variables, and population-responsive policies that respond to given levels of population growth and change.

3. Michael J. Piore, "The Role of Immigration in Industrial Growth: A Case Study of the Origins and Character of Puerto Rican Migration to Boston," M.I.T. Economics Department Working Paper Number 112 (May 1973).

4. Everett S. Lee, "A Theory of Migration," in J.A. Jackson (ed.), *Migration* (Cambridge: Cambridge University Press, 1969), pp. 282-297.

5. Donald J. Bogue, "Internal Migration," in Philip Hauser and Otis Dudley Duncan (eds.), *The Study of Population* (Chicago: University of Chicago Press, p. 504).

6. Charles Tilly, "Migration to American Cities," in Charles Tilly, ed., *An Urban World* (Boston: Little, Brown and Company, 1974), p. 350.

7. S. Stouffer, "Intervening Opportunities: A Theory Relating Mobility and Distance," *American Sociological Review* 5 (1940): 845-67.

8. A proposal to provide greater amenities to smaller cities in Japan as a means of inducing people born there to remain, and those who have migrated elsewhere to return, is a central feature of Prime Minister Tanaka's book, *Nippon Retto Kaizoron (Remodeling of Japanese Archipelago)*. For a discussion see T. Kuroda, "Trends in Internal Migration and Policy Questions in Japan," *International Union for the Scientific Study of Population, International Population Conference*, Liege, 1973.

9. Stanislaw H. Wellisz, "Economic Development and Urbanization," in Leo Jakobson and Ved Prakash (eds.), *Urbanization and National Development* (Beverly Hills: Sage Publications, 1971), p. 145.

10. John Friedmann, *Urbanization, Planning and National Development* (Beverly Hills: Sage Publications, 1973), p. 145.

11. See Wayne Cornelius, "The Impact of Government Policies & Programs on Rural Outmigration," CENIS, 1974, (mimeo.).

12. John R. Harris and Michael P. Todaro, "Migration, Unemployment and Development: A Two-Sector Analysis," *American Economic Review*, March 1970, p. 127.

13. Michael P. Todaro, "Income Expectations, Rural-Urban Migration and Employment in Africa," *International Labor Review*, 1971, pp. 387-413.

14. J. Gugler, "On the Theory of Rural-Urban Migration: The Case of Sub-Saharan Africa," in Jackson, *Migration*, pp. 134-155.

15. Todaro, "Income Expectations," p. 395.

16. Mexico and Argentina, though federal systems, are notable exceptions, for both have high primacy. Federalism in many Third World countries has often masked highly centralized political systems with no real devolution of political power and governmental resources. For this reason federal systems in Third World countries may not have the same effects upon urbanization as they did in the United States and West European countries. Wayne Cornelius called this difference to my attention. For an analysis of the effect of shifting the national capital of Brazil from Rio de Janeiro to Brasilia, which concludes that the transfer did not significantly affect the growth of the largest coastal cities, see David Epstein, *Brasilia: Plan and Reality* (Berkeley and Los Angeles: University of California Press, 1973). See also John J. Harrigan, "Political Economy and the Management of Urban Development in Brazil," and Joel Bergsman, "Urban Growth Policy in Brazil: Intended and Accidental," in Wayne A. Cornelius (ed.), *Urbanization and Inequality: The Political Economy of Urban Development in Latin America*, Latin American Urban Research, Vol. 5 (Beverly Hills, California: Sage Publications), forthcoming.

17. For a review of the ways in which governmental expenditures uninten-

tionally affects population distribution in the United States, see William Alonso, *Problems, Purposes, and Implicit Policies for a National Strategy of Urbanization*, Institute of Urban and Regional Development, University of California, Berkeley, Working Paper No. 158, August 1971.

18. Bernard Berelson (ed.), *Population Policy in Developed Countries* (New York: McGraw-Hill Book Company), p. 785. See also Lloyd Rodwin, *Nation and Cities: a Comparison of Strategies for Urban Growth* (Boston: Houghton Mifflin, 1970), which compares urban growth policies in Venezuela, Turkey, Britain, and France. For a case study of a planned effort at regional development and its relation to urban growth, see Lloyd Rodwin et al., *Planning Urban Growth and Regional Development: The Experience of the Guayana Program in Venezuela* (Cambridge: M.I.T. Press, 1969).

19. Alonso notes that the siting of federal installations, the allocation of defense contracts, and the location of federally funded highways can influence migration by affecting the pattern of private investment and shaping the growth of employment. For an excellent examination of the determinants of industrial location, see William Alonso, *Industrial Location and Regional Policy in Economic Development*, Institute of Urban and Regional Development, University of California-Berkeley, Working Paper No. 74, February 1968. A central theme of Alonso's study is the tension between the goals of national economic growth and interregional equality of incomes, the absence of any technical formula to resolve the conflict, and the ultimate importance, therefore, in making political choices.

20. Berelson, *Population Policy in Developed Countries*, p. 758.

21. Alonso, *Industrial Location*, p. 52. For a case study illustrating this proposition, see David Barkin, "Regional Development and Inter-regional Equity: A Mexican Case Study," in Cornelius, *Urbanization and Equity*.

22. Albert Hirschman, in *Exit, Voice and Loyalty* (Cambridge: Harvard University Press, 1971), argues that there is an inverse relationship between opportunities for migration and political protest. For an interesting examination of the corollary proposition that high levels of labor militancy in the countryside tend to reduce outmigration, see J.S. MacDonald, "Agricultural Organization, Migration and Labour Militancy in Rural Italy," in *Economic History Review* 16, 1 (1963): 61-75. Restrictions on the movement of upwardly mobile (usually middle income) people probably creates more articulated resentment than when the restrictions are imposed on low income groups.

23. In recent years a few developing countries have adopted policies that require selected urban dwellers, especially medical graduates, to relocate in rural areas and small towns. The most comprehensive policy of this sort is the Chinese program of "rusticating" urban educated youth to live and work in rural communes. See Pi-chao Chen, "Overurbanization, Rustication of Urban-Educated Youth, and Politics of Rural Transformation: The Case of China," *Comparative Politics* 4 (1972): 361-386.

24. Brinley Thomas, *Migration and Economic Growth: A Study of Great Britain and the Atlantic Economy* (Cambridge: Cambridge University Press, 1973), p. 130.

25. The U.S. Population Commission provides another recent example of the impact of immigration policies on internal policies affecting manpower use. The commission notes that the policy of utilizing immigrants to remedy shortages in skilled manpower has reduced the pressures for expanding public expenditures for medical schools, a policy, says the commission, that has reduced the opportunities for minorities while expanding opportunities for doctors from developing countries. For a study of the effects of brain drain on the sending countries, see *Brain Drain: A Study of the Persistent Issue of International Scientific Mobility*, Government Printing Office, Washington, D.C., 1974.

26. Charles P. Kindleberger, *Europe's Postwar Growth: The Role of Labor Supply* (Cambridge: Harvard University Press, 1967).

3

Planning to Cope: Administrative Consequences of Rapid Population Growth

John D. Montgomery

Governments that fail to provide for incremental changes may eventually find themselves dealing with crisis changes. Muddling through—relying on the excess capacities of the system or the unlimited patience of the citizens to accommodate demands—is no longer considered desirable practice in responsible government. But how can governments do otherwise? Administrative sciences have not achieved the exactness that leads to useful predictions of changing capacities; nor do they enjoy the status necessary for making major decisions regarding the use of public resources. Most administration decisions still occur as an accidental by-product of other decisions. There is no real shortage of knowledge of administrative behavior and bureaucratic sociology, but what there is has rarely been used to help decisionmakers identify distant crises or to compare and assess the capacity of administrative systems to respond to change in the growth and distribution of a population. Only the urgent discovery that the population-food race is being lost in so many countries has made it feasible for politicians and planners to contemplate the need for predicting and coping with crises before they arrive.

One reason for the lack of attention to this problem is that "demand" is not a constant factor in administrative management. Increments do not occur evenly, nor do administrators normally expect to determine which elements of the population will be entitled to the services they plan and provide, and which elements will be turned away. Presumably the political system will decide "who gets what, when, and how." It is for politicians to identify the point at which a service is to be provided by the government or an intervention is to be withdrawn. Once these "demand" factors have been considered, it is usually left to administrators to attend to the "supply" side.

The most feasible way for them to approach demand as a planning problem has been to assume constant ratios between supply and demand; that is, for example, to plan their "loads" so that any population shifts will automatically and proportionately increase or reduce the total claims on public services. But even this simplifying assumption—which can be abandoned whenever politics changes the rules—has not provided a realistic basis for responding to rapid population change (RPC). For RPC is not a uniform phenomenon even if politics were to leave distributive rights intact. Administrators therefore need to make subtler assumptions about the relationship between supply and demand of public services under conditions of RPC.

The assumed administrative goal is maintenance of service levels. But this goal has to be differentiated in both time and context. If the population growth is *slow* (e.g., a result of fertility rather than migration), an administrative system will try to absorb the increments as they come, by overloading some elements and transferring some responsibilities, perhaps even allowing the quality of service to deteriorate if necessary rather than introduce quantum changes in the system itself. Population growth in the United States, for example, has already produced such administrative responses as gradual deterioration of metropolitan drinking water quality, slower and less frequent mail deliveries, abandonment of graveyards in favor of commercial uses, the subcontracting of urban garbage collection to the private sector, the decline in maintenance of public streets, reductions in free citizen access to advice in the preparation of income tax returns, and, most recently, the attempts to find new uses for excess-capacity school buildings that had originally been built in anticipation of an indefinite baby boom.

In preparing for slow incremental changes, the administrator's best strategy is to predict just which straw it is that will break the camel's back, and to try to arrange alternative means of transporting it.

Even if a population change is *rapid* (e.g., a result of migration or of catastrophic losses), planners will still seek to make use of the excess capacity in the system, and direct it where the demand is greatest, before abandoning existing technical and bureaucratic mechanisms. Thus, during periods of transition, they will tolerate urban squatting and they will continue to staff underutilized and obsolescent agricultural extension services, until at some point the system breaks down or becomes hopelessly antiquated.[1]

The contextual problems of maintaining service levels are even more intricate. The demand effects caused by RPC are more severe in some countries, and in some regions, classes, or sectors within a given country, than in others. Administrative planners cannot simply project that a 3 percent annual population increase will require budget, staff, and facilities increases at a steady 3 percent rate[2]: some services, possessing an excess capacity, can absorb increases with no new costs; some will actually encounter reduced usage; some cannot absorb additional loads without changing their whole technological infrastructure. Planning for rapid population change therefore requires analysis both of changed demand structures and of the services themselves.[3] This chapter will attempt to show how these interactions can be predicted by disaggregating anticipated incremental demands and responses.

The best known changes in the demand structure are those arising from shifts in age distribution and population totals caused by a declining death rate among babies, which produces "bulges" first in the infant population cohort, then, with the passage of time, in older groups. School committees have grappled with such factors for generations, just as market analysts have been able to predict changes in the commercial demands which changing age structure will make upon the baby-food manufacturers. But more complex distortions in demands for government services arise from the fact that RPC, whether caused by growth or migration, nearly always occurs in combination with other social changes. RPC does not occur evenly across the subdivisions of a society; changed demands cannot be predicted from demographic data as conventionally presented because of the conjunction with so many other changes in the demand structure. The requirements for appropriate administrative responses are twofold: planners must be able to identify, in timely fashion, the danger signals sent by an administrative system when it is already beginning to show signs of breakdown because of incremental overload; and they must be able to predict future shifts in the demand structure caused by the conjunction of RPC with other social changes. The sections that follow are intended to suggest (1) types of evidence that could be used to identify stress in administrative systems in order to avoid imminent breakdown (Section I); (2) selected combinations of social change which, in conjunction with RPC, could represent future danger-points (Section II); (3) characteristics of administrative systems in terms of their capacity to expand (Section III); and (4) some macro-level aggregations in the form of suggested country profiles (Section IV). The conclusion describes characteristic governmental responses to threatened administrative overload and proposes a planning instrument for anticipating potential crises.

I. Trends: RPC as a Problem in Incremental Change

Administrative planners can consider any population change as "rapid" when increases in the numbers or demands of actual or potential clients threaten to overload the anticipated "delivery" capacity of the system. No statistical standard will define population growth or movement as "rapid" in all administrative contexts. A 1 percent total increase (which might at some point mean a 20 percent increase in five to seven year olds) may be rapid to school committees in a jurisdiction with every classroom full, but not to the highway department. Conservationists have begun to build campaigns defining a global population explosion as a result of the interactions among (a) population growth; (b) anticipated changes in per capita consumption; (c) rates of resource growth (Gross Domestic Product (GDP) plus imports) per capita; and (d) presumed rate of depletion of natural resources. But such campaigns cannot carry the same conviction in every country. Indeed, in only a very few countries is the rate of increase of the population greater than that of the GDP, in fewer still is there imminent danger of resource depletion.[4] In spite of recent fuel and food crises, most countries still increase productivity faster than population; thus far technology, foreign trade, and self-restraint have been able to cope with resource scarcities. The Doomsday soothsayers have not yet won any elections for conservationists. The Distant Early Warning has been sounded for Planet Earth, but the warning is not perceived anywhere as an urgent national problem yet.

If Doomsday prophecying is not viable politics, declining services and dwindling supplies may provide a more modest spur to action. To administrators, the population crisis is not so much Armageddon as a state of siege. And in the end political repercussions are likely to be felt only when customary government services come more slowly or at greater cost, or when they decline in quantity or quality, resulting in reduced access or satisfaction to the citizens. Changes in the volume or pace of demand cause tremors throughout an administrative system, which can usually be detected by measuring changes in cost or quality. A system's responses can be read as Distant Early Warning signals, automatically transmitted as administrators cope with unexpected demand. Detecting and interpreting these signals require close examination of each system under stress since administrative responses are not uniform across countries, regions, and sectors. The warnings may be only a "blip" on the radar screen.

The following indicators of stress suggest the range of data that might be consulted as an administrative equivalent of the Distant Early Warning System:

1. Changes in Inputs (Resource Requirements)
    a. Drastic budget or staff increases for services performed at a constant level of quality
    b. Horizontal shifts in budgetary allocations among different branches or agencies working at a constant quality level
    c. Increased unit costs of service at constant quality and salary levels
    d. Regional shifts in caseload or personnel
    e. Rise in procurement levels.
2. Changes in Performance or Management
    a. Unseasonal and unscheduled increases in total caseload
    b. Reduction in service standards at constant levels of staff and budget
    c. Cumulative delays in processing routine cases
    d. Vertical shifts in administrative functions from central to local units
    e. Failure to reach planned goals
    f. Changed procedures for dealing with routine cases
    g. Increased resort to coercion and fines to maintain normal functions
    h. Transfer of functions out of the public sector.
3. Public Responses
    a. Complaints or criticism of agency performance
    b. Evidence of corruption in the distribution of public services
    c. Increased exhortations of the public to be patient.

Some of these indicators may turn up with a negative valence, suggesting a decline in demand possibly caused by regional or national population decreases.[5] Some of these signals, of course, may have no connection with RPC. But they are warnings to be examined, explained, and perhaps dealt with. Deterioration in the performance of administrative services may result in demands for a restoration of functions that may not be easily supplied in the face of rising unit costs and other emergent needs.[6]

By the time these warning signals have been transmitted, received, and interpreted, it may be too late to act. Administrators and political planners also need longer-range indicators of impending change.

II. Predicting Demand: Conditions Produced by Interaction of RPC with Other Social Changes

Demographic changes alone are capable of producing the incremental effects registered on the Distant Early Warning system. Many of them, especially those caused by fertility changes rather than migration, are predictable and thus to some extent manageable. More complex interactions are also at work in most cases, however, occurring simultaneously with RPC: changed age structure has different effects in rural and urban locations; population increments can be absorbed by a dynamic industry more readily than a dynamic agriculture, and both sectors produce still different consequences if the other is sluggish; and RPC also interacts with ethnic and regional differences, usually magnifying administrative problems (some with "instant" timing, others delayed by a generation or two). Some of these intersecting forces are likely to produce severe demands on government services, calling for major action (reducing service levels, for example, or investing in new public works, or, in extreme cases, discouraging birth or migration). Other interactions can also produce augmented problems for administrators, but these are the most familiar.

Rural-to-urban migration usually draws the younger, more ambitious elements of the work force from farm to town, creating an age distribution in both places that would not be predicted by a demographic model. There are four possible combinations of interaction between age and location, producing quite different effects: (A) a "youth explosion" in an urban location; (B) the same demographic pattern in rural areas; (C) middle-and-older age groups dominating urban settlements; (D) an aging rural population. Each configuration produces its own set of administrative demands:

		Changes in Age Structure	
		Greater Increase in Young Age Groups	Greater Increase in Middle and Old Age Groups
Locational Effects	Urban	A	C
	Rural	B	D

Figure 3-1.

Figure 3-1 (cont.)

A. Thanks to prevailing migration patterns, most Third World cities show rapid increases in the numbers of young workers available.[7] The newest immigrants, drawn by the "urban magnet," tend to find jobs, but at the cost of displacing older residents. Their success encourages further immigration (and displacement). Those who come with families will expect schooling and housing,[8] which will cost the government more than it would have in rural areas; others will think of their stay as temporary, and settle for substandard housing, but in so doing contribute to other problems in administering public health and safety services.[9] (Examples: Korea, urbanized Java, Iraq; England and Wales.)[a]

B. In rural areas where there is comparatively little out-migration, and where the population has high birth and survival rates, land becomes scarce in proportion to the supply of labor. Government intervention may be needed to develop labor-intensive agricultural technologies to keep productivity high. The rising demand for schooling will be harder to satisfy on a standard basis than in cities; youthful activists are likely to demand land reform if they feel exploited by the landowners.[10] Local elites, in turn, will demand security precautions. (Examples: Mexico,[11] Panama, Bangladesh, Sri Lanka, Burma.)

C. Cities and suburban areas with limited immigration and stable birthrates may seek to stabilize tax rates by resisting further industrialization. They tend to place high demands on social recreation facilities, adult education, programs specifically oriented towards women, public welfare, public housing, and public medical services. They tend to place relatively low demands on new schooling for young people. They may tend to be relatively conservative on issues such as racial integration programs. If agriculture becomes less important to the overall economy, unemployment of women may increase.[12] (Examples: Iraq, United States,[13] parts of Taiwan.) (Familiar cases: Singapore, Algeria, Britain, and other developed areas. Primate cities are still growing rapidly in most LDCs.)

D. Rural areas out of which younger age groups have migrated often seek government labor-saving (and, by implication, capital-intensive) technologies to maintain production levels. Such technologies tend to be associated with land consolidation programs. A combination of situations C and D could result from the projected rapid aging of the populations of Asia and Latin America.[14] (Taiwan has areas in this situation. Other examples: Iraq, United States.[15])

Kenya is attempting to cope with situation A by influencing location choices made by its growing population. The plan is to invest public funds to encourage the growth of several regional centers to which migrants can move as alternatives to Nairobi and Mombasa. The plan involves an ambitious program for the year 2000[16] to provide minimum levels of services, including administration (courts, police, fire), social services (health, education, recreational), and a communications, commercial, and industrial infrastructure in 1,015 local centers, 420 market centers, 140 small towns, and suburban centers, and 9 principal cities (in addition to the two primate cities). Besides creating a more evenly distributed urban base in the country, Kenya's planners hope the strengthened central services will improve rural life by encouraging productive innovation in agriculture. But thus far the plans have been inhibited by the insatiable demands of Nairobi and Mombasa, which are absorbing increasing shares of the funds available for regional development. It is not easy to escape from situation A.

Possibly all four of these sets of events will occur at once in different areas of a country. Since (as the Kenya case illustrates) situations A and B are inherently more crisis prone and require more government action than C or D, national planners should be more acutely aware of them in allocating public resources.

---

[a]Examples of this and the following situations refer to countries or regions at the present time, unless otherwise specified.

The reader may find it convenient to use the matrix in Figure 3-1 to assess priorities among relationships.

A second set of interactions are those between RPC and economic variables which also produce four distinct sets of possible administrative consequences. The most conspicuous sectoral differences are those occurring when both agriculture and industry are relatively stagnant or are relatively dynamic. If either sector is stagnant, the contrasting interactions are quite different. Ordinarily, any surplus population in the society can be more productively absorbed on the farms than the cities, but often at a cost of changes in the tenure system and the technologies in use. If both sectors are in a dynamic phase, the absorptive capacity of industry may be greater, but with the opposite effect on land tenure arrangements as labor becomes scarcer. If one sector is stagnant and the other is not, a migration effect will be introduced,[17] attended by further variation in government programming. The extreme possibilities again present four prototypical situations: (E), in which both sectors are relatively sluggish; (F), where agriculture is stagnant and industry rising; (G), where agriculture is more dynamic than industry; and (H), in which both are on the rise (see Figure 3-2).

		Agricultural Production Per Capita	
		Holding	Rising
Industrial Production Per Capita	Holding	E	G
	Rising	F	H

Situation E. In countries like Burma, Haiti, and Bangladesh on this scale, population increases tend to produce fragmentation of land ownership in rural areas, assuming equal inheritance rights and no undeveloped land to which younger children can migrate. Nor are they likely to be content with migrating to cities, where there is growing unemployment. In rural areas there may be demands for new but competitive labor-intensive technologies to absorb surplus labor. (Other examples: Sri Lanka, Algeria, Uruguay).[18]

Situation F. Increasing urbanization may result in abandonment of farms by new "surplus" population with combined "pull" and "push" effects. If there are labor shortages caused by a highly labor-absorbtive industrial sector, there may be demand for capital-intensive farming technologies, accompanied by a need for urban improvements. If there are labor surpluses, there will be demands for increasing the number of available jobs in both rural and urban areas. If peasants do not share in industrial-based economic development, they will become increasingly alienated from the government. (Examples: Mexico, Argentina, Tunisia. China is attempting to restrain urban flows.)

Situation G. A relatively more dynamic agriculture may bring increased rural land values; demand for tax and terms-of-trade intervention between sectors; rising competition for labor. (Examples: Cyprus, Israel, Pakistan in the 1960s.)

Situation H. The two sectors are dynamic. This may result in consolidation of land holdings; some rural unemployment if capital-based technology advances; possible migration to cities; eventually, increased urban unemployment followed by demand for rural-based food processing and export industries. (Examples: Japan, Taiwan, Colombia, Venezuela in the 60s, Thailand in the 60s, Andhra in India.)

Figure 3-2.

The third set of interactions take place in polyethnic communities, where RPC occurs unevenly. The effect is to exacerbate demand for government interventions if the economic characteristics and political opportunities of the groups are unequal. Among underprivileged groups, RPC tends to increase differentiation and discrimination because their numbers increase faster than their opportunities. Demands for new opportunities could affect governmental services if politicians decide to respect rising group expectations, to capitalize on the awareness of group differences, or to respond to potentially effective organizational activity on the part of emergent groups.[19] This response creates serious strains on governmental resources; the relative investment necessary to keep per capita income at a constant level in LDCs is three times that required in developed countries—65 percent as opposed to 25 percent.[20]

Malaysia has perhaps recognized this problem more explicitly than any other country, not only addressing itself to the balancing of ethnic group demands across sectors (economic with political power, for example), but also undertaking a series of public investments to create opportunities for disadvantaged groups. It is significant that some of these interventions may very well affect the relative fertility among ethnic groups, causing further shifts in their comparative demands.[21]

In the abstract formulation of the four extreme demand situations, (I) would describe a case of equal growth rate among the different ethnic groups where opportunities are restricted to a preferred elite community; (J), where growth rates are uneven and the opportunities are differentiated; (K), with even growth rates and undifferentiated opportunity, and (L), unequal population growth in communal situations of undifferentiated opportunity.

The predicted demand structure is shown in Figure 3-3.

		Ethnic Group Functions	
		Restricted Opportunities	Undifferentiated Opportunities
Distribution of RPC Rates Among Ethnic Groups	Even	I	K
	Uneven	J	L

Situation I. The ethnic groups that are restricted to low productivity or marginal economic functions will be disadvantaged by RPC and will agitate for education, employment preferences, and unemployment and other social benefits. (Examples: Canada, Rhodesia.)

Figure 3-3.

Figure 3-3 (cont.)

Situation J. If the increase occurs in economically marginal ethnic groups, a highly volatile situation arises (if rural, the group will demand urban access; if urban, they will demand increased welfare services or equivalent amenities); in more favorably situated ethnic groups, the possibility of volatile responses would still remain if they lose their preferred status because of excessive growth rates. This situation is common because restricted opportunities tend to relegate certain groups to below-average socioeconomic levels, which in turn leads to above-average birthrates. For the same reason, Situation I is rare. (Examples of Situation J: Lebanon.[22] Egypt, Sudan, Kenya, S. Africa, Congo (Brazz.), Bolivia, U.S., USSR, Yugoslavia, Malaysia.)[23]

Situation K. RPC does not magnify ethnic conflict as a source of demand for government services. (Example: Tanzania.)

Situation L. Foreshadows possible future ethnic specialization leading to Situation I or J because fastest growing groups may gain control of certain occupations. Differential cultural compatibility with requirements and opportunities of modernization in either Situation K or L could also lead to Situation I or J. (Examples: China; Zaire; the southern Nigerian states.)

Densely populated regions are easier to mobilize than sparsely settled areas are.[24] But the larger the area, the more difficult political organization becomes, as the homogeneity of the population is attenuated by distance, geographical differences, and ethnic and cultural diversity. Administrative responses to RPC-induced demands will be structurally different in (M) large areas with low densities, as compared with (N) large areas of high density, (O) small areas of low density, and (P) small areas of high density (see Figure 3-4).

		Size of Area	
		Large	Small
Density of Population	Low	M	O
	High	N	P

Situation M. Increased population increases potential for political mobilization and thus demand for decentralized services. (Examples: Sudan, Argentina, Brazil.[25])

Situation N. Demand depends upon stability of older, more established settlers; recent immigrants, especially in urban areas, are willing to accept substandard employment without protest.[26] Demand for new services may be muted at first despite apparent deterioration of amenities. (Examples: India, Turkey.)

Situation O. Increased population increases national integration without seriously impairing homogeneity. (Examples: Liberia, Nicaragua, Panama.)

Situation P. Population increases tend to increase class-based client demands, producing more "government" and greater bureaucratization. Situation becomes volatile as population approaches saturation point of prevailing technologies. (Examples: Hong Kong, Burundi, Sri Lanka, El Salvador, Haiti, Lebanon, Mauritius, Switzerland, Taiwan, Egypt.)

Figure 3-4.

Analyzing these trends requires access to administrative information, demographic data, and political intentions. It is depressing to learn that most countries ignore demographic data in both long-term and short-term planning (only 27 of 70 countries examined by Stamper in 1973 recognized "population" as a "problem" for planning purposes).[27] The proposed Population Planning Unit in Malaysia is a promising beginning because of the strategic location proposed for it (reporting at Cabinet level) as well as its global point of view.[28] National efforts at regional development, resettlement schemes, and family planning programs are only policy fragments; explicit consideration of interacting elements in the demand structure is necessary if governments are to cope with RPC comprehensively.

III. Alternatives: Responsive Capacities of Administrative Systems

The conditions produced by interactions among demographic elements, spatial distribution, and economic and ethnic factors suggest possible trends in demand structure, but they do not predict civil service recruitment levels, ascertain the need for new public service technologies, or develop strategies for improving intergovernmental administrative relationships. Characteristics of the system itself define the alternatives that are available for coping with demand changes. The alternatives usually include adding or transferring personnel, reorganizing functions, adding facilities, or changing technologies.

Some public services require additional personnel to supply new needs because under the prevailing technology their function requires a fairly fixed ratio of public employees to citizens served regardless of their numbers (e.g. schools, welfare programs). These "client-based" services can be expanded up to the point where (1) the administration becomes unwieldy, or (2) the capital infrastructure can no longer bear the weight of increased use. Planners recognize the likelihood of breakdowns from the latter cause (cramped schools or parks, overburdened streets or sewers)[29] more readily than they do those caused by personnel increases (few administrators perceive the moment when their own staffs become too large). Thus those sectors whose thresholds of physical capacity have been crossed receive attention more speedily than those whose staff is swollen beyond the limits of effective administration.

"Area-based services," in contrast, do not show much sign of strain with population increase, since they are indifferent to the size or density of clients served. Border defense, for example, does not change much as population shifts, but a program of counterinsurgency does. Similarly, radio and television broadcasting do not consume more resources as population changes, as opposed to newspapers and mail deliveries. Meteorology and crop dusting services are also indifferent to client size, while extension or credit services are not. In the former cases, RPC is at worst a neutral factor; it may even create special benefits (the broadcast industry can levy greater tribute on advertisers as the population increases; defense services can more effectively deal with border-crossings insurgents or smugglers if the region is populated by loyal citizens).

The strategy for dealing with client-based services, once the personnel threshold is reached, is to delegate authority and responsibility to local units (devolving education and welfare responsibilities to small communities, for example); for capital-exhausted services, new technologies are required (rooftop parks or buildings setbacks, for example; new forms of waste collection and disposal; and rapid urban transit). For area-based services, no action at all may be necessary when RPC occurs, though in some cases governments may decide to pay close attention to abuses of the system to see that the public sector does not suffer if the benefits of RPC are misallocated (for example, that the broadcast industry does not, Gresham-style, indulge the lowest tastes of the society for its own profit; or that the population supports government efforts to discourage smuggling and insurgent violence).

But there is a difference when these two thresholds are reached. When new staff personnel exceed the number which can be effectively managed, administrators can reorganize, decentralize, delegate, and reallocate. But when facilities are overcrowded, and no more additional units can be constructed (e.g., when traffic-choked streets devour the cities they serve), it is necessary to underwrite new technologies if the service is to be provided. The relationships may be diagrammed as shown in Figure 3-5.

IV. Country Profiles and Projections

In appraising the actual effects of the RPC-induced demand upon a government's administrative capacity, two other variables must be considered. Governmental responses depend first upon the *political* conversion of potential into effective

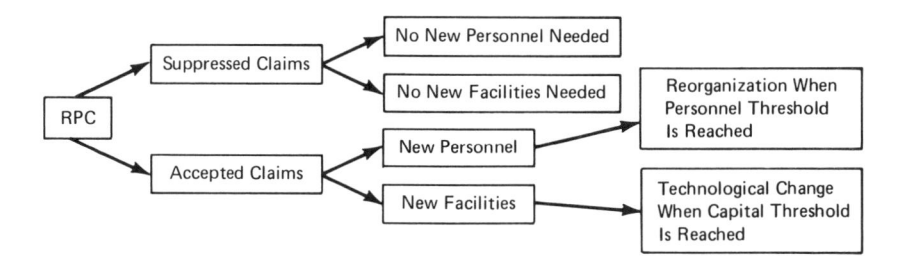

Figure 3-5.

demand, that is, a decision to increase a given service instead of ignoring certain elements of the population. Reducing existing services causes absolute privation—a serious political act. Slowing down the expansion of limited service can also be serious, but it is a relative privation. Making such decisions is what politics is "all about."

The second factor is that of *administrative* conversion, that is, the system's ability to mobilize resources effectively for the purpose of increasing the services in demand. Changes in the system sometimes make it possible to spread its benefits without adding to its cost. In the education sector, for example, a government could attack illiteracy by opening the primary schools to all children between six and ten, an objective that can be met in the face of RPC only by increasing the total educational effort. Alternatively, it could decrease services to other age groups or change the educational technology entirely. A government could also defer public education to a later age, perhaps at the option of the citizen himself, which would permit families and other institutions to provide for early education, at the same time speeding up the learning process for those who approach the primary skills at a later age so that fewer years would be required, with less duplication, to reach the intended educational levels. Other sectors of public service could be similarly redesigned to take advantage of new technologies or economies of scale.[30]

The four polar possibilities can also be used to define the extreme conditions: (Q), with political decisions intensifying the demand, and a government with high administrative potential; (R), the same in situations of low administrative potential; (S), political efforts to contain or reduce demand for services, but

		Political Conversion of Demand	
		Intensification	Reduction
Administrative Potential for Increasing Services	High	Q	S
	Low	R	T

Situation Q. Because politics multiplies demands, the government has to increase services in the sector involved, whether by increasing total resources allocated, by improving the efficiency of conversion, or by reducing services elsewhere. (Examples: Singapore, Malaysia; Venezuela, Lebanon, Argentina, Bolivia, Sri Lanka, Guatemala, Syria, Israel.[31])

Situation R. Unsatisfied demand produces political crises unless suppressed. (Examples: Indonesia under Sukarno, Guinea, Ivory Coast, N. Korea, Rumania, Ghana.)

Situation S. Because demands are muted, a given sector reduces its services, producing resources for transfer elsewhere. (Example: China, Sudan.)

Situation T. Stable demand-conversion relationship. (Examples: Iran, Central African Republic, Chad, Zaire, Dahomey, Gabon, Mali, Niger, Senegal.)

Figure 3-6.

where high administrative resources are available; and (T), the same but with low administrative potential. Thus governmental conversion decisions depend partly on objective circumstances, partly on political judgments of priorities.

Projecting a country's total situation in these terms requires extensive data-gathering. Even in the absence of such data, however, it is possible to make rough comparative judgments. By developing profile indicators we can suggest the problems and policies that might be anticipated in different circumstances.

Using the situational dimensions presented in Sections II and III (see Figure 3-7), China (c. 1965) appears with the profile ABKNS. The proportion of youth is high; urban areas are expanding only slightly faster than rural areas; gains in overall productivity are said to be exceeding population growth.[32] Minority groups like the Kazakhs, who inhabit sparsely settled regions, are multiplying less rapidly than the Han Chinese. The prediction is that rural demands will

I

Location — Age Cohort Pressures

	Young	Middle/Old
Urban	A	C
Rural	B	D

II

Industrial — Agricultural Production

	Holding	Rising
Holding	E	G
Rising	F	H

III

Distribution of Ethnic Growth Rates — Ethnic Opportunities

	Restricted	Undifferentiated
Even	I	K
Uneven	J	L

IV

Density of Population — Size of Area

	Large	Small
Low	M	O
High	N	P

V

Administrative Response Capabilities — Political Conversion of Demand

	Intensification	Reduction
High	Q	S
Low	R	T

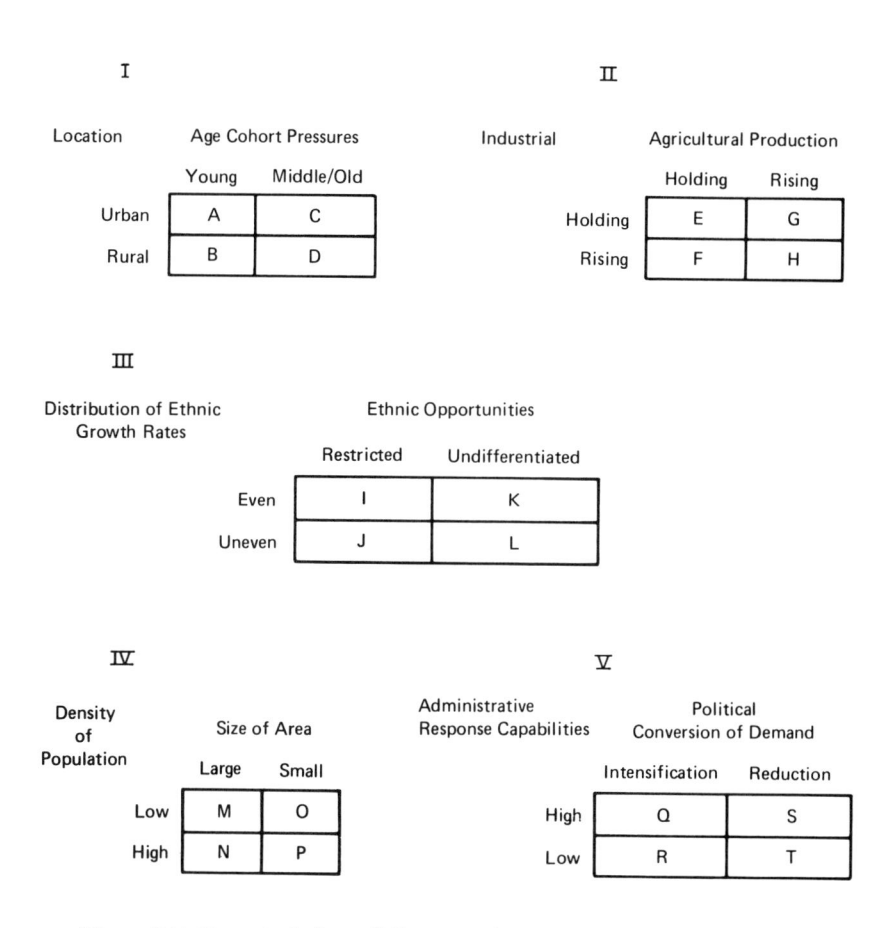

Figure 3-7. Recapitulation of Situational Dimensions—Country Profiles

become increasingly important constraints on policy; new configurations of centralization and decentralization of the government's administrative responses can be expected along functional lines.

Indonesia under Sukarno would have had the profile AEJNR. The youthful cohorts were growing, and even the rural areas (especially in Java) were becoming heavily populated. Both industry and agriculture were stagnant, while RPC accentuated communal differentiation and rivalry. The leadership was responding by encouraging demands the government could not meet, yet the nation was too large and scattered to be managed under strong authoritarian central patterns. The nation did not have a gross population problem: its per capita GNP growth rate, though very slow, was proportionately better than its absolute growth rate in 1950-65. The inherent instability of the situation was magnified by the population distribution, however, a fact which does not appear from casual demographic data. Today Indonesia is progressing to a profile AFJNQ.

Nepal in 1972, when I last visited it, was AEIPT. It had a youthful population, and was becoming slowly urbanized although the inhospitable mountains and the less forbidding Terai region were also pressed by increased numbers.[b] There was a seasonal migration of job-seekers, but since neither agriculture nor industry could absorb more workers, many migrants went to India. Rural and urban poverty was severe among underprivileged ethnic groups, for whom RPC accentuated their absolute and relative privation. Administrative capacity was low and many regions were inaccessible,[33] but for the moment the political system was able to restrain the demand by suppressing party activity and by controlling and channeling local self-expression through the panchayats. Decentralization was in the wind. The situation was potentially more volatile than the current government appeared to recognize, however.

A comparison between Mexico (BFJMR) and Costa Rica (AHKOQ) would show the much greater volatility of the former case, where rapidly growing, underprivileged Indian population and other youthful, politically active *campesinos* create a potential for the political intensification of demand on a government of low administrative capabilities; while in Costa Rica there is little expectation of ethnic conflict arising from RPC, and the administrative potential is likely to be equal to the political demand for new services. In both countries population growth greatly reduced their relative standing in per capita growth rates of GNP.

Kenya (ABFJPQ)[c] and Tanzania (ABHKOQ) are both undergoing high rates of population growth. In Kenya, this situation has led to extreme overcrowding of agricultural land, and a high rate of youthful, rural-urban migration. Because

---

[b]Improved malaria control may be on the verge of reducing the hazards of the Terai region. There are some reports that the population there may be increasing.

[c]Although the overall density of Kenya's population is low, most of it is concentrated in a small area. Thus, Kenya is considered F for the purposes of this profile.

of a thriving industrial sector, an expanding (both in size and capacity) government bureaucracy, and a charismatic president, demands stemming from unemployment, income inequalities, land hunger, and ethnicity have so far not led to political instability. These problems may continue to fester, however. Although Tanzania also faces a serious unemployment problem, ethnic conflicts are not serious, agricultural land is relatively plentiful, and income inequalities are not as severe as those in Kenya. Furthermore, the government has made more progress than the government of Kenya in building a network of decentralized institutions in anticipation of an increased potential for political mobilization. Thus, the government of Tanzania is in a better position to cope with RPC than the government of Kenya.

Although the United States is not suffering from rapid population growth, some authorities believe it has a population problem. Over the decades its GNP growth, while not spectacular, has kept ahead of the population growth. Its profile would be CHJMQ. The growth in birthrate is slowing and so in the future, middle-aged and older groups may increase their demands more rapidly than other age cohorts will. Most of the growth is in urban areas. Both industry and agriculture are dynamic in 1973, but technology favors the absorption of added population in industrial and service rather than agricultural pursuits. Ethnic specialization works against the black and brown minorities, which, in turn, are growing in numbers more rapidly than the majority white groups. RPC's differential impact on minority ethnic groups accentuates an inherently volatile situation as their organizational and political capacity increases. The administrative potential for increasing services is high in spite of the politicization of these demands, and there are further potentials for deconcentration and decentralization of federal programs.

The utility of such profiles will presumably become much greater as additional empirical data are gathered. With the exception of the growth rate data, the preceding classifications are relative judgments. They do, however, permit us to make distinctions that are generally ignored in conventional groupings of stages of economic development or rates of economic growth. Classifications of this type, done in a historical context, may also permit us to predict situations of greatest urgency and to establish some priorities among policy options in different country situations.

After such country studies have been replicated and the thresholds of change have been determined quantitatively, dynamic relationships and time sequences can be explored. This step should make it possible to determine in a given case the comparative importance of such factors as age, location, and ethnic differentiation as variables or influences on administrative capabilities in different sectors. One means of accomplishing this goal would be to group countries according to the cells developed in the preceding matrices. Countries showing ethnically undifferentiated functions, for example, could be further grouped in cells showing young and old population structure changes, then separated into urban and rural location (four cells). Finally, countries showing ethnic differentiation and an unevenly divided population growth would reduce to four more cells by the same process. These twelve cells could then be examined to identify the relative force of the component elements in each grouping in terms of administrative outcomes by sector, using the overload indicators suggested in the introduction.[34] Eventually more exact statistical devices might also be used to identify and clarify these relationships. Situations of resource exhaustion and replenishment could be incorporated into the analysis to explore international and environmental implications. The model as conceived here would be empirically self-correcting, since the variables and dimensions can be constantly redefined and corrected in the light of new evidence. But policymakers can benefit from pursuing this inquiry on a country-by-country basis long before these international comparisons become possible.

V. Coping

In dealing with the administrative consequences of RPC at the national level, planners will have to consider the extent to which service levels in different sectors are vulnerable to decline in the face of changing demands. Such judgments will also have to reflect the national context, but one might project the outcomes along the following spectrum of probabilities:

1. *Most vulnerable*—client-oriented services at the threshold of existing technology, where no additional facilities can be provided (e.g., in the United States, individualized urban transportation and supervised recreation facilities for children).
2. *Endangered*—client-oriented services incapable of expanding their infrastructure resources without significant technological change (e.g., water and sanitation, crowded educational systems).
3. *Relatively invulnerable*—area-based services convenient to the government, and client-oriented services which are capable of absorbing required additional staff if administratively reorganized (e.g., information, research, and communication services and welfare programs).
4. *Least vulnerable*—"state-essential" area-based services capable of expanding personnel base and using multiple or interchangeable technological systems (e.g., military defense, mechanical tax collection systems).

Countries with a profile like China's (ABKNS), where labor-intensive technologies and decentralized administrative authority are appropriate, would present problems to the administrative planner that are not high on the priority list of economists: beyond the food problem, which is being solved by adopting new technologies and incentive systems, there lies a slower-fused problem, the modernization of the urban infrastructure, especially in matters like sanitation and rapid transit. The category of "endangered" services would not appear to present a very serious problem in China's case, since so many client-oriented functions can be performed by communal organizations. Both urban and rural problems were exacerbated in Sukarno's Indonesia (AEJNR), suffering simultaneously from a bulging youth cohort, urbanization, ethnic division, and relatively low technological and administrative flexibility: the planner's problem was maintaining a marginally functioning system while devising new administrative and technological responses to mounting demands in the services deemed most essential (administrators were clearly concerned with these issues on my last visit there in 1974). Nepal's services were still not threatened (AEIPT), because the government's effectiveness created such low expectations that demands remained minimal. This condition was dramatically attested by a fire in 1973 that destroyed the records and equipment of the entire central ministerial apparatus: it caused few inconveniences to the public even though the government came to a standstill. Indeed, more demands flowed from external factors like tourism than from the still inarticulate citizenry or the archaic political system.

The country profiles may also define characteristic situations in which food shortages are most likely to pose administrative problems of different kinds. For example, the low agricultural productivity profile in Burma, Mexico, Sri Lanka, and Bangladesh is significantly associated with low rates of urban migration, which probably means that labor-intensive processes can be employed. This strategy often requires both land reform and technological innovation, each of which calls for significant government intervention.

These typological devices, like any other taxonomies, can be used in preliminary planning to identify salient characteristics for further study. Beyond taxonomy lies the possibility of diagnosis and prescription, two forms of applied knowledge that require detailed information not ordinarily available for dealing with RPC. Few countries now gather information about population changes except through census bureau and academic centers for demographic studies. To perform the diagnostic functions described here would require additional skills and access. Moreover, in order to aggregate the data latent in a system's Distant Early Warning signals, analysts would need access to budget, personnel, and operational documents from agencies performing all of the vulnerable client-based services receiving financial support from the central government. A unit organized to analyze the other incremental and impending changes in an administrative system should therefore be situated near a budget office, finance ministry or economic development unit.

A population planning office would also need access to top administrative decisionmakers in each agency likely to be affected by RPC, so that if necessary, interdepartmental adjustments could be made in staff, organization, facilities, and technologies. Governments whose senior civil service is organized on an

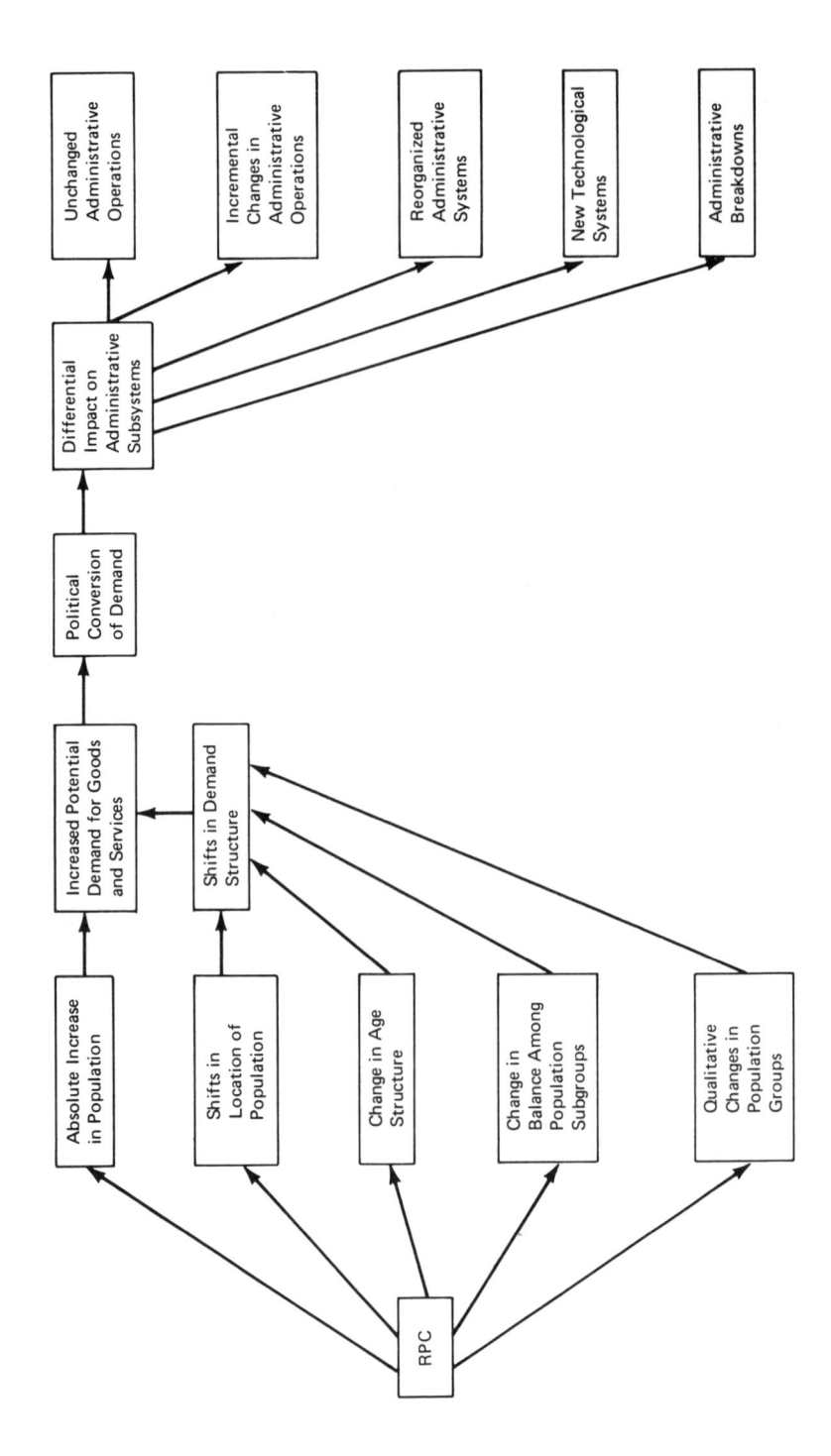

Figure 3-8. Simplified Model of Administrative Consequences of Rapid Population Change

interministerial basis could situate a population unit so it had access to each participating agency by placing it within the permanent secretariat, while still keeping the decision-making responsibility interdepartmental and cooperative.

Some findings and recommendations a population analysis unit will make are likely to be politically sensitive, especially if they involve possible shifts of the resources and services supplied to ethnic groups and regions. But governments that ignore unpalatable facts of RPC do so at the risk of a future crisis. A first step to reducing those political sensitivities is through routine administrative action, which can give time and warning to the leadership, permitting needed interventions as the issues become both public and compelling.

An administrative action like creating a population analysis unit is not a substitute for political decisions; building an organization is not the same as solving a problem. But insofar as any effective intervention by government can cope with the problems of RPC, the first step in creating political will is to recognize it and prepare to respond to it.

Notes

The author is grateful for comments by his colleagues Harold D. Lasswell, Warren Ilchman, and Myron Weiner, and from Garry Brewer of RAND, and for suggestions and data from his research assistant, Clay Wescott.

1. Edward L. Katzenbach, Jr., "The Horse Cavalry in the Twentieth Century: A Study on Policy Response," in *Public Policy* 8 (1958): 120-149.

2. Nathan Keyfitz points out in a study of Indonesia that a 3% yearly increment in the adult rural population is equal to an 18% increase in the adult urban population and that a 2.5% growth rate conceals a 7% rate in certain age groups. "The Youth Cohort Revisited," in W. Howard Wriggins and James F. Guyot, *Population, Politics and the Future of Southern Asia* (New York: Columbia Univ. Press, 1973), pp. 255, 239F.

3. Gunnar Myrdal, *Population: A Problem for Democracy* (Gloucester, Mass., Peter Smith, 1962), (original ed. 1940). See also Cicely Watson, "Population Policy in France: Family Allowances and Other Benefits," *Population Studies* 6,3 (March 1954) and 8,1 (July 1954).

4. Joseph L. Fisher and Neal Potter, "The Effects of Population Growth on Resource Adequacy and Quality," in National Academy of Sciences Study Commission, *Rapid Population Growth, Consequences and Policy Implications* (Baltimore: Johns Hopkins Univ. Press, 1971).

5. Roger Revelle, "Population," *Science Journal*, Oct. 1967, pp. 113-119; William Rich, "Smaller Families through Social and Economic Progress," Washington: Overseas Development Council, 1973.

6. Satisfying them may mean sacrifice to development goals, of course.

Ansley J. Coale and Edgar M. Hoover, *Population Growth and Economic Development in Low Income Countries* (Princeton: Princeton University Press, 1958), Chapter II.

7. Urban migration is positively associated with youthful migration in a number of studies. Cf. Gerry Hendershot, "Characteristics of Migrants to Manila and other Urban Places from Two Rural Communities," University of Philippines, Manila, 1968; Michael Todaro, "A Model of Labor Migration and Urban Unemployment in the Less-Developed Countries," *American Economic Review* 59 (1969); T. Paul Schultz, "Population Growth and Internal Migration in Colombia," (Santa Monica: RAND, 1969). Similar findings are reported for Malaysia: Siew-Ean Khoo, "Development Planning and Internal Migration, West Malaysia 1957-1970," paper prepared for Population Policies Workshop, Harvard University, 1974.

8. Wayne A. Cornelius has demonstrated that in Latin America, expectation levels on the part of new urban immigrants are relatively modest, however. The political demand effect of such movements becomes most pronounced among older and second-generation immigrants. "Urbanization and Political Demand-making: Political Participation among the Migrant Poor in Latin American Cities," *American Political Science Review* 68,3 (Sept. 1974). For a comparable situation in India, cf. Myron Weiner, "Urbanization and Political Protest," *Civilization* 17, 1/2 (1967); 44-50.

9. Such problems are likely to worsen in Latin America and Africa because of projected increases in dependency ratios. These dependents will be disproportionately youthful. *Bulletin of Labor Statistics—Labour Force and World Population Growth* (Geneva: International Labour Organization, 1974), p. 73.

10. Such demands for land reform will be most likely in countries combining large agricultural labor forces with high inequalities of land ownership. Samuel P. Huntington, *Political Order in Changing Societies* (New Haven: Yale University Press, 1968), p. 383.

11. Secretaria de Industria y Comercio, Direccion General de Estadistica, *Proyecciones Demograficas de la Republica Mexicana Poblacion* (Mexico, D.F.: Secretaria de Industria y Comercio, 1966), p. 54, cited in Ellen M. Bussey, *The Flight from Rural Poverty—How Nations Cope* (Lexington, Mass.: Lexington Books, D.C. Heath and Company 1973), p. 35.

12. Women play a disproportionate role in the agricultural economies of most developing countries. By the year 2000, it is projected that in most LDCs, employment opportunities for women will decline along with the diminishing economic importance of agriculture. *Bulletin of Labor Statistics*, pp. 45-46, 65.

13. Lincoln H. Day, "The Social Consequences of a Zero Population Growth Rate in the U.S.," in Charles F. Westoff and Robert Parke, Jr. (eds.), U.S. Commission on Population Growth and the American Future Research Report, Vol. 1, *Demographic and Social Aspects of Population Growth* (Washington: Government Printing Office, 1972), pp. 661-674; Gene E. Rainey, "Arkansas'

Aging Trend: A Portent of Future Politics," *Southwest Social Science Quarterly*, June 1964, pp. 37-49.

Increased demand for housing will result from the declining size of private households, which in turn will be caused primarily by the rising proportion of adults in the population and declining levels of fertility. Department of Economic and Social Affairs, *The Determinants and Consequences of Population Trends* (N.Y.: United Nations, 1973), pp. 353-56.

Demands on social recreation facilities will increase both because of increases in the aged population, and because of increased needs of children whose parents are both working. Demands for public welfare programs will increase because the increasing aged population will continue to have the highest poverty rate of any age group, and will demand more public assistance as they obtain increasing political power. Lower birthrates will not significantly reduce the welfare demands of families with middle-aged parents. Frank A. Pinner, Paul Jacobs, and Philip Selznick, *Old Age and Political Behavior* (Berkeley: University of California Press, 1959); Jackson K. Putnam, *Old Age Politics in California* (Stanford: Stanford University Press, 1970); Research Report of the Commission on Population Growth and the American Future, *Population and the American Future: Report of the Commission* (Washington, D.C.: Government Printing Office, 1972).

Utilization of all forms of health care except dental visits tends to rise with age. National Center for Health Statistics, *Vital and Health Statistics*, Series 10, No. 70, April 1970.

The preceding configuration of demands may be somewhat different in deteriorating "core" cities. Jay Forrester, *Urban Dynamics* (Cambridge, Mass.: MIT Press, 1969).

14. Demographic Yearbook, 1970; J.I. Clark and W.B. Fisher, *Populations of the Mid-East and North Africa* (N.Y.: Africana, 1972), pp. 373-403.

15. For example, the average age of the population of South Asia is projected to increase from 34.3 years in 1970 to 38.0 years in 2000. This aging will result from fertility declines, and increases in life expectancies. *Bulletin of Labor Statistics*, p. 72.

16. Clay G. Wescott, "Growth Centers and Primacy in Kenya," Chapter 5 in this volume.

17. The sometimes deceptive economic causes of migration are described in Corazon Mejia-Ragmundo with respect to the Philippines in a paper prepared for the Population Policies Seminar, Harvard University, 1974.

18. Department of Economic and Social Affairs, Statistical Office, *Statistical Yearbook*, 1973 (N.Y.: United Nations, 1974).

19. Allan E. Goodman, "The Political Implications of Urban Development in Southeast Asia: The 'Fragment' Hypothesis," *Economic Development and Cultural Change* 20,1 (October 1971).

20. George Zaiden, *Population Growth and Economic Development, Studies in Family Planning*, No. 42, Population Council, New York City, 1969.

21. The evidence is, of course, only inferential. Vivien Ponniah, "An Appraisal of Population Policy to Affect Fertility in West Malaysia," paper prepared for Population Policy Seminar, Harvard University, 1974.

22. David Yavkey, *Fertility Differences in a Modernizing Country* (Princeton: University Press, 1961), pp. 29, 35, 42.

23. Department of Economic and Social Affairs, *The Determinants of Population Trends*, Vol. I (N.Y.: United Nations, 1973).

24. Weiner, "Political Demography: An Inquiry into the Political Consequences of Population Change," in National Academy of Sciences Study Commission, *Rapid Population Growth*, p. 587.

25. Interuniversity Consortium for Political Research, *World Handbook of Political and Social Indicators, II.*

26. Joan N. Nelson, *Migrants, Urban Poverty and Instability in Developing Nations*, Harvard, Center for International Affairs, Occasional Paper No. 22, September 1969. Harley L. Browning, "Migrant Selectivity and the Growth of Large Cities in Developing Societies," in National Academy of Sciences Study Commission, *Rapid Population Growth*.

27. B. Maxwell Stamper, "Population Policy in Development Planning," *Reports on Population/Family Planning* (N.Y., Population Council, May 1973). For a brief survey of attempts that have been made to apply demographic considerations to planning, see *Determinants of Population*, pp. 557-630.

28. L. Saunders and S.L. Hardee, "Rationale and Suggestions for Establishing a Population Planning Unit," Kuala Lumpur, Government of Malaysia, 1972.

29. Robert A. Dahl, "The City in the Future of Democracy," *American Political Science Review* 61,4 (December 1967): 966; Roger Revelle and Harold A. Thomas, Jr., "Population Growth and Environmental Control," Cambridge, 1971 (processed); Werner Z. Hirsch, "Expenditure Implication of Metropolitan Growth and Consolidation," *Review of Economics and Statistics* 41,3 (August 1959); and Edward F. Penshaw's "Comment," *Review of Economics and Statistics* 43,1 (February 1961).

30. Such systems choices in education and other services are described in John D. Montgomery, *Technology and Civic Life* (Cambridge: MIT Press, 1974).

31. Arthur S. Banks and Robert B. Textor, *A Cross-Polity Survey* (Cambridge: MIT Press, 1963).

32. Kang Chao, *Agricultural Production in Communist China 1949-65* (Madison: Univ. of Wisconsin Press, 1970). Lee Orleans, *Every Fifth Child: The Population of China* (Stanford: Univ. Press, 1972), pp. 67-72, 104, 125-27, 143-54.

33. A.S. David, "Nepal: National Development, Population, and Family Planning," Population Council, Studies in Family Planning, No. 42, May 1969.

34. Henri Theil, "Estimation of Relationships Using Qualitative Variables," *American Journal of Sociology* 76,1 (July 1970).

4

Population Change and Policy Sciences: Proposed Workshops on Reciprocal Impact Analysis

Harold D. Lasswell

Introduction: Population Policies

Public policies toward population are official measures affecting, intended to affect, or responsive to changes in the numbers, composition or movement of the members of any group at any location. The chief concerns of the present book are policies of fertility and migration. It is evident that fertility policies pertain to births. Migration policies, when effectual, influence the attributes of a population, movements across boundaries, and movements within boundaries.[1]

Population decisions are statutes, treaties, and regulations; they are official commitments in the name of the public order. Population choices, on the other hand, are private acts; they are part of the civic order.[2] Direct population policies are perceived by those involved as expressly related to population changes and as employing strategies that are specifically adapted to making these changes. Examples are the pursuit of fertility effects by disseminating birth control information, or the attempt to influence migration by the compulsory movement of population. Indirect policies affect population change as a side effect of measures aimed at other results (or measures usually directed toward the attainment of objectives other than population control). Examples are housing and labor policies. It is also useful to distinguish between the intended and unintended effects of policy, especially since experience demonstrates that results may be the opposite of what is sought.

In the contemporary world population policies have gained new prominence as leaders in both developed and underdeveloped countries are alarmed by the potentially devastating impact of the uncontrolled growth of numbers on the quality of life.

It is not to be assumed that all are in agreement about the characteristics of the preferred quality of life to be sought and protected by public policy. Nevertheless, the world community is not entirely without authoritative language that partly clarifies the fundamental goals of public order. The Universal Declaration of Human Rights, for example, shows how human relationships in the several sectors of the social process can be fruitfully considered. These preferred events (or values) exemplify the desired quality of life.[3]

1. *Power* (political relations). The Declaration asserts the right "to take part in the government," "to be recognized as a person before the law," and "to

effective remedy by competent national tribunals." Criteria of fair trial are enumerated together with a right of asylum. There is a right to "a social and international order."

2. *Enlightenment* (knowledge and interpretation). There is "freedom of opinion and expression" and a right "to seek, receive, and impart information and ideas through any media and regardless of frontiers."

3. *Wealth* (economic relations). Recognition is given to the "right to own property" and to a "standard of living adequate for the well-being" of the individual and his family.

4. *Well-being* (safety, health, comfort). The Declaration recognizes the right to "life, liberty and security of person" and condemns "torture" as well as "cruel" or "inhuman" treatment or punishment. There is a "right to rest and leisure" and a general right to "social security."

5. *Skill* (occupational, professional, artistic). Recognizes the "right to work, to free choice of employment," and "to protection against unemployment." Also "everybody has a right to education" and "to participate freely in the cultural life of the community, to enjoy the arts and to share in scientific achievement and its benefits."

6. *Affection* (intimacy, loyalty). The Declaration specifies the "right to marry and to found a family" and to engage in congenial association with others ("peaceful assembly and association"). And there is right to be identified with a national community ("right to nationality").

7. *Respect* (recognition). The first article affirms that "all human beings are born free and equal in dignity and right. . . . Everyone is entitled to all rights and freedoms . . . without distinction of any kind." Obviously, there must be no "slavery or servitude," no arbitrary interference with "privacy, family, home or correspondence," and freedom from attacks on "honor and reputation."

8. *Rectitude* (ethics, religion). The Declaration affirms "freedom of thought, conscience and religion. . . . Everyone has duties to the community," and there is no right to destroy the freedom of others.

Uncontrolled population growth is expected to impair the aggregate output of values in every sector of society and to sharpen inequalities of distribution everywhere. An overcrowded world can be expected to swing between extremes of political conflict and massive apathy, and between exaggerated personal hostility and indifference. The control of values such as enlightenment, wealth, skill, and respect will be concentrated in the control of a few. From shortages of food and medicare will rise crises of malnutrition, disease, and defect. As numbers multiply and competition intensifies, human conduct will grow progressively egocentric and socially irresponsible.

It is not necessarily true that the consequences of the uncontrolled expansion will affect the quality of life of every national or sub-national community around the globe at the same time or to the same degree. Nor is it to be taken for granted that every population policy, whatever the intention of its initiators, will accomplish the ends for which it is intended. If we are to be informed about the fluctuating quality of life and particularly about the impact of population change, we must arrange for dependable, comprehensive, and prompt reporting. Policy review and appraisal must also analyze and report the effect of public population policies on the population changes whose impacts have been observed on the quality of life.

A technical requirement of adequate policy appraisal is the choice of indicators of the changes to be pursued or prevented.[4] Indicators differ from one society to another and within a single society. We know, for instance, that "votes" in the political process may be by voice, by stereotyped movement, or by manipulating a physical resource (a ball, a machine, etc.). The problem of indicators is to discern "equivalents." Frequency of exposure to opportunities for enlightenment may be indicated by "minutes of broadcasting time listened to by representative audiences" (and similar measures). "Per capita wages" (and other income transfers) are standard indicators of economic transactions (wealth). "Days of work lost on account of illness" is one obvious indicator of well-being. "Days in school" counts in describing skill. "Individual quarrels and fights per capita" provides a partial indicator of the level of affection (congeniality). "Percentage untouchable or outcast" indicates the size of the low-respect class (or caste). One indicator of rectitude is "per capita attendance at worship sites."

Since indicators are bound to be no more than semi-satisfactory referents of the category for which they stand, both scientists and policymakers are well-advised to keep their critical wits about them in the choice of indices. A situation or a dimension cannot always be described on a 0-100 scale. It may be that a simple rank order will suffice to characterize the quality-quantity of change. Often it is feasible to classify visual records into categories that are sufficiently detailed to disclose significant trends. For instance, the declining strength of a traditional culture may be partially estimated by comparing photographs from year to year of the most sacred festivals. Results may show that there is less and less traditional ornamentation used on dress or paraphernalia.

The Policy Sciences Approach

The preceding pages have exemplified some characteristics of the approach that we recommend for the analysis and guidance of population policies. Phrased in more systematic terms the recommended policy sciences approach is contextual, problem-oriented and multi-method.[5] Although general familiarity is assumed, it may be useful to summarize the policy sciences method.

The approach is *contextual*, which implies that a particular problem is considered in relation to the larger context of the social process in which it is embedded and with which it interacts.

The policy sciences are *problem-oriented* and involve five intellectual tasks, as indicated by these questions: What are the value *goals* of policy in this situation? What are the *trends* to date in goal realization? What conditioning factors (*conditions*) account for the direction and intensity of these trends? What are the most probable *projections* of future developments in the realization of goals? What policy *alternatives* will yield the highest net realization of goal values?

Scientific observers seek to increase knowledge of policy processes and to expedite the use of relevant knowledge in these processes. The goals postulated for scientific purposes may be those of selected active participants or of the scientist himself. Each intellectual task may be approached with full conscious awareness, marginal awareness, or no conscious awareness. (The latent content of marginal awareness can become fully conscious with no experience of anxiety. The latent content of an unconscious process, on the contrary, typically calls for the overcoming of anxiety.)

The policy sciences are *multi-method*, which implies that they rely on whatever procedure seems promising for theory formation, data gathering and processing.

The Interplay of Population and Policy:
A Conceptual Map

The contextual character of the policy sciences requires a conceptual map that depicts the interplay between population and policy. The goals of population policy are doubly contextual: the population changes to be effected involve an entire community or group; both the changes and the strategies by which they are pursued are intended to be compatible with the goals of public policy considered as a whole. A realistic evaluation of a policy or set of policies calls for a conceptual map to guide the process. The map must be revised from time to time in the light of experience.

The scope of the conceptual map is to locate population and policy in the social process of the world community or of any component situation. A social process occurs whenever and wherever human beings interact with one another and with their physical and biological environments. The human participants pursue preferred outcomes (values) through practices which, when stabilized, are the institutions of the interactive situation.

Figure 4-1 presents a conceptual map that begins with "population" and moves to "policy" and again to "population." These phenomena are put in relationship to one another by employing categories selected with the five problem-solving tasks in mind.

Figure 4-2 uses seven terms to characterize policy outcomes. The seven categories in Figure 4-2 apply to private choices as well as to public decisions (e.g., to family or government outcomes).

in a *social context*
of specifiable characteristics
(space, time, culture, organized, unorganized)

population changes
(i.e., births, deaths, migration)

affect the *focus of attention* (initial perspectives)
of some participants immediately or
mediated through channels of communication
(or fail to reach the focus of attention)

influencing subsequent *perspectives*
of identities (or non-identities)
of expectations (or matter-of-fact assumptions)
of demand for net value advantages

(P power, E enlightenment, W wealth,
B well-being, S skill, A affection,
R respect, D rectitude)

(in terms of direction and intensity,
or the tension level—the image and
mood level—of individuals and groups)

of myths (ideologies, counter-ideologies)
(doctrines, formulas, mirandas)

of *participants* with equal or unequal
base values
(e.g., elite, mid-elite, rank and file)

generating *strategies*
of indulgence (gain/blocked loss)
of deprivation (loss/blocked gain)
utilizing symbols and signs (e.g., diplomacy, propaganda)
utilizing deeds and resources (e.g., economic, military)
of isolation or coalition (individual, group)
adapting the tension level (private motives, displacements, justifications)

affecting *outcomes* (see Figure 4-2)
through public order decisions
constitutive, ordinary
through civic order choices
constitutive, ordinary

with post-outcome *effects*
on population change
on public order values and institutions
(producing later impacts on the policy process)
on civic order values and institutions
(aggregate levels of shaping and sharing;
innovation, diffusion and restriction of
institutional practices)

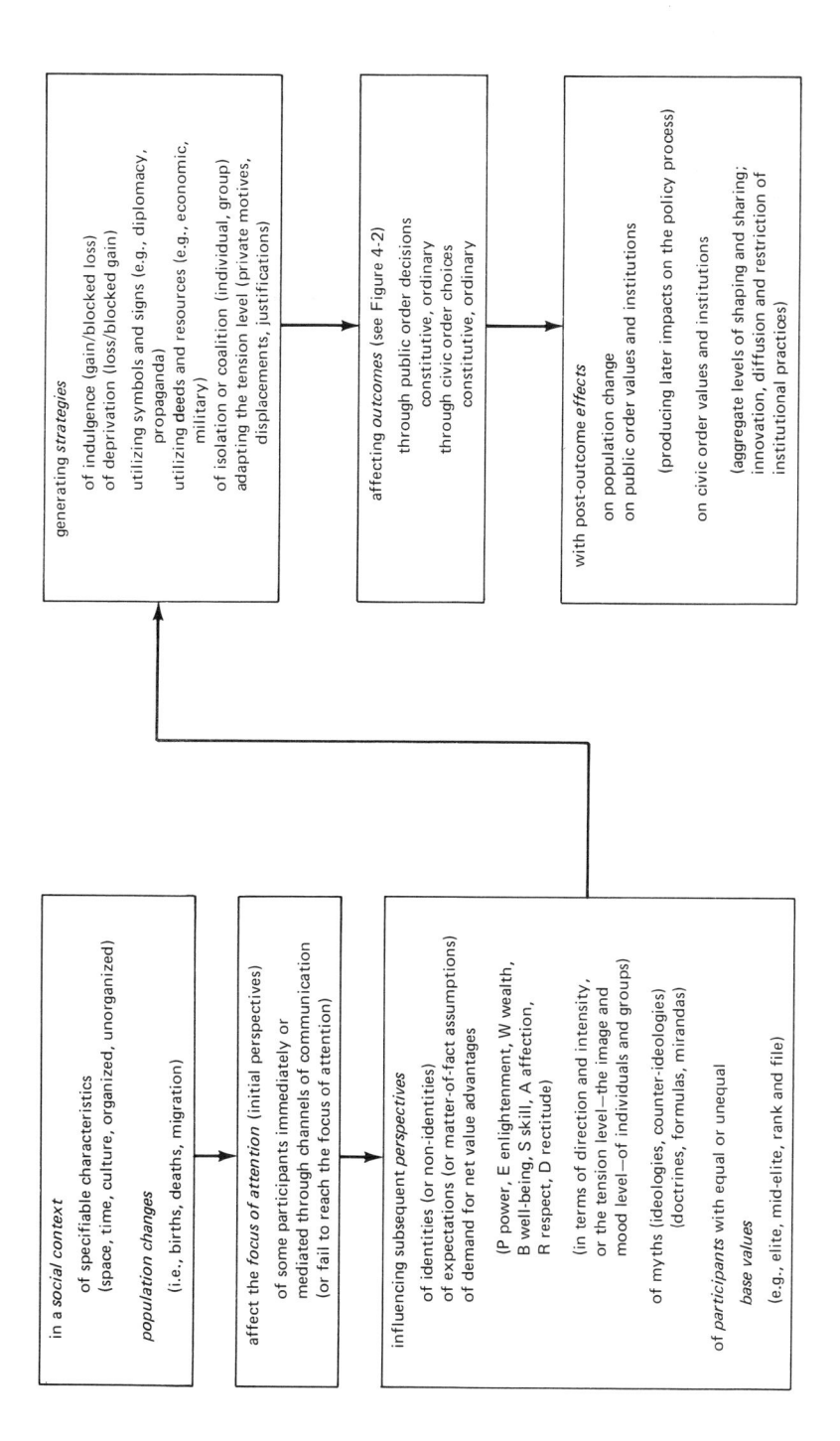

Figure 4-1. Social Process

intelligence, or the gathering, processing and dissemination of information to participants in policy decisions and choices;

promotion, or the use of persuasive or coercive means of influencing decisions and choices;

prescription, or the formulation of authoritative and controlling norms and sanctions;

invocation, or the initiation of action to relate prescriptions provisionally to specific circumstances;

application, or subsequent operations involved in relating prescriptions to circumstances;

termination, or the ending of a prescription and the adjustment of claims based on expectations developed when the prescription was in effect;

appraisal, or the analysis and reporting of the degree to which policy goals have been achieved, and the allocation of imputed or effective responsibility for results.

Figure 4-2. Policy Outcomes

Intelligence Structures and Functions

A conceptual map is especially important for the adequate analysis or execution of the intelligence phase of population policy. Policy forming and execution are steps into the future that, when conducted in a disciplined manner, take advantage of the information that becomes available as the future unfolds.

Realistic planning for future feedback of information proceeds with the five intellectual tasks in mind (goals, trends, conditions, projections, alternatives). As information becomes available during the future it is possible to appraise in more adequate fashion the previously adopted goals and priorities of population policy. At the same time it becomes feasible to evaluate the past projection of events now current, and to assess the adequacy of the methods by which such projections were developed. In turn, these exercises indicate how more satisfactory projections of population can be formulated for future times (at T^1, T^2 and so on).

The data obtained by feedback often raise questions about the dependability of past studies of population trends and conditioning factors. Future inquiries will be turned in two directions: one intended to improve knowledge of the past; the other designing investigations to disclose the patterns of causation in future interactions.

The inflow of information during the future will produce data of relevance to the task of appraising the policies that were in effect during the period in question. These results are then available for use in inventing, pretesting and selecting policies for the control of population changes in immediate or remote time intervals.

Births and Intelligence Concerning Births

As a means of posing problems that relate to the intelligence phase of policy, and of explaining Figures 4-1 and 4-2, we concentrate in this chapter on a single component of many if not most intelligence operations, namely, the reporting and interpretation of births.

In advanced industrial societies it is taken for granted that intelligence agencies will report births, together with much more detailed population data. For working purposes we adopt the postulate that the goals of intelligence services include the accurate and prompt reporting of births to all who participate in the policy process of the relevant social context. It is probable that population policies will be more realistic if public policy is made on the basis of valid information and critical conjectures about trends, conditions, and projections related to births.

Most of our attention will be given to the analysis of trends and conditions that have affected the reporting of births in the past. We are also interested in examining the impact of dependable (or undependable) intelligence about births on population policy as a whole, and on particular population changes.

By focusing on the "birth-decision-birth" pattern we bring out in detail some characteristics of the policy-oriented approach and indicate why these characteristics are to be taken seriously. We are told that many different factors have conditioned the scope of population counts taken in the past.

In primitive tribes, no specialized arrangements are needed for a population count, partly because the numbers are usually small, though chiefly as a consequence of the enormous emphasis that is typically given to kinship identities. Genealogies are already firmly in mind, particularly among the old. Births are usually welcomed since they are perceived as means of ensuring the future of kinship groups. The demand for a written record and a count of births was hardly thinkable before the rise of urban civilization, an event that is approximately dated seven millennia ago and located in the valleys of the Nile, the Tigris-Euphrates, and the Indus. Urban civilization marked the appearance of states of literacy and record keeping, and the relative decline of kinship. It is perhaps surprising for non-specialists to learn that the U.S. census is the oldest continuous periodic count (beginning in 1790), and that the shift from households to individuals did not occur until the middle of the nineteenth century. Infants and youth are said to be undercounted everywhere, and varying degrees of importance have been attached to enumerating the newborn.

We cannot provide an utterly comprehensive list of the factors that have led to the introduction of counting (and especially the counting of births) in historical circumstances. Nor are we able to formulate with much confidence the quantitative impact of these determining factors. Nevertheless, by scrutinizing the past we obtain clues to the identity of the conditioning factors to be looked for and followed as future events unfold. If we describe the strength or weakness of present propensities to count, it will be possible to gather data that confirm or disconfirm predictions made on the basis of interconnections discerned in the past. As future events are followed in selected situations it will be feasible to identify new conditioning factors. Previously observed routines of mutual influencing may no longer apply without revision. Deliberate interventions can be made in future situations for multiple purposes: to test explanatory models;

or to assess the strategies designed to utilize conditioning factors (base values) in operational patterns that culminate in preferred outcomes.

At this point it is convenient to consider the "birth-decision-birth" sequence in reference to the conceptual maps outlined in Figures 4-1 and 4-2. It may be helpful to comment that the social process as a whole or any particular interaction that occurs within it can be described for analysis and comparison in reference to the questions raised in Figure 4-3.

We indicated above that with the rise of cities public authorities were the participants who took the initiative in instituting body counts for purposes of taxation, military service, labor or public works and other objectives. We are also aware that participants in empires, city-states, and nation states have been far from unanimous in support of census-taking activities. Resistance has come from peasants and minority groups differentiated by race, language, origin, and other traits, as well as from slave-holding elites liable to property taxes.

How are we to explain the direction and intensity with which participants in different contexts demand or counter-demand counting in circumstances in which births increase, decrease or remain constant? *Effective demands are a function of net value indulgences or deprivations perceived by the sufficiently influential members of the relevant context, and of the most skillful use of strategies to influence outcomes.*

The advent of a newborn participant in society has consequences that depend in part on the focus of attention. The focus of attention includes the initial perspectives of a participant, and the most significant point is whether attention is initially focused or unfocused on the changes in which the scientific observer is interested (such as births). The focus may be immediate as in the case of a mother, or mediated, as with those who listen to announcements or news.

The initial perspectives of participants are elaborated by participants in terms of identities, expectations, and demands. In industrial societies these elaborations facilitate the conduct of activities intended to establish an intelligence process that gathers many more details than the simple fact of birth.

Who are the *participants*?

What *perspectives* affect their participation?

What *situations* (in terms of space, time and organization) are the settings in which the participants interact?

What *base values* (assets and liabilities) are at the disposal of participants?

What *strategies* are employed to render the base values effective influences on outcomes?

What *outcome* demands succeed or fail?

What are the ensuing *effects* on values and institutions?

Figure 4-3. Social Interaction

The evaluation of the child by various members of the body politic influences the presence and the intensity of demand to count or not to count the newborn. Consider the significance of a child to the mother. A convenient mode of analysis is in terms of the eight value categories employed in our social process map. The pain and discomfort may be perceived as more than justified by the somatic gratifications of motherhood. Therefore the *well-being* value is positive. The child may be a target of deep and enduring love and a source of pride as a vindication of one's potential as a human being (*affection, respect*). For the devout the infant is a religious and ethical fulfillment (*rectitude*). In economic terms the newborn may represent an investment in social security (*wealth*). It is evident that political *power* is a consideration in the case of the queen who retains her position when she has produced a prince. The political weight of any influential family may be perceived as dependent on the production of another potential soldier, candidate or official. For mothers the infant is a challenge to acquire the knowledge and technique necessary to do a good job of child rearing (*enlightenment, skill*). If the mother is gratified by the birth, and if she sees that society welcomes the newborn, she will presumably interpose no obstacle to recording and counting the latest addition to the population. If on the contrary the larger society is seen as an enemy, as in the case of a persecuted minority, attempts may be made to conceal the fact of birth (or in extreme circumstances to destroy the infant).

It is not to be taken for granted that a child is a source of gratification to the mother. Physical and mental complications may affect both mother and child. The mother may find herself unable to love the offspring of a hated husband; and she may feel the shame at having given birth to a defective child. If the infant is born out of wedlock the mother may experience the guilt of the offender against the laws of God and man. The child may be an unwelcomed economic burden or a source of political deprivation if a male heir and not another female is required by the dynasty. The infant may seem to present problems that go beyond the mother's knowledge or skill. When on balance the infant is more a depriver than a source of value indulgence to the mother, she may seek to get rid of it and to avoid registration.

The mother is rarely the only person in a given context whose evaluation of an infant contributes to the demand or counter-demand for census-taking. For the father or husband the child may be a positive or negative object in many or all value categories. Similarly for the siblings, and for grandparents or other relatives.

The perspectives of participants other than family or friends affect the propensity to count or not to count. Americans have not forgotten the rivalries of towns and counties, cities and states, in the "numbers game" of a developing country.

The categories of identity, demand, and expectation have been used to characterize the perspectives of mothers or of other relevant participants in preliminary fashion. For explanatory purposes it is necessary to connect these categories and data to the analysis of myth. A myth is composed of the relatively stable perspectives of a group (or of a personality taken as a total field of reference). A myth is affirmed as ideology by those who accept an established order. Those who reject the system may reject it in the name of a counter-ideology. Each myth is divisible into doctrines, or the most abstract statements of philosophic orientation; the formulas, or the enforcible codes; and the miranda, or popular lore.

A mother's evaluation of her infant, and her disposition to report or to withhold information from official agencies, may be largely determined by the political, religious, ethnic, and other ideological perspectives that she incorporated into her personality during the formative years (of socialization). She has obtained net value advantages by talking, behaving, and feeling in harmony with the myth. Perhaps she has gone through rebellious periods that made her vulnerable to value deprivations from family, friends, and neighborhood, and eventually led her to conform to "woman's destiny."

So far as most of the population is concerned the popular miranda are more important socializing influences than the presentation of complex theological, metaphysical or ethical arguments. The popular lore includes rumors and stories of the rewards of conformity and the punishments of deviation.

We began by selecting a social context. It is important to take note of the sub-situations within the larger setting, especially when there are grounds for hypothesizing that sub-situations exert a causal impact on significant events. Some relevant situations are unorganized; others are organized.

Among the important unorganized situations are attention zones. These may diverge sharply from one another in reporting births. Urban-centered zones may give negligible amounts of attention to natal events in agricultural districts. Nations with a primary city of overwhelming prominence may bestow little notice on lesser cities or peripheral regions. Perhaps audience focus is more evenly dispersed over the country if the urban structure is multi-centered.

A smaller zone of involvement is a promotional (or opinion) zone that actively supports or opposes such policies as the registration of births. Both attention and promotional activities may be deeply conditioned by tribal, religious, linguistic and other identities.

Organized zones can be variously described which appear to be affected by births and in turn to influence population policy. The interconnections of births, organized zones, and policy are affected by other factors occurring in the context. Therefore it is not to be assumed without appropriate investigation that any routine relationship can be predicted involving such situational characteristics as the following: the degree of centralization and decentralization, concentration and deconcentration of authority at any level; monopoly-pluralization of any functional operation; autocracy-oligarchy-democracy; military-civilian control. For instance, high population densities would appear to favor demands for centralized structures.

Propositions about effective demand refer to the perspectives of those in control of the base values employable as strategies to influence outcomes. Often it is not difficult to locate the participants who launch campaigns to inaugurate or to modify a census. Where there is a direct connection between numbers and representation the politically active and influential individuals and organizations can be expected to favor counting—to the degree that a favorable result can be anticipated. Declining areas often succeed in deferring or falsifying a count. Real estate groups also define their interests in different ways, depending on their interpretation of whether accurate population figures are to their expected net advantage. In societies where the demand for scientific and scholarly knowledge of social facts is great, professional and scientific societies add strength to the forces in support of an adequate census. In fact, the rise of professional demographers appears to be a critical factor in the establishing and extending of modern population counts. We note, for example, that the International Demographic Congress of 1878 spoke firmly in favor of international action to improve the data provided by population inventories. The International Statistical Institute evidently took rather effective action toward the end of the last century. When public health considerations grow in importance, we expect to find that exact population figures are in demand, notably in regard to births. Where educational programs go beyond the local neighborhood, planning and administrative operations intensify the demand for data. Welfare, housing, and related family programs have the same result. Human rights projects are likely to be concerned with prompt and accurate population figures. If churches obtain fiscal advantages based on numbers, they can be expected to join the quest for accurate information.

The most inclusive proposition about the role of various participants in a social context can be formulated as follows: *Elite perspectives are likely to have more impact on the intelligence process than the perspectives of non-elite members of the body politic.* If the elite of a developing nation favors a census the plan may at first be blocked by peasants who put so many difficulties in the path of enumerators that the costs are high and results are of dubious validity. Before long, however, the elites are likely to get what they want.

Results depend on the strategic measures employed. In addition to the volume of assets utilized in promotion much depends on the skill with which they are managed. Strategies are aimed at different audiences and skill is exhibited in choosing the "critical minimum" required to obtain the response sought. When appealed to, audiences are (1) favorable, (2) opposed or (3) uncommitted. It is evident that many strategic combinations are conceivable such as: intensifying the support of the favorable, taking care not to arouse latent opposition, splitting the opposition, focusing on a pivotal section of the uncommitted. Poor strategy includes "talking to the convinced" and neglecting the swing groups.

Strategists can manipulate value impacts efficiently to affect perspectives. The indulgences may be gains or blocked losses; the deprivations may be losses or blocked gains. Some campaigns may rely on presenting an inclusive census as valuable and necessary to modernize the nation, appealing to the evolving national identity, and the general demand to step into the twentieth century. Others may focus on the costs of ignorance of population matters. Often the issues are meaningless to those who fill out ballots. Their support may be mobilized on the basis of traditional loyalty, small payments or penalties, and other value inducements or deprivations.

Skillful strategies typically combine the fundamental elements of an act in joint operations. Propaganda, information, and education use *signs* and *symbols* directed to mass audiences. Diplomacy and lobbying are communications aimed to reach particular influentials. The economic instrument employs labor (*deeds*) and *physical resources* to affect production, investment, and consumption. The military-police instrument is used for defense or attack. When parts of the population are predisposed against a census, perceiving it as a means of invading privacy and increasing taxes or improving the efficiency of conscription, pro-census campaigns have sometimes sought to deny or deemphasize possible deprivations by prohibiting the use of the military or the police as advocates or enumerators.

When the actual or potential impact of strategic measures is under consideration it is important to examine the degree to which the tension level has entered the picture. The very taking of a census may sharply enhance the possibility of conflict by providing a target for the displacement of private hostilities toward public objects.

This contingency is always present in some degree and is a manifestation of the fundamental dynamic of politics. A basic view of the political process emphasizes three components: (1) the private motives of participants; (2) displacement toward public targets; (3) justification in terms of common interest. At any given time the tension level—the disposition to act in a given way—may be high or low. Private motives are generated by an enormous number of factors in the life situations of each person. Sometimes it is easy to recognize that several conditioning factors have contributed to the prevailing mood of the body politic, as when unemployment or disease is rampant. Moods of desperation, disappointment, or hostility may predispose individuals to attribute their sense of deprivation to whatever persons and issues come to the focus of their attention. In such circumstances the negative attitudes toward a census may have next to nothing to do with a well-considered evaluation of the advantages or disadvantages of such a practice. When the crops are good and prices are satisfactory, and when plagues are past, the euphoric moods prevailing may lead to the acceptance of information gathering as a valuable step toward a modern state.

The point of emphasis is that a continuing description of politics calls for the use of appropriate methods for the appraisal of the intensity and direction of attitudes referring to images and moods.

At any given time the proportion of public objects available for collective action (such as party programs) is less than the many internal and environmental factors that condition the direction and intensity of individual impulses (motives). If the dominant moods are positive, the affirmatively presented political symbols may benefit. If the dominant moods are negative, the affirmative symbols may be rejected (or, e.g., negatively presented symbols may be more vigorously rejected). The advantage of persistence in support of a political demand is that it may coincide with opportunities to obtain further support from "accidental" displacements.

Strategies culminate in successful or unsuccessful policy outcomes and effects. Figure 4-2 displays the seven outcomes included in our model of the policy process. Our immediate concern is with the intelligence phase of policy, and focuses on the distinctive outcomes of data gathering, processing and dispersion. The outcomes of a census bureau, for instance, flow to the structures specialized to each of the policy components designated in the figure. The data provided by the intelligence flow may pertain to any one of the five intellectual tasks as they contribute to a particular policy. In regard to birth information, for example, the outputs may be goal formulations, historical trends, analytic causation, future projection, or alternative programs. Instead of piecemeal releases the intelligence outcome may be a comprehensive plan intended to guide the activities of all who participate in the policy process.

Any investigation of intelligence outcomes explores effects of two kinds: first, on other decision phases; second, on post-policy events in the social process. Concerning the phases of decision:

Consider *promotion*. We have mentioned the possibility that political leaders may interpret a reduced birthrate as a precursor of declining power in the arena of world politics. They may therefore engage in persuasive or coercive activities intended to check a declining birthrate.

Continue with *prescription*. Further, distinguish a *constitutive* from an *ordinary* prescription. A constitutive outcome is an allocation of *authority* to exercise *control*. Hence a statute or a decree that establishes an intelligence agency (such as a census) is a constitutive prescription. It is to be observed that a completed prescription includes (1) *norms*, or generalized statements of required conduct; (2) *contingencies*, or statements of the circumstances in which the norms are required; and (3) *sanctions*, or the values to be mobilized as indulgences or deprivations of conformers or non-conformers to the norms. An example is a statute that requires a mother (or other parent) to register a child within ten days of birth or pay a fine.

By referring to a statute (which is presumably written) we may convey the impression that authoritative prescriptions ("laws") must be written. Not so: The essential point is *uniformity of expectations about enforcible norms in various contingencies*. In literate societies the act of voting affirmatively on a written or printed draft may be the moment that crystallizes expectations among enough members of the elite or non-elite members of a body politic to meet the minimum requirements laid down by a scientific observer of "law in the formal sense." In a non-literate society an act of announcement or proclamation may be the required practice. In all bodies politic some prescriptions cannot be traced to any particular moment. They gain acceptance without routine enactment.

A formal prescription is not necessarily a "law" in the sense of a definition specifying that "effective enforcement" must occur a certain number of times in the appropriate contingencies. Before it is a "law" a constitutive statute that establishes a census bureau must be made and applied. The officials in tribal or in remote peasant villages may take no steps to appoint a census agent or to provide a register; and they may take no action against those who impermissibly fail to register a birth. In various districts conformity may be so low that a "national" prescription cannot be accurately described as more than a regional regulation. However, despite an inauspicious beginning, an intelligence structure may eventually be set up and operated with enough vigor to overcome insufficiencies. Of course, the trend may move in the opposite direction, passing from conformity to non-conformity.

The reports issued by an intelligence agency may affect invocation. For instance, they may raise a presumption that prescriptions intended to reduce the number of births are neglected and that active measures are now needed to get results.

Intelligence reports may affect application, perhaps by showing that little has been done by responsible legal agencies to follow the steps that were initially taken to activate a newly acquired authority.

An official agency may be authorized to recommend the termination of prescriptions under various circumstances, and to compensate those whose expectations of advantage were generated when the prescriptions were in force. Perhaps the intelligence services provide a list of people who were promised an income if they had no more than two children. If the general prescription is terminated the compensation may be continued for those who adhered to the former norm.

Intelligence reports of births may be combined with other reports to enable an agency of appraisal to summarize (a) the degree to which population policies have been put into *internal* operation, and (b) the profile of *external* effects on all value-institution sectors of society, including the flow of population changes.

The data for (a) have been outlined in the immediately preceding paragraphs, which track the sequence of policy phases as given in Figure 4-2. The data required for (b) are specified in Figure 4-1, in connection with "post-outcome effects." Since that section is highly condensed it seems useful to add Figure 4-4–*Effect Appraisal (Intelligence Policy)*–whose function is to clarify what is involved in appraising the *external* effects of the intelligence outcomes of population policy. Intelligence reports may reach beyond the focus of attention

Population Policies	Population Effects	Quality of Life Effects: Values	Quality of Life: Institutional Changes
i e., fertility policies direct indirect i.e., migration policies	e.g., births ↑ ↓ → e.g., composition influx efflux rates	aggregate level (+, −, 0) distribution pattern (equality, inequality) (power enlightenment wealth well-being skill affection respect rectitude)	innovation or diffusion (+, −, 0) restriction (+, −, 0)

Figure 4-4. Effect Appraisal (Intelligence Policy)

of government officials and gain the notice of individuals or organizations in the civic order.

What are the effects on population of the intelligence obtained, processed and disseminated by the agencies of intelligence? Two sets of influences are involved. Some policy outcomes that were affected by population intelligence had distinguishable effects on population. Intelligence reports also may exert direct influence on the policies of individuals and organizations in the civic order. For instance, the migration of workers from north to south may come as a consequence of the job opportunities reported by the census and disseminated through the media of communication. This "direct civic order effect" may be in addition to the facilitation of migration by policies of free transportation that were stimulated when intelligence reports first reached various departments of government.

Policy appraisal is not complete until it has linked the effects of a particular act or set of acts with changes in the quality of life. For example, inclusive appraisal of population intelligence outcomes in the public order (a) identifies the policy outcomes influenced by these reports, (b) examines the population effects of these policies, and (c) determines the changes in value levels and distribution, and in the relevant institutional practices of diffusion or restriction.

Consider in more detail the effects on quality of life. We are aware of the possibility that during a given period population changes may strengthen or weaken the power position of a nation state in the regional balancing of power, or modify the internal power position of those who are identified with, or opposed to, the established legal and governmental system. Appraised in terms of equality, we may find that population changes have strengthened or weakened the voices of individuals in local or national matters. Institutional practices of enlarged representation may supercede traditional privileges.

Population changes may affect the level of public enlightenment by creating more effective demand for mass media facilities, and for more equal service in cities and towns outside the capital. Perhaps new listening and broadcasting arrangements consolidate an enlarging audience.

Population changes may modify the levels of wealth production and investment, and alter the gradation of income among groups and individuals. Traditional practices of production, saving, investment, and consumption may not remain as before.

Levels of life expectancy and freedom from disease and defect (well-being) may fluctuate with population; and the incidence of birth, death and morbidity may become more or less equalized. Folk practices may incorporate more patterns related to the "universalizing civilization of science and technology."

Skill levels respond to population change by modifications of level and distribution, as well as by diffusion of new and restriction of old practices (including modes of artistic expression and taste).

Population changes influence affection values and institutions by modifying family formation and dissolution, as well as by affecting levels of personal congeniality and of loyalty to collective groups.

Population shifts may contribute to changes in the respect position of a national community among nations, or modify the standing of a group among the classes and regions of a body politic. Individuals may enjoy wider or narrower opportunities to overcome discriminatory treatment; and individualistic practices may rise or fall in terms of traditional conduct.

Changes in numbers or mobility may accelerate or retard the development of demands to adopt and conform to common standards of responsible conduct (rectitude). Standards may become more or less diversified and contrasting, and new practices may spread slowly or with great rapidity.

In the previous paragraphs we have considered some of the potential effects of population changes on quality of life as though the relevant frame of reference was always the past. This is undoubtedly true for many final acts of policy appraisal. At the same time it is important to recognize that active policy processes occur in the present and call for anticipatory consideration of future events. The conceptual map of Figure 4-1 emphasizes the point that an act of decision or choice, since it is a step into the future, cannot be fully known in advance. However, all is not chaos. For one thing the intelligence phase of policy can stabilize goals, which are the preferred events. A stabilized conception increases the likelihood that analysts and decisionmakers will recognize preferred events when they occur, and that they will be ready to take advantage of opportunities in the social process to bring them to effective realization. It is also possible in intelligence operations to describe trends in realizing goals up to the present, and to estimate the intensity with which participants in the social process support or reject these goals. Such estimates are of obvious importance in the projection of future developments and especially in inventing, evaluating, and selecting policy alternatives.

The past also provides grounds for inferring the conditions that may exert a causal impact on preferred future events. In the past ten years outside financial aid may have accelerated desired trends. A relevant question is whether, if outside aid is cut, inside aid can be obtained if it is still judged necessary to sustain or increase change. Clearly the constellation of expected conditioning factors in coming time periods (T^1, T^2 ...) may differ from the constellations that shaped the past.

Continuing Workshops or Decision Seminars

A major implication that we draw from the study of policy processes in general and of population policies in particular is that a more inclusive and systematic approach is needed, especially in the civic order. Investigation shows that public population policies are deeply affected by the interplay of the civic with the public order. There are innumerable examples of the importance of civic order as a means of stirring the public order into action on behalf of population changes that affect the preferred quality of life. In one respect, at least, the history of developing countries is usually the same. As a rule the critical approach to population policies is initiated in the civic order.

It is correct to assert that the population specialists of the globe comprise the combined public and private intelligence services of the world community on questions of population policy. Contemporary demographers often work in interdisciplinary teams whose members are recruited widely from such knowledge institutions in the civic order as universities and bureaus of research and development.

When we investigate in detail the significance of population specialists for public policies, we find that the overall results are less than satisfactory. It is true that theorists of population change have affected the ideological framework of debate. This influence is hardly matched by solid evidence of behavioral changes resulting from recommended policies.

Analyzing the record in the perspective of the policy sciences it appears that certain limitations curb the adequate performance of the most distinctive policy functions for which specialists are trained, namely, intelligence and appraisal. Scholarly centers have typically failed to anticipate future developments, to formulate future objectives and strategies, to plan continuing feedback of information as events unfold, and to engage in continuing revision of policy analysis or impact on the context.

We therefore emphasize the importance of developing a chain of population centers that contribute to knowledge of population by means of programs that include a "decision seminar technique" of focusing on chosen social contexts.[6] The context may cover a national, trans-national or sub-national area; and it may be initially launched to give special attention to a significant component of population change. Whether the starting point of maximum concern is fertility, migration or some other dimension of the phenomenon, the fundamental purpose is to view these events in the context of the population process as a whole. In turn a complex intellectual discipline is required since in principle the challenge is to obtain sufficient mastery over theory, procedures, and data to provide dependable guidance for any participant in the formation and execution of population policy in any chosen situation. In practice such comprehensive potentialities will be trimmed down, partly because many scientists of population will refuse to be client servers if service implies the strengthening of policies that contravene their conceptions of public interest. The point must be underlined that knowledge specialists do not necessarily lose their role as citizen-participants by acquiring knowledge.

The implication of the foregoing is that a continuing workshop or decision seminar that focuses on a particular country, for example, will plan to cover such points as the following:

1. Whose goals in reference to population policy are to be realized?

A first step is to make explicit assumptions about the identity of effective decisionmakers during different time periods (immediate, later, eventual). The policy scientist, we have said, either adopts the perspectives of some other participant in the context or thinks and acts on his own.

2. What quality of life is postulated as desirable for the context at what time? Indicated how?

Quality of life is the degree to which a preferred pattern of equality-inequality is achieved and sustained at a chosen population level.

3. What direct and indirect population policy outcomes, approved and put into effect, would most efficiently, promptly and stably contribute to the realization of the preferred quality of life (by $Time^1$, $Time^2$ ...)?

Presumably several policy combinations may be evaluated as achieving equivalent results.

4. What proposed preferred policy outcomes, if pursued by what strategies, are likely to be most efficiently and promptly adopted and put into effect?

5. What observational positions and procedures would most accurately, efficiently and promptly provide the data required to monitor (a) the degree to which preferred policies are efficiently and promptly adopted and put into effect, and (b) the degree to which the impact of policy outcomes contributes to goal realization; projected events are realistically projected; past trends are continued; past conditioning factors interact as before?

The continuing seminar requires a permanent nucleus of members with shared common purposes who are willing to contribute to the results of inquiry as well as to engage in the consideration of a continually revised visual environment portraying the goals, trends, conditions, projections, and alternatives salient to the context. The interconnected aims of the undertaking are to utilize knowledge for action and action for knowledge.

Notes

1. A summary of the many uses of "population policy" is in Richard L. Clinton, "The Decisional Environment: Knowledge and Attitudes of Elites as a Determinant of Antinatalist Policy Formation," University of North Carolina at Chapel Hill, Prepared for the Battelle Population Study Center Workshop, Seattle, Washington, May 1974.

2. Distinctions elaborated in Harold D. Lasswell and Abraham Kaplan, *Power and Society* (New Haven: Yale University Press, 1950).

3. The Universal Declaration of Human Rights may be used as a provisional clarifier of the quality of life. Harold D. Lasswell, *A Pre-View of Policy Sciences* (New York: Elsevier, 1971), pp. 42-43.

4. Daniel Lerner, John D. Montgomery, and Harold D. Lasswell, *Values and Development* (forthcoming).

5. Lasswell, *Pre-View of Policy Sciences*. On economic dimensions: Warren F. Ilchman and Norman T. Uphoff, *The Political Economy of Change* (Berkeley: University of California Press, 1971).

6. Concerning the "Continuing Decision Seminar," see Lasswell, *Pre-View of Policy Sciences*, pp. 142-159. See also the distinctions between "prototyping," "intervention," and "experimentation," Lasswell, *Pre-View of Policy Sciences*, pp. 69-72.

**Part II:
Country Studies**

Introduction to Part II: The Importance of Context in Population Policy Analysis

David C. Korten

The preceding section of this volume presents a series of conceptual papers seeking a framework for a policy sciences approach in the area of population. These chapters were the work of four important scholars in the policy sciences field and reflect their collective effort to bring their many years of experience to bear on developing a policy capability for dealing with crucial population issues. It was recognized from the beginning, however, that the work done in developing these chapters would become meaningful only as it was applied in a country context.

The literature search carried out by the seminar members revealed that the population field still lacks the type of comprehensive country specific analyses required to extend our insights into a number of crucial aspects of the policy process, including: (1) the processes through which political support or acquiescence is developed for various population policies; (2) the dynamic decision processes through which specific policy choices are made and programs designed; and (3) the contextual aspects of the implementation process which are often central to the success or failure of a given policy.

As a result, students in the seminar were each asked to take a population policy from their own country and apply one or more of the conceptual frameworks to its analysis. Working under the direction of its four faculty participants,[a] the students produced the papers which are presented in the following section of this volume. These papers reflect the fact that they necessarily were developed from relatively scarce data, focusing as they do on analytical approaches that have not become conventions in the field. It is hoped that future seminars will incorporate field trips to facilitate data gathering. Thus the results presented in this volume must be considered as preliminary and only suggestive of future directions rather than as examples of fully developed country policy analyses.

The Importance of Context

The ultimate purpose of applying the policy sciences to population problems is to strengthen the capacity of national policy-making bodies to deal effectively

---

[a]The author of this Introduction joined the seminar only in Spring of 1975 and was not among the faculty of the seminar during which the student papers presented in this volume were prepared.

with population issues. To accomplish this it is necessary that the policy scientist ultimately approach these issues from the perspective of an individual or body faced with making a policy choice. This means that the resulting analysis and recommendations must be relevant to the actual choices faced by the policy-maker whose concerns are being addressed, must be geared to the level of aggregation with which he must deal, and must reflect the social, economic, and political complexity of the environment in which the choice is being made.

Analyzing policy choices and processes in specific country contexts can demonstrate the implications of the diverse range of situations in which actions must be undertaken. Through the study of actual decisions such as the students have undertaken it becomes possible to identify the types of choices open to consideration, and the wide range of contextual issues to be addressed, including relevant political pressures and alignments, the sequence and timing of policy actions relative to the state and readiness of the politically relevant public, unique considerations of objectives and strategy, the strengths and weaknesses of the local institutional infrastructure, and other specific situational requirements relating to such factors as culture, education, and religion.

It is in dealing with this contextual richness that the country analysis can make a unique and important contribution. It offers the opportunity to draw together quantified data where it is available with more informal data and observation where it is not, or where the variables themselves do not readily yield to quantification.

As Ilchman has pointed out in his chapter for this volume, much of the work in the population policy field takes into account too few variables and suffers from excessive aggregation of those variables. The result is studies attempting to test the results of broad categories of policy inputs such as education for women, or family planning programs, directly against measurable outcomes such as contraceptive acceptance or fertility declines, which too often produce inconclusive and contradictory results. (See McGreevey and Birdsall, 1974, for an excellent current review.) At the same time too little attention is given to what Lasswell refers to as *contextuality*.

An Example of the Problem:
The Family Planning Controversy

Many of the current controversies in the population field could be approached more fruitfully with greater efforts to disaggregate data and to give attention to contextual circumstances. An example is the current controversy over whether family planning service delivery has proven to be an effective policy instrument. The fact that relatively few family planning efforts have to date been able to demonstrate proof of measurable national fertility decline that can be attributed to the program has led a number of observers and some policymakers to conclude that people at lower levels of socioeconomic development cannot be motivated to accept family planning, or at least that family planning efforts are irrelevant. Such conclusions are methodologically unwarranted and probably empirically unsound.

The type of highly aggregated input-output analysis on which such conclusions tend to be based can be quite misleading. Dealing with such issues in a meaningful way requires disaggregating the data, looking more closely at intervening variables, and taking into account such factors as lead times. Looking at the family planning effectiveness issue from this perspective is a useful way to illustrate why it is important to take such considerations into account before drawing policy conclusions from the aggregated data.

Disaggregation

Indonesia presents an excellent example of the importance of disaggregating national data. The national data, while showing continued growth in acceptors, produce an estimate of active family planning service users among married women of only 7.4 percent for January 1974 (Nortman 1974). While respectable performance for a country in which the government did not begin a serious services delivery effort until 1970, this figure is too low to expect any important demographic impact or to establish that acceptance levels might eventually be reached which would show definite results in reduction of fertility rates.

Disaggregation provides a much more interesting and useful picture. Until 1974, the government concentrated its program efforts on the islands of Java and Bali, which account for only about 66 percent of the national population. Thus the results achieved within this area are diluted when prevalence of family planning service use is averaged out over the entire national population. Furthermore, results were unevenly distributed among the provinces within the program area, with the best results coming from provinces such as Bali and East Java known for their especially innovative and dynamic leadership. By late 1974 officials were estimating prevalence of contraceptive use among eligible couples at 30 percent in Bali Province and 20 percent in East Java Province (Wasito 1974). Good results were being shown with low income, low education groups (Soetedjo and Clinton 1974) with community-centered program activities described by Keeny (1973). Furthermore, preliminary surveys in East Java suggest that unusually high continuation rates were being achieved (Sullivan et al. 1974).

Intervening Variables

Programs can be evaluated by the quality of the effort as well as their social output. One of the first considerations in evaluating such intervening variables is the substantial variation in national programs in the extent to which they offer a broadly based programmatic effort, are adequately funded, and reach all elements of the population, especially the higher fertility rural populations. Lapham and Mauldin (1972) have documented in considerable detail the differences between twenty countries in the quality and scope of their program efforts and have shown a clear relationship with levels of program acceptance. Berelson (1974) has pointed out that results are also a function of general administrative capacity of the country to in fact implement a programmatic family planning effort. He suggests that one reason programs tend to be more effective in nations at more advanced levels of socioeconomic development is due at least in part to lack of effective administrative infrastructure in the less developed nations through which to carry out effective program activities.

Another important intervening variable is the accessibility and quality of the service offered. A brief visit to a family planning clinic typical of those commonly found in programs throughout the world, and observation of the inconvenience and indignity which a woman must endure to obtain the simplest and most basic contraceptive assistance, adds greatly to understanding why acceptance in some programs is limited. Women who have traveled for hours or even days are told the doctor is not in and they must return another day, or after waiting hours in a hot, crowded waiting room they are asked irrelevant and embarrassing questions such as when they had their first sexual experience or whether they have been a prostitute, and are denied the most basic respect and privacy during unaccustomed vaginal examinations, and finally if they accept pills or condoms, are told they must return every month or two to obtain new supplies. Such conditions have not been universal and progress is being made in correcting them in other programs, but it is obvious that in the recent past, poor quality of service has reduced acceptance rates.

Indonesia is not alone in experiments to improve the quality and accessibility of service and preliminary reports suggest that impressive evaluation results from community based service delivery efforts in Colombia, Brazil, Thailand, and others should eventually be forthcoming.

Lead Time

Consideration of lead times is also quite important in program evaluation and there has been a tendency to draw conclusions prematurely before program results, particularly as measured in terms of fertility decline, could realistically be expected. Getting a program organized, training personnel and winning their support for family planning, publicizing the availability of the service, and finally convincing women accustomed to assuming control over relatively few aspects of their own lives that they can and should assume control over their fertility involves inevitable lead times. Finally there is normally at least a year's delay between acceptance of a method and observable fertility results. Given the massive logistical and educational requirements involved, as well as the basic biological lead times, it would be quite remarkable to demonstrate national demographic impact from even an effectively designed and managed family planning effort in less than five to ten years, particularly if it is being undertaken in a nation with a weak administrative infrastructure among isolated rural populations of minimal educational levels.

An Overview

A brief overview of the Indian, Philippine, and Indonesian programs helps to illustrate the interplay between various contextual and timing variables. India is a country that has made substantial investment in family planning with uneven results. The success of its vasectomy campaigns suggests the presence of substantial demand for services when effectively promoted and delivered (Berelson 1974), yet the performance of its regular clinical delivery system remains unimpressive, apparently due to a combination of a rigid centralized bureaucracy and the vacillating commitment of its political leaders, which together tend to stifle local interest and initiative.

The Philippine program for a time was expanding rapidly with strong backing from the political leadership. More recently, however, it has experienced a substantial decline in recruitment of new acceptors. The data emerging suggest that this results from its reaching the limits of its clinic-based delivery system. Acceptances should increase again as it implements plans for a more community-oriented approach, though possible weaknesses in basic national rural administrative infrastructure may hinder the successful implementation of such efforts.

Indonesia, which combines strong political support for reduction of population growth rates with a fairly effective decentralized civil administration, and a family planning program design increasingly geared to a service-oriented community-based delivery system seems to be enjoying uninterrupted success in the expansion of its program.

The real question is not *whether* family planning services can be an effective population policy tool, but *what type* of family planning effort can and under what circumstances. In answering such questions it is often more valid to look in the short term at more localized efforts and base the evaluation on intermediate outcomes such as acceptance and continuation, since fertility results can normally be measured only indirectly and after a long lead time.

The evidence seems strong that efforts to disaggregate the data and to give greater attention to contextual variables may prove quite important in extending the capability of the policy sciences to provide useful inputs to the policy-making process in the population field.

A Program Design Model

Policy models useful for identifying and responding to important contextual variables can be developed out of even relatively informal cross-national observations of program efforts. An example is a simple typology of program organizational forms described in Korten (1975) derived from observations in Latin America and Asia.

The elements of the typology are represented in terms of five stages of program development. The presentation of order of the stages represents not only a common or modal sequence of program evolution, but also an order of increasing organizational complexity. At each of the more advanced stages the population program tends to have more elements, and is increasingly dependent on organizations with a greater multiplicity of objectives over which there is only indirect population program control. Each successive stage offers greater opportunities for program success if certain contextual preconditions are met, and greater likelihood of failure if they are not.

Stage 1: The Single Purpose Organization. Commonly the first stage of a population program's development is initiated within a single purpose family planning organization, most often a private association devoted exclusively to family planning. With external financing and virtual autonomy in budgeting, personnel assignment, and supervision it is normally able to establish a foothold even in the context of a relatively unsupportive political climate and/or a weak governmental health infrastructure. Its single purpose concern for matters related to family planning makes it a relatively simple organization to manage.

Stage 2: The Multipurpose Health Delivery Organization. Once officially accepted by the government as a legitimate service, family planning is normally introduced in the government health programs. This stage may involve a fairly wide range of organizational alternatives ranging from those such as in the Nicaraguan Ministry of Health, where the family planning program operates almost as a separate organization within the Ministry (Korten et al. 1975); to a completely integrated program such as in the El Salvador social security program, where family planning services are offered but the program has almost no separate organizational identity (Ickis 1974). The greater the integration, the more the success or failure of the family planning program depends on the strength and coverage of the broader health system, the receptivity of its personnel to family planning, the availability of sufficient capacity to handle the additional work load, the nature and effectiveness of supervisory, reporting, and incentive systems, and a number of other complex factors. While the opportunity for referrals increases with the degree of integration, the possibility that family planning will get little attention from medical staff also increases if the necessary preconditions are not met.

Stage 3: The Population Agency. Stage 3 is normally reached when the government decides to undertake a more broadly based population effort involving other than the health sector. Then the need is felt for a central planning coordinating body, with the result that an independent population office, board, or commission is created to perform the coordination function. Its success depends on a number of factors related to its structure and composition, its authority, the amount of governmental political support for its programs, the political and managerial acumen of its leadership, and the existence in the government of adequate coordination and control mechanisms to give clout to a central planning body. Timing is also important as creation of such a unit may serve little purpose and only create administrative redundancy if the government is not ready to support a more broadly based population program and in fact the unit does nothing more than channel funds to or attempt to exercise authority over a ministry of health family planning effort (Montague 1975).

Stage 4: Decentralized Civil Administration. Stage 4 most directly reflects the trends and concerns highlighted at the World Population Conference held in Bucharest. These concerns include a focus on rural development and the treatment of population activities as an integral part of the development process. An aggressive rural development effort requires the activation or creation of mechanisms to achieve decentralized coordination of rural development activities. The success of an aggressive rural development effort is necessarily dependent on the presence of an effective administrative infrastructure through which appropriate initiatives and support can be channeled to activate and coordinate local development activities. This ordinarily means that provincial governors, district officers, and even village heads may assume major responsibility for the direction and coordination of all or most governmental projects and personnel within their jurisdictions. When this happens the role of the responsible national level ministries must shift from that of operational control to one of providing essentially staff support in technical planning, training, and supervision. Variations of this structure are found in Indonesia and Korea, where responsibility for fulfilling population targets rests directly with the governor or district officer. Whether or not the population program can successfully undertake to enter this stage of organization depends on the overall national development strategy, the amount of central political support given to the population effort, and the strength and sophistication of the rural administrative infrastructure.

Stage 5: Beyond the Population Agency. The creation of an independent population agency in Stage 3 to perform the central coordinating function normally indicates that the planning board, planning ministry, or ministry of finance responsible for other national planning activities lacks the required skills or commitment in the population area, or that the population agency will actually retain responsibility for some operational activities. Two important trends, one toward decentralization of operational activities away from the population agency, and the other toward developing greater expertise and commitment with regard to population matters in national planning bodies would suggest that at some point it may become appropriate for countries to phase out the population agency.

The above model, presented here only in brief outline, attempts to provide the policymaker with an organized framework helpful in identifying: (1) the choices which are open to him; (2) the contextual and timing variables most important in making these choices; and, (3) the dependent relationships which determine the fit between the policy choice and the condition of significant contextual variables most likely to produce satisfactory program outcomes. If there is a good fit between the organizational choice and the contextual conditions under which that choice is made, then it is expected that performance will be higher than if he fails to achieve such a fit. This is the dimension on which the model is predictive and may be subjected to experimental validation.

Conclusion

One of the great values of intensive observation and analysis of policy processes on a country specific basis is the opportunity to work from the policymaker's perspective and to study the policy in context, exploring in all their rich variety the broad range of variables which may influence the policy outcome. At the same time the development of models useful for dealing with contextual variables is inevitably dependent on exposure to a broader range of data and experience than can be generated by one country. Thus there must be sufficient theoretical underpinning to the country analysis to provide some degree of comparability and there must be a sufficient variety of countries studied, reflecting differing approaches to policy development and implementation, to allow the detection of important underlying patterns.

Bibliography

Berelson, Bernard. "An Evaluation of the Effects of Population Control Programs." *Studies in Family Planning* 5, 1 (January 1974): 1-12.

Ickis, John C. *El Salvador Country Report: A Management Oriented Description of Its Family Planning Programs.* Managua, Nicaragua: INCAE, 1974.

Keeny, Sam. "Over the Green Mountains: A Report from East Java." *People* 1, 1 (October 1973): 20-21.

Korten, David C. "Population Programs 1985: A Growing Management Challenge." *Studies in Family Planning* (In press).

Korten, Frances F., David C. Korten, Deirdre Strachan, and Carmen de Benard. *Family Planning in Nicaragua: A Description of Program Management.* Managua, Nicaragua: INCAE, 1975.

Lapham, Robert J., and W. Parker Mauldin. "National Family Planning Programs: Review and Evaluation." *Studies in Family Planning* 3, 3 (March 1972): 29-52.

McGreevey, William P., and Nancy Birdsall. *The Policy Relevance of Recent Social Research on Fertility.* Washington, D.C.: Smithsonian Institution, 1974.

Montague, Joel G. "Efforts to Coordinate Population Planning in Developing Countries." Presentation on research in progress to the Department of Population Sciences Faculty Seminar, Harvard University, January 20, 1975.

Nortman, Dorothy. "Population and Family Planning Programs: A Factbook." *Reports on Population/Family Planning*, No. 2 (Sixth Edition), December 1974.

Soetedjo, M., and J.J. Clinton. "Contraceptive Use in the Indonesian National Family Planning Program 1973-74." Technical Report Series Monograph No. 8, Preliminary Edition. National Family Planning Coordinating Board, Jakarta, October 1974.

Sullivan, J., W. Bahrawi, S. Haryono, and A. Hartoadi. "Contraceptive Use—Effectiveness in Mojokerto Regency, East Java." Technical Report Series Monograph No. 9, Preliminary Edition. National Family Planning Coordinating Board, Jakarta, October 1974.

Wasito. Interview by the author with Dr. Wasito, Chairman of the Family Planning Coordinating Board for East Java, November 12, 1974.

5 Growth Centers and Primacy in Kenya

Clay G. Wescott

I

Governments have always been interested in regulating the size and distribution of their respective populations. Although much has been written on policies to regulate population growth,[1] relatively little has been written on migration policies. Goodrich et al. have written a detailed critique of "New Deal" migration policies in the U.S., of the political and economic consequences of these policies, and of the interests that supported and opposed them.[2] A more recent U.S. Commerce Department study has concluded that population distribution in the United States is almost completely the result of private economic forces rather than public policies.[3] This study has not analyzed the political coalitions that were responsible for these policies. Comparative studies of migration policies have generally focused on legal developments[4] or economic consequences[5] rather than political variables. Perlman has studied the political culture of migrants in Rio, and shown how these migrants are affected by political and economic circumstances and policies.[6] There are few other major studies of migration related policies in developing countries.

Perhaps one reason for the paucity of such studies is that they must be interdisciplinary. Until quite recently, it was a rare act of courage to bring together the tools of geography, demography, political science, and economics in a single study. Without such a joining of disciplines, studies of migration related policies are incomplete, if not impossible.

The fundamental question to be raised in this interdisciplinary study is: can the Kenya government design and implement policies that *alter the "choice budgets" of urban migrants* so that a higher proportion of them remain in intermediate cities rather than primary cities, and can the government bring this about *at an acceptable cost of economic and political resources*?[7]

Kenya is an interesting case to look at because it is more developed than many other developing countries. Thus, locational problems, which are beyond the means of other nations to consider, have already been addressed by the Kenya regime. The government of Kenya is boldly planning for the development of urban and rural service centers which can accommodate anticipated population growth up to the year 2000. The government envisions that these service centers will act as stimuli to rural socioeconomic development, provide jobs and

Table 5-1

Socioeconomic indicators place Kenya in the following percentiles in relation to other countries:

Indicator	Percentile (100% = Least Developed Country)	No. of Countries in Sample
Telephones/1000	67%	126
Mass media (Newspapers, radio, T.V./1000)	74%	131
Infant mortality	90%	102
Food supply (Protein/cap., calories/cap.)	54%	107
Physicians/million	64%	135
GNP/cap.	80%	135
Per. cap. energy consumption	70%	129
% in cities 100,000+	87%	109
School enrollment	67%	134
Literacy	72%	130

Source: Charles L. Taylor and Michael C. Hudson, *World Handbook of Political and Social Indicators*, second edition (New Haven: Yale University Press, 1972).

services for Kenyans who choose to live in urban areas, and relieve Nairobi and Mombasa of some of the pressure of rural-urban migrations.

We will examine the process of "gathering, processing, and dissemination of information to participants in policy decisions and choices"[8] regarding growth centers. In doing so, we will suggest some practical considerations that should be taken into account in order to facilitate the implementation of the expressed goals of the Kenya regime.

II

Since 1967, the Town Planning Department (now Department of Physical Planning) of the Kenyan Ministry of Lands and Settlement has issued a "regional physical development plan" for each of the seven official regions of Kenya.[9] These plans have been drawn up in response to a number of projected trends. The government expects that by the year 2000, Kenya's population will increase from its present level of approximately 11 million to between 28 and 34 million. These predictions are based on a projected population growth rate of 2.56%-3.5% for the smaller estimate and 3.5%-3.9% for the larger, as compared with a rate of 3.5% today.[10]

There are good reasons for making these predictions. Except for the possibility of long-term famine,[11] the death rate in Kenya will continue to decline. Thus any hope of decreasing the population growth rate will depend on the family planning program. Although Kenya was the first country in Africa to institute a family planning program, the program has many opponents among both the masses and certain high government officials. As a result, it has continued to function as a voluntary maternal/child care and birth-spacing program rather than a birth control program.[12] Kenya does not yet have all of the socioeconomic characteristics that some believe are prerequisites for a successful family planning program:[13] even with more official support there would be no grounds for expecting the family planning program in Kenya to significantly reduce the population growth rate in the near future.

The long-term prospects are more favorable. It is possible that as the population becomes better educated, and as further progress is made on more widespread income distribution, the family planning program may begin to make a significant dent in the birthrate. Surveys have already begun to show that some rural women in Kenya who want to have smaller families are unable to restrict family size because they lack adequate birth control information.[14] If such information can be speedily transmitted to these women, the national birth rate might begin to diminish. It is not likely, however, that present family planning activities can take effect soon enough to bring the population of Kenya below the government's present projections.[15]

Government interventions must begin elsewhere. Because of pressure on the land,[16] rising agricultural productivity, and the attraction of towns, the government expects a minimum 7.1% annual increase in urban population during this period. By the year 2000, urban areas will have to accommodate 26%-32% of the population (7.3-10.9 million) as compared with 9.9% (1.082 million) in 1969.[17] The regional physical planning effort is an attempt by the Kenya government to plan for the systematic and equitable distribution and development of urban centers capable of servicing this tremendous increase in urban population. At the same time, the government hopes to slow down the rate of rural-urban migration by improving the quality of rural life. This objective is to be accomplished by promoting the maximum development of rural areas by means of a rural growth center strategy.

Physical planners began in the mid-60s defining the existing hierarchy of service centers, in accordance with Christaller's central place theory and Grove and Huszar's study of central places in Ghana.[18] This was done by rating the levels of services in each center according to a point system. For each center, the total point value of all the different services was added. Each center was then ranked in increasing level of importance as a sublocal center, local center, market center, rural center, urban center, and principal town. The centers were superimposed on a population density map to identify servicing gaps in the region. Planners also analyzed communication patterns, potential resources, and in some cases the wishes of the local people as expressed through the District Development Committees and the District Development Advisory Committees.[19]

On the basis of all these factors five grades of centers were designated for future growth. *Local centers* will have no more than 200 residents by the year 2000. They will have locational administration facilities, a police post, a public water supply, a sub-post office, manual telephone facilities, local bus service, a full primary school, a nursery school, and be served by a secondary/minor road. So far, there are 1,015 such centers planned in Kenya.[20] *Market centers* will have no more than 1000 residents. They will have all the facilities of a local center, and in addition a secondary school, dispensary, and family planning service. So far, there are 420 such centers planned in Kenya. *Rural centers* will grow into small towns of between 2,000-5,000 residents by the year 2000. They will have divisional administration facilities, a police station, a sewage disposal system, grid water supply, electricity, a departmental post office, a secondary school to at least form IV, a village polytechnic, a health center with a maternity unit, a sports field, a social hall, a mobile cinema and library service, and will be served by a primary/secondary road. So far, there are 140 such centers planned in Kenya. *Urban centers* will have resident populations of between 10,000 and 50,000 by the year 2000. They will have district administration facilities, divisional police headquarters, an airstrip, a secondary school to form VI, a technical school at the primary level, a hospital, a stadium, a public library, a recreational park, a cinema, and a showground. So far, there are eighty-six urban centers planned in Kenya.

Overall, the government hopes to provide one local center for every 5000 people in the country, one market center for every 15,000, one rural center for every 40,000, and one urban center for every 120,000.

In addition to these rural growth centers, principal towns will be planned for populations of 100,000-200,000 by the year 2000. These towns will form the major administrative, commercial, and industrial centers of the country. In addition to providing the services and infrastructure of smaller centers, these towns will have the headquarters of the provincial administration, a fire station, an airfield, a teacher training college, a technical school, a hospital, a museum/art center, and will be served by an international/trunk road and a regional bus service. So far nine of these towns are planned for Kenya in addition to Nairobi and Mombasa.

The two primary cities will be planned for populations of three million and two million inhabitants respectively. They will offer the most complete range of urban services and infrastructure of any of the principal towns in Kenya. Government plans for the development of Nairobi and Mombasa must be explored in greater detail.

III

The Kenya government is committed to a policy giving priority to the development of other principal towns besides Nairobi and Mombasa. Yet the government projects that by 1980, 88% of the urban population of the eleven largest urban centers will live in one of the two primary cities. This proportion has not significantly changed since 1948. Furthermore, the level of primacy (proportion of urban population of four largest urban centers living in largest city) of Nairobi has steadily increased from 0.53 in 1948 to 0.61 in 1969, and is projected to rise to 0.63 by 1980.[21] The apparent reasons for these projections are that Nairobi and Mombasa have not yet reached optimum size, and that they will continue to be attractive to new industries because of the availability of business services, access to transportation, access to social and cultural amenities, and access to the principal concentrations of purchasing power.[22]

The continuing importance that the government places on the development of the primary cities can be seen from development estimates for infrastructure and government services. Although the stated government policy has been to give priority in the allocation of development funds for services and infrastructure to the designated growth centers, the total allocation of such funds to Nairobi and Mombasa is at a disproportionately high level (60%) in 1973/74, and actually increased between 1972/73 and 1973/74.[23] Furthermore, a disproportionately large share (71%) of projected public investments in urban "main infrastructure" for 1974/78 is allocated to the primary cities.[24]

There is a long standing debate among social scientists over the role of "primate cities" in developing countries.[25] Some have maintained that the presence of cities vastly larger than other cities and dominant in national influence tends to swallow up investment and manpower at the expense of the rest of the country, and may lead to higher consumption rates than production rates.[26] Others have argued that many countries can afford only one major city and/or that economies of scale are such as to make intermediate cities inefficient and unnecessary.[27]

To an extent, each of these opposing arguments is plausible. In the earliest stages of development, the level of primacy may be relatively high but may still increase further because economic development does not occur fast enough, or evenly enough, to support large intermediate cities. The nature of the colonial experience, the lack of a tradition of urbanism, and a small national area are other factors that may lead to high levels of primacy. As the level of economic activity continues to increase, political conflicts between the largest city and its periphery are resolved in favor of the periphery. Intermediate cities become more economically viable, and begin receiving a larger proportion of public resources. These cities, in turn, offer relatively large markets for agriculture and industry, which leads to employment opportunities and modern services for an increasing proportion of the rural population.[28]

In some situations there are structural, political, cultural or geographic factors which prevent this decrease in primacy from taking place. Where this is the case, there is a disproportionately high level of migration to the primary city, skimming off young men from the rest of the country.[a] The process of diffusion

---

[a]Although this helps to reduce overcrowding in rural areas, it may also reduce the economic vitality of these areas. Furthermore, it removes an energetic constituency for government assisted rural development.

of innovations to the countryside is hampered.[29] Services tend to be concentrated in the primary cities, making access by the majority of the population very difficult. Job opportunities in the primary city do not keep pace with the inflow of job seekers, a situation which may create political instability.[30]

This general description applies in full measure to Kenya. Soja has shown that Nairobi is the major nucleus for the generation and diffusion of socioeconomic development throughout Kenya. As a result, districts in relative proximity to and having close interaction with Nairobi tend to have relatively high levels of development. This pattern is largely the result of the attitudes and objectives of the former colonial government and settler population.[31] Extensive rural-urban migration compounds these problems by leaving behind very old and very young people, the uneducated, and large numbers of women in rural areas.[32]

This highly uneven pattern of modernization has resulted in a situation where three-fourths of the national area is "... functionally not part of the Kenya nation ... political allegiance is unsettled and erratic ... the level of participation is extremely low and, more important, the frequency of internal conflict is such that the impress of the central government appears weak and ineffective."[33] Partly as a result of this uneven pattern of modernization, agricultural production per capita is not increasing.[34] In addition, the inability of large numbers of workers in the primary cities to earn a reasonable income may in the long run lead to political instability.[35]

It would seem that the level of primacy of Nairobi acts to retard the level of development of a large part of the country. Thus, it is not surprising that Kenyan physical planners have adopted the goal of expanding other principal towns and service centers. However, the government must also take steps to insure that the level of primacy of Nairobi will decline. The range of actions possible include enacting regulations which would give strong incentives or even requirements to new industries to locate in cities other than Nairobi as much as possible. Policies and administrative actions might be invoked to reduce factor price distortions between different urban areas in the country.[36] These policies could be supplemented by encouraging the development of labor intensive industries outside of Nairobi and Mombasa.[37] Careful consideration should be given to increasing the proportion of urban infrastructure development expenditures that are allocated for projects outside of the two primary cities. Other policies should also be considered to discourage rural-urban migration,[38] to repatriate migrants, and to encourage their remigration to another principal town besides the two primary cities.

Some combination of all of these policies would help to redirect migration flows to intermediate cities, thereby relieving the strain on public services and employment opportunities in the primary cities. Intermediate cities would be additional nuclei for the diffusion of socioeconomic development. They could be the link that will make the rural growth center strategy effective.

Rural growth centers would provide basic services and infrastructure to local farmers and businessmen located in their respective hinterlands. They would be the links between large urban areas and the overwhelming majority of the population living in rural areas. By providing improved transport, warehouse, and marketing facilities, and more accessible agricultural extension personnel, they will help to increase agricultural productivity, which will in turn increase agricultural surpluses that can be used to finance additional investment in new industries. The combination of reduced migration to the primary cities, improvement in rural life, and increased agricultural productivity should help to reduce the danger of political unrest in Kenya.

It is possible that in the near future, intermediate cities may be almost as economically efficient as Nairobi and Mombasa. Improved building construction methods, transportation, and communication systems will be developed which may alter the cost structure of various industries such that it would be advantageous for them to locate in an intermediate city.[39] Improved global communication systems would facilitate the inexpensive use of skilled personnel from all over the world at almost any location.[40] Such systems could also help to bring cultural amenities such as movies, education courses, and public health services of the same quality as found in the primate cities to other locations.[41] Negative considerations arising from the deterioration of services and conditions in Nairobi and Mombasa might also make intermediate cities increasingly attractive.[42]

It has been argued that a developmental emphasis on intermediate cities in Africa would be a misapplication of scarce investment capital which would otherwise be applied directly to agricultural development.[43] However, because of projected rural-urban migration rates, and because of the political influence of urban interest groups that will be discussed shortly, the Kenya regime will have no political choice but to allocate substantial investments to urban areas. The only choices will be the proportions of public investments to be allocated to each urban area, and the extent of government efforts to direct private investment and labor migration to intermediate cities.

This brings us back to the arguments presented by the Kenya government in support of its policy of allowing Nairobi and Mombasa to continue to grow. There is no doubt that at the present time there are certain efficiencies to be gained from allowing the unrestricted growth of the two largest cities. But such a policy would jeopardize rural growth and maintain the chronic pressure on employment opportunities in the primary cities. The government must choose whether these outcomes are politically more or less acceptable than maximizing short-term economic efficiency.

IV

Like any political action affecting the opportunities of identifiable sectors in the country, growth center policies designed to change the urban balance in Kenya would have important political consequences.[44] Since the general outline of these consequences is predictable, it can become an element in the application of growth center policies. Although it is not possible to make precise predictions about prospective political behavior, pursuing such a line of inquiry permits decisionmakers to appraise in much greater detail the prospects for these or any other policies that require widespread support for their success.

The present and known individual characteristics and values of the proposed target group will affect the success of the policies in altering the behavior of this group, and will also influence the extent to which it will support or oppose the regime. The primary target group of urban growth policies in Kenya are the potential urban migrants. In the past these migrants have been disproportionately male[45] and concentrated between the ages of fifteen and about thirty-nine years.[46] In the recent past, high rates of migration have characterized the largest ethnic groups in Kenya (Kikuyu, Luo, Luhya, Kambaa)[47] as well as some of the smaller ones (Tharaka, Iteso, Nandi, Pokot, Sabaot, Kipsigis, Elgeyo, Pokomo, Riverine, Swahili-Shiraze, and Bajuni), while low migration rates have characterized other relatively small groups (Gusii, Embu, Mbere, Meru, Tugen, Marakwet, Somali, Galla, and Samburu).[48] The ethnic diversity of migrants, and differential migration rates of different ethnic groups are likely to continue in the future.[b]

In the past, decisions to migrate have been influenced by the interrelationship of three factors: the influences that push migrants away from their home bases (high birth rates, fragmentation of land holdings, increased education, high unemployment and underemployment), the attractions of urban areas (access to services, more jobs at higher wages, "bright lights") and the relative ease with which these groups can get from one place to another.[49] Most migrants go first to the town nearest their rural residence, and they prefer remaining there if they can obtain adequate employment.[50] Most recent migrants to Nairobi have not developed a firm commitment to the city.[51]

Given these characteristics and values of urban migrants, it is likely that they could be persuaded by appropriate government policies to migrate to an intermediate city. A policy of increasing employment opportunities in intermediate cities would have the most direct effect on altering the direction of urban migration. Such a policy would have the greatest effect if it concentrates on increasing the number of jobs most commonly sought after by males between fifteen and thirty-nine.[c] A policy of improving transport and communications facilities between intermediate cities and their rural hinterland, in conjunction

---

[b]The migration rates of certain of the smaller ethnic groups might change in the near future. For example, if transport facilities were improved for the Galla-Somali, their migration rate would undoubtedly increase. Substantial increases in world agricultural prices might tend to lower the migration rates for the smaller ethnic groups that produce export crops. However, the larger ethnic groups because of their numbers and the resulting pressure on their land, will continue to have high migration rates.

[c]Allowances should be made for ethnic age variation. (See note 37.)

with increasing employment opportunities in these cities, would give urban migrants a chance to live close to their original locations, while partaking of urban incomes and amenities. The improvement of transport and communications facilities between areas which are the principal national sources of migration (Lake Victoria basin, highland area, east of the rift, the hills of Machakos and Taita, and the populated strip along the coast)[52] and intermediate cities would also help to alter migratory flows in the desired direction.

If all of these policies were put into effect, urban migrants would not only alter their behavior in the desired direction, but they would continue to be favorable towards the regime. Recent surveys have shown a high level of support among Nairobi and Mombasa residents, most of whom are migrants, for the current regime.[53] There is every reason to believe that if these people and other potential urban migrants were able to find the same opportuities in other cities, they would be equally supportive of the regime.

Policies to change the urban balance in Kenya will not be feasible for the regime without the support of other politically significant interest groups besides potential migrants. The support of such groups is likely to be mixed.

The Kenya civil service is a strategic interest group with a wide range of interests.[54] In order to make intermediate cities viable, a greater proportion of the civil service would have to be stationed in intermediate cities rather than in primary ones. These bureaucrats will be needed both to administer development programs, and to insure that the central government channels adequate resources to intermediate cities.[55]

Many civil servants now stationed in primary cities will view the prospects of life in intermediate cities as unglamorous and undesirable. If these individuals feel in danger of being transferred, they will oppose policies to change the urban balance. Even civil servants who remain in the primary cities may oppose the new policies when they find that the shiny new medical center that was planned for their neighborhood is now being built in Nakuru.

On the other hand, senior civil servants have tended to support the notion of rural development in the past, and they would probably also support policies for changing the urban balance to facilitate rural development. By the same token, divisional civil servants, most of whom have been actively involved in rural improvement programs, will become actively involved in intermediate cities policies.[56] Some provincial civil servants will welcome the challenge of increased responsibilities and resources that the new policies will provide, but others who might feel threatened by the infusion of new bureaucratic blood would have to be reassured about their status.

There will be a variety of opinions about the new policies among other influential groups based in Nairobi.[57] Businessmen and property owners may be expected initially to oppose policies to change the urban balance, seeing in them a threat to markets and property values. This opposition will help to turn the city council against the policies, both because of the considerable influence of these interests, and because most city councilors are themselves businessmen and property owners. The city council will be particularly opposed to any undermining of its already strained financial position by the central government. The Nairobi council will be in a particularly strong position to oppose such policies because of the influence of Mayor Margaret Kenyatta, daughter of the president.[58] One countervailing argument would pursue the possibility that the squatter communities, which the Nairobi council has been trying unsuccessfully for years to control, might now be lured away to other cities. Large segments of the unemployed and street hawker population, which have been a continuing irritant to the council, may be expected to leave for other cities. Thus even though urban growth policies would not be intended to benefit Nairobi, some of their direct consequences would be welcome.

Most of the other interest groups in Nairobi are poorly organized and incapable of exerting much influence on the central government. Among the few organized groups, tribal organizations would not oppose the policies, since migrants from all of the major tribes and many of the smaller ones would benefit from them. The Kenya Federation of Employers, which has considerable influence in the Kenya regime, has come out many times in favor of wage restraints.[59] Most of the labor force would oppose overt wage restraints. However, Kenya trade unions have demonstrated in the past a responsible attitude towards nation-building efforts, and have submitted to considerable government regulation. Thus, if the regime is tactful, it should be able to enlist the support of organized labor for a new wages policy.[60]

A significant political gain for the regime will come as an indirect effect of the new policies. Even if the national level of unemployment remains high, the unemployed will no longer be concentrated in Nairobi. The danger of mob violence and assassinations in the capital city might be expected to decline. Furthermore, there would be less of a danger that leaders of the unemployed will be able to organize a powerful, radical youth-wing of KANU, of the type that overthrew the governments of Togo and Congo-Brazzaville.[61]

Although the inhabitants of rural areas do not constitute an interest group in any corporate, institutional or class sense, the views of rural citizens are sought and heeded by the Kenya regime.[62] If urban decentralization makes rural growth centers viable and increases overall employment opportunitites and the level of socioeconomic development in rural areas, then support for the regime will probably be maintained or even increased in these areas. The citizens of areas which are not major sources of migration, and which have difficult access to an intermediate city, will gain little from the policies, and may oppose them.[63] But these areas represent relatively small numbers of people. Barring the unlikely renewal of Shifta-like activities, these areas will not constitute a political threat to the regime.

Given the preceding configuration of interests, it should be possible for the government to build a politically significant constituency which would support policies of urban decentralization. Senior civil servants and politicians could be the opinion leaders for such a constituency. They will be joined by divisional civil servants, many provincial civil servants, local politicians, private citizens who are loyal supporters of the regime, the target group, and the rural masses. To be sure, there will be opposition or lack of support from large numbers of bureaucrats, and from Nairobi and Mombasa based businessmen, property owners, and labor leaders.

The regime can help to minimize this opposition in a number of ways. First, the government should try to avoid the involuntary reassignment of civil servants from the primary cities to posts in intermediate cities. Instead, the government might make service in an intermediate city a requirement for promotion. (Such a system is successfully operating in Tanzania.) Second, the regime should try to demonstrate the linkages between controlling squatters and street hawkers, and growth center policies to the city council, business and professional groups in Nairobi. This should help to increase the support of these groups for the policies. Third, the government should make a special effort to provide ICDC loans to Nairobi and Mombasa based businessmen to finance branch operations in intermediate cities.[d] This would help both to appease a politically significant group and to provide an economic stimulus to the intermediate cities. Fourth, the government should make a particular effort to explain to ethnic groups that do not migrate in large numbers, that they will benefit from the policies by their proximity to dynamic intermediate cities and rural growth centers.[64] Since it will not be economically feasible to develop intermediate cities on an equitable basis, the regime should be prepared to deal with criticism from the various tribes concerned. Fifth, the government should not attempt as part of these policies to restrain salaries of upper level manpower. Not only would this stir up a great deal of animosity toward the policies among a group of politically influential people, but it would have no effect on altering the vast majority of migration decisions.[65]

Finally, all appropriate opportunities for increasing local participation in the planning and implementation of the policies should be utilized. Admittedly, consultation with the target population will be sometimes feasible and sometimes not. In general, it will be feasible in the following situations: (1) When a project requires client cooperation (e.g., family planning service, pass laws); (2) When the technology involved is relatively simple and internal to the community (e.g., low cost housing); and (3) When the project is relatively autonomous, and requires a minimum of coordination with other projects and target populations (e.g., sewage disposal system).[66] In designing communication and feedback mechanisms, policymakers should also consider the beliefs, values, and attitudes of all affected social groups, their potentialities for change, and the costs of change. Anthropologists, sociologists and/or psychologists might be able to make useful contributions in these areas.[67]

---

[d]This recommendation may have to be modified depending on the results of the research proposed on page 160 of this chapter regarding foreign owned vs. locally owned businesses.

Although policies to change the urban balance could successfully alter the behavior of target groups, and would be supported by a politically significant constituency, they will only be implemented if the government has the capacity to do so.

The Kenya government is one of the most efficient in Africa.[68] Furthermore, in the particular fields of spatial and population planning, the government can draw on valuable studies by Soja and Ominde, unusually comprehensive regional physical plans, and the work of the first and only conference on regional planning in Africa.[69] The question is whether or not the government is capable of implementing the logical conclusion of all of this work—an intermediate cities policy.

In November 1973 the government approved a cabinet paper accepting most of the recommendations of a study by the International Labor Office that calls for an attack on imbalance and disparities in incomes.[70] Up to now, however, the government has shown little sign of actually restraining private enterprise in order to bring about these and other reforms.

Although the influence of domestic business interests and international diplomatic and business interests should not be underestimated, the government could act to regulate these interests in certain ways without suffering major political losses.[71] As long as Kenya is a "model of stability" in Africa, businessmen will continue to invest there, and foreign countries will continue their aid programs.[e] The regime has not chosen to restrain private enterprise because, as one diplomat has said: "This is one of the most conservative governments in the world."[72] Yet this government, with its broad base of political support and high administrative capability, is in a much better position to regulate private businesses than most other governments in developing countries and many developed ones. For the same reasons, Kenya is unusually attractive to international investors, who might finance much of the infrastructure development in intermediate cities.

The task of changing nine provincial towns into modern cities will create an enormous financial and administrative burden on the government. Granted, the recent official guidelines for adopting standards for accommodation, buildings, and services which are closely related to what the country can afford, will lower the cost of developing intermediate cities. Furthermore, as coordination between the Physical Planning Department and other development related agencies improves, physical planners may be able to obtain better assurances of adequate

---

[e]This is not to say that the government will have an easy time selling these new policies to international interests. For example, foreign aid granting organizations, which now finance about 30% of development expenditures, have traditionally tied much of their aid to purchases of their own capital equipment. If these organizations are going to support some of the new Kenyan policies, such as labor intensive industry, they will have to alter this approach. However, given the intensive questioning of aid policies that is currently going on in the donor countries, and given the increasing threat of political instability in countries such as Kenya, it is probable that aid-tying practices will begin to change.

financing, which will in turn make an intermediate cities policy more viable.[73] In addition, the regime should concentrate at first on a few key cities such as Nakuru, Kisumu, and Eldoret, which are located in areas that have already proven to be attractive to migrants.[74] As these cities expand and become economic catalysts to the development of their respective hinterlands, political pressures will increase on the government to divert an increased share of development resources towards building up other intermediate cities.

V

The suggested combination of growth center policies in Kenya, including efforts to change the urban balance, are consistent with current theories of spatial and economic development. These policies are politically feasible for the Kenya regime to undertake, and will diminish the chances of future instability caused by the high level of unemployment in the primary cities, and frustration over economic stagnation in the rural areas.

These findings must be expanded in much greater detail before the regime makes the massive commitment of resources that these policies will entail. Additional research would be particularly valuable in five areas: (1) What factors have influenced the location decisions of firms already located in intermediate cities? Do foreign enterprises find it easier to function in intermediate cities than locally based companies?[75] What are the implications of these findings for policy-making? (2) What are the demonstrated capacities of governmental institutions (e.g., Kenya Industrial Estates, Ltd., Industrial Court, Development Finance Co. of Kenya, Ltd.) in related areas? (3) What are the competing demands of politically significant sectors regarding the policies? Although we have outlined some of these demands, a more precise formulation could be obtained through private interviews and close analysis of public statements and behaviors; (4) Can anything be learned from the experiences of other countries in developing migration and decentralization policies?[76] and (5) Are the long-run consequences of delaying action on these policies serious enough to warrant paying the short-run political and economic price of adopting them?

The last of these topics is crucial. At some point, the government may have to evaluate the available evidence and decide to act. There is no question that the suggested policies will cause political and economic strain on the Kenya regime. These policies are important enough, and the regime is strong enough, to endure that strain if it chooses to do so. Inaction will produce even greater strains in the future.

Notes

The author is grateful for comments by Warren Ilchman and John Fletcher of Boston University, John D. Montgomery of Harvard, and Myron Weiner and John Harris of MIT.

1. Department of Economic and Social Affairs, *The Determinants and Consequences of Population Trends*, Vol. 1 (N.Y.: United Nations, 1973), pp. 631-66.

2. Carter Goodrich et al., *Migration and Economic Opportunity* (Philadelphia: University of Pennsylvania Press, 1936).

3. U.S. Department of Commerce, Economic Development Administration, *Federal Activities Affecting Location of Economic Development*, prepared by the Center for Political Research, Nov. 1970, Vols. I and II.

4. Richard Plender, *International Migration Law* (Leiden: A.W. Sijthoff, 1972).

5. Ellen Bussey, *The Flight from Rural Poverty—How Nations Cope* (Lexington, Mass.: Lexington Books, D.C. Heath & Co., 1973); Trevor Bell, *Industrial Decentralizaion in South Africa* (Capetown: Oxford University Press, 1973).

6. Janice Perlman, "The Fate of Migrants in Rio's Favelas: the Myth of Marginality," Ph.D. Thesis, M.I.T., 1971.

7. Cf. Warren F. Ilchman and Norman T. Uphoff, *The Political Economy of Change* (Berkeley: University of California, 1971), pp. 257ff.

8. Harold Lasswell, "Population Change and Policy Sciences: Proposed Workshops on Reciprocal Impact Analysis," Chapter 4 in this volume.

9. Town Planning Department, Ministry of Lands & Settlement, *Nyanza Province, Regional Physical Development Plan* (Nairobi: Government Printer, 1970); *Eastern Province* (1970); *Western Province* (1970); *Central Province* (1967); *Rift Valley Province* (1970); *Northeast Province* (1971).

10. The larger estimate is based on the population growth rate rising from 3.5% in 1970-75 to 3.9% in 1995-2000. The smaller estimate assumes that the current birthrate falls to half its present level by 1995-2000, leading to a reduction in the population growth rate to 2.56%. Republic of Kenya, *Development Plan, 1974-78*, Vol. 1 (Nairobi: Government Printer, 1974), pp. 100, 117.

11. Nota bene. William and Paul Paddock, *Famine—1975* (Boston: Little, Brown and Co., 1967).

12. C.N. Ejiogu, "The Kenya Programme: Policy and Results" and J.J. Russell, "The Kenya National Family Planning Programme" in S.H. Ominde and C.N. Ejiogu, *Population Growth and Economic Development in Africa* (London: Heinemann, 1972), pp. 374-377, 387-392; Kivutu Ndeti and Santo Koesoebjoro, "The Background to Kenya's Population Policy," *Journal of Eastern African Research & Development* 3, 1 (1973): 75-88.

13. Ejiogu, "Kenya Programme"; William Rich, *Smaller Families through Social and Economic Progress* (Washington, D.C.: Overseas Development Council, 1973).

14. According to a K.A.P. survey reported in Ejiogu, "Kenya Programme."

15. The current rate of population growth is adding 126,000 persons to the labor force each year, which is causing increased rural unemployment, increased migration to urban centers, and increased urban unemployment. In addition,

large families are a drain on family income and a deterrent to savings and investment. Increased numbers also force the government to invest in more schools, hospitals, and other services which are relatively unproductive to the economy. Although a high population growth rate is likely in the forseeable future, any decrease in this rate will increase the standard of living in Kenya. M.P. Todaro, "Income Expectations, Rural-Urban Migration and Employment in Africa," in *International Labor Review* 104, 5 (November 1971): 387-413.

16. Kenya has one of the highest levels of rural population per sq. km. of arable land (678) in the world. This compares with a level of 93 in Tanzania, 280 in India, and 543 in Indonesia. R.K. Som, "Population Prospects in Africa," in Ominde and Ejiogu, *Population Growth and Economic Development*, pp. 95-110. Department of Economic and Social Affairs, Statistical Office, *Demographic Yearbook, 1972* (N.Y.: United Nations, 1973), pp. 147-49; *F.A.O. Production Yearbook, 1971* (Rome: F.A.O., 1972), pp. 3-8.

17. The government defines "urban area" as a town with a population greater than 2000. Kenya, *Development Plan, 1974-78*, p. 114.

18. Walter Christaller, *Central Places in Southern Germany* (Englewood Cliffs, N.J.: Prentice-Hall, 1966); Arthur Getis and Judith Getis, "Christaller's Central Place Theory," *Journal of Geography*, May 1966, pp. 220-226.

19. Although the overall planning process was avowedly based on Christaller, many of the particular methods employed seem to have been derived from a comparable study by David Grove and Laszlo Huszar, *The Towns of Ghana: the Role of Service Centers in Regional Planning* (Accra: Ghana Universities Press, 1964). The regional physical plans in Kenya are expected to have more influence on the future development of Kenya than the Grove and Huszar study had on the development of Ghana.

19. For additional considerations that might be used in the designation of growth centers, see Clay G. Wescott, "Regional Physical Planning in Kenya: Problems and Prospects," in Robert Obudho (ed.), *Urbanization and Development Planning in Kenya* (forthcoming); S.M. Kimani and D.R.F. Taylor, "The Role of Growth Centers in Rural Development," Working Paper No. 117, Institute for Development Studies, University College, Nairobi, August 1973.

20. This and the following lists of services are based on the revised guidelines in Kenya, *Development Plan, 1974-78*, Vol. 1, pp. 145-46.

21. Ibid., p. 118.

22. Republic of Kenya, *Development Plan, 1970-74* (Nairobi: Government Printer, 1969).

Peter Marris has suggested to me some additional reasons: (1) Poor people in Nairobi can become a political force more easily than poor people living elsewhere because of their proximity to government officials; (2) Large cities provide the greatest opportunities for the formation of voluntary organizations, which in turn act as vital stimuli to the kind of creativity necessary for economic development; and (3) Large cities provide the greatest range of opportunities for occupations such as street hawking.

23. Figures are the result of my computations made on the basis of Republic of Kenya, *Development Estimates 1972/73* (Nairobi: Government Printer, 1973); Republic of Kenya, *Development Estimates 1973/74* (Nairobi: Government Printer, 1974) cited in Wescott, "Regional Physical Planning."

24. Kenya, *Development Plan, 1974-78*, p. 123.

25. For our purposes, primacy exists in a country which is dominated by one or more very large cities, and which has fewer intermediate cities than one would expect from the rank size rule. Cf. UNESCO, *Report by the Director-General on the Joint UN/UNESCO Seminar on Urbanization in the ECAFE Region* (Paris 1956).

26. B.F. Hoselitz, "Generative and Parasitic Cities," *Economic Development and Cultural Change* 9 (July 1961): 572-88; Joseph J. Spengler, "Africa and the Theory of Optimum City Size," in Horace Miner, *The City in Modern Africa* (N.Y.: Praeger, 1967), pp. 55-90; Akin L. Mabogunje, "Urbanization problems in Africa," in Salah El-Shakhs and Robert Obudho, *Urbanization, National Development, and Regional Planning in Africa* (N.Y.: Praeger, 1974), pp. 13-26.

27. Gerald Breese, *Urbanization in Newly Developing Countries* (Englewood Cliffs, N.J.: Prentice-Hall, 1966), pp. 44-45; William Alonso, "The Economics of Urban Size," in John Friedmann, *Methods of Regional Planning and Analysis* (Cambridge: MIT, 1960).

28. Wescott, "Regional Physical Planning"; Salah El-Shakhs, "Development, Primacy and Systems of Cities," *The Journal of Developing Areas* 7, 1 (October 1972): 11-36; Brian J.L. Berry, "City Size and Economic Development," in Leo Jakobson and Ved Prakash, *Urbanization and National Development* (Beverly Hills: Sage Publications, 1971), pp. 111-56.

29. Donald A. Schon, *Beyond the Stable State* (London: Temple Smith, 1971), pp. 80-94.

30. Most migrants to primary cities benefit economically from their migration, and probably tend to be politically conservative. However, if the children of migrants remain in primary cities and are unable to obtain satisfactory employment, they may advocate radical political solutions. Myron Weiner, "Urbanization and Political Protest," *Civilizations* 17, 1/2 (1967): 44-50.

In Hirschman's terms, these dissatisfied second generation migrants will have no "exit" options, since there will be even fewer economic opportunities outside of the primary cities. Thus, they will be forced to resort to "voice." Albert O. Hirschman, *Exit, Voice and Loyalty* (Cambridge: Harvard University Press, 1970).

31. E.W. Soja, *The Geography of Modernization in Kenya: a Spatial Analysis of Social, Economic, and Political Change* (Syracuse: Syracuse University Press, 1968).

32. According to one estimate, about a third (400,000) of all rural households are headed by women whose husbands are away in town. *Employment, Incomes and Equality* (Geneva: International Labor Office, 1972), p. 47.

33. Schon, *Beyond the Stable State*, pp. 90-92; Soja, *Geography of Modernization*, p. 112.

The Kenya government has clearly been aware of this situation. So far, it has responded by trying to improve postal service in the countryside, granting increased authority over local affairs to local townships, creating a national radio and television network, building new roads, schools and industries outside of Nairobi, and undertaking a vast agricultural resettlement program in the former white highlands. However, it is uncertain whether or not these and other programs have had much effect on large sections of the country. John Friedmann, *Urbanization, Planning, and National Development* (Beverly Hills: Sage Publications, 1973), p. 158.

34. F.A.O. *Production Yearbook, 1972* (Rome: F.A.O., 1973).

Although the value of agricultural production has steadily increased, rapid population growth has prevented any significant change in per capita agricultural production.

35. According to one study based on 1971 figures, 20% of adult males and 50% of females working or unemployed in Nairobi are unable to earn a reasonable minimum income. *Employment, Incomes and Equality*, pp. 51-64.

36. A number of forces in Kenya have led to underpriced capital and overpriced labor, which in turn has caused increased migration to the primary cities, and increasing unemployment. Policies to discourage the importation of capital intensive equipment, combined with policies of wage restraint in the primary cities and wage subsidies paid to employers of workers in intermediate cities, all would tend to lessen these distortions. Todaro, "Income Expectations," pp. 396-97.

In addition, tax reforms which brought a greater proportion of middle income groups within the scope of direct taxation would both help to improve overall income distribution and would provide increased tax revenues with which to finance intermediate city development. Nizar Jetha, "The Budgetary Constraint in Kenya," in James R. Sheffield, *Education, Employment and Rural Development* (Nairobi: East African Publishing House, 1967), pp. 447-469.

37. It has been argued that the development of labor intensive industries would lead to lower levels of urban unemployment, would be consistent with the government's priorities in Sessional Paper #10, and would probably not lead to higher monetary costs of production. Others have argued that labor intensive industries would have higher production costs because of reliance on "outmoded technologies." However, such an argument may underestimate the potential for development of "intermediate technologies" in the areas of both production and manpower training, which could make labor intensive industries more efficient. John R. Harris and Michael P. Todaro, "Wage Policy and Employment in a Developing Economy," Discussion Paper #72, Institute for Development Studies, Nairobi, November 1968; O.D.K. Morbye, "Long Term Employment Prospects and the Need for Large Scale Rural Works Programmes," in Sheffield,

Education, Employment and Rural Development, pp. 243-44; E.F. Schumacher, *Small Is Beautiful: Economics as if People Mattered* (N.Y.: Harper & Row, 1973); Republic of Kenya, National Assembly, *Report of the Select Committee on Unemployment* (Nairobi: Government Printer, 1970), pp. 10, 20.

38. Ibid., pp. 11-13.

39. Alvin Tofler, *Future Shock* (N.Y.: Random House, 1970).

40. Communications investment in Africa, both in microwave facilities and satellite earth stations, should be on a tremendous scale during the next ten years. There is presently in the planning stage a proposed Pan-African telecommunications network which would link most African countries with new, modern equipment. In addition, many African countries either have or intend to build INTELSAT earth stations.

For a brief overview of how new communications technologies can lead to increased employment opportunities in rural areas, see Peter C. Goldmark, *The New Rural Society* (Stanford, Conn.: Goldmark Communications, 1972).

41. Some experts believe that a battery-powered television set costing less than $20 might be feasible before the end of this century. Such a television could include an antenna that would pick up transmissions directly from an orbiting satellite. Thus, it could bring sophisticated urban entertainment and educational programs to any location. Herman Kahn and Anthony J. Weiner, *The Year 2000: A Framework for Speculation on the Next 33 Years* (N.Y.: Macmillan, 1967), p. 55.

Educational TV is already being used in African schools. For example, Niger and Ivory Coast have a program that brings ETV to schools at an annual cost of sixty-five dollars per pupil. Edward M. Corbett, *The French Presence in Black Africa* (Washington: Black Orpheus, 1972), pp. 30-31.

42. Shanti Tangri, "Urbanization, Political Stability and Economic Growth," in John Friedmann, *Methods of Regional Planning and Analysis* (Cambridge: MIT, 1960).

43. Bob J. Walter, "Planning for Whom?" in El-Shackhs, *Urbanization . . . ,* "Development, Primacy and Systems of Cities," pp. 93-109.

44. Warren F. Ilchman and Norman T. Uphoff, *The Political Economy of Change* (Berkeley: University of California, 1971), pp. 257ff.

45. However, the proportion of women and children migrants increased between 1948-1962, and is likely to further increase in the future. S.H. Ominde, *Land and Population Movements in Kenya* (Evanston: Northwestern University, 1968), p. 189.

46. There is some variation outside of this age range among ethnic groups. Ibid., pp. 188-89.

47. Ibid., p. 189.

These four groups combined make up about 58% of the total population. Republic of Kenya, *Kenya Population Census, 1969*, Vol. 1, p. 69.

48. Ominde, *Land and Population Movements*, p. 189.

The largest of these smaller groups, the Meru, make up about 5% of the population.

49. Ominde, *Land and Population Movements*, pp. 184-88.

50. Henry Rempel et al., "Rural to Urban Labor Migration: a Tabulation of Responses to the Questionnaire used in the Migration Survey," Staff Paper No. 39, Institute for Development Studies, Nairobi, March 1970: *Public Opinion Poll No. 17: Kenya Leadership* (Nairobi: Marco Publishers, 1967), pp. 19-20; *Employment, Incomes and Equality*, p. 46.

51. Richard Vengroff, "Urban Government and Nationbuilding in East Africa," *Journal of Modern African Studies* 9, 4 (December 1971): 588.

52. Ominde, *Land and Population Movements*, p. 188.

53. Raymond Hopkins, "Code Book for the Kenyan Study of Social Mobilization and Political Participation," 1971, and Marc H. Ross, "Grassroots in the City: Political Participation and Alienation in Nairobi After Independence," 1971, both cited in Henry Bienen, *Kenya: the Politics of Participation and Control* (Princeton: Princeton University Press, 1974).

54. Ibid., pp. 58-65.

55. Progress is already being made in this direction as a result of *Report of the Commission of Inquiry*, D.N. Ndegwa, Chairman (Nairobi: Government Printer, 1971), pp. 112-113.

56. John Nellis, "The Administration of Rural Development in Kenya," *East African Journal* 9, 3 (March 1972): 15-20.

57. Most of these opinions would be supported by corresponding groups in Mombasa. However, because of factors such as distance from the capital, these groups have less influence on the central government than Nairobi-based groups.

For a much more complete account of Nairobi politics, see Herbert H. Werlin, *Governing an African City: A Study of Nairobi* (N.Y.: Africana Pub. Co., 1974).

58. There have been numerous instances which suggest that this influence is considerable. For example, in 1967 the Minister for Local Government proposed a redistribution of a major part of the GPT tax collected in Nairobi and Mombasa to the county councils. This was vigorously but unsuccessfully opposed by the Nairobi City Council. Yet after a little over a year in office, Mayor Kenyatta managed to terminate this practice. *Official Report, National Assembly* 13, December 18, 1967: cols. 3461-3462; *East African Standard*, December 3, 1968; Werlin, *Governing an African City*, pp. 215-16.

59. Alice H. Amsden, *International Firms and Labour in Kenya: 1945-70* (London: Frank Cass, 1971), pp. 99-102, 156.

60. Ibid., pp. 104-159.

61. Peter Gutkind, "The Energy of Despair: Social Organization of the Unemployed in Two African Cities—Lagos and Nairobi," Parts I and II, *Civilizations*, Vols. III and IV, (1967).

62. Bienen, *Kenya.*

Granted there are aberrations from the general pattern of accountability to the masses, such as the recent KANU resolution making President Kenyatta the life president of the ruling party. *Daily Nation*, July 5, 1974.

63. See speech by Mr. Makokha opposing the development of Nairobi and Mombasa at the expense of other regions. Republic of Kenya, *Offical Report, House of Representatives* 5, (June 22, 1965): cols. 635-36.

64. According to one survey, a large majority of Kenyans believe that the government should improve infrastructure and services for the smaller tribes, even if this means spending less on the more advanced tribes. Thus, if there is public understanding of the goals of growth center policies, these policies should enjoy widespread support. Donald Rothchild, "Ethnic Inequalities in Kenya," *Journal of Modern African Studies* 7, 4 (1969): pp. 689-711.

65. Significant wage restraints on this group will only have the effect of encouraging many of them to find higher paying employment in other countries, thus aggravating what is already a serious high level manpower shortage in Kenya. See Oladejo O. Okedifi and Francis O. Okediji, "African Brain Drain to the Highly Industrialized Nations," *The African Review* 1, 2 (September 1971): 44-52.

66. Adapted from John D. Montgomery and Milton J. Esman, "Popular Participation in Development Administration," *Journal of Comparative Administration* 3 (November 1971): 358-83. See also W. Ouma Oyugi, "Participation in Development Planning at the Local Level," Discussion Paper No. 163, Institute for Development Studies, University of Nairobi, 1973.

67. Glynn Cochrane, "What Can Anthropology Do for Development?" *Finance and Development* 2, 2 (June 1974): 20-23.

68. Bienen, *Kenya*, pp. 25-65.

The bureaucracy in Kenya could always be improved. For example, the bureaucracy has proved incapable and/or unwilling to increase local participation in development planning. The reasons for this may be fears by the regime of excessive political claims on too few public resources. The regime may also believe that the membership of local development organizations would have insufficient expertise to make wise decisions. The regime may be sincerely in favor of increasing popular participation, but is unable to get provincial civil servants to cooperate. In any case, the regime has not only failed to bring about local participation in development policy, but has warned national politicians not to interfere with the work of civil servants. W. Ouma Oyugi, "SRDP: An Assessment," *East Africa Journal* 9, 3 (March 1972): 34-40; Robert H. Jackson, "Planning, Politics and Administration," in Goran Hyden, Robert Jackson, and John Okumu, *Development Administration: The Kenyan Experience* (Nairobi: Oxford, 1970), pp. 172-199; Cherry Gertzel, "The Provincial Administration in Kenya," *Journal of Commonwealth Political Studies* 4, 3 (November 1966):213.

69. Soja, *Geography of Modernization*; Ominde, *Land and Population Movements*; M. Safier, *Urbanization and Regional Planning in Kenya* (Nairobi: East African Publishing House, 1971).

70. *Employment, Incomes and Equality.*

71. As mentioned previously, such regulations might provide for locational incentives and penalties, reduction of discrepancies in factor prices and wages between different urban areas, and increases in the labor content of production.

As long as the government can limit its use of such regulations so that there are adequate high level manpower available to administrate them, there is a good chance that the regulations can be used successfully. *Who Controls Industry in Kenya?*—report of a working party (Nairobi: East African Publishing House, 1968), p. 248.

72. *New York Times*, December 16, 1973, p. 28.

73. *Development Plan, 1974-78*, pp. 122-24.

74. Ominde, *Land and Population Movements.*

This type of strategy has already been adopted regarding the development of industrial estates by Kenya Industrial Estates, Ltd.

75. It has been argued that foreign enterprises in Kenya tend to be 20-30% more labor intensive than comparable locally-based ones, because the foreign concerns can recruit supervisors more easily and use them more effectively. *Employment, Incomes and Equality*, pp. 450-51, 184.

Foreign businesses may be relatively more successful in intermediate cities, since they can draw on the expertise and business services of their parent company, and thus have less need for the sophisticated business services available in the primary cities. In addition, they can make more efficient use of the relatively low-cost labor force available in intermediate cities.

76. For brief statements of comparable problems and approaches in Tanzania, see Zygmunt Pioro, "Growth Poles and Growth Centers Theory as Applied to Settlement Development in Tanzania," in Antoni Kuklinski, *Growth Poles and Growth Centers in Regional Planning* (Paris: Mouton, 1972), pp. 169-94; "Achieving the Objectives of the Arusha Declaration: Managing Rural Development," unpublished paper by the Government of Tanzania, 1971; Paul Collins, "Decentralization and Local Administration for Development in Tanzania," *Africa Today* 21, 3 (Summer 1974); J.K. Nyerere, "Decentralization: the People's Role in Planning," unpublished statement to the NEC meeting in Iringa in May 1972.

Policies to control the growth of large urban centers have been adopted by other nations such as Greece, Finland, Holland, Brazil, Japan, Britain, Zambia, Indonesia, France, Sweden, Togo, South Korea, and P.R. China. Ronald Freedman and Bernard Berelson, "The Human Population," *Scientific American* 231, 3 (September 1974): 38.

The World Population Plan of Action adopted in Bucharest on August 30, 1974 supported the notion of urban decentralization: "In planning development, and particularly in planning the location of businesses and the distribution of social services and amenities, governments should take into account not only short term economic returns of alternative patterns, but also the social and environmental costs and benefits involved as well as equity and social justice in the distribution of benefits." *New York Times*, August 31, 1974, p. 6.

6 Government Policies and Interests in Nigerian Migration

Paulina Kofoworola Makinwa

In a historical perspective, the study of migration patterns in Nigeria falls into three periods; the pre-colonial, the colonial, and the post-independence, which reflect the peoples' response to widely divergent economic and social situations. In pre-colonial times large-scale movements of people took place all over Nigeria and this led, in some parts, notably among the Yorubas of Western Nigeria, to the formation of large towns.[1] Primarily for security reasons, group movements as opposed to individual migration accounted for the vast of bulk of pre-colonial migration. Thus, the imposition of a rather coercive colonial administration is properly seen as the major stimulant to individual migration for economic reasons which laid the foundation for the rural-rural and rural-urban migration patterns still prevalent in Nigeria. Since World War II, the process of industrialization set in motion by the political and economic policies of the federal and regional governments has further reinforced this migration pattern. Imbalanced economic development and unequal access to economic opportunities are the results of policies that have allocated to the urban areas a lion's share of all government's developmental efforts to the detriment of the rural areas. Consequently, the volume and pace of rural-urban migration has greatly increased in recent years.

This chapter will focus mainly on the role of government policies in shaping the direction and volume of population movements in Nigeria. A brief review of the general characteristics of rural-urban and rural-rural migration in Nigeria serves as background to the chapter. The second and main part shows rural-urban migration as side effects of government policies aimed at modernization and rapid industrialization especially since the period after the Second World War. The third part reviews governments' attempts to stem the tide of rural-urban influx. The fourth and concluding section examines policy implications of current migration patterns.

Rural-Urban Migration

The most prevalent pattern of internal migration in Nigeria is from rural areas and from smaller towns to the urban centers. This, more than natural increase (which is about 2.5 percent), has accounted for the alarming rate of urban growth in recent years. For example, between 1950 and 1963, Lagos grew from 267,000 to 665,246 inhabitants and spread beyond its city boundaries, engulfing several small adjacent communities to form a metropolitan complex of 1,089,868 persons. The present growth rate in Greater Lagos is about 8 percent per annum within the city limits, nearly 20 percent in the urbanizing outlying areas, and 11 percent overall.[2] It is estimated that for every child born in Lagos during the intercensal decade (1953-1963), three more migrated into Lagos.[3] The total number of migrants into Lagos during the intercensal decade was estimated at over 644,000. Of these 510,000 originated from Western Region, 106,000 Eastern Region, 23,000 Mid-Western Region and over 6,000 from Northern Nigeria. No previous movement of this magnitude has ever been recorded in Africa's history.[4]

As the Lagos figures show, ethnic groups migrated freely throughout Nigeria for economic reasons. Thus Ibo and Yoruba traders journey northwards and often settled permanently, while Hausa and Fulani traders and herders migrated southwards. Both in the north and the south "strangers" (those not belonging to the predominant ethnic group) tend to live in Sabongari or strangers' town on land usually adjacent to the native city and given to the strangers by the native chief.[a]

Migrations into urban centers from rural areas or smaller towns are of three types:

1. Seasonal movements, predominantly of young adult males, occurring during the time of agricultural slack season (the dry season). After an absence of several months, most of these migrants return home to cultivate their farms with the onset of the next wet season, but a few settle permanently in the towns as traders. In Northern Nigeria seasonal migrants are called *masu cin rani* "men who while (? eat) away the dry season." Among these, the long-distance migrants are known as *yan tuma da gora*, "sons of jumping with gourd." They take their name from one of three essential personal belongings the migrants usually carry a bottle-shaped gourd for drinking water. The other two essentials are a sleeping mat and a sword or bow and arrows.[5]

2. Short-term movements of "target" workers, again predominantly adult males who spend short periods working in the city to earn enough money for specific purposes such as payment of poll tax, a bride price, the purchase of a bicycle or some other consumer product.

3. Definitive movements where migrants stay in the cities for indefinite periods of time. Migrants in this group include unskilled laborers and traders from rural areas, as well as large numbers of primary school "dropouts," predominantly male, from rural areas and smaller towns.

[a]This custom of strangers living in "Sabo" made the Ibos an easy target for the Hausas in the aftermath of the coup d'etat in 1966. Although movements of different ethnic groups have again resumed after the Civil War and Ibos have returned in large numbers to resume permanent residence in Lagos (the capital city) it is doubtful that more than a few have returned to the North.

A survey of migrant labor undertaken in Sokoto Province of Northern Nigeria during the dry season 1952/53, following the population census of 1952, found that "between a quarter and a third of the labour force of the Province" had migrated.[6] All their destination have in common the fact that their economic development was far in advance of that of migrants' origin.[7] A rural sample survey conducted throughout Nigeria during 1965/1966 confirmed the findings of the Sokoto Study.[8]

In 1963, only seven years after the introduction of free primary education in Western Nigeria, a government-sponsored study found that of the over 100,000 children in the region who left primary schools yearly, only half of them gained admission into other schools for further education, or were able to find useful employment. Most of these unemployed had migrated to the towns.[9]

Regular wages usually higher than the expected incomes from agriculture (in money if not in real terms) or the opportunity of making money is a very important attraction of the urban centers. The opportunities for paid employment are much higher in towns than in the countryside, and in larger towns than in the small towns, both for the educated and the unskilled. The educated seek employment in manufacturing, commerce, the civil service, etc., and the unskilled seek employment as houseboys, messengers, apprentices or as beggers. Begging is a very important occupation, particularly among Hausa migrants.[10] Although the prospect of employment is often more apparent than real, it has been shown that given a politically determined high minimum wage, the continued existence of rural-urban migration, despite overt and covert urban unemployment, is an economically rational choice on the part of the individual migrant.[11]

Rural-Rural Migration

Although less important than rural to urban or small town to large town migration, a great deal of rural-to-rural migration goes on. As in migration to the urban centers, the main motive for migrating is economic. Because of the traditional method of shifting cultivation farmers constantly move in search of new farmlands. In areas of population pressure and shortage of farm lands, farmers travel long distances away from their tribes to become stranger farmers or tenants on lands belonging to other tribes. Compensation is paid to the landlords in cash or in kind. This group of migrants usually stays for several years. In addition, farm laborers move seasonally into cocoa, groundnuts, and cotton-growing areas to augment the labor force at harvest time.[12]

1914-1944

In 1914, when the British government amalgamated the Southern and Northern Protectorates into a new country and christened it Nigeria, the country consisted of thousands of largely self-sufficient communities engaged in the traditional occupations—farming, crafts, and trade. Trading and communications was by the slow tedious method of traveling on foot or on animals. Travelers were continually at the mercy of raiding armies and marauding bands. Heinrich Barth, who traveled in these areas during the mid-nineteenth century, noted on his journeys that small groups of travelers joined to form larger groups for the purpose of mutual protection.[13] Although trade was not at a standstill under these conditions, activities were restricted and this would have left little scope for small-scale individual initiative. An externally imposed government soon introduced important structural changes in the economy. Notable among these changes were the introduction of laws and their enforcement, a monetary system, the development of a communications network-roads and railways, and the presence of intermediary European traders who offered cash rewards for the sale of particular crops—palm produce—mainly palm oil and kernels—and later, cocoa, cotton, and groundnuts. The peaceful and stable conditions increased opportunities for the development of trading activities among Nigerians themselves. The trade in kola nuts was started. These nuts are grown in the southern forested region but are sold mainly in the north where the people chew them as a form of stimulant. In addition, tin ore and coal were discovered and exploited on the Jos Plateau and the Udi Hills, near Enugu, respectively.

On the aggregate, these factors completely changed the scale of social and economic values. The rail lines effectively linked the north and the south and the locomotives and lorries reduced traveling distances. Christian missionaries introduced primary and secondary education. The economic development which offered employment for migrants—cultivation of export crops, kola nuts and tin and coal mining—also provided a strong stimulus for the growth of old urban centers and the addition of new ones. British administrative headquarters and commercial headquarters of the private foreign firms were often located in the same towns. The growth of the export trade created produce collection centers, usually along the newly built railways and motor roads. Several small ports, among them Lagos and Port Harcourt, became important for handling the growing exports and imports. Many people migrated from the rural areas and towns which were located away from the roads and railways.[14] According to Mabogunje, "irrespective of their size traditional urban centers which were not on the rail-line or on other major routeways found themselves shunted into the backwater of economic decadence, losing many of their virile young men to centres now better favoured locationally."[15] Then, as now, the towns promised wage employment and they contained a disproportionate amount of all the new amenities such as schools, hospitals, and in some places, electric power. People journeyed to the towns to find jobs, to go to school, to trade or just to get a taste of town life. The influx of people to towns is reflected in census counts. Centers with populations of 20,000 or more which contained a total population of about 0.8 million in 1921, had by 1931 increased their total population to nearly double, about 1.4 million.[16]

A small check census undertaken at Illo, Northern Nigeria, in November 1936, to collect some information on the characteristics of seasonal migration gave the estimated number of migrants passing through the check point as 66 per day. Information was collected from 289 migrants, many of whom were migrating to Ghana (then Gold Coast) with a few heading for Western Nigeria. (At this time the Gold Coast was more economically developed than Nigeria.) These movements were attributed to a progressive decrease in productivity in the Sokoto Province over a period of ten years combined with a demand for a higher standard of living.[17]

In this period, the colonial administrative policy was one of maintaining law and order and the development of infrastructure, all geared toward the orderly conduct of export trade. It was "a fatherly rule that the Colonial Service rendered from Gambia to Nigeria."[18] In effect, the introduction of wage labor, differences in economic opportunities in the towns, and greater security for individual migrants all encouraged migration into the rapidly developing towns.

The Modern Period

Since World War II, the federal and regional governments have taken an active role in promoting economic development in general and industrialization in particular. Nigeria's first development plan was launched in 1946. Since 1955, in addition to the plans of the federal government, each region has had separate regional development plans. For various reasons, the plans (excepting the Second National Development Plan, which ends in 1975) have had little effect on the course of economic development in the country. Nevertheless, government policies and public investment have been of critical importance in determining both the path and the speed of economic development. These policies direct and indirect, which were adopted primarily to hasten economic development, have had a very great impact on internal migration. The direct measures to foster economic development are fiscal incentives, support activities, and direct public investment in manufacturing. Indirect measures include the provision of social infrastructure such as the construction of roads, railways, health centers; the introduction of free primary education; guarantees to private investors against uncompensated nationalization; and freedom for foreigners regarding the sale of their assets and repatriation of profits.[19] We shall first consider the role of the direct methods on internal migration.

Direct Measures and Imbalanced Development

The pre-decision forces responsible for the policy of deliberate government intervention in the economy are the low per capita income of the people (about $80); the general poverty of the country and inadequate supply of economic and social infrastructure; the availability to government of large amounts of internal revenue as well as foreign gifts, grants, and loans; and the philosophy of "pragmatic socialism" which the Nigerian governments profess. From these arose governments' policy of intervention for the purpose of inducing social and economic change. But the innovation and application of the policy were also all calculated to keep the governments in power. As will be seen in the analysis that follows, policymakers kept their eye on the general electorate by introducing popular measures such as free primary education while also satisfying the powerful coalition of professionals, labor unions, and businessmen. The passage of minimum wage laws, governments' technical and financial aid to businessmen, the preparation of industrial estates, as well as the concentration of social amenities in urban areas were designed primarily to benefit this coalition. On the other hand, farmers, though numerically the most powerful group, were (and are still) unorganized and so were more or less ignored as is evident by the fact that while farmers generated the bulk of governments' investment capital (via the marketing boards)[b] rural areas still lack basic amenities such as pipe-borne water and electricity.

As the largest source of investment capital and the most important employer in Nigeria, the central and regional governments together possess economic and political resources with which to achieve their "preferred outcomes." With these resources and supported by businessmen, the professionals, the labor unions, and the farmers (who were content mainly due to the introduction of the free primary education, which is the most rural based of all educational institutions in Nigeria), all incumbent political parties retained control of the regional and central governments until the military coup d'etat of 1966. Thus, governments' intervention in the economic and social status quo succeeded admirably in keeping the politicians in power and led to rapid development and modernization of some areas. But the experiment also had some offshoots for which the policymakers, focused as they were on their narrow sectional goals, were unprepared. The most serious of these and the most dramatic in its impact and visibility is the rising tide of rural-urban migration.

The Growth Zones

Since the end of the Second World War, the development of Nigeria has been marked by rapid commercial, manufacturing, and urban growth, all of which are concentrated in four areas. These areas are:

1. In the southwest: centered on metropolitan Lagos—a vast industrial hub, which is also a port city, University town, and the capital of both the Lagos State and the Federal Republic of Nigeria;

---

[b]The role of marketing boards is discussed on pages 178-181.

2. In the southeast: consisting of a well-knit network of cities chief of which are Port Harcourt, Onitsha, Aba, and Enugu;
3. In the mid-western state: an industrial zone centered on Warri, Benin and Sapele; and
4. In the north: a densely populated zone which is industrial, commercial, and administrative in character and is dominated by Kano and Kaduna.

This concentration of urban and industrial development in the four areas has not been entirely accidental but has resulted from deliberate policies in the past by the governments of Nigeria to modernize and so industrialize the capital and one or two other provincial capitals in the former four regions, the North, the East, the West, the Midwest and the Federal Territory of Lagos. In an attempt by federal and regional governments to develop certain cities as show pieces of rapid economic growth, governments used direct public investments, fiscal incentives, and support activities particularly the siting of industrial estates to lure industries into the favored areas.

An industrial estate is "a tract of land which is subdivided and developed according to a comprehensive plan for the use of a community of industrial enterprises."[20] Industrial estates provide essential services such as feeder roads, railway sidings, water, electric power, telephone services, means of drainage of industrial effluents and sometimes, as in the case of the Yaba Industrial Estate, factory buildings. New industries were, naturally, attracted to these estates, which are usually on the outskirts of the few favored towns. Metropolitan Lagos, for example, contains no fewer than four such estates.

The fiscal incentives extended by the federal government include tariff protection, import duty relief, accelerated depreciation allowances, tax holidays, and pioneer industry status. All these measures successfully entice and also influence the location of industries (both foreign and native-owned) since it is easier for new firms to locate in prepared industrial estates. One Nigerian study has shown that "when all the small, medium sized and large industries are considered the overall pattern of the industries, and particularly those that enjoy pioneer and other fiscal incentive grants, reveals a high degree of concentration in a few industrial estates."[21]

Support activities undertaken by agencies of the federal and regional governments include the provision of debenture and equity capital by the regional Development Corporations, the Federal Loans Board, and the Nigerian Industrial Bank. In addition, government agencies have undertaken direct industrial investment both as minor and in some cases as major shareholders (when governments provide over 75 percent of the capital). Nearly all of these partially government-owned establishments are located in urban centers within the four growth zones.

Pattern of Industrial Location

Of the 318 most important establishments which accounted for about 90 percent of total industrial investment in 1965, 35.2 percent were located in Lagos State, mainly within Metropolitan Lagos; 8.8 percent were located in the Port-Harcourt-Aba area; Kano and Kaduna areas accounted for 15 percent; and Benin, Sapele and Warri in the Mid-West State, 6 percent. This meant that these four "growth zones," which together account for less than 2 percent of the land area of Nigeria, contained at least 67 percent of the number of main industrial investments or 45 percent of total capital investments. Eighty out of a total of 105 firms whose investments were 250,000 Nigerian pounds (approximately $750,000) in 1965, were located in these four growth areas.[22]

The main result of this pattern of industrial location is to leave several heavily populated areas in each region and much of the hinterland with very little modern industrial enterprises. A severe imbalance in economic opportunities between urban and rural areas has been created.

The Role of Marketing Boards

Capital for government participation in industries has primarily been derived from the rural areas as "surpluses" from the export earnings of the marketing boards. The marketing boards are statutory monopsonies which handle all Nigeria's major agricultural exports. There is the Cocoa Marketing Board in the Western Region, the Palm Produce Marketing Board in the Eastern Region, and the Cotton and Groundnut Marketing Boards in the North. The Nigerian Commodity Marketing Boards were established by the colonial government during World War II in order to ensure orderly marketing of West African produce and to protect the United Kingdom's supplies of raw materials. Their main functions, as stated in the terms of the laws establishing them were:

(a) to stabilize produce prices by fixing legal minimum prices for a whole season at a time. The Boards were also charged with responsibility for minimizing price alterations between one season and another, through appropriate use of price stabilization funds which they were to build up by retention of part of their trading profits;
(b) to maintain and control an efficient organization for the purchase of commodities from primary producers, through the appointment of licensed buying agents to work under the Board's directions;
(c) to improve the quality of export produce by all suitable means and to maintain legally-prescribed grades and standards of quality;
(d) to promote the development of areas of production and the prosperity of the producers through allocating funds to appropriate authorities for suitable projects in the fields of economic development and research.[23]

In effect, the marketing boards, by paying fixed prices (usually lower than world prices) to farmers, became and still are effective means of mobilizing rural domestic savings. The period of the early 1950s witnessed very high prices for all commodities as the demand of the industrialized countries for raw materials increased rapidly after the war. Consequently, large sums of money was withheld from farmers as Marketing Board surpluses. Furthermore, moneys were withheld from farmers as export duties and produce purchase tax.

The 1953 World Bank Mission had estimated that liquid reserves of 25 million pounds were adequate for price stabilization and recommended that the remaining surplus (or second line reserves) be used as long-term loans to government for development purposes.[24] The Bank Mission also recommended that no further stabilization reserves be accumulated. The various governments took the World Bank at its word and did much more. "Having seen semi-accidentally, the enormous potential for the raising of revenues which the price-fixing function of the Marketing Boards offers, first the Western Region, and then the Eastern Region as well, began consciously to take advantage of it for development purposes."[25] Table 6-1 summarizes government withdrawals from the agricultural export sector between 1947 and 1962, and Table 6-2 the disposal of the marketing board funds in the period 1955-61.

Rural-Urban Income Differentials

It has already been noted above that government taxes and withdrawals by marketing boards is an important force which influence rural-urban differential. A second important force is governments' policy of adjusting money wages every few years for workers in the controlled sector of the economy that is, the Civil Service and industries employing more than ten workers.

Government wage determination has usually been dominated by institutional (such as the trade unions) and political considerations while supply and demand factors take second place. Thus, while export prices to farmers have not shown appreciable increase in the years following independence, wage legislations have sharply increased the wages of urban unskilled labor. Since no such legislation governs wages in the uncontrolled sectors of the economy including small-scale agriculture, wages of farm laborers have tended to be much lower than those of their urban counterparts.

Some of the marketing board "surpluses" were ploughed back into agriculture as input subsidies for fertilizer, pesticides, crop research, etc., and on balance, it would be difficult not to conclude that the earning and subsequent spending of trading and other surpluses by the marketing boards were beneficial to the economic development of Nigeria.[26] The net effect, however, has been a substantial transfer to the non-agricultural sector usually in the urban areas.

Table 6-1

Government Withdrawals from Major Components of the Marketing Board Controlled Agricultural Export Sector in Nigeria Cumulative (1947-1962)

	Export Duties		Marketing Board Trading Surplus		Produce Purchase Tax		Total withdrawals pounds 000's	Potential producer income pounds 000's	Total withdrawals as a % of potential producer income
	Pounds 000's	% of potential producer income	Pounds 000's	% of potential producer income	Pounds 000's	% of potential producer income			
Cocoa 1947/48 to 1961/62	64,481	17.8	46,638	12.8	4,553	13	115,672	363,046	31.9
Groundnuts 1947/48 to 1960/61	32,154	12.9	25,743	10.4	3,998	1.6	61,895	248,436	24.9
Palm Kernels 1947-61	26,997	11.1	36,978	15.2	4,327	1.8	68,303	242,996	28.1
Palm Oil 1947-1961	17,002	11.0	10,849	7.0	4,592	3.0	32,442	154,028	21.0
Cotton 1949/50-1960/61	8,458	12.9	5,272	8.0	792	1.2	14,522	65,767	22.1
Total	149,092	13.9	125,480	11.7	18,262	1.6%	292,834	1,074,273	27.2

Source: Adapted from Gerald K. Helleiner, "The Fiscal Role of Marketing Boards in Nigerian Economic Development, 1947-61," in Carl K. Eicher and Carl Liedholm (eds.), *Growth and Development of the Nigerian Economy* (Michigan: Michigan State University Press, 1970), p. 123.

Table 6-2
Disposal of Nigerian Regional Marketing Funds Cumulative Grants, Investments and Loans Outstanding, 1955-61* (000's Pounds)

	Eastern Region (Dec. 31, 1961)	Northern Region (Oct. 31, 1961)	Western Region (Sept. 31, 1961)	Total (Sept. 30- Dec. 31, 1961)
Cumulative Grants to Regional Government	7,500.0	–	25,589.1	33,089.1
Cumulative Grants to regional development and finance corporations	2,800.0	1,883.2	–	4,683.2
Other Cumulative Grants and expenditures	212.1	3,226.7	5,717.4	9,156.2
Loans outstanding to Federal Government	1,816.9	3,323.6	–	5,140.5
Loans outstanding to Regional Government	–	6,811.2	10,000.0	16,811.2
Loans outstanding to Regional Development and finance corporations	500.0	–	4,200.0	4,700.0
Equity investment in Nigerian private companies	3,545.0	276.0	3,080.0	6,901.0
Loans outstanding to Nigerian private companies	–	800.0	6,288.2	7,088.2
United Kingdom Securities	3,202.2	6,578.0	1,721.6	11,501.8
Federation of Nigeria Securities	–	3,025.1	–	3,025.1
Total	19,576.2	25,923.8	56,596.3	102,096.3

Source: Gerald K. Helleiner, "The Fiscal Role of Marketing Boards in Nigerian Economic Development, 1947-61," in Carl K. Eicher and Carl Liedholm (eds.), *Growth and Development of the Nigerian Economy* (Michigan: Michigan State University Press, 1970), p. 134.

Unequal Distribution of Social Amenities

Compared with the urban centers, rural areas in Nigeria are noted for their lack of electricity, pipe-borne water supply, and health facilities. In the Second National Development Plan covering the period 1970-75, only 19 percent of the public capital investment in health, education, social welfare, electricity, town and country planning, water, and sewage is in the rural areas. By 1971, there was no major industry in Nigeria located outside an urban area.[27] Higher educational institutions, secondary, technical, teacher-training colleges, and universities are located predominantly in urban centers. By contrast, primary schools abound throughout the countryside; government investment in primary institutions being higher for the rural areas than for the urban areas. The gross imbalance in investment allocations to urban and rural areas becomes more noticeable when it is realized that only an estimated 20 percent of the total population can be described as urban dwellers.[28]

Indirect Measures and "the Revolution of Rising Expectations"

Indirect policies adopted by the governments of Nigeria to hasten general development includes the provision of social infrastructure, the initiation of internal commercial airline, television network, the construction of new roads and railways and the introduction of free primary schools. Subsequently, a combination of imbalanced economic growth and the false aspirations created in graduates and dropouts of primary schools resulted in rural-urban migration of a magnitude for which the government was not prepared.

Free Primary Education

As a result of the introduction of free primary education, enrollment in primary schools increased threefold. Although the rate of educational development in Northern Nigeria has not been as phenomenal as in the South, the percentage increase has been no less spectacular. By 1956 the total number enrolled in primary schools was more than triple the enrollment in 1947. By 1963 enrollment had increased by about one million pupils. Total number of primary school children for the country is reported as 3,515,827 in 1970, an increase of more than half a million.[29] From its introduction, the free primary education scheme was plagued by many problems, including shortage of trained teachers and classroom space, mainly due to the fact that educational planning had been undertaken without adequate statistical data. In order to compensate for the shortage of classrooms there is a widespread resort to the use of the "shift system" in schools, which has resulted in a reduction, by a third, of the number of hours spent in school each day.[c] Furthermore, in an effort to cut down costs and to bring primary education to a wider section of the community, primary school education was reduced from eight years to six years.[30]

The cumulative result of untrained teachers, very low teacher to pupil ratio, shorter school hours per day, and fewer years in primary schools is a drastic fall in the quality of primary education. About 60 percent of the primary school graduates will gain admission to secondary schools (there is shortage of secondary schools) or find useful employment, while the remaining 40 percent will join the ranks of the unemployed who will eventually make the journey to

---

[c]The "shift system" in Nigerian Schools is a means of getting double usage out of existing classrooms during each school day. Although the times vary slightly from town to town, the shift system usually works as follows: A set of pupils attend school from 8.00 A.M. to 12.00 noon, and another set attend the same school (with a different set of teachers) from 12.30 P.M. to 4.30 P.M. Consequently, pupils get an average of four hours of schooling a day where formerly primary schools lasted about six hours a day from 8.00 A.M. to 2.00 P.M.

the towns. Recent sample surveys taken in Ibadan and in nine other principal urban centers show that many school leavers have been unemployed for two or three years or even longer.[31] Primary education broadens the pupils' horizon and create expectations which certainly cannot be fulfilled in the rural areas with their appalling lack of the good things of life.

Governments' Reactions

Since independence in 1960, the imperfections of previous policies which developed certain areas of the country as showpieces of modernization to the neglect of the rural areas has become more and more perceptible through undesirable social outcomes, for example, the rising number of unemployed youth in the cities and the breakdown of urban services such as public transportation and refuse collection. The undesirable social outcomes of previous policies thus became the pre-decision forces which led to the formulation of new policies. The method of application and the timing of these policies militated against achieving their desired outcomes. The programs in the application phase of the policies were designed to win votes for the politicians. The hasty introduction of the farm settlement scheme in Western Nigeria in 1959 on the eve of the federal elections is a case in point. Farm settlements were pointedly located in key constituencies sometimes without regard to the geographical suitability to types of crops grown. The project yielded political dividends. It held promise for the unemployed youth and the farmers and at the same time did not upset the status quo in the urban areas, thereby retaining the support of trade unionists and businessmen. As the following analysis will show, a great deal of financial resources were committed to farm settlements, but pre-decision intelligence gathering was incomplete and sometimes ignored. The policy was hastily executed and in the end provided very few jobs.

Farm Settlements

Farm settlements are in operation in the Western, Mid-Western, and Eastern regions in Southern Nigeria.[d] In 1964 there were nineteen such settlements in the

---

[d]The former three regions of southern Nigeria now consists of six states: Lagos, Western, Midwestern, East Central, Rivers, and Southeastern. An earlier attempt had been made at farm settlement in Northern Nigeria in 1949. This was the Mowka Land Settlement Scheme (also known by the name of the company that operated it as the Niger Agricultural Project Limited was to operate commercially and fulfill two aims, population of food, oilseeds for export and subsistence crops for local consumption, and settlement of peasant farmers on hitherto empty land in Northern Nigeria. Patterned after the Gezira scheme in the Sudan, the scheme failed after a few years. Among reasons for failure of the project was the haste with which the project was conceived and implemented, attempt by the Nigerian government not only to introduce farmers to new farming techniques, but also to bring a change in his manner of living by trying to make him live in model villages which bore little resemblance to the type to which he had been accustomed, and the fact that although northern farmers migrated seasonally during the dry season they did not migrate permanently. In addition, settlers were discouraged on political grounds from permanent settlement.

West with 3,002 settlers, four in the mid-West with 795 settlers, and six in the Eastern Region with 570 settlers. The Western Region's farm settlement scheme was formally launched in 1960, although the first settlers had moved in and started opening up land in thirteen settlement areas in 1959. They were based on the operating principles of Israeli Moshavim, that is, individually-owned and operated farms with some cooperatively-owned and operated central services. The general objectives of all the farm settlements was to curb rural-urban migration and provide jobs for unemployed primary school leavers. In the West, the stated objectives were:

(a) To test and later demonstrate carefully planned farming systems designed to attract young, educated persons to take up farming as a satisfying and lucrative means of obtaining their livelihood.
(b) To demonstrate that by careful planning farms can be established and operated by young, educated farmers, with reasonable assistance in the form of advice and loans from the Government or another, which will provide a comfortable standard of living for the owners, comparable with or higher than that gained by persons of their own status in other forms of employment.
(c) To develop another extension method with a view to accelerating agricultural development in the Region. It is planned that, by concentrating development on widely scattered "areas of concentration" in order to secure the best possible results from the limited staff available, these will serve as examples to the rest of the country and enable experience to be gained by the staff in the operation of a 'supervised credit' scheme which can later be applied to individual farms.[32]

In addition, five institutes of agriculture were established for training purposes.

The Eastern Nigerian Farm Institute and Settlement Project was proposed in 1962 to serve the following purposes:

(i) Attempt to reverse the trend of migration from the rural to urban areas by making rural life more attractive and more congenial than it has been hitherto.
(ii) Provide some employment and livelihood for Primary School Leavers who cannot be absorbed in Industry, Public Services and Commercial houses at the present level of the Region's development.
(iii) Make better and fuller use of land where it is sparsely populated or after fragmented holdings have been consolidated.
(iv) Increase and maintain the output of food and agricultural products by making rural areas more productive.[33]

During that period of the first six-year Development Plan (1962-68) 75 percent of the combined Western and Mid-Western capital expenditure on agricultural development projects and 20 percent of the Eastern Regions was spent on farm settlements. Several writers have criticized the scheme as too expensive; location of some of the settlements have been influenced only by political considerations; and generally the scheme has been of financial benefit, either directly or indirectly, to an insignificant proportion of total rural populations. An FAO team evaluated the farm settlement schemes in 1968 concluded as follows:

The capital outlay per settler on the present Farm Settlement Schemes, renders it impossible for them to make any contribution to the employment problem in a country where the population is growing at the rate of some 1.1 to 1.4 million per annum. So far, there has been little to learn by adjacent farmers from the existing settlements and results from another major aim of the Schemes—the creation of a prosperous and enlightened class of farmers from primary school-leavers—have been negative and expensive. In the meantime, the improvements of standards on the very large numbers of existing small holdings has been largely neglected.[34]

But there is also evidence that some of the farm settlements have been successful and are attracting new settlers. A March 1974 statement from the Western Region Ministry of Agriculture claims that four settlements (at Ilora, Ogbomoso, and Onisere) average income per settler for 1970-71 was ₦400 to ₦800 ($600 to $1,200) more than a settler would earn in one year in government employment. However, the statement continues, "the present government is not too keen on the farm settlement scheme and the whole thing is under review."[35]

The National Youth Corps

This is a newly initiated federal government scheme to make young graduates work in rural areas. Originally, it was assumed that a Youth Corps would absorb unemployed (perhaps unemployable) school leavers, but eventually it was recent university graduates who were conscripted to serve mainly in the rural areas. The first members were 2,000 graduates of the five Nigerians universities who completed their courses and were below the age of thirty years in June 1973. Each member was assigned to rural areas in states other than the state of origin the assumption being that these students would have preferred, if left to their own initiative, to work in urban areas in their states of origin. They received salaries commensurate with what they would earn in private industry. Although it is too early to evaluate the process of the program on rural-urban migration, the program is generally considered by its originators as successful. A survey to appraise the impact of the scheme found "36.3 percent of members ready to take up employment in the states where they have been deployed."[36]

Delivery of Urban Services

The combination of natural increases and increasing rural-urban migration has resulted in high urban population growth rates. The impact of the rapid influx of population on the urban services has been disastrous. For example, in Lagos a street plan which formerly served a town of 30,000 traveling mainly on foot is now severely strained by the more than the twentyfold increase of traders, clerks, administrators, etc., who struggle to their work on assorted automobiles. An observer of the Lagos scene described the general conditions:

In Metropolitan Lagos, chaotic traffic conditions have become endemic; demands on the water supply system have begun to outstrip its maximum capacity; power cuts have become chronic as industrial and domestic requirements have both escalated; factories have been compelled to bore their own wells and to set up standby electricity plants; public transport has been inundated; port facilities have been stretched to their limits; the congestion of housing and land uses has visibly worsened and living conditions have degenerated over extensive areas within and beyond the city's limit, in spite of slum clearance schemes.[37]

The situation in Lagos is not unique. Other urban centers, notably Ibadan and Kaduna, are reported as exhibiting the "Lagos symptoms."

Housing estates and slum clearance schemes are governmental attempts to accommodate the rapid influx of migrants into the urban centers. For example, a large slum clearance and resettlement program was embarked upon in Lagos in 1955 which included seventy acres of central Lagos and involved about 200,000 people who were eventually relocated on new estates at Surulere. All regional capitals have new housing estates which are located outside the area of main population concentration. The inadequacy of housing estates to stop the proliferation of urban slums is once more exemplified by conditions in Lagos. The "new" estate at Surulere is now completely engulfed by low-cost housing (including large tracts of slums) due to the rapid rate of in-migration.

Conclusions and Policy Implications

The development of growth zones, the building and the distribution of marketing board "surplus," the labor wage laws, and the free primary school system were all designed to produce the following outcomes; ensure the power of the politicians, induce social and economic change through increase in per capita wealth, develop skills and create enlightenment and rectitude through education; in general, as stated in the second National Development Plan, to create "a land of bright and full opportunities for all citizens."[38] In effect these opportunities were neither full nor were they equal for all citizens. Rural-urban migration is one attempt on the part of the people to correct the imbalance. Increasing rural-urban migration is thus the unintended side effects of the prescription, promotion, and application of policies aimed at economic development. The policy implication is therefore clear, that in order to stem the rising tide of migrants into the cities, conscious effort will have to be made to modernize the rural area which generated most of the capital investment in the country.

Policymakers will need to consciously assess the impact which governments' policies and programs may have on peoples' decision to migrate. For example, if policymakers want to use marketing boards to mobilize domestic savings and simultaneously curb rural-urban migration, then farmers' incomes should be augmented through government subsidies of farm inputs.

Efforts to curb rural-urban migration will require more gathering and dissemination of information about:

1. the target population,
2. the reasons for migrating,
3. the availability of financial resources, and
4. how best to use available resources to generate the maximum number of jobs.

In the Nigerian context the target population is the youth who come to the towns seeking higher education and jobs. Also, despite the fact that the oil industry has replaced agriculture as the foremost foreign exchange earner, agriculture must still be regarded as the employment-generating sector for the next ten to fifteen years. According to one estimate, the non-agricultural sector can increase employment by no more than 3 percent per year.[39] And since unemployed school leavers constitute a large segment of migrants, policymakers will want to appraise the content of present primary school curriculum with the view to making it more rural oriented. In addition, the standard of life in the rural areas will have to be upgraded through the provision of more social amenities including more secondary schools if government seriously intends to lower the rate of rural-urban migration.

Notes

1. N.C. Mitchell, "Yoruba Towns," K.M. Barbour and R.M. Prothero (eds.) in *Essays on African Population* (London: Routledge and Kegan, Paul, 1961); Akin, L. Mabogunje, *Urbanization in Nigeria* (New York: African Publishing Corp., 1968).

2. Mabogunje, *Urbanization in Nigeria*, p. 270.

3. "Lagos Descent into Chaos," *West Africa*, February 13-19, 1971, pp. 183-185.

4. Leslie Green and Vincent Milone, *Urbanization in Nigeria: A Planning Commentary*, Ford Foundation, International Urbanization Survey, March 1971, p. 7.

5. This last item is no longer important. An interesting and very informative account of seasonal migration from Northern to Southern Nigeria is to be found in Prothero, *Migrant Labour from Sokoto Province Northern Nigeria* (The Government Printer, Northern Region of Nigeria, 1958).

6. Ibid., p. 22.

7. Ibid., pp. 26-27.

8. Federal Office of Statistics, Lagos Nigeria. *Rural Demographic Sample Survey 1956-1966.* Mimeo.

9. Ibadan, Western State, Ministry of Economic Development, Statistics Division.

10. Abner Cohen, *Custom and Politics in Urban Africa: A Study of Hausa Migrants in Yoruba Towns* (Los Angeles: University of California Press, 1969). In a Hausa settlement in Sabo, Ibadan, Cohen noted that several categories of beggers are highly organized. Thus blind beggers are organized and have a titular Chief of the Blind, Sarkin Makoh; chief of the lame beggers is Sarkin Guragu; and the chief of leper beggers is Sarkin Kutare, pp. 44-46.

11. Michael P. Todaro, "A Model of Labor Migration and Urban Unemployment in Less Developed Countries," *The American Economic Review* 59 (March 1969): 137-48.

12. M. Kola Onasanya, "Population Movement in Nigeria," *The Geographer* (May 1972), (University of Lagos), pp. 59-64.

13. Prothero, *Migrant Labour*, p. 37.

14. For comprehensive survey of the economic development of Nigeria, see Gerald K. Helleiner, *Peasant Agriculture Government and Economic Growth in Nigeria* The Economic Growth Center, Yale University (Homewood, Ill.: Richard D. Irwin, Inc. 1966), Chapter 1.

15. Akin L. Mabogunje, "The Economic Implications of the Pattern of Urbanization in Nigeria," *The Nigerian Journal of Economic and Social Studies* 7, 1 (March 1965): 16.

16. Federal Republic of Nigeria, Digest of Statistics. These figures are highly suspect. These are not comprehensive enumeration of population.

17. Prothero, *Migrant Labour*, pp. 18-21.

18. Laura Boyle, *Diary of a Colonial Officer's Wife* (U.K.: Alden Press, 1968).

19. Peter Kilby, *Industrialization in an Open Economy: Nigeria, 1945-1960* (Cambridge University Press, 1969), pp. 22-25.

20. Bredo William, *Industrial Estates* (Glencoe, Illinois: The Free Press, 1960), pp. 1-2.

21. S.A. Aluko, "Fiscal Incentives for Industrial Development in Nigeria," Mimeographed, University of Ife, May 1967, p. 135.

22. A.N. Hakam, "The Motivation to Invest and the Locational Pattern of Foreign Private Industrial Investment in Nigeria," *The Nigerian Journal of Economic and Social Studies* 8, 1 (March 1966); S.A. Aluko: *Fiscal Incentives*, pp. 135-136.

23. United Nations, FAO, *Agricultural Development in Nigeria, 1968-1980*, Rome, 1966, pp. 349-350.

The Nigerian Commodity Marketing Boards, each of which dealt with all the relevant aspects of a single export crop, were abandoned in 1954 as a result of constitutional changes in favor of increased regional autonomy. Consequently, the commodity boards were replaced by Regional Marketing Boards which were granted somewhat similar control powers over all major crops (excluding rubber) within the boundaries of each administrative region.

Gerald K. Helleiner, "The Fiscal Role of Marketing Boards in Nigerian Economic Development, 1947-61," in Carl E. Eicher and Carl Liedholm (eds.), *Growth and Development of the Nigerian Economy* (Michigan State University Press, 1970).

24. International Bank for Reconstruction and Development, *The Economic Development of Nigeria* (Baltimore: Johns Hopkins University Press, 1955), p. 88.

25. Helleiner, "Fiscal Role," p. 129.

26. Ibid., p. 142.

27. S.A. Aluko, "Resource Allocation and Overall Strategy," *The Quarterly Journal of Administration*, Ife University, 5, 3 (April 1971). Special issue devoted to the Second National Development Plan, 1970-74), p. 282.

28. Federal Ministry of Information, Second National Development Plan 1970-74, Lagos, 1970, p. 63.

29. Federal Republic of Nigeria, *Statistics of Education*, 1970.

30. *Second National Development Plan 1970-74*, pp. 315-317.

31. Western Nigeria, Statistics Division, Ministry of Economic Planning and Social Development. Report of a sample Survey of unemployment among school leavers, Ibadan, Vol. 11, 1967, Vol. III, 1968, Vol. IV, 1970.

32. *Agricultural Development in Nigeria 1968-1980*, p. 339.

33. Ibid., pp. 339-340.

34. Ibid., p. 347.

35. Reported in *West Africa*, March 4, 1974, p. 236.

36. Ibid., Feb. 18, 1974, p. 173.

37. Leslie Green and Vincent Milone, *Urbanization in Nigeria*, pp. 14-15.

38. *Second National Development Plan*, p. 32.

39. Eicher and Leidholm, *Growth and Development of Nigerian Economy*, p. 384.

Bibliography

Books

Aluko, S.A. "Fiscal Incentives for Industrial Development in Nigeria." Mimeographed, Ile-Ife, University of Ife, 1967.
American University, Foreign Area Studies: *Area Handbook for Nigeria*, 1972.
Baldwin, K.D.S. *The Niger Agricultural Project*. Cambridge: Harvard University Press, 1957.
Barbour, K. Michael and Prothero, R. Mansell. *Essays on African Population*. London, Routledge and Kegan Paul, 1961.

Beckinsale, R.P. and Houston, J.M. *Urbanization and its Problems.* Essays in honour of E.W. Gilbert. Oxford, Blackwell, 1968.

Beyer, Glen H. *The Urban Explostion in Latin America.* A Continent in Process of Modernization. Ithaca, New York: Cornell University Press. 1967.

Bogue, Donald J. "Internal Migration." In Philip Hauser and Otis Dudley Duncan (eds.), *The Study of Population: An Inventory and Appraisal.* Chicago: University of Chicago Press, 1959.

Brass, W. et al. *The Demography of Tropical Africa.* Princeton: University Press, 1968.

Bredo, William. *Industrial Estates.* Glencoe, Ill.: The Free Press, 1960.

Breese, Gerald William (ed.). *The City in Newly Developed Countries: Readings on Urbanization.* Englewood Cliffs, N.J.: Prentice-Hall, 1969.

Caldwell, John C. *African Rural-Urban Migration. The Movement to Ghana's Towns.* New York: Columbia University Press, 1969.

Caldwell, J.C. and Okonjo Chukuka (eds.). *The Population of Tropical Africa.* Longmans, 1968.

Cohen, Abner. *Custom and Politics in Urban Africa. A Study of Hausa Migrants in Yoruba Towns.* Berkeley and Los Angeles: University of California Press, 1969.

Eicher, Carl K. and Liedholm, Carl (eds.). *Growth and Development of the Nigerian Economy.* Michigan State University Press, 1970.

Green, Leslie and Milone, Vincent. *Urbanization in Nigeria: A Planning Commentary.* The Ford Foundation, International Urbanization Survey, 1971.

Hance, William Adams. *Population, Migration and Urbanization in Africa.* New York, Columbia University Press, 1970.

――――. "Urbanization in West Africa," Chapter 13. In *The Geography of Modern Africa.* New York: Columbia University Press, 1974.

Helleiner, Gerald K. *Peasant Agriculture, Government and Economic Growth in Nigeria, The Economic Growth Center.* Yale University. Homewood, Ill.: Richard D. Irwin, Inc., 1966.

International Association for Metropolitan Research and International Development Research Center (IDRC). *Town Drift: Social and Policy Implications of Rural-Urban Migration in Eight Development Countries.* Final Conference on "Rural-Urban Migrants and Metropolitan Development," November 24 to December 1, 1973, Istanbul, Turkey.

Kilby, Peter. *Industrialization in an Open Economy: Nigeria, 1945-1960.* Cambridge University Press, 1969.

Kuczynski, R.R. *Demographic Survey of the British Colonial Empire.* Oxford University Press, London, 1949.

Kuper, Hilda (ed.). *Urbanization and Migration in West Africa.* Berkeley: University of California Press, 1965.

Little, Kenneth Lindsay. *Some Contemporary Trends in African Urbanization.* Evanston: Northwestern University Press, 1966.

Mabogunje, Akinlawon Ladipo. *Urbanization in Nigeria*. New York: Africana Publishing Corporation, 1971.

Marris, Peter. *Family and Social Change in an African City*. Evanston, Ill.: Northwestern University Press, 1962.

Miner, Horace (ed.). *The City in Modern Africa*. London: Paul Mall Arlie House, 1967.

Ominde, S.H. and Ejiogu, C.N. (eds.). *Population Growth and Economic Development in Africa*. London: Heinemann, 1972.

Prothero, R. Mansell. *Migrant Labour from Sokoto Province Northern Nigeria*. The Government Printer, Northern Region of Nigeria, 1958.

Roider, Werner. *Farm Settlements for Socio-Economic Development*. The Western Nigerian Case. Munchen: Welt Forum Verlag, 1971.

The Royal Institute of International Affairs. *Nigeria*. London: Oxford University Press, 1969.

Journals and Periodicals

Aboyade, O. "Industrial Location and Development Policy: The Nigerian Case." *The Nigerian Journal of Economic and Social Studies* 10, 3 (November 1968).

Akinola, R.A. "Factors in the Geographical Concentration of Manufacturing in Greater Lagos." *Lagos Notes and Records: University of Lagos Bulletin of African Studies* 1, 1 (June 1967).

Asiodu, P.C. "Industrial Policy and Incentives in Nigeria." *The Nigerian Journal of Economic and Social Studies* 9, 2 (1967).

Caldwell, J.C. "Determinants of Rural Urban Migration in Ghana." *Population Studies: A Journal of Demography* 22, 3 (Nov. 1968): 361-377.

Callaway, Archibald. "Unemployment Among African School Leavers." *The Journal of Modern African Studies* 1, 3. Cambridge, U.K.: University Press, 1963.

_____. "Expanding Nigeria's Education: Projections and Achievements since Independence." *The Nigerian Journal of Economic and Social Studies* 11, 2 (July 1969).

Eke, I.I.U. "Population of Nigeria, 1952-65." *The Nigerian Journal of Economic and Social Studies* 8, 2 (July 1966).

Frank, Charles R., Jr. "Industrialization and Employment Generation in Nigeria." *The Nigerian Journal of Economic and Social Studies* 9, 3 (Nov. 1967).

Gugler, Josef. "Comparative Urban Growth in Subsaharan Africa." *Nkanga*, 6 Makerere Institute of Social Research, 1970.

Gugler, Josef. "On the Theory of Rural-Urban Migration. The Case of Subsaharan Africa." In J.A. Jackson (ed.), *Migration*. Cambridge, U.K.: University Press, 1969, pp. 134-155.

Hakam, A.N. "The Motivation to Invest and the Locational Pattern of Foreign Private Industrial Investments in Nigeria." *The Nigerian Journal of Economic and Social Studies* 8, 1 (March 1966).

Harris, John and Todaro, Michael P. "Migration, Unemployment and Development. A Two-Sector Analysis." *The American Economic Review* 60 (March 1970): 126-142.

Imoagene, Stephen O. "Mechanism of Immigrant Adjustment in West African Urban Community." *The Nigerian Journal of Economic and Social Studies* 9, 1 (March 1967).

Morrison, Peter A. "Policy Aspects of Population Redistribution in the United States, IUSSP, pp. 389-401; M. Kola Onasanya, "Population Movement in Nigeria." *The Geographer* (University of Lagos) Vol. 4, May 1972, pp. 59-64.

Pool, D.I. "Development of Population Policies." *Journal of Modern African Studies* 9, 1 (1971).

Sada, P.O. "The Rural-Urban Fringe of Lagos: Population and Land Use." *The Nigerian Journal of Social and Economic Studies* 12, 2 (July 1970).

Schatz, Bayre P. "Aiding Nigerian Business. The Yaba Industrial Estate." *The Nigerian Journal of Economic and Social Studies* 6, 2 (July 1964).

Todaro, Michael P. "Income Expectation, Rural-Urban Migration and Employment in Africa." *Labour Review*, July 1971.

Wander, Hilda. "Population Policies Affecting Internal Migration and Urbanization." Proceedings of the International Union for the Scientific Study of Population, Liege, 1973, (IUSSP) pp. 359-371.

Official Publications Regional and National Government, U.N., etc.

Federal Ministry of Information (Nigeria). *Second National Development Plan*, 1970-1974, 1970.

Federal Republic of Nigeria. *Annual Abstract of Statistics*.

Federal Republic of Nigeria. *Statistics of Education in Nigeria*. Series III, Vol. III, 1970.

United Nations, FAO. *Agricultural Development in Nigeria 1968-1980*. Rome, 1966.

7

Migration Policies and the Shaping of Sudanese Society

G.A. Balamoan

The contemporary Sudan, unlike any developing country in Africa, is multi-ethnic; unlike other African countries, its multi-ethnicity has not been shaped by the drawing of international boundaries but rather by the large-scale international movements of populations into the Sudan.

This chapter examines the role that government played in determining the ethnic composition of the Sudan. We will look at the policy interventions by the British Imperial rulers and how these interventions significantly shaped this contemporary ethnic distribution. Some of these policies were deliberate attempts to affect the composition of the country while other policies were indirect. The same policies have been continued by all the successive national governments of the Republic of the Sudan since independence, though for very different reasons.

In the present area of the Sudan, the population has increased from less than 1.5 million in 1898 to 10.26 in 1956. Had there been no immigration the population of the Sudan would have been about 3 million in 1956. My projections for the period 1957 to 1975 reveal that the Sudan population in 1975 will be over 22 million persons.

It is very difficult to estimate the many ethnic units of this population because the Sudan Population Census 1955-56 was woefully inadequate for this purpose.[1] An individual's tribal allegiance or origin was never questioned by the Census takers. If a person was asked which language he spoke he almost invariably said it was Arabic; this was especially true in the north. It was entirely up to the individual to say what he was.[2] This made things particularly easy for the latest immigrants from the Congo-Chad-Niger who had not yet "assimilated" and who felt it politically and socially advisable to claim Sudanese origin when in fact they had no claim. Therefore, the figures produced by the Census of 1955-56 are unreliable. Only 537,000 persons reported themselves as West African, a figure in no way revealing the magnitude of the migrations. Moreover, according to the same Census, 51 percent of all Sudanese speak Arabic;[3] but in fact, there are 450 tribes speaking 110 different languages. However, there is a vital cultural link in Islam and Arabic which British Imperial rulers and Egyptian policymakers had fostered in central and northern Sudan until 1955 and since then Egypt and the (independent) Republic of Sudan.

This is a story of deliberate policies to attract international migration. These policies were laid down and carried out by British Imperial administrators from 1900 through 1955 then continued from 1956 to the present by all the Sudanese national governments after independence. One might ask why did the Sudanese governments after independence foster this immigration? One who evaluates the consequences of overpopulation might conjecture that it was inertia to change, or refusal to recognize that any problem exists; but it may be much more than that: it could be a policy to preserve a particular ethnic composition within the Sudan.

A major obstacle to the Sudan's future development is therefore not only its 2.5 to 3 percent net annual natural increase in population, which will exceed 42 million by 1966, but the continuing migration into the Sudan from countries west and southwest of the Sudan. In 1974 alone more than one million refugees, victims of one of Africa's worst drought, migrated to the Sudan.[4]

Immigration from West Africa was noted as early as 1900, and the immigrant villages which suddenly mushroomed were mentioned in Governor-General Wingate's report of 1903, when the population was estimated at 1.8 million. The immigrants found land, water, and capital in the Sudan and many were assisted by the government to obtain these necessities to start their own small farms. Also as tenant farmers on the Sudan Plantations Syndicate, (later known as the Sudan Gezira Board) they were given hawashas, 10 to 40 acre land plots on the irrigation scheme. The immigration was a result of British population policy in the Nile Valley. There were at least four major policy interventions. In the following pages I will very briefly enumerate how so few (about five or seven men) British Imperial administrators were able to make these major interventions which were:

1. The Closed Districts Order in 1902 for the Southern Sudan, which prevented Southern Sudanese people from going to work in Northern Sudan.
2. The planned importation of Congo-Chad-Niger-Senegal peoples to fill up the Northern and Central Sudan with the full cooperation of West African British and French Imperial Administrators.
3. The elimination of Egyptians and "contaminated Sudanese and others" from the Sudan, estimated at 510,000 persons in three months, in 1924-25.
4. Financial assistance obtained from Egypt to finance the infrastructure in the Sudan which exceeded $260 million between 1895 and 1936 and about $100 million between 1936 and 1946.

These policies were facilitated by the condition of the Sudan, especially between 1880 and 1936. The estimated 1880 population was 8.5 million, but by 1898 it had declined to 1.5 million with a probable death rate from disease and famine to suggest a declining population after 1898.

Since about 1900 there has been large-scale migration from the Congo-Chad-Niger-Senegal Regions into the Nile Valley. All this took place without benefit of law, though it has nowhere been called "illegal." At least seven in ten of all the Sudan's population as of 1956 could be described as aliens within "The Definition of Sudanese Ordinance of 15 July 1948." This ordinance specified that a person is Sudanese if he or his father or his grandfather were born in the Sudan before December 31, 1897 and domiciled in the Sudan ever since, or if domiciled in the Sudan at the beginning of the Mahdia, 1881 to 1884, but taking refuge in Egypt with the intention of returning to the Sudan. The 1936 Anglo-Egyptian Treaty permitted unrestricted Egyptian immigration into the Sudan, but British Imperial Administrators did not implement this treaty.

Demographic History of the Sudan During the Mahdist Regime 1884-1899

What was the demographic condition of the Egyptian Sudan immediately after the collapse of the Egyptian government in about 1880? And what was the demographic condition of the Mahdist Sudan during the crucial period 1884 to 1898? To answer the first question, we have only the doubtful estimate given by Sir Reginald Wingate in his 1903 Census that the Sudan's population in or about 1880 was over eight and a half million people. Considering the geographic, economic, and political condition of the Egyptian Sudan up to the collapse of Egyptian rule there in about 1880, it is perhaps unlikely that the population in 1882 would have equalled that again for 1950—after almost fifty-two years of peaceful government.[5]

Mohammed Ahmed El Mahdi, an Arab Sudanese (a Dongolawi, from Northern Sudan), proclaimed himself the Mahdi in 1881. From insignificant beginnings, but favored by a general discontent due to previous maladministration, he met with a series of astonishing successes which were crowned by the murder of General Gordon, and he was soon master of all Egypt's southern provinces. The Mahdi died after an attack of typhus fever on June 22, 1885. Before his death the Mahdi named as his successor, Khalifah Abdullahi El Ta'aishi, perhaps a Takruri from the Western Sudan.[6] During the reign of Khalifah Abdullahi there were many inter-tribal wars, famines, and diseases. Finally came the reconquest of the Sudan. The combined effect of these factors depopulated the country by at least 80 percent of its inhabitants.

For the purpose of defending the Sudan against Anglo-Egyptian invasion the Khalifah Abdullahi had forbidden pilgrimages to Makkah, having substituted pilgrimages to the Tomb of the Mahdi. This policy dammed the sluggish stream of Muslim West Africans who passed through the Sudan on their way to and from Makkah. During the Mahdist period Niger-Chad pilgrimages probably increased. This caused an inevitable increase in the numbers of recruits into the Dervish army loyal to the Khalifah. Large quantities of grain, animals, and other supplies were requisitioned from the people and stored or stabled in the city.

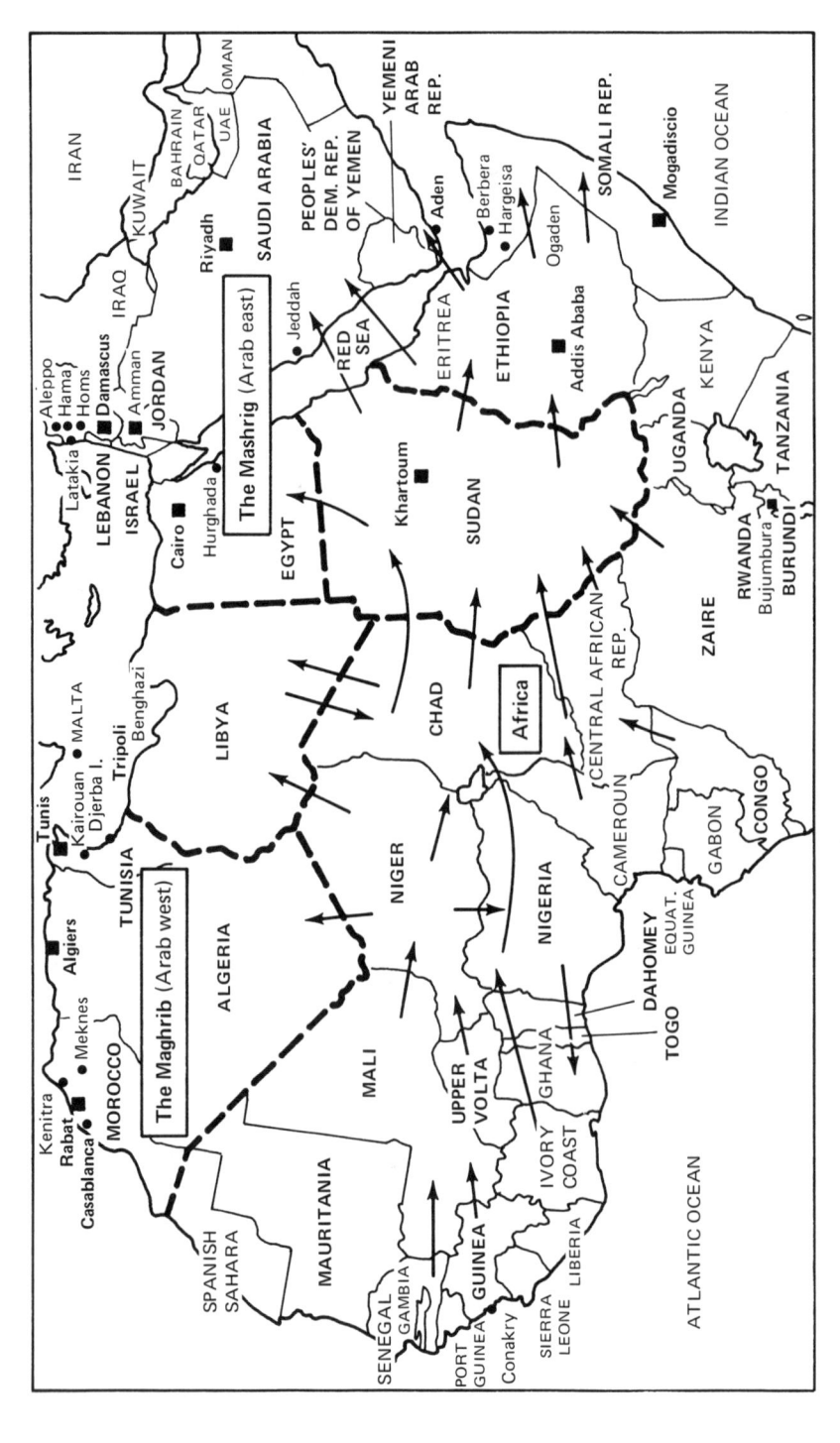

Figure 7-1. Approximate Migration Pattern

The discontent to which this arbitrary taxation gave rise was cured by a more arbitrary remedy. As many of the doubtful and embittered tribesmen as could be caught were collected in Omdurman. This policy caused a further depopulation of the grain producing areas, and a further shortage of foodstuffs. Prices in Omdurman and Khartoum were said to have been fourteen times higher than pre-1880. The Khalifah sent the Kordofan troops to fetch grain from the Jaalin in the North. The Jaalin tried to reason with the Khalifah that they already had too little grain, but their entreaties were probably misunderstood. After stubborn resistance, the Jaalin people were methodically exterminated.[7]

The land lay prostrated and utterly exhausted. Sixteen years of fierce convulsion had reduced the once teeming population of the Sudan by more than 75 percent. Wide regions were depopulated. Great tracts had passed out of cultivation. The villages had fallen back into sand. The date-palms had been cut down. Most of the female camels were either eaten or dead.[8] "There were formerly 3,000 sakias (waterwheels) between Dongola and Khartoum, but by the end of 1898 there were not more than seventy."[9] Nearly all the young men had perished. The balance of the species had followed all else to destruction. "There is," to quote an official euphemism, "a great dearth of population."

The Anglo-Egyptian Condominium
1899-1955

Anglo-Egyptian Sudan Census 1896-1903
and Subsequent Population Estimates

Before 1896 no reliable census had been made of the Sudan; but in view of the importance of arriving at some approximate estimate of the population Her Brittanic Majesty's Consul-General to Egypt and the Soudan directed Sir Reginald Wingate's *"very special attention to that question."*[10]

The result of Sudan's First Administrative Census, which took place between 1896 and 1903, as shown in Table 7-1.

In forwarding the Census figures, Sir Reginald Wingate made the following remarks:

It will be observed that the total population of the Soudan before the period of Dervish Rule is estimated at 8,525,000 that 3,451,000 persons are said to have died of disease, that 3,203,500 to have been killed in external and internal war, and that the existing population is estimated at 1,870,500 persons.

... One has only to travel through the country to realise the terrible ravages of Dervish misrule, of which there is such painful evidence in the wholesale destruction of towns and villages, and the enormous tracts of once cultivated land now either a barren wilderness or overgrown with thorns and high grass necessitating immense labour to clear and bring again under the plough.

Table 7-1
Estimated Population Prior to Dervish Rule, Losses During Dervish Rule, and 1903 Estimates of Population by Province

Province	Province Population Prior to Dervish Rule 1880	Approximate Loss During Dervish Rule — Disease	Approximate Loss During Dervish Rule — Warfare	1903 Population
Bahr El Ghasal	1,500,000	400,000	700,000	400,000
Berber	800,000	450,000	250,000	100,000
Dongola	300,000	110,000	80,000	110,000
Gezirah	550,000	275,000	125,000	150,000
Wadi Halfa	55,000	12,000	13,000	30,000
Kassala	500,000	300,000	120,000	80,000
Khartoum	700,000	400,000	210,000	90,000
Kordofan	1,800,000	600,000	650,000	550,000
Sennar	1,100,000	500,000	450,000	150,000
Suakin (Town)	20,000	4,000	5,500	10,500
Suakin (Arabs)	300,000	100,000	150,000	50,000
Kodah (Upper Nile)	900,000	300,000	450,000	150,000
Approx. Totals	8,525,000	3,451,000	3,203,500	1,870,500

As an instance, I might cite one among the many cases which have come under my personal observation. Prior to 1882 the district comprising the banks of the Rivers Rahad and Dinder contained upwards of 800 villages. When this country was examined some two years ago not a village remained; but through the energetic action of the Governor, Colonel Corringe, 28 new villages have sprung up.[11]

These twenty-eight new villages were the beginning of West African settlements, and were included in the census as Sudanese in 1903.

Sir Reginald Wingate's critics have regarded the 1903 estimates as too low. He was, so it was suggested, anxious to censure the Mahdist regime for its barbarity. Certainly he gave prominence in his early reports to evidence of depopulation both in the Northern and the Southern Provinces.[12] If the estimates of 1903 were faulty, it was in respect of the figures assigned to losses by warfare and disease, and consequently to his overestimation of the population in 1882, rather than to error in 1903. While it may be objected that the 1903 estimates were also probably in error, and may be underestimates, they were after all the result of careful observations by people who were actually in the country, assessing for taxation on the basis of numbers in tribes.[13] I must also reiterate that all but the hard core of loyalists saw that a new power had come to stay and hastened to make their peace and were expected to cooperate in the Census. This process was made easy by the presence of Sir Rudolf Von Slatin Pasha, who was personally known to every man of consequence.[14] On the other hand the estimates for 1882, and for losses, could be little more than guesses; for neither Slatin nor Ohrwalder had any other basis for estimation. Since the Egyptian regime before 1882 was accompanied by much maladministration it is most unlikely that the population in 1882 would have equalled that for 1950.[15] The latter figure was reached after half a century of peace, economic development, and substantial immigration. The verdict on the 1903 table is that the estimates of losses during the Mahdiya were probably exaggerated; and hence the population for 1882 was overestimated; but the total given for 1903 which was reached during seven years (1896 to 1903), was probably not far wrong.[16]

Method of Investigation

Under the leadership of the Commander of the Anglo-Egyptian Army of Restoration of the Sudan, and later on under the leadership of the Governor-General Sir Reginald Wingate, the administrative Census was carried out in this manner:

As the Army of Restoration advanced, the population of the hamlets and villages were counted by the Shaikhs, whose figures were checked by the Omda, rechecked by the Mamur of the District, and again rechecked by the British District Commissioner and again rechecked by the Provincial Military Governor. These triple-checked figures were later submitted to Sir Rudolf Von Slatin Pasha, who was Commissioner for Labour Resources and who at the time of the administrative Census made extensive tours to each Province to satisfy himself that the Census was being carried out correctly. At the same time the Rev. Father Ohrwalder (although not in any official capacity) was able with his great and thorough knowledge of the Sudan to verify figures simply because he made personal visits to all places with which he was acquainted before the Mahdiya, and because the land was almost empty of people except along the banks of the Nile.

The Shaikhs and Omdas in particular gladly cooperated with the District Commissioner.[17] Heads of tribes and Shaikhs El Khut need not tell a lie by deflating the numbers of their people. The new regime was military, and its might was too fresh in their minds as were also the horrors of the Mahdiya. Heads of tribes knew that the truth was expected; also there was no obvious reason why the heads of villages, at times of severe famines, should not tell the numbers of their people. It may well be that they even exaggerated their numbers because the new government distributed free corn especially imported from India and Egypt, and as further famine relief money was even loaned without interest. Government needed to know the numbers so that famine relief rations might be adequately distributed; at least an approximate answer, therefore, was a matter of life or death. Hence one is even inclined to accept the assumption that the numbers given could well have been higher so that a larger share of grain might be obtained.

In 1905 Sir Reginald Wingate's Report stated: "... including two year's growth in numbers, these figures have more pretence to accuracy.... I think the returns now rendered may safely be taken as a fairly accurate basis on which to build up the statistics of future years."[18]

The population was still estimated at just below two million. The returns for the population of Bahr El Ghazal put the Nilotic tribes at 400,000. Officially, the Governor-General came out for all Sudan at the figure of 1,852,818.

It was not until a year later that Wingate increased the figures for 1906 for all Sudan by 61,000: "... because it was almost impossible to compute the nomad population." The 1906 population for all Sudan was put at 1,913,800.[19] At this stage the sudden migration from West Africa had already started and the presence of the migrants began to be felt not only in Kordofan and the White Nile but as far as Gedaref. It is likely that most of these 61,000 were additional immigrants from West Africa.

At the turn of the century and for many decades the Sudan would have been very meagerly populated had there been no immigration at all. Malaria, yellow fever, and malnutrition, though not very frequently a direct cause of death, continued to be the most important general factors adversely affecting the health of the Sudanese. Smallpox, sleeping sickness, and cerebrospinal meningitis had caused great ravages in all British and French Dependencies. Leprosy affected 1 percent of the population.[20] Venereal diseases and syphillis were a frequent cause of sterility. The space between two children was rarely less than two or three years. Natural growth could have been very low, or perhaps 1 percent at the very highest, during the first fifty years of this century.

Due to immigration, in 1914 the population of the Anglo-Egyptian Sudan was again raised—this time by 400,000 persons, bringing the total to 3,400,000.[21]

In 1916 Sultan Ali Dinar, who had ruled Darfur Province on behalf of the Anglo-Egyptian government of the Sudan, was conquered and Darfur came under Direct Rule.[22] Ali Dinar had not been able to find suitable men to fight, since there was a general condition of malnutrition, if not actual starvation, which was accentuated by poor rainfall not only in Darfur but in all Sub-Sahara Africa. The riverain inhabitants had also suffered severely and a widespread famine had been only partly averted by the government's importing of corn from India,[23] for there was no surplus in Egypt, and this was mainly distributed in the seven towns; almost all of the villages had to go without.

The Sudan Intelligence Service had put Darfur's population at 270,000 in 1903, but at 320,000 in 1913. In 1920 Darfur's population was put at 498,974, including immigrants from the Senegal-Chad-Niger Regions.

During World War I (1914 to 1918) there was no census.

Despite every evidence that the rate of Sudanese natural net annual increase in population was nil or very low, there is a net increase of just under two millions between 1899 and 1914. It is conceivable that both the 1903 and 1913 figures are incorrect by a seriously wide margin. Nevertheless, that statistical inaccuracy and natural growth cannot possibly account for the very sharp rise in the estimated population. We are, therefore, left with the conclusion that probably two million people must have immigrated into the Sudan in the first thirteen years of this century.

The Closed Districts

The Southern Region of the Sudan was divided into three provinces: Fashodah, Mongalla, and Bahr El Ghazal. In 1902 Fashodah Province was renamed Upper Nile and the town of Fashodah became known as Kodok. In 1940 Bahr El Ghazal and Equatoria (the Old Mongalla) were amalgamated and became known as Equatoria Province, until 1948 when Bahr El Ghazal again became a separate province. The British government had decided in 1902 to treat "the South" separately so that it might best be administered by, and become part of, Uganda and possibly Kenya.

From 1922 until 1955 the Closed Districts comprised not only the three Southern Provinces but included the southern districts of Sennar on the Blue Nile and the Nuba Mountains. All these had a population estimated at 585,000 in 1903, but was increased to 1,620,000 persons in 1912.[24] The land area was approximately a third of the total area of all Sudan of one million square miles. The object of that policy was to build up a series of self-contained racial and tribal units with the structure and organization based upon the indigenous customs, traditional usage, and beliefs. The creation of a firm barrier to "Arabization" was considered an essential prerequisite of this absolutely Closed Districts policy.

There appears a marked difference between Lebon/Balamoan's figures on one hand and Barbour on the other[25] (see Table 7-2), but this is easy to explain: Lebon/Balamoan's estimate of 750,000 was for the Nilotic Sudanese only, not all the population of the Closed Districts, which had included politically, all the Nuba Mountains, most of Southern Kordofan and southern Blue Nile Provinces, as stated above. Barbour's and Lebon/Balamoan totals for all Sudan for the same year are in almost complete agreement.

Lebon/Balamoan had put the population of Bahr El Ghazal at 350,000 in 1913. Barbour's 810,000 included immigration from the Congo. Both figures should earn credibility. The reduced figure of 350,000 in 1913 by Balamoan has been for native Sudanese Nilotics excluding any immigrants from the Congo who had been moved to Central Sudan—certainly Balamoan's figures for Central Sudan are higher than Barbour's. It is not unlikely that there has been an even earlier immigration from the Congo, through the Bahr El Ghazal and Equatoria to Central Sudan, as the evidence amply shows. The difference in population for all Sudan in 1913 between Balamoan and Barbour is approximately 28,000, but

Table 7-2
Estimated Population of Sudan by Province 1903-1955

Province	1903 Lebon Balamoan	1907 Barbour	1910 Barbour Lebon Balamoan	1913 Barbour	1913 Lebon Balamoan	1920 Balamoan	1921 Balamoan
Northern	240,000	280,459	260,000	302,067	280,000	354,490	363,969
Khartoum	90,000	140,874	110,000	125,672	115,000	185,184	186,400
Kassala	140,000	158,260	135,000	110,200	160,000	190,603	195,986
Blue Nile	300,000	334,287	400,000	416,600	475,000	551,638	563,838
Kordofan	550,000	486,937	590,000	523,858	635,000	779,944	804,433
Darfur	270,000	—	300,000	—	320,000	498,974	523,924
Total Central and Northern	1,590,000	1,400,817	1,795,000	1,478,397	1,985,000	2,560,833	2,638,550
Bahr El Ghazal	400,000	400,000	315,000	810,000	350,000	1,000,000	1,500,000
Upper Nile	150,000	144,923	200,000	303,470	215,000	323,035	501,346
Equatoria (Mongalla)	(?) 35,000	55,000	150,000	115,000	185,000	228,510	213,270
Total Southern	585,000	599,923	665,000	1,228,470	750,000	1,551,545	2,214,616
Total—All Sudan	2,175,000	2,000,740	2,460,000	2,706,867	2,735,000	4,112,378	4,853,166

(?) The 35,000 given opposite Mongalla in 1903 was the figure for the Lado Enclave and does not represent Mongalla, which was not enumerated by 1903 as a separate unit, but was included with Upper Nile and Bahr El Ghazal, because the provincial boundary was not determined.

The figures for Darfur by Lebon are the guesses of the Sudan Governor-General. Darfur was under Sultan Ali Dinar, it came under direct rule after it was taken over and incorporated within the Anglo-Egyptian Sudan. For a detailed and most interesting account see: A.B. Theobald "Ali Dinar Last Sudan of Darfur 1898-1916" (London: Longmans, 1965).

Balamoan's figures were obtained from the Public Record Office, London, File No. F.O./E.5828/296/16 dated July 7, 1924.

Errors in Arithmetic: In the original document there was a mistake in adding up the 1922 Sudan Population Statistics which gave a total of 5,912,402. The correct sum is 5,842,402.

In adding up the 1932 Professor Barbour's figure should read 5,796,806, not 5,605,806. Professor K.M. Barbour's figures are found in "Population Shifts and Changes in the Sudan Since 1898," *Middle Eastern Studies* 2, 2 (January 1966).

Province	1922 Balamoan	1923 Balamoan	1923 Barbour	1932 Barbour	1936 Barbour	1948 Barbour	1955 Krotki
Northern	369,245	376,697	363,969	376,111	446,695	616,300	873,000
Khartoum	185,181	188,749	186,400	261,852	260,458	329,000	505,000
Kassala	207,419	199,326	195,986	378,067	419,875	717,900	941,000
Blue Nile	507,445	597,524	563,401	1,234,637	1,287,347	1,465,400	2,070,000
Kordofan	910,126	948,946	804,433	1,047,202	1,162,651	1,518,900	1,762,000
Darfur	298,130	460,541	523,924	875,873	715,534	882,800	1,329,000
Total Central and Northern	2,477,546	2,770,583	2,638,113	4,173,742	4,292,560	5,530,300	7,480,000
Bahr El Ghazal	2,500,000	2,500,000	2,500,000	666,495	475,505	714,500	991,000
Upper Nile	569,278	497,118	501,346	607,863	502,163	711,500	889,000
Equatoria	295,578	288,644	213,270	348,706	449,600	590,900	904,000
Total Southern	3,364,856	3,285,762	3,214,616	1,623,064	1,427,268	2,016,900	2,784,000
Total – All Sudan	5,842,402	6,056,345	5,852,729	5,796,806	5,719,828	7,548,200	10,264,000

the difference between us for the three Southern Provinces is approximately 478,470 persons, which I explain as having been caused by immigration from the Congo (see the section on the Congo). As for the reduction in the numbers in 1936, as compared with 1932, this was due to government policy in "repatriating" West Africans, Northern Sudanese Arabs, and French and Belgian Congolese from the Southern Region, and allowing them to settle anywhere they wished in the melting pot of Central and Northern Sudan. We notice from the statistics now collated that there has been a very sharp rise in the numbers of peoples in the Central Sudan while there was a remarkable decrease in the numbers for the three Southern Provinces taking place simultaneously between 1913 and 1936. In addition we should seriously consider the probability that the population in the three Southern Provinces remained static for at least a generation or two—the fact that the birth rate somewhat counterbalanced the average annual mortality rate was itself a sign of success. Nevertheless one should not be puzzled that in 1903 there were 585,000 Southern Sudanese, but that in 1955-56 there were 2,784,000 Southern Sudanese.

It may not be that all of the population in Nilotic Sudan (750,000) or the entire Closed Districts (1,228,000) would have gone to the plantations in the Centre and North, but at least 100,000 working men and women might have done so if they had been given the opportunity to work and earn a better living. We must not forget that the Nilotic Sudanese woman works on equal basis with the man and sometimes even works harder; hence both sexes would have worked on the fields and in the towns or perhaps, with training, in the army, police, and the railways. To speak of a 100,000 persons of working age moving to the Centre and North was more than double the entire unskilled labor requirements of all Sudan until, perhaps, 1940. The artificial "gap" in labor forced the Sudan, including the Sudan Plantation Syndicate, to turn to "other" sources. It may be true that: "the primitive and unsophisticated natives of the Southern Provinces who have little or no economic value and in most cases do not repay the cost of their administration"[26] were not suitable *at that particular time* (1912), but the British Sudan government policy to prohibit natives of the Closed Districts from moving freely within their own country was indefensible. This had indeed created an artificial labor shortage. No doubt special training would have been necessary but so it was also in the case of the Congo-Chad-Niger immigrants. The Vagabonds Ordinance (1905) should have been extended to include the Closed Districts. Thus the Sudan was robbed of half of its original population and forced to accept the settlement of a colossal number of its neighbors' surplus population, the great majority of whom could not contribute much to the National Product. On the other hand there was no doubt that the Muslim North would not have easily tolerated the pagan or Christian Nilotic, but the British administration in the Sudan could have seen to it that any form of prejudice was stamped out rather than give in to a policy which ultimately destroyed the economic and social framework.

To make the Southern Sudan absolutely closed, the policy was pursued on the following lines: the immediate problem faced in regard to this was to eliminate all Northern influence, since this, unless checked, would have spread and increased "Egyptian contamination." And it was at this point that the artificial barriers erected between the North and the Southern Sudan, began: all the Muslim colonies were removed from the Southern Provinces—the Nigerians and some Northern traders who were conservative Mohammedans were removed from such places as Raga and Kaffia Kingi en bloc to Darfur, the Blue Nile, and Kassala. It was announced that the licenses of Northern traders would not be renewed after 1930 and that they would have to leave the Southern Sudan at the latest by January 31, 1931. Orders were issued throughout the Sudan that "Arabs" from the Northern Provinces would not be allowed to enter the three Southern Provinces to trade, hunt or for any other purpose, except under permits, which were usually not given. It was made a punishable offense for natives of the Southern Provinces to visit Central or other Northern Provinces. To create maximum contrast Islam was intensified in the North.

In Bahr El Ghazel any Nilotics living in the Kaffia Kingi area were removed further to the South; Kaffia Kingi itself was abandoned; Raga was removed to its present spot; and no one was allowed to live on the old stations. The result was the falling into decay of Raga and Kaffia Kingi. The more devout Muslims among the Southern police were dismissed; Arabic names were not recognized by the British authorities and the wearing of Northern dress by chiefs and natives was discouraged. Some district commissioners punished anyone who failed to register his name within a fixed date or anyone who continued to use his Arabic name. In these circumstances, a native was given a number, e.g., 1212 or 3131 or 4567, until his tribal name was ascertained or until the evangelical missions could persuade him to accept "James" or "Ephraim" or "Cesar" or "Philip" or even such exotic names as "MacPherson" as an alternative! Northern civil servants and police subordinate to the Mamurs were transferred to the North. Local labor was, therefore, abundant and the forces of supply and demand depressed wages to a piaster or two per day (four cents). The missions were directed by government not to offer high rates of pay.

By 1955, the policy had achieved great success. The Southern Sudanese continued as a separate unit increasing continually by immigration from the Congo, their numbers having risen from 585,000 in 1903 to 2,784,000 in 1955, and had formed an almost independent nation. On the eve of Sudan's political independence (1955-56) the Southern Sudanese declared civil war against the North, which itself was 70 percent West African, demanding complete independence.

The Importation of Congo-Chad-Niger Peoples to Fill Up the Central and Northern Sudan

Contrary to Mather[27] and Barbour's[28] erroneous conclusions that there is no documentary evidence to prove these waves of illegal immigrants from west of the Sudanese Western frontiers, the archives in Kaduna, Ibadan, and Lagos in

Nigeria, and the Public Record Office and the Royal Commonwealth Society's Library in London contained sufficient evidence, albeit scattered and extremely difficult to collect.

Perhaps the first official mention of immigration was given by the governor of Sennar Province (on the Blue Nile), who wrote in 1902 that: "... the population is increasing by immigration."[29] The second mention was by the Kordofan governor, who reported: "... The condition of this Province has greatly improved during the past year. There has been a large increase in population due to extensive immigration...."[30]

The third mention, though completely different, in the same year (1902), which indicates the vigilance of the British administration, but from an opposite direction, was contained in the Berber Province Report: "... The population this year shows an increase of 4,304 souls. The Census has been taken with greater accuracy, and the numbers are probably correct. Among the nomad Arabs there have been a large influx of Rashaidah Arabs from Suakin, who have settled on the Atbara, and have brought with them large numbers of camels...."[31]

In the 1909 Report on Kassala Province, we read that: "... Emigration and immigration was nil, *with the exception of the yearly influx of Hausas, Takruris and Fellattas*, who make Kassala a stay on their journey to Mecca. A great number of them find themselves unable to resist the attraction of Kassala, and take up their abode in it for good, while others complete the pilgrimage, but return to stay. A few families go and come to take up their residence...."

And so the reports of Provincial Governors or Governors-General contained evidence every year. However, I shall conclude with one more item:

In Sudan Monthly Record No. 409, August 1928, under the title, "Immigration From French Territory to Darfur Province":

During the month there has been a large influx of natives of French Equatorial Africa into Dar Masalit and Zalingei District. The immigrants are partly Arabs from Abesher and further west, and partly Masalit and Dago from Adre and Goz Beida. According to native reports this migration is due to intensive tax collecting and other drastic measures on the part of the French authorities, and as the majority of the refugees have left their cultivations behind, some even abandoning their cattle, it may be assumed that the measure of their discontent or their fear is considerable. So far no specific requests for the return of refugees have been received from the French authorities.

Immigration from the Congo

Commenting on the Sudan Population Statistics for 1920, 1921, 1922, and 1923, in July 1924, Mr. P. Nichols at the Foreign Office, London, wrote: "A 50 per cent increase in population in four years seems to me an extraordinarily rapid advance, though a part of this increase must be ascribed to immigration."

But John Murray, policymaker at the Foreign Office, appears to have attempted to cover this extraordinarily rapid advance when he commented against Mr. P. Nichols' remarks, also in July 1924, that: "It was really due to the discovery that Bahr El Ghazal Province was much more thickly populated than had been supposed."[32]

It appears as if there was a gigantic error in the statistics for Bahr El Ghazal Province in the years 1920, 1921, 1922, and 1923, but indeed there was no error. It is now certain that there was unrestricted immigration from the French Congo and the Belgian Congo as well.

However, in Appendix 7 in the Sudan Monthly Intelligence Report dated April 1924, the following passage appeared about French Congo, which sheds light on the approximately two million extra people given for Bahr El Ghazal:

... *NATIVES:* M. Marion, who has had 20 years service in French Equatorial Africa greatly deplored the military administration which was responsible for halving the population in some areas. French military operations ended early in 1923. All the country bordering on the western district (Bahr El Ghazal Province) is uninhabited, i.e., no tribes between D'jale and the boundary or between Yalinga and the boundary.

The Circonscription of Dar Kouti is very sparsely inhabited by (1) a few wandering Fellatta, (2) the remains of the Yulu at D'Jale, (3) a Kara tribe under Chief Aug Abu at Birae and (4) a negroid tribe called Gula, living between Birao and Mamun.

The Circonscription of Haute Kotto is chiefly populated by Banda, with a few isolated Zande colonies, showing various invasions in that direction. Yalinga is that most easterly wedge of territory occupied by Banda. From there going westward Dar Banda broadens out north and south. East of Yalinga was originally inhabited by the Kreish Naka, Kreish of Sharadomo and the Afa, *now all in the Sudan. It has no population at present.*

This is evidence that the population of the three Sudanese Southern Province has indeed increased substantially due to immigration into the Sudan.[33]

In contrast to the above state of demographic policy we notice a different picture about Egyptian labor in the Gezira Scheme: "Work which was being done in the northern area closed down on about June 10, 1928, and all the Egyptian labourers employed on this work were repatriated[a] on the completion of their contracts."[34]

The Elimination of Egyptians and "Contaminated Sudanese and Others" from the Sudan

As a result of the 1919 great rebellion in Egypt and the Sudan against British occupation of the Nile Valley, the official policy of the British government in the Sudan, which previously had been to encourage Egyptian immigration, was

---
[a]Meaning repatriation to Egypt proper.

reversed and all that was Egyptian, or even remotely appertained to anything Egyptian, was reversed. The British government wanted to settle the future status of the Sudan in such a way that Egypt would continue to foot the bill for Sudanese expenditure; that Britain should continue not to pay any money for the Sudan Civil Service or the development of the infrastructure; and that an immediate clean cut from Egypt was necessary, i.e., the elimination of all Egyptians and "contaminated Sudanese," including their families and dependents, and all Egyptian forms of government, and the elimination of all those in the private sector. "The Scheme For The Elimination of Egyptian Personnel Serving in the Sudan," devised by Sir Lee Stack and Sir George Schuster, was put into operation immediately.[35]

The British government then tried to procure evidence on the strength of which it might get rid of the Egyptians, and it was at this state that the assassination of the Sirdar of the Egyptian army and Governor-General of the Sudan, Sir Lee Stack, took place in a street in Cairo. This led to the ill-starred ultimatum—and how well the turn of events suited English policy is evident from the words used by the late Sirdar's daughter: "My father's death is a great loss to us; but the service he rendered to the (British) Government in his death is greater than that which he could have rendered to it living."

However, simultaneously with disturbances in Egypt, rebellion broke out in most cities of the Sudan in 1924. The magnitude of the rebellion showed that a very large number of Sudanese were pro-Egypt and anti-British.[36]

The British administrators in the Sudan were remarkably capable in taking control of the situation with very few British soldiers. British military strength was estimated at that time to have been under 5 percent of the combined Sudanese and Egyptian military and civil strength. With exemplary skill and courage the evacuation of the Egyptian Railway Battalians and their families and dependents from the Sudan was completed by September 20, 1924.[37] This was followed by the evacuation of all the Egyptian army units, including those Sudanese units which were considered contaminated by pro-Egyptian ideas.

In a despatch from the Foreign Office, London, Austin Chamberlain to Field-Marshall Viscount Allenby in Cairo, wrote:

"I noticed with interest a statement in the Sudan Agency Report of the 17th December of last year (enclosed in your despatch No. 776 of the 28th December) to the effect that Egyptians of the non-official class are reported to be leaving the Sudan in considerable numbers. It appears from the report of the 28th December, from the same source (enclosed in your despatch No. 14 of the 14th January) that this movement is taking place simultaneously with a reduction in the numbers of Egyptian civil officials and teachers in the Sudan.

2. It is satisfactory that the removal of the Egyptian troops to Egypt should be reflected so soon in a similar movement of the Egyptian civilian population. The sudden ejection of a mass of officials would no doubt create a number of unnecessary and unwelcome problems for the Sudan Government, but I am very definitely of the opinion that the policy of that Government should tend to the

eventual elimination of all Egyptian officials from the Sudan. There should be no undue haste, neither should there be any relaxation of this process.

3. In the meantime I shall be glad to learn what has been done in the matter particularly in regard to teachers, the danger of whose presence is admirably brought out in the report of the Acting Governor, Khartoum Province, enclosed in your Lordship's despatch No. 16 of the 6th instant. (Signed) Austin Chamberlain."[38]

The New Military Regime in Sudan decided upon the disbandment of the remaining "contaminated" Sudanese units (Nilotics and Nuba), and arrangements made for disposal of disbanded men was contained in a report from Sudan Agency Cairo to the First Secretary, the Residency, Cairo, dated January 9, 1925. The correspondence showed that the governor of Nuba Mountains Province preferred that the discharged soldiers should be dispersed among the hills and not allowed to settle together in a colony. These discharged Nuba proceeded in seven parties at intervals according to the arrangements that could be made for their dispersal.

What Was the Number of Eliminated Egyptians?

Something of a multiplier effect appears to have been triggered by "The Scheme for the Elimination of Egyptian Personnel Serving in the Sudan." In a fairly close knit community, in a vast but still sparsely populated region, the elimination of friends and relatives had a significant impact upon those remaining behind. They considered that those eliminated were not only innocent, but that because the Sudan was Egypt's southern province and financed with Egyptian taxpayers' money, the British administration in the Sudan, supposedly working on behalf of Egypt, had no right to eject any Egyptian out of "his home." However, it was not long before most of the undecided members, inspired by a "hero's welcome" in Egypt or by imagined economic as well as cultural-psychological motives, and those afraid of one thing or another, joined the exodus. The result was to add momentum to an already panicky situation.

The numbers of men, women, and children who accompanied the head of the family to Egypt has not yet been ascertained. However, it may be reasonably assumed that each breadwinner had a very large family, which included on an average five children plus his own wife, his (and/or his wife's) mother and father, and in many cases "a relation"; all these constituted on an average an extended family of ten members. If the total eliminated from the Sudan was 400,000, as given by Egyptian sources, then the number of chief breadwinners *in all occupations* could be safely estimated at 40,000, which is a reasonable figure.

In addition to those who had officially declared themselves "contaminated

Sudanese," the British government in the Sudan eliminated all those who were "white" or "light brown" and had them despatched to Egypt proper. There are no precise statistical data about these, but judging from the many persons interviewed, the number could be put at 110,000 individuals who belonged to perhaps 11,000 chief breadwinners. This figure included Syrians, Greeks, Nilotics, and other Negroes who were sympathetic with pro-Egyptian sentiments.

It appears, therefore, that more than half a million women, children, and men were eliminated from the Anglo-Egyptian Sudan within three months and at the expense of Egypt.[39]

The Era of Sir John Maffey

Sir John Maffey, the successor to Sir Lee Stack and Sir Geoffrey Archer, as Governor-General of the Sudan, supported by the Financial Secretary, Sir George Schuster, tenaciously held that:

... I agree under certain conditions to the return of an Egyptian Battalion. I am opposed to the return of Egyptian Personnel to a share in the administration.... A Battalion is a unit. It is not an infiltration. A tooth can be pulled out. Blood poisoning is a more serious matter.... When we first occupied the Sudan thirty years ago it was natural that in the early years we should use Egyptians in the administration in all its branches. We used Egyptians because there was nobody else. We did not use them in the higher grades of service. Makram Ebeid is totally wrong in stating that at the date of the 1899 Convention there was an Egyptian Sub-Governor General, Egyptian Members of Council and Egyptian Mudirs.[40] No such appointments were held by Egyptians. Thirty years have passed and the need for employing Egyptians has become less and less. The Sudanese have developed consciousness of their own claims and the ability to realise them.

Let me call attention here to one very vital consideration: throughout all the early years of our occupation of the Sudan, the British were in full control of Egypt and of everything Egyptian. Consequently all Egyptian employees in those days were subservient to British policy and to British masters. An Egyptian looked to his British Officer for credit and promotion. As Egyptian Nationalism developed they have naturally all become keen Egyptians. For Egypt has a declared policy in the Sudan, namely to hasten the day when the Sudan shall return to its normal position as an ordinary Egyptian Province."[41]

In the year before the above took place, Sir John Maffey wrote to Sir Ronald Lindsay, Foreign Office, London: "My conviction is that it is the right policy to maintain the Condominium, though I would not give Egypt more than the "shadow without the substance"—the phrase with which you closed our interview on June 13, 1929."

The final conclusion to these tedious and fruitless discussions was the inclusion in the new Anglo-Egyptian Treaty of 1936, of a provision that

Egyptian citizens could enter the Sudan, but as a matter of fact, the application of this new treaty was as much honored by Great Britain as the 1899 treaty.

In 1952 Nasser took over power in Egypt, recognized that the Sudan was lost to Egypt, and effectively hastened Sudan's independence from both Great Britain and Egypt.

*The Economic Problems of the
Development of the Infrastructure
in Sudan 1895-1940*

In 1884, General Gordon wrote: "The Soudan is a useless possession, ever was so, and ever will be so." Colonel Stewart added: "I quite agree with General Gordon that the Soudan is an expensive and useless possession."

By contrast, in 1903, Lord Cromer summed up the situation that:

"... without incurring a charge of excessive optimism it may be anticipated that, with the judicious expenditure of capital and continuous application of a system of government, such as that which is now being very skillfully directed by Sir Reginald Wingate and his staff, the future of the country will be far less gloomy than was predicted by the two high authorities quoted above. But progress will be slow."[42]

The possession of the Sudan in 1899, must have seemed likely to prove a white elephant. The following quotation from Harold MacMichael in "The Sudan" explains the economic situation in 1898:

The state of the Sudan was in every way deplorable. Its population had fallen during the Dervish regime from over 8,500,000 to less than 2,000,000 as a result of famine, disease and inter-nicine warfare. Whole villages had been obliterated, cultivation was at a standstill, flocks and herds had been destroyed, date palms cut down; slave raiding was rampant, and there was no security for life or property. Revolts and savage reprisals had left a legacy of bitter feuds, hatred and suspicion in every district. Little tribal authority survived except among those nomadic tribes, such as the Kababish, which lived in areas inaccessible to the Khalifa's soldiery.[43]

In a "Memorandum Respecting the Reaction of Recent Events in Egypt on the Financial Position of the Sudan," the following statement appeared: "Whilst Egypt was a British Protectorate, either virtual or avowed, an arrangement was possible under which we dictated the policy to be followed in the Sudan, whilst Egypt paid for it."[44]

It is clear that the Egyptian government, acting under the guidance of its British advisers, accepted the responsibility for financing such capital expenditure as might prove necessary for providing means of communications for "strategic" purposes, and for developing the country's resources, so as to hasten the day when it could pay for its own administration.

The Civil Subvention. This subvention represented money paid by Egypt to the Sudan government in order to make good any deficit in expenditure on current civil administration over and above revenue collected in the Sudan.

The amount voted for this purpose in the Egyptian government budget was originally fixed on the basis of the Budget Estimates of the Sudan Government. It is clear, from an examination of what actually happened, that the intention in the first years was that the amount granted should be adjusted to cover the actual deficit in the Sudan government's expenditure for any year. If the actual deficit proved larger than the amount voted by Egypt on the basis of the Sudan Budget Estimates, the deficiency was made up by a subsequent supplementary vote, while, conversely, if the vote proved to be larger than the realized deficit the surplus was intended to be refunded by the Sudan government.

From 1902 on, a different understanding appears to have been arrived at. A definite sum seems to have been allotted for each year as the Egyptian contribution to the Sudan current expenses. The amount of such sum was roughly adjusted to the requirements of the Sudan, but the Sudan government was allowed to retain for its own purposes any surplus realized from its total receipts, i.e., its own revenues and the Egyptian contribution combined.

The British Treasury said that the Egyptian Treasury had always debited to the Sudan with the amounts already mentioned, i.e., the sums required to make good the budget deficits, and with the calculated additional cost of maintaining the Egyptian army in the Sudan.

Initially for the reconquest of the Sudan, approximately $10 million was paid by Egypt to equip the 25,000 men of the Egyptian army, including a British contingent of 8,000 men.[4,5] This $10 million did not include the cost of food required by the soldiers, and so perhaps over a period of four years $4 million could have been expended, a sum which included supplies to the starving inhabitants wherever the Anglo-Egyptian army restored law and order. Towards this amount of approximately $14 million Great Britain advanced $3,200,000 as a loan against Egypt's repayment. By 1936 the Egyptian bookkeeping showed that they had expended about $260 million on both capital and on variable expenses, of which nothing was repaid.

The full cost of all military and police expenditure in the Sudan was borne by Egypt from time immemorial to 1955. Between approximately 1946 and 1954 military aid was negligible and was concerned with maintaining three Egyptian garrisons only. Despite the fact that aid and fines varied in quantity between 1925 and 1954, by 1925 the Sudan was able to stand on its own feet, having a good civil service, a fast rising immigrant population, established railways and steamers and communications, a clean water supply in the mushrooming towns and cities, model plantation schemes, and cheap fuel. The financial aid for capital and recurrent requirements was discontinued only when the Sudan gained independence in January 1956, and still continued where education and Islamic religion were concerned.

The Republic of the Sudan 1956-1974

The Consequences of Indiscriminate Migration and High Net Annual Natural Growth Rate

The Republic of the Sudan is a young country, too young perhaps to be called a nation as yet. When it has become a nation, however, as a result of this immigration it will probably become a nation predominantly West African in character and population. Thus the West African immigration into the Sudan will have resulted not in the immigrant being swallowed up by his new country but in his swallowing it.

Thanks to Egyptian money, Arabic has now become the lingua franca of Muslim Africa both north and south of the Sahara. Since Nasser came to power in 1952 the Arab world will accept as an Arab any person who speaks Arabic, irrespective of color or race. As soon as a Negro or a European or even a Chinese starts learning Arabic and settles in an Arab land, he ceases to be thought of as a Negro or European or Chinese and becomes an Arab.

The development of the Sudan and the improvement in the quality of life depends in good part on the solutions which we should be able to apply to the problem of unrestricted entry. There is urgent need to arrest the accumulating social and economic pressures which impose an almost insuperable challenge on the infrastructure.

The net annual natural increase is a phenomenon without precedent in the history of the Sudan. At 3 percent net annual natural increase, at least 639,000 children were added to the population in 1974; of whom 70 percent, i.e., 447,300 are the children of immigrants. The remaining 191,700 are children of "pre-1900 Sudanese." In addition to the above figure (of 639,000) we must add the minimum annual average 125,000 immigrants—this is based on long-term immigration trend, though in 1974 alone over one million persons migrated into the Sudan from the Niger-Senegal Regions alone.[46] Therefore, to have a minimum 764,000 additional inhabitants, subject to further increases each year (though in 1974 alone the population of Sudan increased by under two million persons) is trouble on a very large scale for the infrastructure in Sudan as well as the social relations among individuals.

There have been over nine national Sudanese governments in the eighteen years since independence, but all have failed to control in-migration of unskilled labor. The Sudanese government does not control inter-country migration and as a result the towns and cities are crowded with the unemployed. Historically at least, in respect to inter-country migration, the British Imperial Administration successfully prevented movement of excess populations to the towns and cities, thus confining unwanted surplus to the villages.

The government of the Southern Region is eager to increase the population in the three southern provinces. Rumor has it that the result of the 1973

Population Census was not made public because, among other problems, the Government of the Southern Region refused to acknowledge that the inhabitants under its jurisdiction were about 1.5 million.[b] They maintain that their number is five or six million. The immigration "policy" in the south as in the north permits any person from all countries around the Southern Region to enter and settle as long as the color is distinctly negroid.

I have not seen an improvement in the quality of life in my country and I am sure that there will be none in the foreseeable future unless, among other equally very important factors, the doors are closed against the entry of the indigent of surrounding countries. I would even propose the immediate repatriation of all those who drifted in since, say, 1936? Their own governments should take care of them; Ghana and several other African governments expelled 'aliens.' However, this is unlikely to happen because, as this investigation has shown, most of those who make up the Sudan and the Sudan government are the descendants of the migrants, and the "melting pot" makes it impossible to distinguish who is who on an ethnic basis. To understand the policy of the elite one must understand that the governing social class is itself the product of the policies which the British pursued during the early part of this century.

No Sudanese government considers the Sudan anything but severely underpopulated. Hence a family planning policy does not exist to reduce the birthrate in Sudan, and even if family planning is thought of, it is unlikely to succeed in a land where more than 90 percent of the population is illiterate. Such is the tragedy on the Nile; it has to be seen to be understood.

Notes

1. Donald George Morrison, et al., *Black Africa: A Comparative Handbook* (New York: The Free Press, 1972).

2. "The Population of Sudan," Report of the Sixth Annual Conference, Philosophical Society of Sudan, pp. 48-53. (Khartoum: Ministry for Social Affairs, Population Census Office, 1958.)

3. K.J. Krotki, "21 Facts About the Sudanese," First Population Census 1955-56, p. 23. (Khartoum: Ministry for Social Affairs, Population Census Office, 1958.)

4. I.M. Mansour, Sudan Minister of Finance, reported by *Chicago Daily News* and *Boston Globe*, October 17, 1974.

5. Lebon, *Land Use in the Sudan*, (Geographical Publications Ltd. Monograph No. 4, 1965), pp. 152-158.

6. Rudolf Carl Slatin, *Fire and Sword in the Sudan 1879-1895*, (London, New York: Edward Arnold, 1896), Chapter 4, pp. 128, 129.

[b]The Central government in Khartoum encourages migration from the South to Northern Sudan in an effort to cause assimilation in "the melting pot" through Arabic and Islam.

7. Winston Churchill, *The River War*, Volume I, (London: Longmans, Green & Co., 1899), Chapters 6 and 10, pp. 313-322.

8. Lebon, *Land Use in the Sudan*, (Geographical Publications Ltd. Monograph No. 4, 1965), p. 159, Figure 36, "The Increase of Domestic Animals in Sudan 1920-60."

9. Lord Cromer's Report: Egypt, No. 3, 1899. In report by Her Brittanic Majesty's Agent and Consul-General on Finance, Administration and Condition of Egypt and Soudan in 1898, p. 6.

10. Her Brittanic Majesty's Agent and Consul-General for Egypt and the Sudan Report, 1903.

11. Ibid.

12. Ibid., (Cd. 1951-1904), pp. 79-81; Ibid., 1899 (Cd. 95-1900) p. 44; 1901 (Cd. 1012-1902); 1904 (Cd. 2409-1905) 1.115; Count Gleichen, *The Anglo-Egyptian Sudan: A Compendium Prepared by Officers of the Sudan Government*, 1905, Volume I, p. 106 (for Gedaref) and p. 177 (for Central Kordofan).

13. Lebon, *Land Use in the Sudan*, p. 157.

14. Kenneth David Druit Henderson, *Sudan Republic*, (London: E. Benn Ltd. 1965), p. 45.

15. Lebon, *Land Use in the Sudan*, p. 157.

16. Ibid.

17. H. Macmichael, *The Sudan*, (London: E. Benn Ltd., 1954), Chapter 9 on "The Administration, Policy and System," pp. 102-119.

18. Sudan Governor-General's Report, 1905, p. 30.

19. Sudan Governor-General's Report, 1906, p. 12; Rushdi Henin, "Second Thoughts on Sudan's Population Census," in J.C. Caldwell and C. Okonjo (eds.), *The Population of Tropical Africa*, (New York: Columbia University Press, 1968), pp. 142-151 but particularly p. 146.

20. Robert Rene Kuczynski, *Demographic Survey of the British Colonial Empire*, Volume I (London: Oxford University Press, 1948-53), p. 12.

21. Sudan Governor-General's Report, 1914, p. 10.

22. Harold Macmichael, *The Anglo-Egyptian Sudan*, (London: Faber & Faber Ltd., 1934), Chapter XI; A.B. Theobald, *Ali Dinar Last Sultan of Darfure 1898-1916*, (London: Longman's, 1965).

23. Macmichael, *The Anglo-Egyptian Sudan*, p. 117.

24. Sudan Governor-General's Report Khartoum, 1912, pp. 23-24.

25. K.M. Barbour, "Population Shifts and Changes in the Sudan Since 1898," *Middle Eastern Studies* 2, no. 2 (January 1966).

26. Sudan Governor-General's Report Khartoum, 1912, pp. 23-24.

27. D.B. Mather, "Migration in the Sudan," in R.W. Steel and C.A. Fisher (eds.), *Geographical Essays in British Tropical Lands* (1956), pp. 115-143.

28. Barbour, "Population Shifts and Changes in the Sudan Since 1898."

29. Sudan Governor-General's Report, 1902, p. 83.

30. Ibid., p. 87.
31. Ibid., p. 84.
32. Public Record Office, London, PRO/FO/E 5828/296/16 dated July 7, 1924.
33. Public Record Office, London, PRO/FO/371-13880 (1929).
34. Sudan Monthly Report No. 407, dated June 1928.
35. Allenby to Curzon PRO/FO/E 2889/93/16 dated March 24, 1920.
36. PRO/FO/371/10053 and 10054 (1924).
37. PRO/FO/E. 8366/735/16 (1924).
38. PRO/FO/J. 173/2/16 dated January 26, 1925, No. 96.
39. PRO/FO/371/13140.
40. PRO/J/1070/4/16, dated April 1, 1930; Makram Ebeid: "Egypt and the Sudan," Confidential Print.
41. PRO/J/1882/4/11 dated June 12, 1930.
42. Reports by Her Brittanic Majesty's Agent and Consul-General of Egypt and the Sudan in 1903, p. 99.
43. Macmichael, *The Sudan*, pp. 15 and 73-74.
44. Circular to British Cabinet dated December 31, 1924, PRO/E. 11772/73 and PRO/FO/371/10055, pages 1 and 2.
45. Churchill, *The River War*, Volume II, (London: Longmans, Green & Co., 1899), Chapter 26.
46. I.M. Mansour, Sudan Minister of Finance, reported by *Chicago Daily News* and *Boston Globe*, October 17, 1974.

8

Migration and Fertility in Indonesia

Mayling Oey

When Indonesia conducted its second census of population in 1971, valuable retrospective data were collected on children ever born and surviving children. Although these data provide the basis for only crude estimates of fertility and mortality, this information is important for the understanding of the present demographic situation in Indonesia, where no complete vital registration system is available and hence no accurate demographic parameters can be determined.

Fertility patterns are indicative of the diversity which characterizes Indonesia. Not only are regionally different patterns of fertility observed, but there are also notable differences when women are categorized according to their migration status. A significant difference can be observed when the fertility pattern among migrant women in Lampung, of whom most were born on Java (65%) and came to the province under the auspices of the Transmigration Program, is compared to the fertility pattern of primarily Javanese women residing on Java.[a] The objectives of this chapter are therefore to present a comparative analysis of social determinants of fertility among migrants and non-migrants in Lampung and Javanese on Java. Second, to examine the impact of the transmigration program on fertility and third, to analyze the implications of high fertility among migrants on development of the province.

Before embarking on the analysis however, the following section will be devoted to a description of the Transmigration Program.

The Transmigration Program

The Transmigration Program is the implementation of a government policy whereby people from high density areas are transferred to more sparsely inhabited areas. In its implementation the program largely involves resettling people from Java and Bali to the other islands.

The discrepancy between the densely populated island of Java, which covers

---

I am greatly indebted to Dr. Gordon Temple, who kindly tabulated the data for this chapter, and to Drs. W. Ilchman, J. Fox, Djunaedi Hadisumarto, and Peter McDonald, whose valuable criticisms and editorial comments have greatly improved this chapter.

[a]Although only people from Central Java, Jogyakarta, and East Java are considered Javanese and those from West Java are Sundanese, for purposes of this chapter I will refer to everybody from Java as Javanese.

only 7% of the total land area, but is inhabited by 65% of the total population, and the vast and empty spaces in the outer islands has been recognized for a long time. The idea of moving people from overcrowded Java to the outer islands was considered by Sir Thomas Raffles as early as 1814 and by DeBois de Gesignes in 1827 (Swasono 1970). There was a growing concern about population pressures on Java among various individuals toward the end of the last century. An investigation held in 1903 indicated there was already a fairly large landless peasant class and a very large proportion of the population who were owners of very small plots of land, not sufficient to support a family (Pelzer 1948, pp. 166-67). Rapid population growth on Java has resulted in a growing landless class. Jay (1956), in a study done during the early fifties, reported that approximately 50% of the families of a typical village were landless and 20% had only 1-1.25 acres. In 1963 it was estimated that 60% of the agricultural laborers were landless (Peraturan Dasar 1962, p. 14). Acknowledgment of the problems of population pressures on Java and awareness of the contrasting densities have led officials for decades to seek a solution by moving people from overcrowded Java to the outer islands. In 1905 the Netherlands Indies government designed a program of colonization. After independence the Indonesian government resumed the program, which from then on has been referred to as the Transmigration Program.

When the Indonesian government resumed the program in 1950, the primary objective remained the reduction of population pressures on Java. Various overly ambitious plans were designed and unrealistic targets were determined[b] during the fifties and early sixties. Consequently, the targets set during the past two decades were not achieved. While the plans called for resettling several hundred thousands annually during the fifties, the average achievement was about 25 thousand per annum; the fluctuations may be statistical artifacts rather than real trends (see Table 8-1). During the first half of the decade of the sixties the data show an increasing number of transmigrants being resettled. Here again the drop in 1964 may be due to erroneously compiling the data for the years 1963-65. On the other hand, the drop in 1966-67 indicates a real drop as a consequence of severe social and economic disturbances during the mid-sixties. Thereafter, during the First Five Year Development Plan (REPELITA) of 1969-74, there is again an increasing trend in number of government sponsored settlers, and the largest number of transmigrants was achieved during the past budget year 1973-74.

During the 1950s the Transmigration Service of the Department of Social Welfare was responsible for the implementation of the program. At that time transmigration was considered a social welfare mechanism. Consequently, the same scheme, as first implemented by the Dutch, was followed. The government carried almost full responsibility of resettlement. Most of the migrants are either

---

[b]A detailed description of the plans can be found in H.J. Heeren, *Het Land aan de Overkant*, J.A. Boom en Zoon, Uitgevers te Meppel, 1967: 25-30.

Table 8-1
Number of Transmigrants Between 1951-1974

Year	Number of Transmigrants	Year	Number of Transmigrants
1951	2,944	1961	19,609
1952	17,605	1962	22,169
1953	40,008	1963	32,109
1954	29,838	1964	15,222
1955	21,389	1965	53,362
1956	25,549	1966	4,648
1957	20,045	1967	6,166
1958	20,603	1968	13,742
1959	46,096		
1960	22,078	1969-70	17,848
		1970-71	19,995
		1971-72	18,870
		1972-73	51,918
		1973-74	82,873

Sources: 1951-1968, Report published by the Departemen Transkop, Realisasi Penempatan Transmigrasi 1951-1968, Jakarta, 1973.

1969-74 is based on the budget year which starts on April 1 and ends on March 31 the following year, in *Konsep Pertama Rencana Transmigrasi Pelita II, Tahun 1974-78*, Departemen Tenaga Kerja, Transmigrasi dan Kooperasi, Diroktorat Jendral Transmigrasi, Jakarta, p. 3.

fully or partially supported by the government. Though far simpler, recruitment criteria are the same as those determined by the Dutch. The applicant has to be: (a) an Indonesian citizen; (b) married, in good health, and between the ages of eighteen and forty-five; and (c) their wives may not be pregnant or have an infant of less than six months of age. In 1965 a new requirement was added: (d) the applicant may not have been involved in the 1965 September Coup (Heeren 1967, p. 39; Demographic Factbook 1973, p. 165). Furthermore, under the Transmigration Program migrants are to be given one-fourth ha. for their house and vegetable garden, one ha. of *sawah* and three-fourths ha. of *ladang* (Heeren 1967, p. 66).

It was later felt that transmigration alone would not improve the well-being of the migrants. Combined with the political environment, which was strongly in favor of the development of cooperatives, the conditions were conducive for the establishment of an independent department. Hence, in 1960 the Department of Transmigration and Cooperatives was established. During that time the studies which indicated the futility of transmigration as the solution to population pressures were given greater attention. Professor Widjojo, for instance, stressed the importance of a reduction in fertility rather than outmigration (Nitisastro 1970, pp. 231-35).

When it became less practical to consider transmigration as the only means to alleviate overpopulation in Java, and the emphasis shifted from a Java-centered concern to a nationwide interest, additional objectives, such as promotion of economic development, security, and national unity, were given equal weighting (McNicoll 1968, p. 65). Since the present government took over, in conjunction with the worldwide orientation toward social and economic development, Indonesia has adopted a similar orientation. Transmigration is no longer considered independently but rather as part of the national development scheme. In 1973 another administrative consolidation took place with the Department of Manpower and the new department was named the Department of Manpower, Transmigration and Cooperatives.

The shift in status of the implementing agency should be indicative of changing goals. However, the discrepancy in density between Java and the outer islands remains a rationale for moving excessive labor out of Java to the outer islands where there is an unfulfilled demand for labor. The First Five Year Development Plan (REPELITA) of 1969/70-1973/74 continues to state the objective of transmigration as population redistribution and manpower supply for development (113-15). This persistent orientation is considering transmigration as a social welfare mechanism is also indicated by the aims of transmigration as stated in a transmigration workshop held in 1971:

1. to increase production and the income of the farmer;
2. to widen employment opportunities and community welfare;
3. to increase awareness, order and security on a national scale;
4. to distribute population more evenly (Basic Formulations of the Transmigration Workshop 1971, p. 4).

Consequently, the emphasis in implementing transmigration remains in designing ways and means by which the government is directly involved in the Javanese migration process (Tavanlar 1971). Such a preoccupation leaves little room for recognition of the success achieved by the Dutch under the *bawon* system (sharecropping). Furthermore, although it has been pointed out that it is more important to stimulate a spontaneous migration flow,[c] initiated by the government sponsored program (Keyfitz 1964), this phenomenon does not seem to have received sufficient attention.

Because of the emphasis on the sending areas, little attention has been paid to the growth of the receiving areas. Lampung, for instance, which has the longest history of resettlement and continues to be the most important transmigration area (see Tavanlar 1971), had the highest intercensal growth rate in the country. Transmigration has certainly been a significant contributor to Lampung's high

---
[c]In this chapter, spontaneous migrants are those who come to the transmigration areas with no aid from the government but are eligible to claim land after arrival in the transmigration regions.

growth rate. However, apart from population growth due to migration, the rate of natural increase is one of the highest in the country. Between 1961-1971 the growth rate which may be attributed to natural increase was 2.9%.[d]

Further evidence is shown by the data in Table 8-2. The average number of children ever born to a woman between the ages of fifteen and forty-nine is the highest in Lampung. This is hardly surprising considering that Lampung has such a large migrant population (those born in another province), most of whose members are concentrated in the high fertility age group. It is surprising to note, however, that the age specific fertility pattern of migrants is very similar to the pattern of nonmigrants in Lampung, but significantly different from the pattern of Javanese women residing on Java (see Figure 8-3). It is this striking phenomenon which will be analyzed in this chapter.

Comparative Analysis of Social Determinants of Differential Fertility

The Data Collection System

The data for this chapter are computed from a 10% subsample of the 3.8% sample of enumeration blocks, which varied in size from 60-125 households in rural Java and 30-70 households elsewhere. The sample was stratified by *Nabupaten* (regency) and *kotamadya* (municipality). For each strata enumeration blocks were selected by systematic random sampling (Suharto et al., pp. 5-6).

The data on fertility are derived from the data collected from ever married women ten years and over, who were asked questions on the number of children they had born alive and children still living. With data collected in this manner there are, of course, noticeable flaws, such as:

1. Based on the assumption that in a traditional society, like Indonesia, where more than 90% of the people profess Islam, illegitimacy is nonexistent and therefore ignored.

2. As in any other data collection system on vital events, there will be an undercount of both infant births and deaths due to difficulty in definition of when an infant is alive. In Indonesia there may be an even more excessive undercount because infants are not named until at least seven days after birth, to keep evil spirits away (Geertz 1960, p. 47).

The above mentioned shortcomings in the data point to the possible underenumeration. Hence the data to be analyzed in this chapter are indicators of lower rather than upper limits.

---

[d]In 1961 the population in Lampung numbered 1,667,511 while in 1971 it was 2,223,838. There were approximately 553,000 net-migrants during that period. Using the formula $P_t = P_o e^{rt}$, where P_t is the population at time t and P_o is the population at the base year, r equals 2.9%, which includes, of course, the excess of births over deaths of the migrants.

Table 8-2
Average Number of Children Ever Born to Women Aged 15-49 by Province, Indonesia 1971

Province	Average Number of Children Ever Born
Java	3.10
Jakarta	2.83
West Java	3.63
Central Java	3.08
Jogjakarta	2.67
East Java	2.78
Sumatra	3.46
Aceh	3.20
North Sumatra	3.37
West Sumatra	3.65
Riau	3.08
Jambi	3.37
South Sumatra	3.52
Bengkulu	3.52
Lampung	3.83
Kalimantan	3.12
West Kalimantan	3.07
Central Kalimantan	3.38
South Kalimantan	3.14
East Kalimantan	2.98
Sulawesi	3.04
North Sulawesi	3.10
Central Sulawesi	2.93
South-east Sulawesi	3.07
Other Islands	2.92
Bali	2.76
West Nusa Tenggara	3.42
East Nusa Tenggara	2.45
Maluku	3.17
West Irian	3.12
Indonesia	3.14

Source: Biro Pusat Statistik, unpublished 1971 census of population tabulations.

Concerning mortality, crude measures of mortality are indirectly estimated from the responses to the questions concerning number of children ever born and surviving children. Brass et al. have developed a technique to estimate mortality from these data. According to this technique estimates can be made on the proportion of children ever born who died before reaching ages 1, 2, 3, 5, 10, 15, ..., 35, from the proportion reported as surviving among children ever born to women aged 15-19, 20-24, 25-29, ..., 60-64 (1968, pp. 104-139; United Nations Manual IV 1967).

The census questionnaire included a question concerning one's migration status. Further information was ascertained on province of last residence and duration of stay in present province of residence. Such data do not of course allow identification of intraprovince movements. Although these shortcomings are regrettable, they will not affect the analyses in this chapter.

Due to high repeater rates it was considered more appropriate to collect data on highest level of schooling attained as indicated by letter of completion or certificate. An individual's attained level of education was categorized as follows: no school, not yet finished elementary school, elementary school, general junior high school, vocational junior high school, general senior high school, vocational senior high school, academy, university. Such a classification is unjustified, especially at higher levels of education, because according to such a definition of level of attained education, those who do not graduate with a certificate are classified downward. Thus, a university student is classified as having finished high school only.

The Data Analysis

The 1971 census enumerated 2,777,020 persons in Lampung. Of this number 1,430,000, or 51.5%, were females and 1,347,000 were males. Lampung has a very young population; 49.2% of the population is under fifteen and 63.5% under twenty-five years of age. Being the major recipient area for transmigrants, Lampung has a large migrant population, where 997,028 or 35% of the total population in the province were migrants. A commonly found characteristic among migrants is that the migrating unit consists of a young married couple with small children (Petersen 1969, p. 262; Heer 1968, pp. 71-72). The two peaks representing the young adults and small children can be seen in Figure 8-1. This representation of the age at which migrants arrived in Lampung differs, of course, significantly from their ages during the census. The age and sex distribution of the migrant population in 1971, which is shown in Figure 8-2, is quite different from Figure 8-1. This striking difference between these two population pyramids is that while the largest age group in Figure 8-1 represents children between the ages 0-4, in Figure 8-2 this cohort is very small. The very narrow base in Figure 8-2 is not surprising, considering that this age group represents only those arrivals during the previous four years. Because many migrants are young adults and still in their reproductive ages, they are still capable and do have more children after arrival in Lampung. Consequently, these children are nonmigrants, who in addition to the children of nonmigrant parents constitute an excessively large age cohort of nonmigrant children (see Figure 8-3). This very large cohort of children is indicative of high fertility among women in Lampung.

224

[Population pyramid chart]

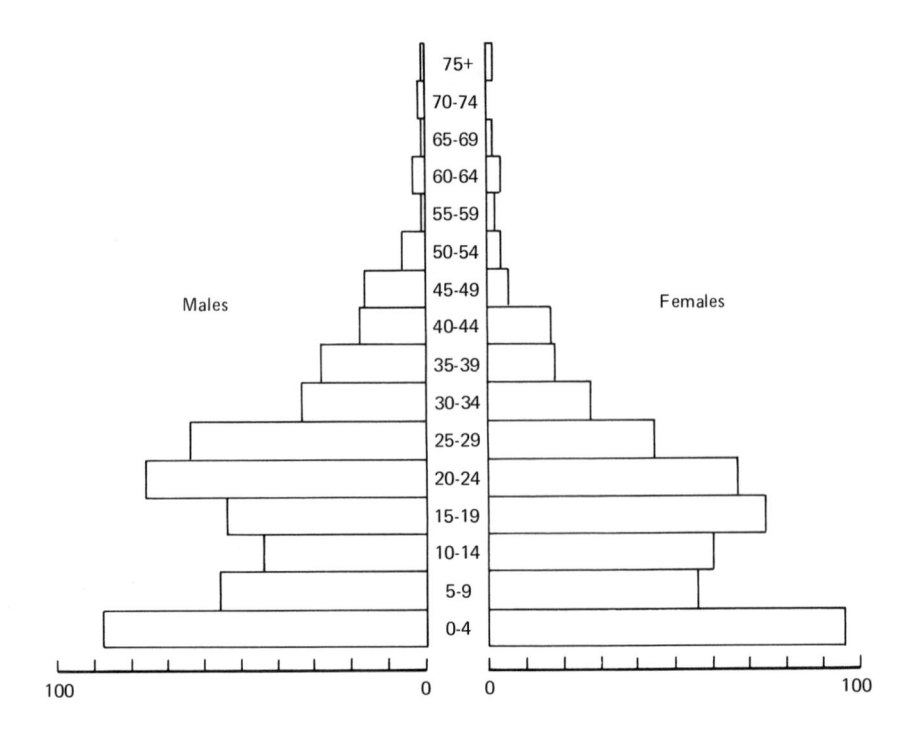

Figure 8-1. Age at Migration into Lampung (in thousands). Source: Based on Biro Pusat Statistik, unpublished 1971 census of population tabulations.

Although the data do not allow for a separation between children born to migrant women from those born to non-migrant women, it was possible to compute separate age specific average numbers of children ever born. It is interesting to note, in Figure 8-4, that up to age 35 migrant women have higher fertility than nonmigrant women. Compared to nonmigrant women, who continue their high fertility pattern throughout their reproductive ages, the pattern for migrant women shows a dip for the age group 40-44 and ends up with a slightly higher rate for those aged 45-49 than nonmigrant women of the same cohort. A similar pattern was found by Goldstein, who compared nonmigrants to life time migrants in rural agricultural areas of residence in Thailand (1973, p. 234). Compared to predominantly Javanese women on Java, the largely Javanese migrant women in Lampung have far higher age specific fertility rates and this difference increases with age.

Differential fertility can be explained by differences in number of children ever born to ever married women or proportions ever married women (Figure

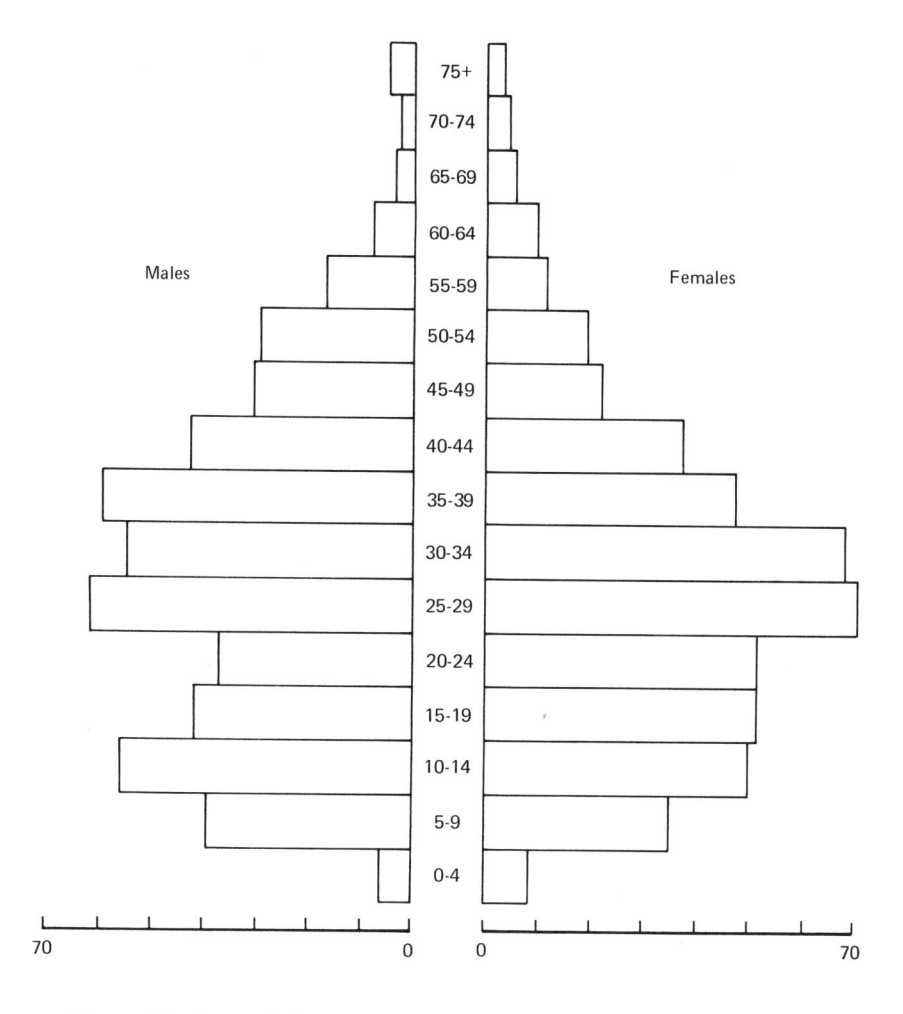

Figure 8-2. Age and Sex Distribution of Migrants in Lampung 1971 (in thousands). Source: Based on Biro Pusat Statistik, unpublished 1971 census of population tabulations.

8-5 and Table 8-3). Of these two components, the number of children ever born to ever married women better explains the differences in Figure 8-4. Migrant women show slightly lower age specific numbers of children ever born to ever married women than nonmigrant women, while Javanese women have for all age groups the lowest number of children ever born to ever married women. Not only are age specific numbers of children ever born to ever married women highest among migrant women, but so are the proportions ever married largest

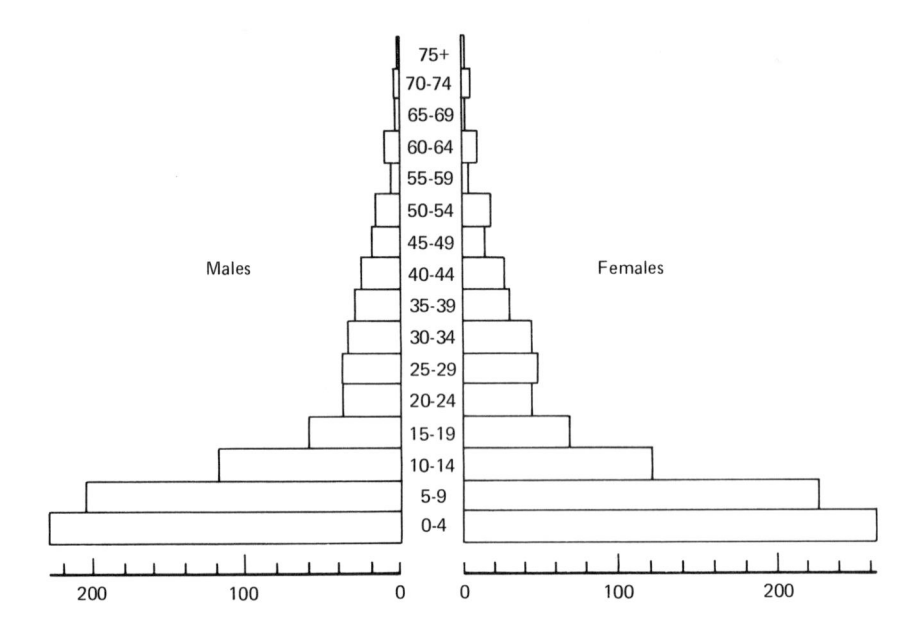

[Population pyramid showing age groups from 0-4 to 75+ with Males on left and Females on right, scale 0 to 200+ thousands]

Figure 8-3. Age and Sex Distribution of Nonmigrants in Lampung, 1971 (in thousands). Source: Based on Biro Pusat Statistik, unpublished 1971 census of population tabulations.

among migrant women. While the direction of the differential rates is the same for fertility measured per women or per ever married women, the data on age specific proportions ever married do not explain differential fertility between nonmigrant women in Lampung and women on Java.

Although no data are available on age at marriage, it is possible to infer, indirectly, the differences between these cohorts. While 99% of all migrant women are married before they reach their twenty-fifth birthday, nonmigrant women and women on Java tend to marry at a slightly later age. When migrant women are compared to the Javanese women, the data tend to support the often found inverse relationship between age at marriage and fertility. If, however, nonmigrant women are included in the comparison, then no relationship can be found.

Though not conclusive, these data tend to indicate a slight possible selection process, for migrants, by age at marriage. Unknown, however, is the direction of the causal relationship between age at marriage and migration status. It can be assumed that recruitment criteria of transmigration, one of which requires them to be married, may have influenced this relationship. Two alternative explanations can be offered. The first alternative is that some young aspirant migrants get married to qualify for the programs; the second is that because they are

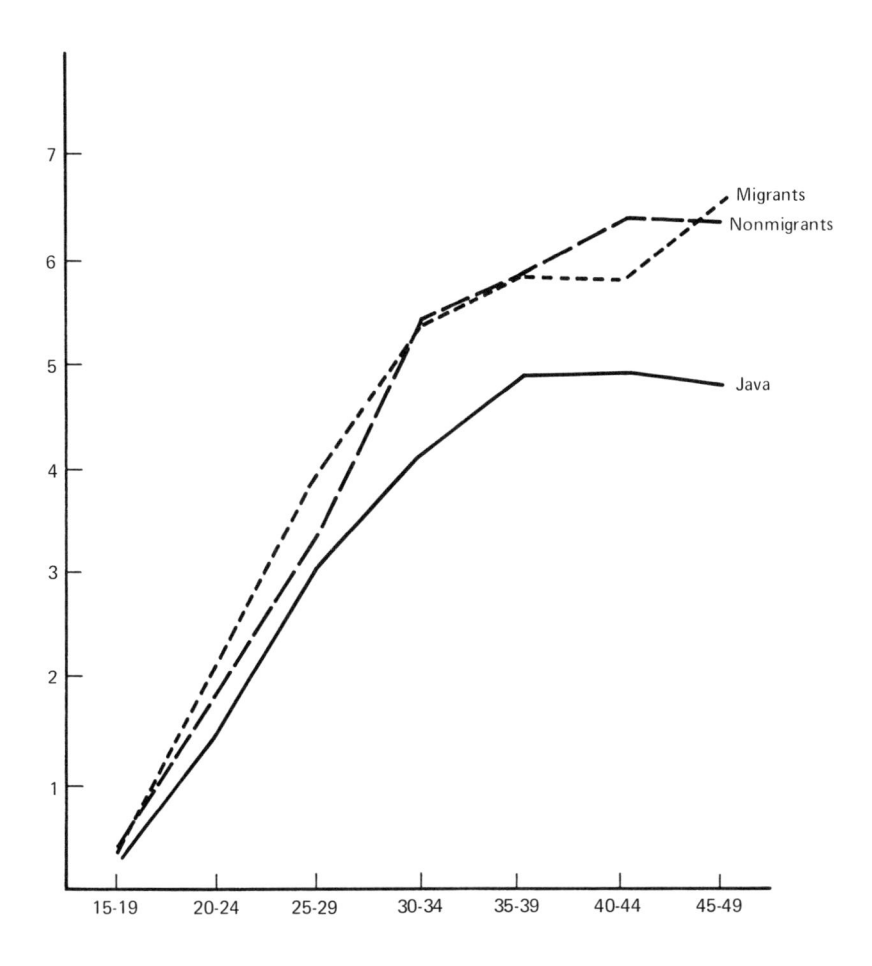

Figure 8-4. Age Specific Average Number of Children Ever Born Per Women: Migrants, and Nonmigrants in Lampung and Java, 1971. Source: Based on Biro Pusat Statistik, unpublished 1971 census of population tabulations.

young and married they qualify to become transmigrants. The first alternative raises the possibility of the danger which Maassen has warned the authorities against (Pelzer 1948, p. 210), while the second is more in line with the purpose of the program—removal of the young and reproductive to reduce excessive population growth on Java.

Another selective characteristic of migrants, which is frequently a good indicator of fertility, is their socioeconomic status. Socioeconomic status is often measured by a combined index of income, occupation, and education.

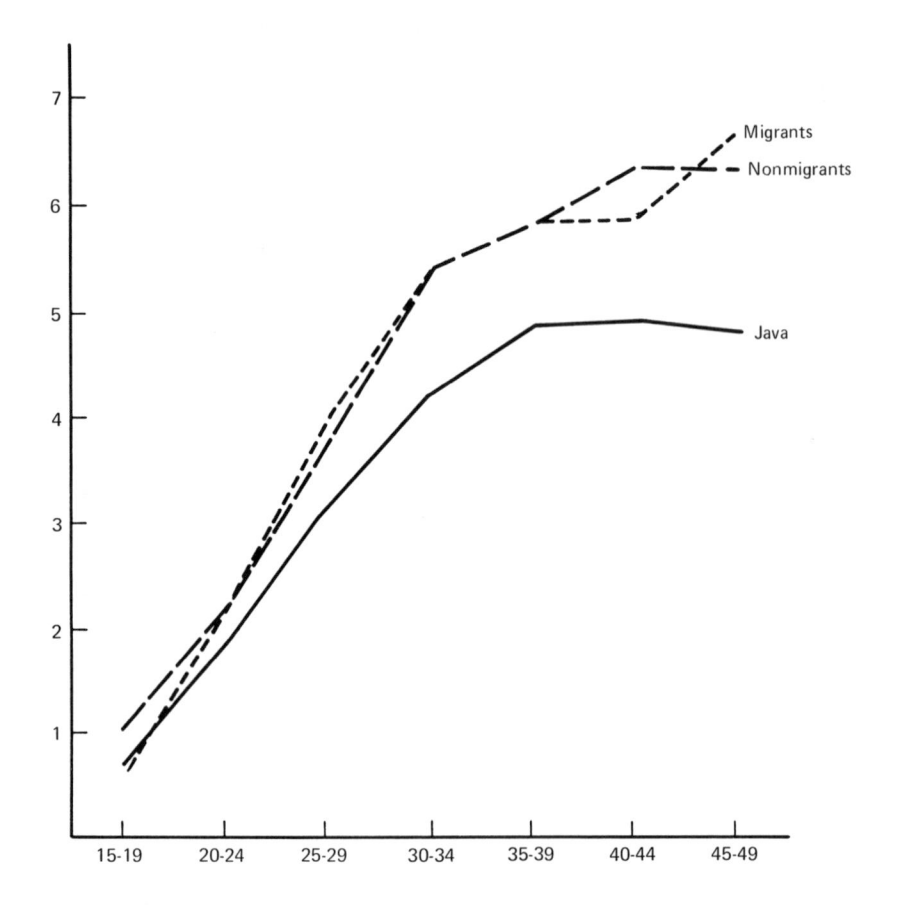

Figure 8-5. Age Specific Average Number of Children Ever Born Per Ever Married Women: Migrants and Nonmigrants in Lampung and Java, 1971. Source: Based on Biro Pusat Statistik, unpublished 1971 census of population tabulations.

Since no data were collected on the first two variables, education will be the only variable which can be used in this study to indicate socioeconomic status. Table 8-4 shows the discrepancy between the levels of education of the population on Java and the migrants in Lampung. The proportion of functional illiterates is 82.4% among the migrant population compared to 75.4% on Java. Consistent with illiteracy figures, slightly smaller proportions of migrants had ever attended school compared to those residing on Java. The slight differences in proportions of the population ten years and over who had ever attended school may be due to the comparatively small proportion of migrants aged ten

Table 8-3

Proportions of Women Ever Married by Age: Migrant and Nonmigrant Women in Lampung and Java, 1971

| | Lampung | | |
Age	Migrants	Nonmigrants	Java
15-19	54.79	43.62	43.14
20-24	98.96	84,94	85.41
25-29	99.58	90.51	96.72
30-34	99.12	99.51	98.36
35-39	100.0	100.00	99.02
40-44	98.51	100.00	99.41
45-49	97.44	100.00	99.35

Source: Biro Pusat Statistik, unpublished 1971 census of population tabulations.

Table 8-4

Percentage Distribution of the Population 10 Years and Over on Java and Migrants in Lampung, by Level of Education, 1971

Level of Education	Java[1]	Migrants in Lampung[2]
No education	42.94	45.51
Some elementary school	32.43	36.85
Finished elementary school	18.24	14.32
General junior high school	2.83	1.32
Special junior high school	1.19	.74
General senior high school	1.13	.45
Special senior high school	.88	.71
Academy	.19	.02
University	.17	.08

Sources:
[1] Biro Pusat Statistik, *Sensus Penduduk 1971*, Serie C. Jakarta.
[2] Biro Pusat Statistik, unpublished 1971 census of population tabulations.

to twenty-four (see Figure 8-2). Since the difference in proportions of migrants and Javanese who had ever attended school is only slight, high fertility among migrant women cannot be justifiably explained by a selection process.

Similarly, the specific data do not support the broad generalization concerning a negative relationship between education and fertility. The data in Table 8-5 separate age specific fertility rates by level of education. No specific pattern of relationship between levels of education and fertility can be ascertained. Hence,

Table 8-5
Age Specific Average Number of Children Ever Born to a Woman, by Level of Education

Age	No School	Some Elementary	Finished Elementary	Junior High School	Senior High School	Academy/ University
			Java 1971			
15-19	.28	.25	.27	.07	.05	–
20-24	1.62	1.62	1.62	.82	.64	.17
25-29	3.09	3.13	3.10	2.31	2.36	.60
30-34	4.12	4.34	4.35	3.37	3.99	1.40
35-39	4.73	5.28	5.17	4.33	4.75	2.35
40-44	4.75	5.66	5.91	4.87	5.37	3.17
45-49	4.68	5.40	5.75	5.13	5.59	3.61
			Migrants in Lampung 1971			
15-19	.27	.35	.14	.41	–	–
20-24	2.35	2.10	2.09	2.26	.20	–
25-29	4.02	3.97	3.92	1.00	2.96	1.00
30-34	5.76	4.67	4.18	6.00	–	7.00
35-39	5.84	6.34	5.51	2.83	3.31	–
40-44	5.78	5.93	5.98	3.00	–	–
45-49	6.29	7.30	9.30	3.00	1.00	–
			Nonmigrants in Lampung 1971			
15-19	.36	.43	.23	.03	–	–
20-24	2.30	1.94	1.39	.56	.40	–
25-29	3.10	3.64	3.20	4.69	2.00	–
30-34	5.16	5.65	5.04	7.18	6.00	1.00
35-39	5.41	5.66	8.43	11.00	–	–
40-44	6.02	8.06	7.27	–	–	–
45-49	6.86	2.57	5.00	–	–	–

Source: Biro Pusat Statistik, unpublished 1971 census of population tabulations.
Note: Some of the unlikely numbers may be due to the small sample size.

it may be concluded that education in itself is not a very strong determinant of fertility differentials among the populations studied.

A general relationship can also be found between mortality and fertility. However, when specific rates are examined, the relationship breaks down. The next set of data is on age specific number of surviving children (see Figures 8-6 and 8-7), which in combination with the data on children ever born provide the data for Table 8-6. A comparison of the data in Figures 8-4 and 8-5, and 8-6 and

[Figure: graph showing age-specific average number of surviving children per woman, x-axis age groups 15-19 to 45-49, y-axis 0 to 7, three curves: Migrants, Nonmigrants, Java]

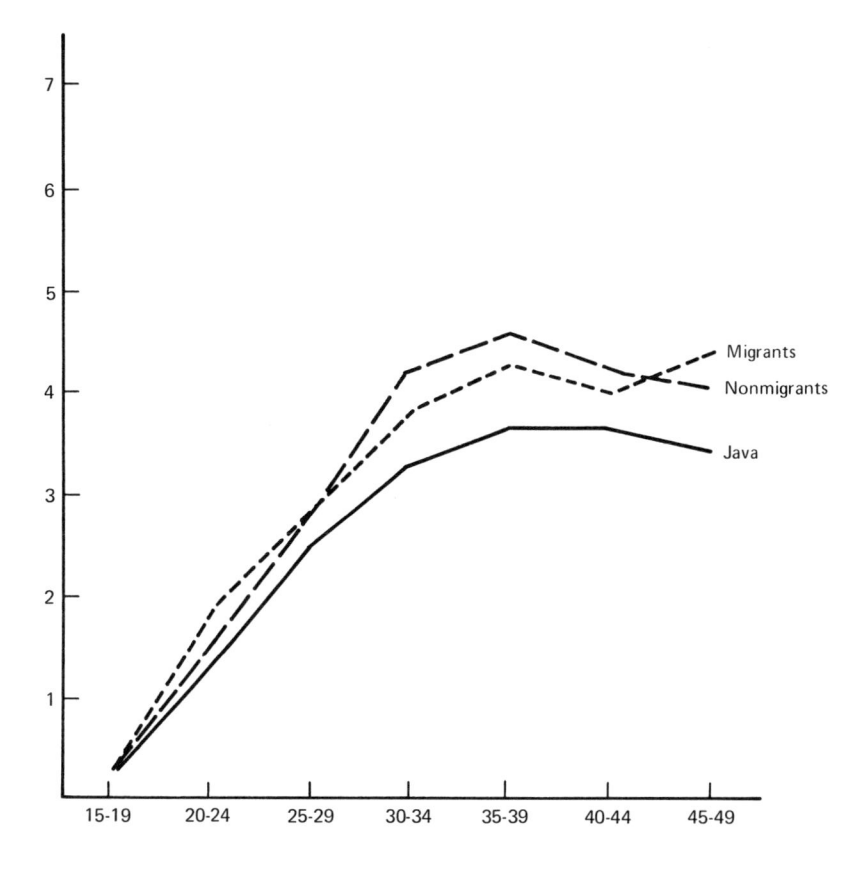

Figure 8-6. Age Specific Average Number of Surviving Children Per Women: Migrants and Nonmigrants in Lampung and Java, 1971. Source: Based on Biro Pusat Statistik, unpublished 1971 census of population tabulations.

8-7, indicate a general positive relationship between age specific average number of children ever born and surviving children. Similarly, there is a positive relationship when a comparison for these data is made between Java and Lampung.

The pattern is, however, quite different when migrants are compared to nonmigrants in Lampung. While the numbers of children ever born are consistently higher for migrants than for nonmigrants, the numbers of survivors of these children are lower for migrant women than for nonmigrant women between the ages 25-44. Similarly, a comparison of data in Figures 8-4 and 8-5 with data in Table 8-6 indicates that in general the difference in fertility between

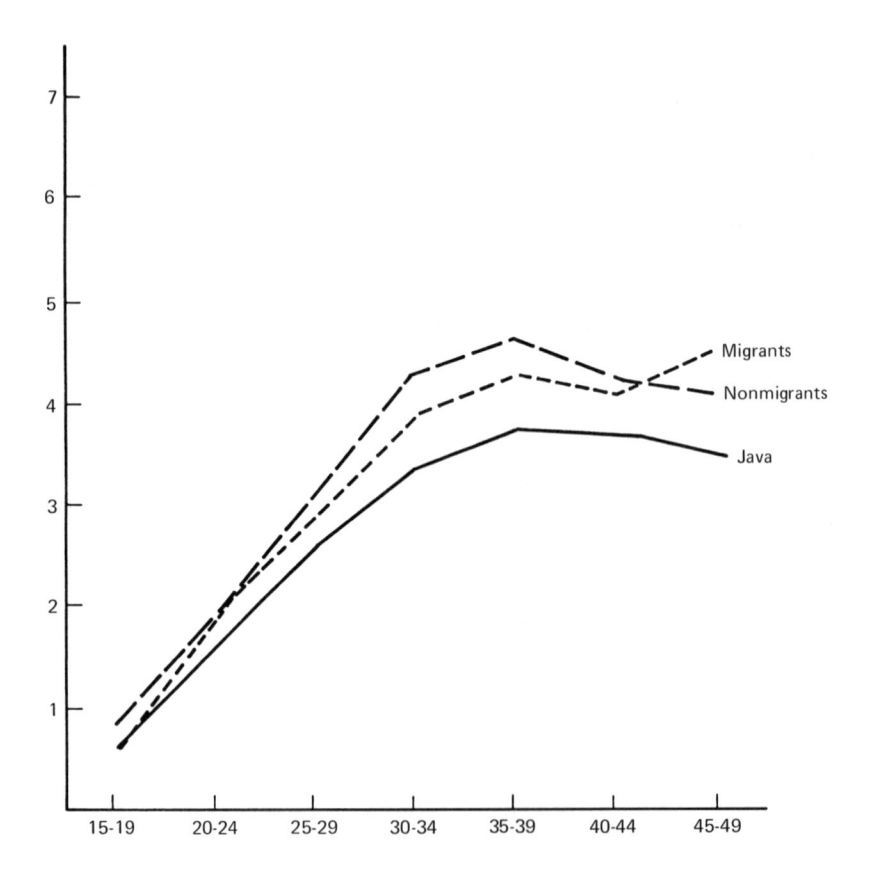

Figure 8-7. Age Specific Average Number of Surviving Children Per Ever Married Women: Migrants and Nonmigrants in Lampung and Java, 1971. Source: Based on Biro Pusat Statistik, unpublished 1971 census of population tabulations.

women in Java and Lampung can be attributed to differences in infant and child mortality (as indicated by column $_xq_0$ of Table 8-6). Java, with its lower age specific number of children ever born than Lampung, is also characterized by lower infant and child mortality than Lampung. This positive relationship between infant and child mortality and fertility breaks down, however, when a comparison is made between migrants and nonmigrants in Lampung. While the average number of children ever born to a migrant women aged 15-49 is higher than those born to a nonmigrant women of the same age group (4.11 as compared to 3.48), infant mortality is higher among nonmigrants than among migrants (206 compared to 152 per 1,000 live births). Hence, here again it may be concluded that infant mortality, in itself, is not always a good determinant of fertility.

Table 8-6
Calculation of $_xq_0$ and $_xl_0$ Based on Children Ever Born and Surviving Children Recorded in the 1971 Census

Age of Women	P_i	S_i	$1-S_i/P_i$	Multipliers	Age x	$_xq_0$	$_xl_0$
\multicolumn{8}{c}{Java 1971}
15-19	.25	.21	.160	1.019	1	.163	83696
20-24	1.52	1.27	.164	1.032	2	.169	83075
25-29	3.05	2.45	.197	1.006	3	.198	80182
30-34	4.12	3.27	.206	1.011	5	.208	79173
35-39	4.85	3.69	.239	1.021	10	.244	75598
40-44	4.93	3.67	.255	.999	15	.255	74526
45-49	4.82	3.45	.284	.997	20	.283	71685
\multicolumn{8}{c}{Migrants in Lampung 1971}
15-19	.28	.24	.143	1.064	1	.152	84785
20-24	2.17	1.80	.170	1.053	2	.179	82099
25-29	3.93	2.82	.282	1.018	3	.287	71292
30-34	5.34	3.83	.283	1.020	5	.289	71134
35-39	5.84	4.27	.269	1.030	10	.277	72293
40-44	5.82	4.01	.311	1.008	15	.313	68651
45-49	6.55	4.38	.329	1.008	20	.332	66837
\multicolumn{8}{c}{Nonmigrants in Lampung 1971}
15-19	.34	.27	.206	.999	1	.206	79421
20-24	1.85	1.49	.195	1.021	2	.199	80091
25-29	3.37	2.80	.169	1.000	3	.169	83100
30-34	5.39	4.25	.211	1.007	5	.212	78752
35-39	5.84	4.61	.211	1.016	10	.214	78562
40-44	6.37	4.23	.336	.993	15	.334	66635
45-49	6.39	4.09	.360	.992	20	.357	64288

Source: Based on Biro Pusat Statistik, unpublished 1971 census of population tabulations.
Note:
P_i = Average number of children ever born.
S_i = Average number of surviving children.
Multipliers are developed by Brass in Brass et al., (1968) and United Nations Manual IV (1967).
$_xq_0$ = Proportion dead before reaching age x.
$_xl_0$ = Proportion surviving before reaching age x.

The preceding analysis of differential fertility leads to the following conclusion. Differential fertility between primarily Javanese migrant women and Javanese women cannot be conclusively attributed to a selection process.

The Impact of the Transmigration Program on Fertility

Because of the inconclusive finding that migrants have higher fertility than the Javanese on Java due to their selectivity, I will propose a contrary but related argument: migrants have responded to their new environment by having more children than if they had stayed on Java. This argument is based on the idea that the number of children a couple has is a marginal rather than an average decision. Furthermore, this argument was proposed by Malthus, who claims that "Population does invariably increase when the means of subsistence increases" (quoted by Keyfitz 1972, p. 48). According to Malthus, population increase under improved economic conditions is not due to a reduction in mortality but instead is a consequence of increased fertility. Malthus argues that an increase in demand for labor reduces the age at marriage and therefore increases fertility (in Heer 1972, p. 308). I will thus argue that higher fertility among primarily Javanese migrants is a consequence of improved economic conditions, or means of subsistence, and the higher demand for labor in Lampung than on Java.

Unlike the previous analysis on social determinants of fertility, there are no comparable data on economic indicators. It is therefore necessary to rely on secondary and older data. Heeren, who conducted a survey in 1965, collected valuable information. Among other variables he gathered data on reasons for migration, size of landholdings before departure from Java, and in the settlement area. His findings are presented in Tables 8-7 - 8-9. These data will, of course, have to be interpreted with caution, considering that they came from a case study of only three settlement areas and the sample was rather small and not representative. Notwithstanding these weaknesses in the data, these are the only available data.

The data on reasons for migration show that 50% of the migrants left their

Table 8-7

Reasons for Migration Among Transmigrants Arriving in Lampung Between 1954-1965

Reason for Migration	Number	%
Landless	149	49.8
For improvement	79	26.3
Following family members	29	9.6
Security	8	2.3
Others	36	12.0
Total	301	100.0

Source: Based on Heeren (1967, p. 65), table 6.6.

Table 8-8
Size of Landholding on Java

Size of Landholding	Number	%
No land	236	78.4
.25 ha.	39	13.0
.5-1 ha.	18	6.0
1.25+	8	2.6
Total	301	100.0

Source: Based on Heeren (1967, p. 65), table 6.7.

Table 8-9
Size of Landholding in Lampung

Size of Landholding	Number	%
.25 ha.	32	11.1
.5-1 ha.	36	12.5
1.25-1.75 ha	26	9.1
2 ha. +	193	67.3
Total	287	100.0

Source: Based on Heeren (1967, p. 66), table 6.8.

place of origin because they were landless.[e] To verify this information Heeren asked the migrants a question about the size of landholdings they owned while still on Java. Table 8-8 shows that 91% of the respondents were landless or owned only .25 ha., barely sufficient for a house and vegetable garden. Only 2.6% were owners of 1.25 ha. or more, a size sufficient to support a family on Java. A comparison of Tables 8-8 and 8-9 shows that most of these migrants have significantly improved their economic well-being. While only 8.6% claimed they had owned more than .5 ha. on Java, 89% owned .5 ha. or more in Lampung.

These numbers are not significant in themselves. What is important is that most of these migrants have changed their economic status from being landless to becoming landowners. During the colonization program it was found that settlers needed extra hands, especially during harvest time. The large-scale colonization program was built on this finding; more hands were needed than were available in the settlement areas, and earlier settlers were willing to pay higher wages to newcomers than the prevailing going rate on Java in exchange

---
[e]Although Heeren did not ask them whether they knew they were to be given land, the migrants know enough about the transmigration program for us to assume that they came with the expectation of getting land.

for services rendered during critical times. Under the colonization scheme pioneers were given only one ha. of land while transmigrants were officially eligible for two ha. of land. With a greater area to farm, but basically using the same traditional technology, it can be assumed the owners of relatively large pieces of land would need more help. Not only are these settlement areas short of labor, but there are several public as well as private agricultural projects being developed in the province (Tavanlar 1971). Thus, the demand for labor in Lampung is relatively greater than the supply.

On the other hand, there is an excess of labor on Java. However, the exact extent of this overabundance of labor is unknown. The census used rather weak definitions of employed and unemployed persons (Biro Pusat Statistik 1972). According to the 1971 census only 1% of the population ten years and over was unemployed. In a less developed economy, such as Indonesia has, where per capita income is a mere $100, it does not seem plausible that Java would have such a low proportion of unemployed persons. It is therefore preferable, and more appropriate to consider the proportion of employed persons. For this category the census enumerated only 49.23% of the population ten years and over on Java as employed. By the census definition the remaining 49% were not economically active, which meant that these people were neither employed nor seeking employment. Here again these statistics are not very meaningful, because this means that only 33.85% of the total population on Java is responsible to support the remaining 66.15% of the population. It is, however, indicative of the magnitude of underemployment and the therefore excessive labor available on Java.

So far, a comparative description between Lampung and Java has been presented. Java, with its extreme density, has a man/land ratio of seven times that of Lampung. Consequently, there is no more arable land available on Java, while in Lampung irrigation networks are being built, which will vastly expand the available arable land (Tavanlar 1971). This discrepancy in means of subsistence has resulted in the discrepancy between demand and availability of labor. These differences suggest that there is an inverse relationship between availability of means for subsistence, demand for labor, and fertility.

Similarly, White (1973) has attempted to show the relationship, between demand for labor and high fertility, with historical data on Java's population growth during the colonial period. Geertz (1973) has argued, in a commentary, that White's model did not fully explain high fertility on Java during colonial times. It is recognized that this chapter does not succeed in fully explaining the exact relationship either. Such a study is, however, beyond the scope of this chapter. Furthermore, since it is unlikely that economic variables alone can explain the demand for children, it is misleading to rely solely on an economic model to explain differential fertility.

It is for this reason that this chapter has attempted to present both a social and an economic analysis of differential fertility behavior between Javanese women who migrate out of Java and those who remain. There are two broad conclusions which can be drawn from the preceding analysis: First, the difference in fertility pattern cannot be attributed to a selection process in terms of age at marriage, education, and infant and child mortality. Second, migrants have higher fertility than those they left behind because they have responded to improved economic conditions, where there are more means of subsistence and greater demand for labor.

Implications of High Fertility on Policy Objectives and Recommendations

Before analyzing the policy implications of the findings, at this juncture, it is necessary to restate the present objectives of the transmigration program:

1. To achieve more balanced and equal population distribution.
2. To transfer labor to carry out development projects (First Five Year Development Plan, pp. 113-15).

Since various studies have already indicated the futility of the first objective (e.g., Pelzer 1948; Nitisastro 1970), the present writer will decline to reiterate the arguments here. Instead, the findings will be analyzed only in terms of the second objective of the program.

With regard to this second objective, it should be kept in mind that the transmigration program does not provide labor, where needed, on a contractual and temporal basis. Instead, the program does provide inducements for Javanese to move permanently. Hence, it is important to consider not only short-term but also long-term consequences of resettling people into new areas to be developed.

Resettling people in development projects, which is synonymous with transmigration areas, is advantageous in that such a program can fulfill the demand for labor in a relatively short period of time. The disadvantage—but one which in this case is a policy objective—is that resettlement allows for families to move permanently. Hence, there are long-term consequences involved. An important finding of this study that is worth considering is that migrants have higher fertility than those remaining on Java. Numerous studies have already indicated that fertility and level of economic development are inversely related. Rather than arguing about the direction of the causal relationship, it may be hypothesized that high fertility in these transmigration areas will retard development. Hence, if fertility remains high in these areas, such areas may never develop. Thus, to consider transmigration as an instrument of development (as recommended by Tavanlar 1971), when migrant fertility continues to be high, may only be a misconceived objective.

Thus, if the development of transmigration areas is a serious objective, other measures, which may hopefully cure fertility, will have to be considered and implemented.

First, if age at marriage is inversely related to high fertility, and if as it seems from this study that lower age at marriage is related to migration states, then it ought to be recommended that the requirement that an applicant be married, should be removed. This requirement was made during the colonization period when there were few Javanese migrants in Lampung and single persons were considered detrimental to the stability of the community. Today, Javanese are the majority in Lampung and such a requirement is no longer necessary.

Second, the findings of this study indicate that age at marriage is not an important determinant of fertility, instead, fertility of ever married women better explains differential fertility. Hence, it ought to be recommended that measures be taken to reduce martial fertility. Heer (1972) found that an increase in income alone results in an increase in fertility. He therefore recommends that a prerequisite to development is to neutralize the income effect of fertility by seriously improving the education and health services. On the basis of the findings in this study, similar recommendations are offered. Since the income of migrants has increased and fertility for them is higher than for those who did not come to Lampung, and where, moreover, education is slightly negatively related to fertility, it is strongly recommended that greater investments be made in education and health services in the transmigration areas. This recommendation is also supported by Heeren's findings that the settlers complained about the lack of educational facilities (1967, p. 70). Furthermore, better provision of health services in these areas should improve the health of the settlers. With better health care it is expected that infant and child mortality will be reduced. Where the findings indicate a slight positive relationship between mortality and fertility, a decrease in infant and child mortality may depress fertility.

Third, the increasing activities of the National Family Planning Coordinating Board, which during the first five-year development plan were concentrated on Java and Bali, should in the shortest possible time be expanded and activated to the transmigration areas.

Recommendations for Further Research

It is apparent from this study that although several reasons have been offered to explain differential fertility, a great deal more remains unknown. An important study should be conducted on the mechanisms which lead to such high fertility among migrants.

Such a study should be an in-depth and detailed study in which migrants are compared to nonmigrants in the immediate vicinity of the place of origin of the studied migrants. The study should not only be concerned with socioeconomic and demographic data, but it should also seek subjective perceptions of those under study concerning their fertility behavior. Such a study should attempt to test the following hypotheses:

1. Migrants have higher fertility than nonmigrants.
2. Migrants tend to marry at an earlier age than nonmigrants.
3. The difference in age at marriage accounts for the difference in fertility behavior.
4. Migrants are less educated than nonmigrants.
5. Migrants had smaller incomes than nonmigrants.
6. The discrepancy in socioeconomic status explains differential fertility patterns.
7. Migrants suffer more from infant and child mortality than nonmigrants.
8. Differential infant and child mortality accounts for the difference in fertility behavior.
9. An increase in real income raises the means of subsistence and therefore the demand for labor, which in turn increases fertility.
10. Migrants perceive a better future than nonmigrants and therefore have more children than nonmigrants.
11. The lack of social and recreational activities accounts for fertility differences.
12. The divorce rate is lower in the settlement areas than in the place of the migrants origin.
13. Differential divorce rates account for fertility differentials.

References

"Basic Formulations of the Transmigration Workshop," 1971.

Biro Pusat Statistik, *Sensus Penduduk 1971*, Serie C. Jakarta, 1972.

Brass, William, et al. *The Demography of Tropical Africa*. Princeton, New Jersey: Princeton University Press, 1968.

Department of Information, Republic of Indonesia. *The First Five-Year Development Plan* (1969/70-1973/74), Volume 2c.

Departemen Tenaga Kerja, Transmigrasi dan Kooperasi, Direktorat Jendral Transmigrasi. *Konsep Pertama Rencana Transmigrasi Pelita II, Tahun 1974-78*. Jakarta.

Geertz, Clifford. *The Religion of Java*. Glencoe: The Free Press, 1960.

———. *Agricultural Involution*. Berkeley, Calif.: University of California Press, 1971.

———. "Comments on Benjamin White's 'Demand for Labor and Population Growth in Colonial Java'." *Human Ecology* 1, 3 (1973): 237-39.

Goldstein, Sidney. "Interrelations between Migration and Fertility in Thailand." *Demography* 10, 1 (May 1973): 225-41.

Heer, David M. *Society and Population.* Englewood Cliffs, New Jersey: Prentice-Hall Inc., 1968.

_____. "Economic Development and Fertility." In William Petersen (ed.), *Readings in Population.* New York: The Macmillan Company, 1972.

Heeren, H.J. *Het Land aan de Overkant.* J.A. Boom en Zoon, Uitgevers te Meppel, 1967.

Jay, Robert. "Local Government in Rural Central Java." *Far Eastern Quarterly* 15 (1956): 215-27.

Keyfitz, Nathan. "Recommendations for Population Study and Demographic Research in Indonesia." *Warta Leknas* 2, 3 (1964), (II, 3).

_____. "Population Theory and Doctrine: A Historical Survey." In William Petersen (ed.), *Readings in Population.* New York: The Macmillan Company, 1972.

Lembaga Demografi Fakultas Ekonomi Universitas Indonesia. *Demographic Factbook of Indonesia.* Jakarta, 1973.

McNicoll, Geoffrey. "Internal Migration in Indonesia: Descriptive Notes." *Indonesia* 5 (April 1968): 29-92.

McNicoll, Geoffrey and Si Gde Made Mamas. "The Demographic Situation in Indonesia." Paper presented at the annual P.A.A. conference, April 1973.

Nitisastro, Widjojo. *Population Trends in Indonesia.* Ithaca: Cornell University Press, 1970.

Pelzer, K.J. *Pioneer Settlement in Asiatic Tropics.* New York: Institute for Pacific Relations, 1948.

"Peraturan Dasar Pokok-Pokok Agraria dan Landreform." Jakarta, 1962.

Petersen, William. *Population.* London: The MacMillan Co., 1969.

_____. *Readings in Population.* London: The MacMillan Co., 1972.

Suharto, Sam; Geoffrey McNicoll; and Lee-Jay Cho. "The 1971 Indonesian Census: An Introduction." Mimeographed.

Swasono, Sri Edi. "Transmigrasi dalam Perspektif Pembangunan." In the daily *Indonesia Raya.* Jakarta, August 3, 1970.

Tavanlar, Eligio, J. "Transmigration as an Instrument of Development." Unpublished report of the Development Advisory Service, Indonesia Project, 1971.

United Nations, Manual IV. *Methods of Estimating Basic Demographic Measures from Incomplete Data.* New York, Series A, Population Studies, No. 42, 1967.

White, Benjamin. "Demand for Labor and Population Growth in Colonial Java." *Human Ecology* 1, 3 (1973): 217-36.

9 Relations of Production and Fertility Levels: The Case of Northeast Brazil

Maria Helena T. Henriques Lerda

Introduction

As Caio Prado, Jr., perhaps the most famous Brazilian historian, testifies:

Undoubtedly, no other Brazilian region has had more written about it than the Northeast... Nevertheless, there is a question that, strange as it may sound, was always deferred to oblivion... I refer to the relations of production and work... that is, how men relate to each other in their productive activities and how they behave, in relation to each other and to the community, in the exercise of their economic functions. This type of analysis, obviously, opens perspectives on the social structure and living conditions of the population and its different classes.[1]

This chapter attempts the type of analysis Prado, Jr. is talking about. It represents an effort to pinpoint the determinants of fertility in the Brazilian Northeastern rural population through the examination of the physical characteristics and economic structure of the area.

The Brazilian Northeast is by all definitions a controversial area. According to the different institutions that orient its economy (SUDENE, Banco do Nordeste), it is composed of the states of Maranhao, Piaui, Ceara, Rio Grande do Norte, Paraiba, Pernambuco, Alagoas, Sergipe, Bahia, and the Territory of Fernando de Noronha. There, in 18 percent of the Brazilian area, live approximately 30 percent of the Brazilian population.

Since the early times of colonization an export economy based on sugar has grown in the area. It conquered the favorable soil of the coastal areas and facilitated the conquest of the interior through its subsidiary economy, cattle-raising. Men followed the animals, which roamed as far as the edge of the Amazon jungle. That was how the region was formed, a region where population growth has always been high. It is not surprising that an accelerated population growth and an export economy occur together. The latter stimulates food production in subsidiary marginal regions, which in times of export crisis develop subsistence economies. As we know a subsistence economy enables a sustained growth of the population even though its productivity remains stable or decreases.

The use of the best soil for growing sugar and the expansion of the sugar plantations brought about another element characteristic of the Northeast economy, the large estates which hinder the development of other economic cultures. As long as the landowners are the ones that retain most of the income, it is very difficult to pass from an export economy to one based on the internal market.

With the decrease in the external demand for sugar it became obvious that the sugar economy could not provide sufficient employment. The unemployed, lacking a source of income, began to migrate to the interior to occupy poorer lands and to set up minifundia. As these areas also became filled, the migration was expanded into the interior in the direction of the dry hinterland, constituting a new focus of population growth.

This is the configuration of a regional economy that lacks dynamism. The problems are multiplied by the geographical characteristics of the Northeastern region: the barrenness of a considerable part of its territory and the periodic droughts. Our discussion of the determinants of fertility and the policies that bear on them will take account of the economic factors described above.

The Northeast as a Geo-Economic Reality

According to Andrade,[2] the Northeast can be divided into five regions: Guiana Maranhense, Meio-Norte, Sertao, Agreste, and Mata.

The Guiana Maranhense embraces a wide area of the Northwest of Maranhao. Two geo-economic zones are easily distinguishable: the North, which was settled long ago, and the South, which was more recently settled. There was a period of economic growth in the North in the nineteenth century, but now the urban centers are decaying. The people in this area are engaged in fishing, hunting, extensive cattle-raising, and the gathering of nuts. The amount of subsistence agriculture is negligible.

The South is crossed by major rivers and, up to the beginning of this century, was occupied by Indians, who hindered the expansion into and agricultural exploitation of the area. The region has a high proportion of "terras devolutas"[a] and this facilitated its settlement. Squatters occupy the land, cut down the forest, and cultivate rice as a commercial crop. Rice, maize, and manioc, as well as fishing and hunting, are their main source of food. The commerce in rice has resulted in the formation of new urban centers. Despite being centers of growth, their social conditions are quite modest.

The type of settlement in the South is disastrous for the area's natural resources. The forest is destroyed (without the lumber being utilized) and soil

---

[a]Extensions of land owned by the federal or state government that are not in use. Most often these areas are occupied by "posseiros" (squatters) that clean and cultivate the land hoping that eventually the legal right of "usocapiao" (ownership of the land after proof that for x number of years the land has been kept productive) becomes reality.

erosion, which is common in equatorial regions, occurs. After the rice harvest, manioc or banana are cultivated and then the area is relegated to cattle-raising. The peasant leaves the area after two or three years of exploitation and looks for another forest area.[3]

Transportation difficulties and control of the rice economy by the rice mill owners, together with the poverty of the soil and the rudimentary agricultural techniques, account for the miserable living conditions of the rural workers. After the workers have cleared and cultivated the land, wealthy landlords acquire them, and then compel the workers to sell them their harvest and buy their provisions from the owners' retail stores. The worker, with no source of credit or support, must depend on the merchant, who is also very often the owner of the rice mill, for his provisions. The merchant also acquires land which the worker has abandoned because it is too difficult to cultivate, and uses it for cattle-raising.

The second sub-region, Meio-Norte, is an old settlement and comprises a large part of Maranhao, almost all of Piaui, and the Northwest of Ceara. It may be subdivided into several zones, based on the major economic activity. The most important ones are related to palm oil trees, carnauba trees, limited cattle-raising and cotton growing, and extensive cattle-raising. Each activity creates a specific landscape and life style in the area it dominates.

The palm oil tree provides the peasant with the sticks and straw used in building his house, as well as the coconut that is his food and source of income. The gathering of the coconut is an exclusive right of the inhabitants of the holdings, who must, however, sell the crop to the landowner. Again, it is through commerce that the owner exercises control over the workers. The workers also engage in some subsistence agriculture. The holdings occupy generally large expanses of land. The cattle range free, changing their grazing area with the seasons. Cattle-raising is the major economic activity of the sub-region.

Carnauba wax from Carnauba trees is a major part of the export economy of the region. It is a secure source of income, despite the constant fluctuation of its price.

The high hinterland, in Maranhao or Piaui, has a quite closed economy devoted almost exclusively to subsistence agriculture and extensive cattle-raising. The distance from the major urban centers and the lack of roads prevent the development of agriculture.

Given its expanse and particular climate, the Sertao is the most characteristic sub-region of the Northeast. It occupies half the territory of the region, but has low demographic densities. Natural conditions and the economic activity of the area vary considerably, suggesting the existence of several zones in the sub-region. Cattle-raising and subsistence agriculture are found here.

The Agreste, despite its small land area, has a high population concentration. It is a narrow strip that, as a transitional region, exhibits both a humid and a dry climate. Cereal and fruit cultivation, as well as cotton and cattle-raising, occur here.

The sub-region of Mata has been the most important in the Northeast since the Brazilian colonization in the sixteenth century. It includes five of the capitals of the Northeastern states, the oldest urban centers in the region, and the great plantations that have remained to the present.

This summary of the region has outlined the difficulties and complexities with which we are dealing. Physical problems, together with a rigid land tenure system, exploitation of the workers, and a past of dependence and underdevelopment, are some of the factors to be considered in the formulation of all policies, whether directly aimed at population or not.

The Historical Roots of the Northeastern Configuration

It is important for us to show that the present characteristics of the economy of the Northeast are not purely due to its geographic predicaments but respond rather to a pattern that was established centuries ago and that was defined by two economic systems: sugar cane and cattle-raising. Characteristics such as the location of the major cities on the coast, the low level of technology in economic activities, the lack of communication and difficulties of transportation across the region, the low level of commercialization within the region will then, we hope, be understood.

The lack of precious metals in Brazil, as opposed to the amounts found in Central America and Peru, led the Portuguese to think of a colonization mainly oriented toward trade.[4] Since the beginning their most important objective was the exploitation of natural resources for the benefit of European commerce. Settlement along the coast indicates the commercial orientation toward the exterior market. Only in the second century of colonization did the conquest of the interior through mining and cattle-raising activities begin.

The basic element in agriculture was the large one-crop plantation worked by slaves. The regime of large-scale agrarian exploitation—the sugar plantation and the large estate—was a natural and necessary consequence of the combination of a series of circumstances, namely the tropical nature of the land, the objectives that inspired the colonialists, and the general conditions of the new economic order—maritime discoveries and the needs of temperate Europe.[5]

With the expansion of the sugar economy and the growing need for draft animals, a dependent economy was created in the Northeast, the cattle-raising economy.[6] The latter was, from the beginning, completely different from the sugar economy. The occupation of the land was extensive, the percentage of land permanently occupied was minimal and the labor force requirements were very small—roughly one cowboy for each fifty head of cattle. The availability of land was the triggering factor and together with the other characteristics explain why cattle-raising was a major factor in the penetration into and occupation of the Brazilian interior.

A subsistence economy developed, based on cattle-raising and a primitive method of agriculture. Even though land was abundant, its ownership was concentrated in a few hands and the majority of the population could not count on it as a source of income.

The subsistence economy required that each family, or individual, provide for itself. The "roça" was the basis of this economy, but did not provide a living by itself.[b] The peasant had to find supplementary work, generally in cattle-raising, where his employer was also the owner of the property on which the peasant had his roca. Within the major economic system the rural worker developed different activities (such as piece-work), for some of which he received an income which provided for his minimal monetary needs.

Even though the peasant's roca is the characteristic land unit in the subsistence economy, the owner of the property on which the roças are situated is more influential than the peasants. It is convenient for the owner to have many peasants living on his land. While their roças take care of the peasants' own subsistence needs, the owner has a ready labor supply, whose ties of loyalty are to him.

Throughout the period of the alternating rise and fall of the sugar, and later the cotton, economy in the Northeast, there was a steady growth in population. The waves of prosperity, followed by periods of depression, threw more and more people into the subsistence sector, which created a structural disequilibrium in that sector. The severe drought of 1877-80 added to the problems. There was a movement to help the affected population by promoting their migration to the Amazon region, where labor was scarce.

The above factors set the limits of population growth in the area. Through an examination of the trends in some demographic indices we will see the process of growth and expansion of the population. This is the objective of the next section of this chapter.

The Trends in Population Growth

A brief survey of population trends in the Northeast shows that the area's own population has been steadily increasing, although its share in Brazil's total population has been decreasing. The consequences of out-migration from the area are shown in Table 9-1.

The Northeast has traditionally been a supplier of unskilled labor to other regions of Brazil. Its people are significantly represented in the two larger metropolises, São Paulo and Rio de Janeiro, and were the major laborers in the construction of Brasilia. More recently they have begun to be seen in what are considered the frontier areas.

---

[b]This is the name given in Brazil to a small plot where basic subsistence crops are planted. They are generally devoted to the cultivation of pulses, beans, and manioc. The "roceiro" is the head of the family, in charge of the roça.

Table 9-1
Proportion of the Brazilian Population in the Northeast (at different population censuses)

Year	Proportion
1872	46.8
1890	42.0
1900	38.8
1920	36.7
1940	35.0
1950	34.5
1960	31.5
1970	30.4

Source: Instituto Brasileiro de Geografia e Estatistics (IBGE), *Sinopse Preliminar do Censo Demografico*, VIII Reconseamento Geral, 1970 (Rio de Janeiro, 1971), table 2, pp. 82-83.

Mobility inside the region is quite high. It is mainly motivated by two considerations: (1) pioneering, which results in the destruction of the forest and appearance of commerce and cattle-raising; and (2) short-term movement for temporary work.

Migration to the larger cities is also very common. Since the number of urban centers of importance is very small, these cities have had a rapid growth in population, with its attendant drain on public services.

The uncertainty of the job market and the effects of periodic droughts in the Northeast result in the peasant's constant movement in search of work, which has given the region's peasants a reputation as Brazilian itinerants.

There has been a great increase in the population densities of Northeast states (see Table 9-2), due both to the high in-migration and the high fertility level. This increase occurred despite the extremely high mortality rate—life expectancy at birth being less than fifty years for both men and women.

Rural population growth has contributed a major share to the overall population of the states. The proportion of urban to rural populations ranges 25.4 to 1 (Maranhao) to 54.5 to 1 (Pernambuco). The latter is the only state in which the urban population represents more than half of the state's total.[8]

It is our contention that the fertility rate in the Northeast region is not only a reflection of a lack of knowledge about contraception, but is also the peasants' method of coping with the hardships of migration and economic struggle. Some evidence that "natural fertility" is not occurring in the region[9] is reflected in recent estimations of fertility levels for groups of state.[10] Their fertility levels, as measured by a summary index such as the Total Fertility Rate, oscillate around a value of 6.0 children per woman. Nevertheless, there are differences in the pathways through which those values are obtained. The fertility contribution of the 15-19 age group is younger in Maranhao and Piaui than the group II states

Table 9-2
Population Densities in the Different States of the Northeast (at different population censuses)

States	Densities per km²			
	1940	1950	1960	1970
Maranhao	3.8	4.9	7.7	9.4
Piaui	3.3	4.2	5.0	6.9
Ceara	14.2	18.4	22.7	30.6
R.G. Norte	14.5	18.3	21.8	30.4
Paraiba	25.2	30.4	35.8	43.4
Pernambuco	27.4	34.6	42.1	53.4
Alagoas	34.4	39.5	46.0	58.1
F. Noronha	...	23.2	55.6	52.4
Sergipe	24.7	29.3	34.6	41.4
Bahia	7.0	8.6	10.7	13.5

Source: IBGE, *Sinopse Preliminar de Censo Demografico*, VIII, Reconseamento Geral, 1970 (Rio de Janeiro, 1971), table 4, p. 86.

and much younger than Sergipe and Bahia. The age-specific fertility rates for the 20-29 age group, where women are generally most fertile, are very similar in all three groups of states. The fertility contribution of women in the 30-39 age group, generally accepted as an indication of late fertility patterns, is highest in Sergipe and Bahia with an age-specific fertility rate of 254.1 births per 1000 women.

Two observations come to mind from the previous consideration. First, there are differences in the observed fertility levels among the groups of states. Second, the relatively low fertility rates indicate that fertility is being controlled, which leads us to search for hypotheses which will explain these phenomena.

The type of research we want to pursue is related to what it generally calls ecological analysis. We intend to examine the predominant economic activity of micro-units (the level of disaggregation is the one provided in the census). We believe the basic characteristics of the land tenure system in the area are the major determinants of rural fertility periods.

The Role of Rural Structure
in Fertility Determination

Our original plan was to develop this analysis for the entire Northeast region using physiographic zones (a census unit) as our smallest unit of analysis. The scarcity of time and problems in data availability led us to concentrate on the state of Maranhao, hoping that the use of a test case would help in the understanding of the formulation and rationale of the hypotheses.

In 1960, the Brazilian government took an agricultural and a population census. Unfortunately, problems occurred during the data processing of the latter and less than half of the states had their final results published. In the Northeast, only Maranhao and Piaui were that fortunate. This placed an immediate limitation on the comparison of 1960 population and agricultural data at the regional level.

The formulation of hypotheses for the state of Maranhao is made at the level of the physiographic zones for the state. Fertility levels are predicted based on the structural characteristics of the ecological units. They are then compared to the actual child-woman ratio in the population.

The choice of this fertility measure is dictated by the available data. We do not claim it to be an ideal measure, but the best under the circumstances. The limitations of such a measure are basically three. First, it is affected by differences in age structure (the proportion of each fertile age group to all the reproductive ages) and fertility structure (the contribution of each age group to total fertility). Second, it is affected by differences in the levels of infant and child mortality (children less than five years old). And third, it is affected by differential exposure to migration, when there are reasons to believe that one of the characteristics that differentiates the migrant population from the rest of the population is their average number of children, or their age and marital status.

We have no reason to assume a priori that there are differences in age structure and mortality levels for the different units of analysis. The limitation concerning selectivity of the migrants may be more serious in terms of distorting the comparisons and we have made an indirect check on that—the sex ratio of the immigrants varies between 87.3 (zone 1) and 120.9 (zone 4), with the other zones having values around 110 (see Table 9-3). Therefore, the differences do not seem to be of a serious magntiude.

The variables chosen as proxies for the structural characteristics of the area were obtained from the population and agricultural censuses and from background information on the different economic activities in the area. Based on the considerations presented in previous sections of this chapter, we prepared the following list of hypotheses:

1. Regions of old settlement, characterized by unsuccessful attempts at agriculture; lack of major economic activity; lack of opportunity for earning a living; and where hunting and fishing, when practiced, are oriented toward survival, are expected to have *low* fertility levels.
2. Regions of new settlement, with high percentages of terras devolutas and opportunities for earning a living in agriculture, are expected to have *high* fertility levels. This expectation is strengthened when both a source of income (i.e., work in commercial crops) and the opportunity for subsistence farming (basically on minifundia) are available, and when there is work for entire families, as in the gathering of coconuts in palm oil tree cultivation.

249

Table 9-3

	Physiographic Zones	Type of Settlement	% Area in Minifundio(1)	% in Area in Latifundio(2)	% Area in Crops	% Area in Postures	% Family Workers	% Employees	Hypotheses	Predicted Levels	Observed Levels (C.W.R.)(3)
1	Litoral Norte	Old: sugar	14.6	50.1	1.4	93.9	72.1	8.2	1,(3)	Low	603.6
2	Baixada	Part old: sugar Part new	30.4	35.4	30.5	9.7	61.6	23.2	2	High	766.2
3	Baixo Mearim	New	49.3	23.2	53.5	24.9	86.4	10.5	2	High	768.1
4	Gurupi	Part old: sugar Part new	2.8	17.4	13.4	11.0	73.6	15.7	1,(2)	Low	746.6
5	Pindaré	New	66.1	—	93.2	6.7	66.8	30.6	2	High	803.9
6	Tocantins	New	18.3	12.4	25.9	38.5	68.0	25.1	3	Low	697.3
7	Litoral Nordeste	New	14.8	43.8	19.0	16.3	73.2	19.7	2,4	High	848.4
8	Baixo Parnaiba	New	2.7	47.5	15.2	18.8	73.6	14.0	2,4	High	788.1
9	Medio Parnaiba	Old: sugar, rice & cotton	0.1	69.2	6.8	32.9	44.8	34.7	1 (4)	Low	712.9
10	Ita Pecuru	Old: sugar rice & cotton	7.7	71.9	14.3	19.8	83.2	9.1	1	Low	695.8
11	Carolina	New	0.1	60.0	1.5	52.6	84.9	14.3	3	Low	658.6
12	Alto Parnaiba	Old: cattle raising	0.2	75.9	1.8	47.4	81.3	17.0	1,3	Low	723.8
13	Alto Mearim	Old: cattle raising	8.2	56.3	14.9	40.3	89.0	8.7	4	High	775.6

(1) Holdings with less than 10 ha.
(2) Holdings with 500 or more ha.
(3) Child-woman ratio (%)
Source: IBGE, Demographic and Agricultural Censuses, 1960.

3. *Low* fertility is expected in the areas where large holdings and extensive cattle-raising prevail, since labor force requirements are minimal and there are no alternative sources for earning a living.
4. Areas where large holdings devoted to agriculture dominate tend to have *high* fertility levels. Since only a rudimentary level of skill is required, most family members can work and, therefore, the more children in the family, the higher the income. The palm oil tree provides everything to satisfy the basic needs of the caboclo of the area's families.

To determine whether our predictions were accurate, we compared the predictions of high or low fertility rates with the observed data.[11] To establish the upper and lower boundaries of the dependent variable, we calculated its mean—737.6; values above this were considered high, those below were considered below. Table 9-3 shows the values of the independent variables and the resulting predictions.

As we can see in Table 9-3, most of the predictions are quite accurate. We would like to make a few specific comments. Three of the zones (3, 5, and 6) are currently experiencing a high population growth rate, and are considered areas of transition. This is especially evident in zone 6, where a pattern is not self-evident. Zones 9 and 10, despite similar characteristics, differ in that zone 9 is a region of palm oil trees, while zone 10 is still the dominion of the cerrados. In zone 10 there is a noticeably higher percentage of employment, which may indicate the presence of a factory and some processing activity.

Reflections on Possible Policies

So far, the development policies attempted in the Northeast region of Brazil have only dealt, directly or indirectly, with the question of scarcity of water. Furtado went beyond that when he suggested, fifteen years ago, that

The first objective should be to create (in the region) an economy resistant to droughts. To achieve this objective we would need to know the region better—its resources of superficial and underground waters, its flora—and to mobilize credit and technical assistance. An economy of higher productivity would probably result in a reduction in the number of cattle in some zones. The overabundance of animals is a deterrent to cotton cultivation and makes the system more vulnerable to droughts. An economy of higher productivity in the caatinga would not be compatible with high demographic densities. Therefore, the organization of the caatinga economy would result in a surplus population that would have to be absorbed elsewhere.[12]

The organization of agriculture and food production would have to occur along with efforts to industrialize. Industrialization, which would provide increased employment in the region, requires cheap labor, energy sources, and abundant raw materials. The Northeast fulfills all these needs.

Two obstacles stand in the way of industrialization and an improved standard of living in the region. They are, first, a regressive income distribution structure and, second, the concentration of rural properties in the extremes of latifundia and minifundia. A change in these conditions would certainly move the population out of its current socioeconomic and demographic inertia. Several studies have already shown that improved socioeconomic conditions will lead to a decrease in both mortality and fertility. We have no reason to expect that such would not be the case in the Brazilian Northeast.

Another development policy in effect is that of moving some of the population to colonize frontier areas. Setting up a basic infrastructure to effectively carry out this policy is the first problem to be solved. The colonization effort has not to date been evaluated, but unless it can produce drastic changes in the present living conditions, the problem of demographic balance will remain.

Notes

1. Andrade, Manuel Correia de, *A Terra e o Homem no Nordeste*, Brasiliense Ed., 2nd edition (São Paulo, Brazil, 1964), p. IX. (Preface by Caio Prado, Jr.).

2. Andrade, Manuel Correia de, *Geografia Economica do Nordeste*, Atlas Ed. (São Paulo, Brazil, 1970), pp. 22-23.

3. "Peasant" is the best available translation in English for "campones," which means anything from farm workers, very small landholders and tenants, community members, to rural workers in general. See, Inter-American Committee for Agricultural Development, *Agrarian Structure in Latin America*, Solon Barraclough and Juan Carios Collarte (eds.), (Lexington, Mass.: Lexington Books, D.C. Heath and Company, 1973), Glossary, p. 292.

4. Caio Prado, Jr., *The Colonial Background of Modern Brazil* (Berkeley and Los Angeles: University of California Press, 1967), Part One, pp. 7-129.

5. Ibid.

6. Celso Furtado, *Formacao Economica do Brasil* (Rio de Janeiro, Brazil, Fundo de Cultura Ed., 1959), pp. 70-82.

7. Andrade, *Geografia Economica*, p. 41.

8. IBGE, *Sinopse Preliminar do Censo Demografico*, VIII, Recenseamento Geral, 1970 (Rio de Janeiro, 1971), table 5, p. 87.

9. The concept of "natural fertility" has a precise meaning in demography. It is defined by Espenshade, "When we speak of the natural fertility schedule of a population we mean the age-specific marital fertility schedule we would observe in the absence of birth control." Thomas J. Espenshade, "A New Method for Estimating the Level of Natural Fertility in Populations Practicing Birth Control," *Demography* 8, 4 (November 1971).

It is necessary to define birth control in the context of natural fertility. It is the practice through which "the behavior of the couple is bound to the number of children already born and is modified when this number reaches the maximum which the couple does not want to exceed; it is not the case of a taboo concerning lactation, which is independent of the number of children already born." See Louis Henry, "Some Data on Natural Fertility," *Eugenics Quarterly* 8 (1961): 81.

10. Elza Berguo, "Un Analisis de la Fecundidad en el Brasil, segun Regiones," CELADE, *Notas de Poblacion*, Year I, Vol. 3, table 1, p. 19. The grouping of states conforms to a classification of regions in Brazil to be used in a coming national fertility study. The regions are assumed to be homogeneous within themselves, and their selection came after a thorough examination of the different states of Brazil in light of several criteria—geography, economy, and history being a few of them. Group I is represented by Maranhão and Piaui; Group II by the states of Ceará, Rio Grande de Norte, Paraíba, Pernambuco, Alagoas and the Territory of Fernando de Noronha; and finally, Group III contains Sergipe and Bahia.

11. Similar treatment is found in Diana Oya, "Land Tenure and Fertility in Northeast Brazil," Harvard University, January 1974, in manuscript.

12. Celso Furtado, *A Operacao Nordeste* (Rio de Janeiro, Brazil: Textos Brasileiros de Economia, Instituto Superior de Estudos Brasileiros, 1959), pp. 32-33.

10 Incentives for Family Limitations and Sterilization in India

Devendra K. Kothari

Objectives

Although sterilizations have been performed in India for many years, they became officially part of the Family Planning Program only in 1956. In recent years sterilizations have become an increasingly emphasized feature of the program. Experiments with increased monetary incentives to acceptors illustrate, however, that the government is relying too much on sterilization to solve the problem of rapid population growth.

The main objective of this chapter is to evaluate the feasibility and effectiveness of the monetary-incentive-based sterilization program to achieve the goals of lower fertility in the shortest possible time. This objective will be analyzed within the framework of the policy sciences as suggested by Lasswell and Montgomery.[1,2] The policy-oriented approach is contextual which implies that a particular problem is considered in relation to the larger context of the social process in which it is embedded and with which it interacts. However, it is observed that most of the administrative decisions usually occur as a by-product of other decisions, not in their own right. Therefore, most of the time, in the long run, they fail to achieve desired goals. This is also observed in India, where at the predecision stage policymakers do not consider the wider social implications of their decisions. Therefore, we shall also suggest lines of possible improvement to achieve the goals of lower fertility in India.

Predecision Forces

The early stages of a decision process involve information-gathering. On April 11, 1951, four years after Independence, a Committee on Population Growth and Family Planning was appointed to suggest a policy on the subject. Though not unanimously, the committee urged family limitation and noted the need of specific governmental measures for it. The interest of the government in the matter of population control was further aroused by the 1951 census report of India, in which the Census Commissioner of India drew the attention to the situation which India would have to face in the future if the population grew as it had grown during the decade 1941-1951, and suggested programs of population control. At the same time the First Five Year Plan recognized the urgency of the problem of population control and allotted money for family planning. Thus at the end of 1952, family planning on medical ground was officially proposed to be started in India on an experimental basis. But the government of India was not sure what to do with the experimental program recently introduced. A change in the governmental approach toward the population question became apparent near the end of the Second Plan period. At that time, one of the National Sample Survey reports revealed that the population of India had been growing at an annual rate of nearly 2 percent. This was confirmed by the 1961 census and it showed that population growth during the preceding decade was thirty million more than it had been expected. This increase in the rate of population growth and the discussion of the possible consequences of a high rate of growth on economic development in the classic work on the subject by Coale and Hoover, helped the government to think less in terms of a family planning program on medical and health ground and more in terms of a population control program on economic grounds.[3] Besides these factors, donor nations and international agencies began urging India to devote greater resources to curtailing fertility and indicated their willingness to provide technical and financial assistance to that end.[4]

In response to these forces, the government of India appointed the Mudaliar Committee in 1961 to suggest an adequate program for implementing the policy of population control from the Third Plan onward. The committee recommended, among other things, including the extension of facilities for voluntary sterilizations throughout the country, the promotion of intensive research on fertility control, and the provision of economic incentives for those who limit their families and disincentives for those who do not, through taxation and Social Security measures.[5]

These predecision settings forced the development-oriented politicians and administrators to recognize that rapid population growth was not merely an ephemeral problem but a major and political enduring obstacle to modernization.

Policy Decisions

In 1964, the government of India accepted population control as an essential element in the strategy of development to achieve a faster rate of economic growth as established in the Third Five Year Plan. It decided also to take the program to the people rather than waiting for them to come to the clinics.

Thus for the first time India approached the population question with confidence that it possessed a technology (I.U.D. and sterilization) which was suitable in sociological, medical, and organizational terms and the government set optimistic goals of fertility reduction, made population policy a prominent feature of its development objectives, and increased the resources and authority of its birth control organizations. India clearly announced that a goal of its birth control program was to reduce the birth rate from an official 41/1000 to 25/1000 by 1978.[6]

But the question was how to achieve this ambitious target in the shortest possible time. Being a democratic country India adopted the "cafeteria approach,"[7] which means making available a variety of scientifically proved and tested contraceptive methods so that couples could choose the one best suited to their requirements. But this should not be interpreted as implying that equal emphasis was given to all methods. In the initial state of the program most emphasis was given to I.U.D.'s.[a] After 1967, the emphasis laid on sterilizations, particularly on vasectomies, was due to the following reasons:

1. Long experience with sterilizations in India led to a decision to place it in the official family planning programs in 1956. India had the required technical know-how for this method.

2. India had trained doctors, administration, and technical personnel to carry out its massive program of sterilization. Moreover, India had an extensive and highly developed health system, including local clinics through which to reach its target population.

3. In comparison to female sterilization, which generally requires days of hospitalization, the male operation does not require a hospital stay and is performed with local anesthesia. Moreover, the male operation is so simple that no special equipment is needed and a really experienced physician can perform the operation in five minutes.[8] Furthermore, it can be performed at any place. (In Maharashtra, vasectomies are done at railway stations, both to convince people that the operation is minor and to reach those whose fear of medical institutions might otherwise hold them back.)

4. Medically, sterilization is regarded as a safe and highly effective birth control method relative to such alternatives as the pill and the I.U.D. and it does not require sustained motivation. Moreover morbidity and mortality rates are very low in the case of vasectomies.

5. The rapid decline in I.U.D. acceptance which followed the early popularity of the method also influenced the policymakers to place greater emphasis on sterilization—particularly on vasectomies.

Thus looking to the Indian conditions, where 80 percent of the population live in rural areas and do not have clinic facilities, sterilization, which can be

a	1965-66	1969-70	1972-73
Sterilizations	671,000	1,422,000	3,019,000
I.U.D. Insertions	813,000	459,000	333,000

Source: Dorothy Nortman, "Population and Family Planning Programs: A Factbook," *Reports on Population/Family Planning*, No. 2, 1972, p. 69.

performed by mobile units and camps and may cover target populations easily, was the most feasible method of population control.

Program and Project Decisions

Infrastructure

To achieve fertility reduction, an organizational set-up from the center to the peripheral level was evolved as a part of the existing medical and health services to reach approximately 100 million couples in the reproductive ages spread out in 56,000 villages and 3,000 towns and cities in a total area of 1.23 million square miles with varying geographic characteristics.

The clinic approach was strengthened by adopting the "extension approach." Following this approach, India made major strides in a remarkably short time in establishing and staffing facilities to bring family planning services closer to the people.

To make sterilization program more effective in the rural areas the extra emphasis was given on mobile units and sterilization camps. The "camp" is a part of the "extension approach." The development of the camp concept has considerably helped in spreading the sterilization program to the vast rural areas. This concept was devised to provide facilities at central points for a group of villages so that people could easily avail themselves of the services.

The camp concept also demonstrated that large numbers of people can be motivated to accept sterilization in a short span of the time through organized and concentrated efforts. "They provide a spectacular example of a family planning program transcending the traditional health and family planning network to become a total community effort."[9]

The camp concept is becoming more and more popular throughout the country and creating a social environment for acceptance of sterilization. Moreover, camps are also easy ways to achieve targets. For example, at the Ernakulum camp, Kerala, in 1971, about 62,193 vasectomies and 505 tubectomies were performed in eight weeks.[10] In another example the Gujarat State Family Planning Bureau in 1971, following the spectacular success of the Ernakulam camp, organized more than 1,000 camps throughout the state and performed 221,933 vasectomies during a two-month campaign.[11]

Budget Allocation

We do not have separate figures for the sterilization program but it is observed that the program has all the necessary financial backups. The available data show that the government of India has increased the budget allocation for the program in the successive plans. The Fourth Plan has allocated Rs. 3000 million for the period 1969-74 for the Family Planning Programs. And it is believed that the major portion would be spent on the sterilization program. As the U.N. Mission observed, the largest share goes toward the operation of the various units through which the program chiefly functions.

After providing all these facilities, there was still a major problem of how to attract couples to the program. This problem attracted the attention of many scholars and a solution was seen in monetary incentives.

Role of Monetary Incentives

Everett Rogers observed in Indonesia that "family planning does not occur *unless* clinic services are provided. Nor does it occur if *only* clinic services are provided." The incentive is required to motivate the people for the family planning. "Incentives are objects of financial value given by a family planning agency to encourage the adoption of family planning methods."[12]

In the late 1950s Professor Enke attempted to determine the value of incentives in preventing a birth.[13] He also discussed his plans for large incentives with Indian leaders, including Pandit Nehru. Since then "incentive" has become a very important point in the Family Planning Program.

Three countries including India currently offer monetary incentives to acceptors of family planning services, mainly for sterilizations,[14] although an official Indian report says "the compensation ... is for meeting out of pocket expenses and is not an incentive as such."[15] But of 297 men asked their primary motivation for the operation, 43 percent cited money; 38 percent a desire to limit family size.[16] Professor Pohlman believes that the idea of compensation for time lost from work and for expenses is, however, good public relations. Since canvassers make a living from their hard work, payments to them must act as incentives.[17]

Whatever the purposes of monetary help, the experiments with increased monetary "compensation" to acceptors illustrate the thinking among decision-makers.[18] The U.N. Mission also observed that more than one-fifth of the total budget of the Family Planning Program goes for compensative money, payments chiefly to sterilization and I.U.D. clients.[19] In certain camps more than 90 percent of the entire expenditure was made as direct benefits to persons including acceptors and canvassers.[20]

Besides official incentives, some private and public organizations are also paying case incentives of Rs. 200 to Rs. 300 over and above paid holidays to boost the program of sterilization among their employees. The government of India is also encouraging such activities by giving income tax exemptions to industrial organizations for expenditures on family planning.[21]

There is some evidence that monetary incentives are important in the program. During 1963, for example, when Tamilnadu discontinued the finder's fee to canvassers, vasectomy acceptance dropped to approximately a third of the original acceptances. When the payment was restored, acceptances rose to the previous level.[22]

Outcome of the Program

The annual rate of sterilizations steadily increased from .02 per 1,000 population in 1956 to 3.6 in 1967, then dropped slightly to 3.2 in 1968 and again rose to 3.98 in 1971.[23] The high rate of sterilizations in 1971 may be attributed to the camp concept adopted in the program together with higher monetary incentives.

Program Appraisal

Appraisal is an important aspect of any study. It helps to analyze whether a program is moving in the right direction and indicates steps that must be taken at various points in its development to ensure achievement of its objectives. Professor Lasswell believes that it helps analyze and report about the degree to which policy goals have been achieved, and the allocation of imputed or effective responsibility of results.[24]

What Are the Trends to Date in Goal Realization?

Sterilization is of demographic significance only if a substantial proportion of the population practices the method. Also of demographic relevance are the age of sterilized persons and the number of children they have at the time of sterilization.[25]

Prevalence

India has performed the largest number of sterilizations in the world—over thirteen million at the end of 1972. But this number represents only a small proportion—about 12 percent—of the population in the reproductive age group.

Table 10-1 shows that the program attained approximately 58 percent of the total target in 1969-70 and 48 percent in 1970-71. The percentages of targets achieved in India also vary by state: from 17 percent in Assam to 80 percent in Orrisa and 82 percent in Andhra Pradesh.

The target-setting is a very interesting aspect of the Indian program. The targets of sterilization were really very ambitious. It has been openly acknowl-

Table 10-1
Target and Performance (in thousands)

Year	Target	Performance	Percentage
1966-67	1,264	887	70.0
1967-68	2,058	1,840	89.4
1968-69	3,163	1,665	52.6
1969-70	2,431	1,422	58.5
1970-71	2,778	1,329	47.8

Source: Programme Informations 1970-71–*Government of India, New Delhi*, June 1971.

edged by the various experts that the sterilization targets were beyond the capacity of the program. Finkle observed that "ambitious goals are not necessarily bad, but the effect of the family planning target was to deny the program realistic objectives which could constitute the basis for detailed plans of action at various program levels. The process of target setting in the Indian family planning program gave primacy to those enthusiasts whose aspirations were intended to please the country's political leaders and impress foreign donors."[2]

Timing of Sterilization

It seems that the timing of sterilization with respect to age as well as to the number of living children is late in India. The various studies reveal, that the husband's age at the time of sterilization averages in the late thirties and forties. The wife's age is more relevant to the timing of sterilization than the husband's, as her reproductive span is narrower. The various studies suggest that the wife is generally in her early thirties when she or her husband is sterilized. This average corresponds to the mean of 32.2 years reported for all India. More than 55 percent of total women were above age thirty when they or their husbands were sterilized.[27]

The late timing of sterilization with respect to number of living children appears to be the main characteristic in India. The mean and median number of living children range from a mean as low as 3.1 to a median as high as 5.6.[28] The official report reveals that the average number of living children is 4.5 at the time of the sterilization. Of the total sterilized persons, 62.8 percent were having more than four children.[29]

Demographic Effectiveness

"The demographic impact of the large number of sterilizations performed to date is not fully established, partly because the frequency of considering couples who used other contraceptive methods prior to the operation is not taken into account and partly because there are important gaps in knowledge of such client characteristics as recent pregnancy history, parity and age of the wife and socio-economic status."[30] However, the demographic effectiveness of sterilization can be determined both by its prevalence and by the timing of such practice in relation to the reproductive span of women.

Looking to the completed fertility per woman, that is an average of 5.5 children in India, under such a situation the timing of sterilization after an average of 4.5 children would only minimally lower her birth rate.

The impact of the sterilization on population growth also depends on the age structure of their adopters. In India, couples generally produce 80 percent or more of their actual family size before the age of thirty-five due to early marriage and low life expectancy. Therefore, the late age of sterilization, which is about 32.2 years, is not going to effect fertility too much.

These points suggest that the program's demographic effect was not as near as it devised. It is estimated that about 500,000 births were averted by the program in 1968-69. Therefore, it is suggested that unless there is a trend toward earlier timing, the program's demographic effectiveness in India would not be substantial.

What Conditioning Factors Account for the Direction and Intensity of These Trends?

Highly motivated couples may have already been reached by the program and realistically the number of sterilizations should be expected to level off. Moreover, the recent trends in target achievement also show that the program is not attracting expected numbers of acceptors. Furthermore, those who are accepting sterilizations are not expected to effect the fertility to the required degree. All these situations can be explained through the following points:

1. *Structural constraints.* The critical medical aspect of sterilization is its finality, because the operation as currently performed cannot be reversed. Therefore, it must be regarded primarily as a means of ending reproduction. Infant mortality is still high in India and there exists fear among parents that their children will not survive to assist them. Besides this, because there are so many other structural constraints, such as negative cultural attitudes, limited knowledge, illiteracy, rurality, superstition, and embarrassment, it is understandable why the program could not attract a good proportion of couples.

2. *Regionalism.* Table 10-2 indicates that the prevalence rate was greater in the Southern states of India than in the Northern states. It has effected the performance in the Southern states in recent years. The table reveals that the Tamilnadu performed about 16 percent of all reported sterilizations during the period 1956 to 1968, with an acceptance rate of 2.78/1000 population in

Table 10-2
Regional Differentials in the Sterilizations Performed

State	Percentage of the Total Sterilizations 1956-1968	Acceptance Rate per 1000 Population 1969-1970	Target Achieved in Percentage 1969-1970	Percentage of the Total Population 1971
Tamilnadu	16.1	2.78	46	7.5
Maharashtra	15.5	4.63	77	9.2
Uttar Pradesh	9.3	.87	15	16.1
Madhya Pradesh	8.3	3.07	51	7.6
West Bengal	7.1	1.82	30	8.1
Andhra Pradesh	6.5	4.84	82	7.9
Orrisa	5.6	4.81	80	4.0
Gujarat	5.5	3.62	60	4.4
Mysore	5.4	1.69	28	5.3
Bihar	5.3	1.18	20	10.2
Kerala	5.2	2.84	47	3.9
Punjab	3.3	2.84	47	2.5
Rajasthan	2.1	1.69	28	4.7
Assam	.7	1.12	19	2.7
Haryana	.7	3.22	54	1.8

Sources: H.B. Presser, "Voluntary Sterilization: A World View," *Reports on Population/Family Planning*, No. 5, 1970, p. 12; R.J. Lapham, and W.P. Mauldin, "National Family Planning: Reviewed Evaluation," *Studies in Family Planning* 3 (March 1972): 44; Census Centenary 1972, *Government of India*, New Delhi, p. 21.

1969-70 and achieved the target by 46 percent, while the population of this state constituted only 7.5 percent of the total population of India in 1971. On the other hand, the most populated states in India, Uttar Pradesh and Bihar with about 27 percent of India's population, have performed less than 15 percent of all sterilizations and have an acceptance rate of only 1/1000.

Looking to these regional trends in the family planning, a well-known political leader from Tamilnadu publicly voiced concern that his state would lose seats in the parliament because family planning had disproportionately lowered the population. Such feeling has also affected the performance of sterilizations in the recent years.

3. *Ethnic and Religious Considerations.* It is found that sterilization is acceptable to those with different religious beliefs including Hindus, Muslims, and Catholics. Most of the population of India is Hindu (82.7 percent), a substantial minority is Muslim (11.3 percent), and the remaining 6 percent are of other religions.[31] It is therefore not surprising to find as Presser reports,[32] that from 83 to 99 percent of the sterilized persons are Hindus, although they seem

to constitute a disproportionate number in the samples relative to their representation in the total population. Muslims seem to be underrepresented in the sterilization studies relative to their share in the total population.

Although ethnic suspicions are relatively minor, religious and caste groups in the country sometimes watch each other's family planning performance out of concern that their relative share not be reduced.[33] In recent years this situation was used by some political parties and it is believed that the program was influenced by their propaganda.

4. *Role of Monetary Incentives.* It is believed that due to the monetary incentives, the program is not able to attract the right acceptors. According to Srinivasan and Kachirayan a good proportion of acceptors who underwent vasectomy were either sterile or subfertile at the time. On the basis of such evidences, Repetto observed in the Tamilnadu that "canvassers sometimes bring men who are bachelors, over age... and they are motivated solely by a pecuniary incentive rather than a concern for family welfare, and in some cases are realising exorbitant incomes."[34]

Thus the picture that emerges of the incentive-motivated vasectomy adopter is an individual who is likely to adopt for the "wrong" reasons, and, in many cases, whose adoption may not lead to the desired consequences of birth prevention.[35] Therefore, it is now felt by many experts that India requires a new set of motivational approaches to attract the right people towards the Family Planning Program.

5. *Administrative Set-up.* It is observed in India that the decision to regard family planning as a health subject had three major consequences affecting the strategy, structure, and performance of the program. The control over vital aspects of the program was retained by the states, which have constitutional authority to manage health services, while the program is fully financed by the center. Due to this constitutional restriction, the central government cannot circumvent the states in working with the districts. This is an important disadvantage to the program as the districts constitute the critical subunits of government, where family planning workers come into direct contact with the target population. Thus this lack of direct communication from the center to the subunits has also affected the performance of the program.[36]

What Are the Most Probable Projections of Future Development in the Realization of Goals?

The program has obtained the "plateau" situation because highly motivated couples may now have been reached by the program. Looking to the trends, the U.N. Mission observed "... it appears that the peak has been reached."[37] Nevertheless the advocates of the program believe that with the higher monetary incentives the hard-core non-receptive population that exists after several years of usual propaganda efforts for the sterilization can be "cracked" and the "plateau" in the rate of adoption can be overcome.

But our past experience tells us that the monetary-incentive-based program cannot influence intricate reproductive behavior of the population too much and after the sixteen years of effort we are able to protect only 12 percent of the fertile couples through the program.

Moreover, the government of India cannot afford the monetary-incentive-based program for an indefinite period, because there are many other pressing needs to which it has to respond. That was the most probable reason why the government of India recently has reduced budget allocation of the Family Planning Program. This followed stinging criticism, especially from abroad, that India is courting a hazardous policy and failing to tackle a fundamental problem—the nation's unchecked birth rate. Despite this criticism, India's family planning budget in 1973-74 remains below the figure approved in the previous year.[38]

Furthermore, India's family planning program is mainly based on external help and it is not very hopeful that the volume of external help would be increased in coming years. The U.N. Mission also observed this situation and remarked that the external aid has "... so far not been commensurate either with the magnitude of the problem or with the size of the efforts of the Government of India to tackle it."[39]

Finally, it can also be said that the increased monetary incentive system would require a good amount of supervision because there will be greater probability of fraud and corruption.

Therefore, looking to these points it can be concluded that the probability of introduction of higher monetary incentives in the program seems not very reasonable. It is expected that the present system will not be able to attract more "quality" adopters to the program in the coming years.

What Policy Alternatives Will Yield the Highest Net Realization of Goal Values?

The above analysis reveals that the program could not generate sufficient motivation for lower fertility among the population overwhelmingly rural, illiterate, and isolated. India's policymakers incorrectly assumed at the decision level that all the fertile audiences would actively seek family planning services, once they were made available. They placed too much hope in the "clinic approach" and when the I.U.D. program failed they did not try for its rehabilitation, but placed greater emphasis on sterilization, while knowing the fact that the majority of the population in the reproductive age group would not welcome the program, due to certain known reasons. They also considered monetary incentive as a panacea and thought it would motivate the couples, and so did not try to develop other methods of motivation. In fact, they did not even try to influence the intricate reproductive behavior and therefore, the program attracted mostly "low quality" adopters, which was one reason why the birth rate remained near 39/1000 population in 1971. Recently the Indian Minister of Family Planning is reported to have publicly recognized that the program cannot hope to reduce the country's birth rate to 25/1000 by 1978. The aim now would be the reduction of the birth rate to 30/1000 by 1980.[40]

By citing the drawbacks, we do not mean that the program has failed. Undoubtedly it has created an environment for further action. We agree with Professor Wilbur Schramm, who stated "... when the acceptance plateau is reached, then it is necessary to be more efficient and skillful with communication and try to devise tactics and messages that will persuade as well as inform."[41]

To date, effective social communication action strategies have been a missing ingredient in the program. Therefore, we propose a societal role in the fertility control programs. Because we believe that "the population problem has no technical solution, it requires a fundamental extension in morality."[42] Therefore, we suggest the following strategies for the post-"plateau" period.

1. In place of family planning we propose "population planning," which according to Elihu Bergman "... takes its cues from requirements for societal welfare. Family Planning has enshrined individual freedom of choice as its controlling norm. Population planning includes the interest of the community and the advantages to the individual in discharging an obligation to the society.... The fulfillment of population planning norms require authoritative action by the political system—some sort of policy action."[43] To achieve the goals of population planning the government must formulate policies which will make it advantageous for people to have smaller families. At a political level it must create confidence among various socioeconomic and regional groups that they will not be at a disadvantage because of their participation in birth control programs.

2. We propose that population planning should not be part of the Health Ministry but should be a separate ministry in itself, and should be headed by a powerful political leader, so he can influence the policies of other ministries to fulfill the objectives of the population planning.

3. We propose that the population should be a central unit so the center can communicate directly with local units and subunits.

4. Rather than give equal priority to all the couples in the reproductive age group, we propose that a selective approach should be adopted. The top priority should be given to the people (15-25 years) who affect current and future fertility trends. Therefore, the government through its policies must influence this group intensively for fertility reduction.

5. We propose that population education should be given due importance

from the post-primary education. We believe population education would bring a change in the attitudes of children and adolescents in favor of a small family.

6. We propose that a birth control program should be truly based on the "cafeteria" approach and should not place too much emphasis on a single method. Looking to the Indian conditions, the government must revitalize the I.U.D. program, because it is an inexpensive and reversible method of clinical contraception and can be used for spacing.

7. The targets should not be overly ambitious and they should be based on the resources available. We propose that the "Population Ministry" should prepare a "Two Year Plan," like the Five Year Plan, for population planning and at the end of every two years the program should be evaluated so that strategies and tactics may be selected or modified in the perspective of experience and research.

The execution of all these proposals does not require huge resources, but does require right political thinking and supervision. Our proposals are directed not against the sterilization program based on monetary incentives as such, but against the assumption that they are an effective means of controlling population growth in the current socioeconomic situation. "The need is not to abandon family planning programs but to put equal or greater resources into other approaches."[44]

Notes

1. H.D. Lasswell, "Population Change and Policy Sciences: Proposed Workshops on Reciprocal Impact Analysis," *Harvard Center for Population Studies*, 1974, mimeo.

2. J.D. Montgomery, "A Strategy of Analyzing the Effects of Rapid Population Change on the Administration of Public Services," *Harvard Center for Population Studies*, Cambridge, 1974, mimeo.

3. T.J. Samuel, "The Development of India's Policy of Population Control," *The Milbank Memorial Fund Quarterly* 44 (January 1966): 53-55.

4. J.P. Lewis, "Population Control in India," *Population Bulletin* 26, 5 (1970): 15.

5. *Christian Science Monitor*, Boston, Mass., December 2, 1961.

6. Shri Govind Narain, "India: The Family Planning Program Since 1965," *Studies in Family Planning* 35 (1968): 2.

7. Ibid., p. 3.

8. E. Pohlman, "How to Kill Population," *The Westminster Press*, Philadelphia, Pa., p. 108.

9. S. Krishnakumar, "Kerala Pioneering Experiment in Massive Vasectomy Camps," *Studies in Family Planning* 3 (August 1972): 177.

10. Ibid., p. 177.

11. V.H. Thakor and V.M. Patel, "The Gujarat State Massive Vasectomy Campaign," *Studies in Family Planning* 3 (August 1972): 186.

12. E.M. Rogers, "A Field Study of Family Planning Incentives and Field Staff in Indonesia," *Indonesia Planned Parenthood Association,* Djakarta, 1971.

13. S. Enke, "The Gains to India from Population Control," *Review of Economic Statistics* 42 (1960): 175-81.

14. J.T. Fawcett, "Psychology and Population," *The Population Council,* New York, 1970, p. 101.

15. Government of India, "Small Family Norms Committee Report," New Delhi, 1968.

16. K. Srinivasan and M. Kachisayan, "Vasectomy Follow-up Study: Findings and Implications," *Institute of Rural Health and Family Planning Bulletin* 3 (1968): 13-32.

17. E. Pohlman, "Incentives and Compensations in Birth Planning," *Monograph II, University of North Carolina*, 1971, p. 3.

18. United Nations, "An Evaluation of the Family Planning Program of the Government of India," U.N. ST/SOA/Ser. R/11, 1969, p. 14.

19. Ibid., p. 14.

20. Krishnakumar, "Kerala Pioneering Experiment," p. 184.

21. Government of India, "Centre Calling," December 5, 1970, New Delhi, p. 6.

22. R. Repetto, "India: A Case Study of the Madras Vasectomy Program," *Studies in Family Planning* 31 (1968): 10.

23. Dorothy Nortman, "Population and Family Planning Programs: A Factbook," *Reports on Population/Family Planning*, No. 2, 1973, p. 69.

24. H.D. Lasswell, "Population Change," p. 4.

25. H.B. Presser, "Voluntary Sterilization: A World View," *Reports on Population/Family Planning*, No. 5, July 1970, p. 10.

26. J.L. Finkle, "The Political Environment of Population Control in India and Pakistan," in Richard Clinton et al. (eds.), *Political Science in Population Studies* (Lexington, Mass.: Lexington Books, D.C. Heath and Company, 1972), p. 113.

27. Sri Govind Narain, "India: The Family Planning Program Since 1965," *Studies in Family Planning* 35 (1968): 3.

28. Presser, "Voluntary Sterilization," p. 13.

29. Narain, "India: Family Planning Program."

30. United Nations, "Evaluation of Family Planning Program," p. 42.

31. Government of India, "Census Centenary 1972—Population Statistics," New Delhi, p. 2.

32. Presser, "Voluntary Sterilization," p. 21.

33. D.K. Kothari, "Population Policy: A Social Framework of Fertility Control," unpublished paper, 1973, p. 12.

34. Repetto, "India: A Case Study," p. 6.

35. E.M. Rogers, "Incentives in the Diffusion of Family Planning Informations," *Studies in Family Planning* 2 (December 1971): 248.

36. Finkle, "Political Environment," p. 114.

37. United Nations, "Evaluation of Family Planning Program," p. 15.

38. *New York Times*, November 11, 1973, p. 6.

39. United Nations, "Evaluation of Family Planning Program," p. 74.

40. *The Asian Student*, A publication of the Asia Foundation, San Francisco, January 1974, p. 3.

41. W. Schramm, "Communication in Family Planning," *Reports on Population/Family Planning* 7 (1971): 19.

42. G. Hardin, "The Tragedy of the Commons," *Science* 162 (1968): 1243.

43. E. Bergman, "American Population Policy Making: The Politics of Do Good, but do not Rock the Boatt," in Richard Clinton et al. (eds.), *Research in the Politics of Population* (Lexington, Mass.: Lexington Books, D.C. Heath and Company, 1972), p. 43.

44. K. Davis, "The Population Policy: Will Current Program Succeed?" in Revelle et al., *The Survival Equation*, National Academy of Sciences (Baltimore: Johns Hopkins University Press, 1971), p. 151.

11 Structure and Decisions in the American Family Planning Program

Korbin Liu

Introduction

For the past fifteen years, family planning programs have been major public policy issues in many countries. In 1969, the United States government created within the Department of Health, Education and Welfare a new agency, the National Center for Family Planning Services (NCFPS), to focus the government's interest in increasing its support of voluntary family planning services. In order to provide additional funds to finance the establishment of the new agency and to subsidize the family planning services, the Family Planning Services and Population Research Act was passed in 1970. The new funds greatly supplemented the existing resources for family planning activities.[a]

After five years of operation, from 1969 to 1973, the National Center was phased out, and family planning services became an integral part of community health services supported by the government through a new bureau in HEW. While categorical family planning services funding is being maintained for the time being, it too is expected to be phased out.

The purpose of this chapter is to present a framework for the analysis of public policies and to illustrate how the use of such a framework might reduce the loss of resources in the course of policy development. To serve this purpose the framework will be illustrated in an analysis of elements of the U.S. family planning policies of 1969-70, the creation of the NCFPS, and the enactment of the Family Planning Services and Population Research Act. It is not the intent of this chapter to make an exhaustive appraisal of those policies. Since this analysis is made after the termination of the policies, it will benefit from some facts which were not available to the decisionmakers in 1969-70. Even from this retrospective view, it will attempt to be more than must an academic case study of past policies. First, such an analysis of the U.S. family planning program might offer policy-related implications to governments of other countries which are considering either the initiation of a national family planning program or the modification of an ongoing family planning program. Secondly, family planning activities will continue in the United States and an account of past experiences

---

[a]The New funds were authorized under Title X of the Public Health Service Act, 1970. Previously, Federal family planning funds were authorized primarily under Title V of the Social Security Act, as amended in 1967, and Title II of the Economic Opportunity Act, 1967.

might help in determining future activities. Finally, the ultimate appraisal of the U.S. family planning program has not been concluded, and this analysis will attempt to add to that effort.

Policy Analysis Framework

The analytical framework will be based on Lasswell's seven policy outcomes (see Chapter 4 in this volume) and Ilchman's five sets of factors which act on and are acted upon by events and actions throughout the course of the policy process.[1] According to Lasswell, the seven policy outcomes represent the logical sequence of events that any policy undergoes from initiation to final evaluation. The seven outcomes are intelligence, promotion, prescription, invocation, application, termination, and appraisal. According to Ilchman, the potential effectiveness of a policy is dependent upon elements other than technical ones. The five sets of factors place technical alternatives within an administrative and political sphere, and policies can thus be evaluated according to the entire context of public action, rather than just in terms of technical costs and benefits. The five sets of factors prescribed by Ilchman are knowledge about the problem to which the policy is directed, regime resources to carry out the policy, sector resources which support or impede the policy, decision rules by which the policy is carried out, and administrative infrastructures which exist to carry out the policy.

Lasswell's seven policy outcomes provide a sequence of phases over time, while Ilchman's five sets of factors represent analytical units that are examined at each one of Lasswell's phases. In Lasswell's scheme, *intelligence* represents knowledge about the problems for which a policy is raised. This phase considers the total context of the problem to be addressed by the policy, and specifically examines the goals that the policy will attempt to achieve, the trends of events representing the problem to be solved, the conditions that underlie the events, in both direction and intensity, projections of the trends if no policy is initiated to intervene in the process, and the delineation and assessment of policy alternatives which can intervene and alter the trends in an effort to achieve the goals. The *promotion* phase is characterized by activities to gain support for the implementation of a policy chosen on the basis of information from the intelligence phase. *Prescription* is the official statement of the policy, and is exemplified in public policies by laws passed by Congress, administrative regulations by the executive branch, or judicial decisions. *Invocation* represents the first stage in the application of the policy. In some cases, the invocation phase specifies events that take place before the official machinery is mobilized to implement the policy. *Termination* represents the final phase in the implementation of the policy, and is effected through modification or elimination. *Appraisal* represents the evaluation of the policy's ability to reach the goals officially prescribed.

The five sets of factors that constitute Ilchman's scheme represent forces that should be critically examined at each phase of the policy process. The forces either add resources to effectuate the desired outcome, or act as obstacles against the desired outcome. The status of the forces changes over time due to the dynamic relationship between each phase in Lasswell's scheme and the other phases preceding it. In choosing the best policy alternative, it is desirable to evaluate the probable status of the factors at each phase of the policy process. As perfect information is never available, policymakers have to make "guesstimates" of changes in the status of the factors, given the effects of preceding events.

The *knowledge* factors provide the policymaker with information to determine the scope of the problem, define alternative approaches to solving the problem, and rationalize the specific policy chosen. At this stage, the policymaker determines the target population and the social outcomes that would result from the policy chosen. He evaluates the types of action that would be necessary to intervene in the target population's choice budgets, and the technical costs that would be incurred. The *regime resources* constitute the amounts of authority, status, information, economic goods and services, and coercion which the regime has available to carry out the policy. The *sector resources* constitute the amounts of legitimacy, status, information, economic goods and services, and violence which different sectors can direct toward the implementation of the policy. Different sectors might be in favor of, against, or neutral to specific policies. The *decision rules* define the administrative behavior of the regime in carrying out the policy. Frequently throughout the development of a policy, decision rules are modified; either established decision rules are deleted or altered, or new ones are initiated. The *administrative infrastructure* describes the machinery through which the policy is implemented. Like the other factors, the administrative infrastructure will be subject to modification throughout the evolution of the policy. It is likely to change in size and composition. For example, new agencies may be established, existing agencies may be combined, or personnel from one existing agency may be transferred to a new agency.

The importance of Ilchman's sets of factors is that they include political and administrative elements, as well as academic and technical ones. It is obvious that an analysis of technical solutions alone cannot determine the likelihood that the desired social outcomes will be achieved, or explain the effectiveness of past policies in achieving their goals.

Once the policy process has progressed to the invocation, application, and termination phase, impact and response decisions are elicited from individuals or groups affected by the outcomes of the policy and others who are not directly affected by the immediate products of the policy. The latter group may derive, for example, moral, psychological, or political benefits from the policy.

In summary, the framework is not a unique process for problem solving. It is simply a structure for considering factors important to the policy process. The essential features of the framework are: (a) the analysis of important policy-related factors, (b) the appraisal of changes in those factors over time, and (c) the appraisal of the interrelationships of the factors.

Application of the Framework

The function of the framework is to organize components of the policy analysis in a systematic order so that decisions can be made to begin the policy process, change courses, or abandon the idea altogether. The longitudinal spectrum of the framework provided by Lasswell's seven policy outcomes forces the decisionmaker to project the relative changes in the nature and quantity of the policy-relevant factors over time. The advantage of this longitudinal perspective is that it allows the policymaker to evaluate the potential success of the policy in light of conditions that may exist after the time the policy is considered.

The first illustration of the policy framework is the issue of the creation of the National Center for Family Planning Services. In 1969, the decisionmakers favored the creation of a single-purpose agency to administer the new family planning services funds over the inclusion of the new service programs in the programs of existing health agencies. At the intelligence phase, an analysis of the policy factors strongly favored the inclusion of the family planning activities under an agency such as the Maternal and Child Health Services. First, there already was an overall federal policy of coordinating health services to reduce duplication and overlapping of categorical programs by the extensive federal health bureaucracy. Second, family planning is logically an element of comprehensive maternal and child health care. Third, the creation of a new agency would necessarily result in the expenditure of additional resources for the maintenance of the new administrative structure. It is usually more efficient to add additional personnel to existing infrastructures than to create new infrastructures. Fourth, strong sector forces, particularly within the federal bureaucracy itself, opposed the creation of the new agency. Finally, there did not seem to be any logical support for the notion that a new group of bureaucrats could promote a new program better than an old group of bureaucrats.

However, the decisionmakers were also subject to the pressure of proponents of the new agency who felt that a National Center was necessary to establish family planning as the national priority that it had been designated by the Administration and by Congress. Further, the decisionmakers projected a loss of flexibility in decision making if an existing infrastructure were given the authority to administer the new family planning program. In the first place, the existing agency would be biased toward funding its traditional grantees such as hospitals and health departments. A new Center would be more flexible in funding different types of projects such as community action agencies, Planned

Parenthood affiliates, and other private nonprofit organizations. Secondly, a National Center mandated primarily to promote family planning services would more effectively ensure that the new funds were utilized for contraceptive care.

In summary, while good arguments were made for and against the creation of a new agency to administer the family planning funds, the decisionmakers decided that the social impact of creating the new agency exceeded the additional costs that would be incurred. As can be inferred from the discussion, the evaluation was made of the estimated loss of resources that would have occurred once the policy process had progressed to the application phase.

A second illustration is the decision against charging fees for services. At the prescription phase of the policy process, the decisionmakers felt that no fees should be charged to any recipient of federally supported family planning services. This judgment was based first on the knowledge that many women in the United States were unable to prevent unplanned pregnancy because they could not afford to obtain the reliable contraceptive methods or sufficient education and counseling about the use of any contraceptive method. Secondly, it was believed that sufficient regime resources would be available over the course of the policy process to subsidize completely family planning care for all women who wanted such services. In fact, family planning activities in the federal government were clearly a priority issue both to the Administration had to Congress. Finally, the decisionmakers felt that, in order for fees to be charged, a screening procedure about family income would have to be initiated. This procedure might have been perceived by some sector groups as a means test. The fear was that sector opposition might have been generated in response to federal attempts to distinguish the poor from the nonpoor. Given the analysis described above, the regulations of the Family Planning Services Act specified that no charges would be made for services provided by the Act.

This decision against charging fees was reversed later in the policy process. It was discovered that the administrational and congressional enchantment with family planning would wane, and the regime resources anticipated for the later years of the program would not meet the original projections. It also became apparent that many of the patients of the federally subsidized family planning clinics desired to pay whatever they could for the care that was being provided. In fact, many women felt that receiving free services was tantamount to being "on welfare," and clearly preferred to pay something for the services. A final discovery was that some private physicians refused to participate in family planning projects because they feared that paying patients, who would ordinarily have gone to their private offices, would now opt to receive services from them at the free family planning clinics. This presented problems to some of the projects, which had difficulty recruiting physicians to serve in the clinics.

Hence, the decisionmakers were prompted to reverse their position on charging fees. Subsequently, the regulations of the Family Planning Services Act were revised to permit projects to establish a sliding scale of fees. This mechanism allowed certain individuals to contribute to the maintenance of the family planning program. In most cases, any charge could be waived if the patient resisted paying for any part of the services. In terms of the framework, the decisionmakers' analysis of important policy factors had not been projected far enough into the policy process to allow them to make the correct decision at the prescription phase. The termination of the original policy provided intelligence input to the formation of a new policy. The subsequent policy exemplifies the use of the entire framework for a new decision.

A third illustration is the issue of abortion as a potential element in the U.S. government funded family planning program. At the intelligence phase, policymakers in the United States were aware of the effectiveness of abortion services in reducing unplanned fertility. There certainly existed logical and empirical justification for including abortions in the total service package. However, in reviewing the sector resources that would be marshalled against the family planning policies if abortion were included as a service component, it became clear that a policy which included abortion services would have been defeated at the prescription phase. As a consequence, the entire family planning effort would have been defeated. Thus, the policymakers decided to exclude abortion as one element of the proposed family planning program so that the other component of the program, contraceptive care, could become viable. In terms of the policy framework, a policy to provide federally subsidized abortion services with contraceptive care was never begun, since projected sector opposition to it at a later stage of the policy would have forced the policy to fail.

Resources Lost

The previous section provided illustrations of how the framework could be applied to assist decisionmakers in policy formulation. The examples were general in nature and were intended to provide overall insights into the utility of the framework. This section will present two further illustrations from the U.S. family planning policies of 1969-70. The purpose of this section is to illustrate evaluation of Ilchman's analytical units to determine the types of resources that would be lost as a consequence of choosing a particular policy.

The first case discusses the resources that were lost as a consequence of the pattern of funding chosen for increasing the federal family planning activities. In terms of the framework, it was important for the policymakers to decide how much and at what rates the regime resource of economic goods and services should be made available to the policy to increase family planning activities. Given any pattern that was chosen, some resources would be lost in the effort to improve social welfare through family planning. This case will discuss specific types of resources lost as a consequence of the specific funding pattern that was experienced. It will also examine the types of resources that might have been lost if an alternative pattern were chosen.

During the promotion and prescription phases of the policy process, the popularity of family planning was manifested by both the executive and legislative branches of government. Family planning was stated to be a priority program by the Administration, and Congress passed the Family Planning Services Act by overwhelming margins. In light of these events, there was optimism that much of the prescribed authorization would be forthcoming and that the government would continue to support the policies until the goal was reached.

One consequence of the prevailing optimism was that the National Center did not exercise due concern that grantees of the federal funds emphasize the recruitment of "hard to reach" and "highly motivated" subgroups of the potential target population equally. Second, the anticipated high levels of funding, and the rapid increase in funding in the early years of the program, resulted in a minimal effort to find funding for family planning from other sources. Third, the rate of funding increases in the early years did not seem to be commensurate with the rate of effective demand for the family planning services. Hence, the utilization of funds was inefficient. A fourth consequence was the ineffective synchronization between the levels of funding for family planning services and the readiness of the administrative and clinical services infrastructure to utilize the service funds. For example, there was not sufficient time to recruit new staff members for the National Center, and to process them through personnel. By the time they were hired, the staff members of the National Center were left with inadequate time to promote the availability of the new federal funding before first year funds had to be obligated. As a consequence, the lack of sufficient lead time required to develop good projects probably resulted in grant awards made to many unprepared and some inferior grantees.

In retrospect, it is apparent that considerable resources were lost because of the high level of funding at the early phases of the program and the poor synchronization between the availability of new levels of funding and the development of the administrative infrastructure to manage the funds. This situation seems particularly ironic when one considers that the federal funding level for family planning services levelled off in 1974 at a time when the public demand to use federally subsidized clinics seemed to far exceed the resources that were available to provide the necessary services.

The preceding discussion illustrates how resources were lost as a consequence of the pattern of rapidly increasing funding for new family planning activities. In light of this experience, a more logical funding pattern would have been to raise the budget levels gradually in order to allow the administrative and clinic infrastructure to develop, and then to make increases in funding levels commensurate with the public demand for services. However, a realistic consideration of this alternative funding pattern might arrive at a different prognosis. While the alternative pattern would have reduced the loss of resources through inefficiencies, the net amount of funding during the course of the policy might in fact have been less if the projected higher levels of funding in the later stages of the hypothetical pattern were never actualized. At the stage when the high levels of funding were needed, new national priorities would have emerged and congressional "funding fatigue" might easily have doomed the family planning efforts to the low levels of the early stages of the process.

In summary, this case illustrates the types of resources that were lost as a result of the funding pattern experiences, and the resources that might never have materialized if an alternative funding pattern were chosen. In general terms of the framework, this case elucidates the types of factors under Ilchman's category of regime resources which need to be evaluated over the projected course of the policy as part of the total process of policy analysis.

The second case in this section examines in more detail the policy to create the National Center for Family Planning Services. Earlier in this chapter, it was noted that creating a new agency like the National Center was important in assuring that the new family planning efforts would not be hampered by the customs of the existing infrastructure. This discussion deals with the types of resources that were lost because the decisionmakers decided to create the National Center. In terms of the framework, such losses in resources are weighed against the ones that would have resulted if the new funds were administered by the existing infrastructure.

Two areas of major concern in this analysis are the relationship of the National Center to the rest of the federal bureaucracy, and the development of the NCFPS itself. The Maternal and Child Health Service (MCHS) and the Office of Economic Opportunity (OEO) were both administering family planning funds prior to the creation of the NCFPS. In fact, the MCHS was awarding the Social Security Act Title V special projects grants until the NCFPS was created, at which point jurisdiction of those funds were turned over to the NCFPS.[b] When the NCFPS was created, it was situated in a part of the existing administrative infrastructure which had preferred that it not exist in the first place. This event clearly became a harbinger of administrative problems for the NCFPS. In addition, the Center was designated the "lead agency" for the federal family planning effort, but was not assigned any administrative authority over the family planning activities of either MCHS or OEO. Without this authority, and with the natural unwillingness of competing agencies to cooperate with each other, federal resources for family planning were lost because of duplications of effort and poor planning. The following two examples illustrate the types of problems that arose, and how resources could have been saved if infrastructure roles were better defined. The first case deals with an OEO community action agency that wanted funding for a family planning clinic. The agency submitted identical proposals to both the OEO and the NCFPS. At a regional level meeting

---

[b]Although the Special Projects Grants under Title V were transferred to the NCFPS, Maternal and Child Health Formula Funds also under Title V continued to be administered by MCHS and continued to stipulate that a portion of the formula grants had to be expended for family planning activities.

between OEO and NCFPS, it was decided that NCFPS would fund the particular project, and the project was duly funded. Just before the end of the fiscal year, the OEO regional office decided that it wanted to supplement the community action agency which the NCFPS had just funded. The consequence of this action was to give the local project twice the amount of money it had originally requested. The cost per patient for family planning care provided by that agency was inappropriately high for the first year of its operation.

The second case deals with a statewide program that was interested in obtaining funding for an automated data system to record information about its family planning patients. The state agency which administered the program was a grantee of both the NCFPS and the MCHS. A request for funds from the NCPFS was rejected because the NCFPS had already initiated a project to develop a regionwide automated data system. A subsequent request to MCHS, however, was approved for $20,000. The lack of cooperation between NCFPS and MCHS resulted in a loss of the $20,000 since that amount was inadequate to implement the system, and the state agency ultimately abandoned its independent data system and utilized the regional system that was initiated by the NCFPS.

It is obvious from these examples that coordination among the family planning funding agencies could have averted both the inefficiency in the utilization of funds or the total loss of them.

The second area of concern in this analysis is the loss of resources in the development of the new agency itself. The NCFPS was created as a unit under the Health Services and Mental Health Administration (HSMHA), which was the next highest level in the HEW bureaucracy. HSMHA directed the activities of most of the HEW health services agencies, including MCHS. Unlike MCHS, and other agencies in HSMHA, the NCFPS was under the direct responsibility of two superiors, the Deputy Assistant Secretary for Population Affairs and the administrator of HSMHA. As a result of being supervised by two separate offices, the NCFPS had to reconcile its policies with the goals and priorities of both of its bosses. The energy expended in fulfilling this dual responsibility might have been better used for other purposes.

The lack of sole affiliation with the HSMHA enhanced the antagonism of the other units of HSMHA, which were naturally envious of a new agency which was projected to receive major increases in its annual budget levels. The immediate consequences of this situation was that the NCFPS experienced difficulties in coordinating program activities with other units and in cutting through bureaucratic "red tape." For example, the NCFPS had extraordinary problems getting cooperation on personnel related matters. As was previously noted, the difficulties with recruitment and hiring enhanced the poor synchronization of high levels of funding with the administrative capability to expend the funds efficiently.

Within the NCFPS itself, a major infrastructure problem was the poor delineation of the roles of the staff, and in particular, of headquarters versus regional staff. While these roles should have been clarified at the invocation phase, the functions of the respective staffs were determined on an ad hoc basis. The problem of roles was further complicated by the dual responsibility of regional staff to the director of NCFPS and to the regional representatives of the administrator of HSMHA; this was an analogous problem to the one encountered by the director of NCFPS.

During the implementation phases of the policy, it became obvious that the ambiguity of roles was a meaningful factor in the loss of resources and in the neglect of important activities. Specifically, headquarters and regional conflicts in policy formulation for the agency resulted in delaying or totally omitting actions on important policy issues. In short, division of labor among the NCFPS was not effectively specified, with a resulting loss of considerable resources and the omission of important policy actions.

In summary, this case illustrated the types of resources that were lost as a result of the creation of the new National Center. An evaluation of the wisdom of the policy to create the Center has to weigh the amounts of such resources lost against those that would have been lost if the Center were not created. In the general terms of the framework, this case illustrates the types of details under Ilchman's category of administrative infrastructure which have to be evaluated as part of the total process of policy analysis.

Summary and Conclusions

This chapter has presented a framework for policy analysis based on Lasswell's seven policy outcomes and Ilchman's five sets of analytical factors. The purpose of the framework is to provide a structure by which important elements in the analysis of public policies can be projected over the course of the policy process. In the illustration of the framework, examples have been taken from the U.S. government's policies creating the National Center for Family Planning Services in 1969 and enacting the Family Planning Services and Population Research Act of 1970. The illustrations have attempted to provide overall insights into the utilization of the framework and to demonstrate the utility of examining resources that would be lost as a consequence of pursuing a particular policy.

The terms "decisionmaker" and "policymaker" have been loosely used throughout this chapter. They refer to various persons, groups of persons, or institutions, depending upon the specific example that was being discussed.

While all decisions that are made are based on some level of structure, it is the belief of the author that formalized structures for policy analysis, such as the framework presented in this chapter, can be of value even to the most astute decisionmaker. At the least, formalized structures offer a schema for classifying important policy factors. Beyond that, formalized structures can facilitate the visualization of the relationships among policy factors and the analysis of the dynamic interactions of such factors over time.

Note

1. Warren F. Ilchman and Norman T. Uphoff, *The Political Economy of Change*, University of California Press, Berkeley, 1971.

12 Organizing for Population Change in Malaysia

Zakaria Haji Ahmad and
Siew-Nyat Chin

Introduction

Planning to cope with the consequences and effects of rapid population change is both an administrative and political task. Once the problems of population change is perceived by a regime to be salient political necessities, and the essential political decisions follow, there remain important questions of organizational dynamics or "demonics"[1] of bureaucratic policies. This chapter presents an historical and structural analysis of Malaysia's attempts at organizing for population change. As an example of incremental problem-solving by a responsible government (see Chapter 3 in this volume), the Malaysian case is an almost unique example of a "developing country" that is preparing to meet the problems of population growth and population distribution. For purposes of historical analysis, we shall consider the case of the Malaysian government's attempts to control fertility; for purposes of structural analysis, we shall evaluate the suggestive spectrum of Malaysian population policies and its organizational aspects in terms of past, present, and future perspectives (see Chapter 4 in this volume).

Malaysian population policy has been viewed primarily as an economic issue. There was no conscious effort on the part of the government in organizing for population change in Malaysia until 1966. That some kind of population policy was officially initiated at that time was a consequence of inferences arrived at by Malaysia's economic planners and political decisionmakers that real gains in economic development and economic growth in the early and mid-60s—top priorities of the regime—were being offset by the high rates of natural increase in the population. Critics pointed out that "under the Second Five-Year Development Plan (1961-65), production increased by an average of 4.5 percent a year, but because of the increase in population there was only a slight increase in per capita income during this period of moderate economic expansion. An increase of approximately 22 percent in economic output during the Plan period was largely offset by a population increase of nearly 19 percent."[2] Basically as a policy of controlling fertility, then, the Malaysian government set up the National Family Planning Board (NFPB) in 1966 and began in 1974 to establish a Population Research Unit.[3]

The absence of politics in embarking upon a population program in Malaysia is a result of the strong and centralized political party in authority that views its consolidation of political power through the development process. There was decisive executive action for fertility control once it was demonstrated that population increase was and is inimical to economic development.

"Population change" refers to changes that occur in the size, structure, composition, and distribution of any population. Population change variables include fertility and mortality, in- and out-migration, rural-urban migration, urbanization, land settlement, dependency ratios, restriction of movements of peoples, and regional development. The spectrum of population change covers the causes and consequences of these variables in question. Thus, the political effects of increased urbanization, or the anticipated increase in numbers of school-age children, can be viewed as elements of population change.

"Organizing" refers to cognizance, intelligence-gathering, reflecting, thinking, and acting upon problems of population change, and the variety of responses taken to act—by declaring a policy, debating its merits, garnering support for an issue, preparing the machinery to act, and implementing such policies. However, population change may be the result of not only so-called population policies, but also other government policies. Thus, the domain of population policies may span "non-population" policies. As an example, a decision by the Malaysian government to enhance the development of "New Villages" may in effect curtail out-migration from these areas since such development may conceivably result in more employment opportunities, etc., in these areas.[4] Policy evaluation is also part of "organizing." The more conscious the various steps in organizing, the higher the level of organization. In the Malaysian case, organizing for population change has centered around both individuals and groups as well as government and private bodies, both local and foreign. In terms of fertility control, family planning had been organized in the beginning by Family Planning Associations, which were private groups, and later on a national scale by the NFPB.

Malaysian Demographic and Socioeconomic Profiles

The Federation of Malaysia comprises thirteen states, of which eleven (formerly known as Malaya and now officially termed Peninsular Malaysia) are in the Malay peninsula and the other two (Sabah and Sarawak) are on the island of Borneo. The 1970 population was 10,810,000, with 9,181,000 in Peninsular Malaysia, 653,550 in Sabah and 976,000 in Sarawak. Of the total population, 55% were Malays and other indigenous peoples, 34.4% Chinese, 9.1% Indians and Pakistanis, and 1.5% others. In Peninsular Malaysia, 52.7% of the population were Malays, 35.8% Chinese, 10.7% Indians, and 0.8% others.[5]

Because Sabah and Sarawak present a distinct situation, and also since most of the monitored population change has been focused on Peninsular Malaysia, our discussion is primarily on the latter region. Although Sabah and Sarawak together make up more than 60% of the total area of the country, they account for only 16% of the population. It is not surprising then that the family planning program has confined its activities to Peninsular Malaysia thus far. However, this is not to imply that population density was the sole determinant of the decision to restrict the family planning program to the peninsular part of the country; there are myriad political and other factors involved in this decision.

Peninsular Malaysia has a high rate of population growth. The annual crude rate of natural increase for 1970 was 26.5 per thousand. The present rapid growth is not a new phenomenon but rather a continuation of long-term rapid growth by immigration prior to the Second World War and natural increase from sometime after the 1920s. Between the first census in 1911 and the 1957 census, the population in Malaya had increased from 2,340,000 to 6,280,000, i.e., at an annual growth rate of 3.7%. By 1973, the population had increased to 9,900,000, reflecting an annual growth rate from 1957 of 3.0%.[6]

The growth of population in the late nineteenth and early twentieth centuries was caused by the influx of immigrant Chinese and Indian labor attracted by the nascent rubber and tin industries, as well as a result of British colonial migration policies. Although this large-scale migration has stopped since the 1930s, significant effects persisted for a long time in the ethnic composition, sex ratio, and age distribution of the nation. By the present time, the population no longer shows strong evidence of immigration except in the ethnic composition.[7] What is salient, especially in political terms, is that Malaysia contains, in its Chinese community, proportionately the largest minority in Southeast Asia and is the only country in which a national minority forms the urban majority. Within the ten most populous urban areas the racial composition was 27% Malays, 57% Chinese, 13% Indians, and 2% others.[8] Or, to put it differently, "whereas 85% of the Malays live in communities of less than 10,000, only 53% of Chinese and 65% of Indians do so."[9]

The separation of the population into its three main ethnic groups in Peninsular Malaysia, and an even more complex ethnic composition pattern in Sabah and Sarawak, has determined the communal nature of the country's politics. As stated succinctly by Milne, "It dictates the pattern of the economy, has helped to shape the Constitution, and has influenced the democratic process and the party system."[10] Also, the racial factor was an important consideration in the formation of Malaysia.

Mortality levels are low, female life expectancy at birth being sixty-six years in 1970. Fertility level, however, is still high, although there has been a substantial decline since 1956. The crude birthrate in 1971 was 32.6 per thousand.[11] However, there are significant mortality and fertility differentials among the major ethnic groups, as well as between the rural and urban populations (see Table 12-1). There are also significant urban-rural differentials in the ethnic composition (see Table 12-2).[12,a]

---

[a]A more detailed account is given in Appendix A.

Table 12-1
Crude Birth Rate by Year and Race

	Malays	Chinese	Indians
1957	48.1	43.3	49.7
1960	43.3	37.5	43.4
1963	42.4	35.8	40.0
1966	41.3	33.7	36.5
1969	36.5	30.0	31.2

Source: L.J. Cho, J. Palmore, and L. Saunders, "Recent Fertility Trends in West Malaysia," *Demography* 5, 2 (1968): 742-743.

Table 12-2
Total Fertility Rate in 3 Regions

TFR	Metropolitan	Non-Metropolitan	Rural
1957-61	5170	5830	6280
1962-66	4615	4805	5775

Source: L.J. Cho, J. Palmore, and L. Saunders, "Recent Fertility Trends in West Malaysia," *Demography* 5, 2 (1968): 742-743.

While the basic problem in Malaysia is not yet one of an excessive level of population in relation to resources, the present rate of rapid population growth poses a number of socioeconomic problems. The first such problem is a rise in the youth dependency ratio. In Peninsular Malaysia, the ratio rose from 82.1% in 1957 to 85.3% in 1970.[13] Although the dependency ratio is expected to fall in the period 1971-75 and after, with declines in the rates of population growth, it will still remain high, implying the need for a continuous increase in public expenditures in health, education, and other social services, which might otherwise be diverted to expanding the productive capacity of the economy.

A second problem arising from the age composition is that the very large number of young people who are and will be maturing to reproductive age means that, even though fertility rates continue to decline as they have been, population growth will continue at a relatively high rate for several decades. Between 1970 and 1975, the number of females in childbearing age is expected to increase twice as fast as the total population, due to the age structure of the population. This underlines the serious need for efforts in family planning.

A third problem is the increase in the number of young people entering the labor force each year in search of jobs. Due largely to high growth rates in the pre-1957 period, the increase in the labor force has averaged 3.2% per year, thus adding some 625,000 new entrants into the labor force for the 1970-75 period.[14] Job creation and keeping the unemployment rate down has thus become the top priority in the government in the calculus of a population policy.

Family Planning in Peninsular Malaysia

A 1973 article by Lee, Ong and Smith entitled "Family Planning in West Malaysia: The Triumph of Economics and Health Over Politics" and a 1971 article by Ness and Ando entitled "The Politics of Population Planning in Malaysia and the Philippines" have covered extensively the historical background and current issues facing the family planning program in Malaysia. This section will rely heavily on the two articles.

Family planning in Malaya began with sporadic activities carried out in some of the states by individual physicians and nurses in conjunction with their routine duties in the 1940s.[15] The first organized and sustained efforts at family planning began in 1953, when several nurses and doctors met in Kuala Lumpur to form the first family planning association (FPA) in Malaya. A large part of the encouragement and example for the formation of this first family planning group in Malaya came from the Singapore Family Planning Association, which had been organized in 1952.

Throughout the 1950s and early 1960s, the traditional pronatalist attitude of the Malayan government toward the provision of family planning services could be described as at best tolerant, at worst hostile. It was tolerant of private activities as long as the FPAs kept a low profile; it was hostile to governmental support of family planning programs.[16] However, by 1964 government attitude had changed slightly. Khir Johari, the Minister of Agriculture, who had earlier held the Education portfolio, made a statement to the effect that the only way Malaysia could achieve self-sufficiency in essential foodstuffs within a decade was to reduce the rate of population growth.[17] This was probably the first time that a high-ranking minister had publicly expressed a concern with the population growth rate; it had come thirteen years after the formation of the first FPA. Khir Johari's concern was shared by other members of the Cabinet:

Malaysia can support more than its present population, but any increase in population must not be out of proportion to existing social and economic facilities and levels of development. The economic and social development programme of the government can be nullified unless the demographic trends are harmonized with the development programme.[18]

Although the statements seem to be fairly lukewarm in terms of the level of expressed concern, they nonetheless paved the way for the formation of a subcommittee in the Cabinet in November 1964 to study the issue of family planning. The decision reached in this subcommittee eventually led to the formation of the National Family Planning Board (NFPB).

Concomitant with the awareness of the relationship between population growth and economic development, the Malaysian government changed its position with regard to family planning practice from hostility, to tolerance, to support, and finally to sponsorship of the program. The question of interest is:

at what points along the continuum moving from a traditional pro-natalist attitude to an intermediate phase of concern over the obstacles to economic development posed by high rates of population growth, to a final phase of adopting an anti-natalist policy, did the change take place? A general outline of the process of policy formulation for family planning in the Malaysian government reveals the following steps:

1. The beginning of government interest in the population growth rates;
2. A statement by a responsible official concerned with the adverse effects on per capita economic development of high population growth rates;
3. The establishment of the Cabinet subcommittee on family planning;
4. The conducting of baseline research in the form of KAP surveys;
5. Statement of a target—a reduction in the population growth rates;
6. The establishment in the government apparatus of a family planning authority, the National Family Planning Board.

The growing awareness of the interrelationship of population growth with other problems of economic development began when the government's planning arm, specifically the Economic Planning Unit (EPU), began to be aware of the adverse effects of high population growth rates on the economic development efforts of the government. Although the EPU has roots that go back to 1952, it was not until the enlargement and reorganization in 1960-61 that it could be said to have gained the competence needed to assess accurately the impact of population growth on economic growth. Such an assessment occurred in 1962-63 with the interim evaluation of the current five-year plan. This evaluation "had the effect of sharpening the perception of the high economic costs of the nation's three-percent plus rate of population growth."

"The large-scale mobilization of natural resources for public investment under the development plans was not generating enough new jobs for the expanding labor force, but it was increasing the minimum level of public services, which produced a long-ranged commitment to rapid increases in public expenditures just to keep up with the high level of population growth."[19]

The decision to introduce public policies designed to reduce fertility was not made overnight. Up to now, Razak, the then Deputy Prime Minister, who was also in charge of rural development, had vetoed the inclusion of family planning clinics in the rural development efforts. Rapid population growth was seen as a condition that made rapid economic growth imperative, and not as a condition that had to be overcome.

The first sign of change in this "pure development" approach came when Khir Johari began to speak out in public in favor of family planning. As early as 1958 he had proclaimed that "unless the country was able to find some ways and means of raising money, we have got to do something in the form of compulsory family planning."[20] Up to 1964, Khir Johari was practically the only high-ranking government official who spoke publicly in favor of family planning. The intelligence which helped to bring about Khir Johari's early awareness of the problems of rapid population growth must have been the familiar social problems that he had been sensitized to as Minister of Education, such as the increasing burden of education expenditures on government budgets and the shortage of teachers and overcrowded schoolrooms.[b] Later, as Minister of Agriculture, he must also have realized that although the agricultural sector was expanding (land utilization was still low), it was expected that the dependency on agriculture would decrease in the 1970s. Since more than 60% of Malaysia's labor force was engaged in agricultural employment, there was the added problem of creating employment opportunities in other sectors of the economy in order to stem the expected increase in unemployment and underemployment.

By 1964, the government had completely reversed its policy.[21] Population growth had been redefined and was seen as an obstacle to economic development. The subcommittee on family planning in the Cabinet was established in November 1964. The Cabinet faced a series of limiting factors to any efforts at government involvement in the provision of family planning services. Chief among these is the significant fertility differential between the Malay and non-Malay segments of the population.[22] The main cause of this differential has been attributed to the tremendous economic disparity between the two segments of the population. For instance, the mean monthly income of Malay households in 1970 was M$179, while that of Chinese and Indian households in 1970 were M$387 and M$310 respectively.[c] Although significant changes have occurred in the structure of Malay employment, with rising shares in manufacturing, commerce, and services, nearly 70% of the employed Malays are still to be found in agriculture. These economic and occupational differentials between the two groups seemed to dictate that the government proceed gingerly with any attempt at reducing the population growth rate.

The chief activities of the subcommittee were (1) an agreement with the Ford Foundation for technical and financial assistance in the conduct of a KAP survey,[23] and (2) the commission of a study on the impact of changes in the population growth rate on the per capita economic indices.

In the middle of 1965, the subcommittee recommended to the Cabinet the creation of a national family planning board. The target would be a reduction in the rate of population growth as stated in the First Malaysia Plan. This plan,

---

[b]In addition, there is also the tendency for the "bulge" in primary schools to be transmitted to secondary schools and universities in the absence of alternative training and occupational opportunities for primary school leavers.

[c]In addition, Malay households accounted for nearly 85% of all households in the income range below M$100 in Peninsular Malaysia. The share of Chinese and Indian households in this income range was 9.6% and 4.9% respectively. In contrast, in the middle income range of M$400 to M$699, Chinese households predominated with nearly 56% of the total. Malay households constituted over 31%, and Indian households about 12% in this income range.

which was drafted in 1965 for the period 1966-1970, in anticipation of the passage of the Family Planning Bill in Parliament, stated among its objectives the need to "lay the groundwork for less rapid population growth by initiating an effective programme of family planning."[24] The projected reduction in population growth rate was stated to be from 2.7% per annum in 1970-75 to 2.2% per annum by 1980-85.

In the manner of Malaysian government agencies, little publicity was given to the establishment of the National Family Planning Board. After the subcommittee presented its recommendations to the Cabinet, the Family Planning Bill was presented to Parliament, and was passed. The NFPB was subsequently established in June 1966.[d] Whatever latent political opposition there was was apparently effectively quelled by the description of the NFPB as an organization aimed at improving the health of mothers and children. Family planning is similarly identified with the promotion of maternal and child health in government publications as well as in the mass media.[25]

Administratively speaking, the performance of the NFPB shows strong resemblance to other Malaysian governmental structures. As noted by Ness and Ando, "the family planning program is oriented to an increase in the provision of goods and services that the administrative structure is already capable of providing. The provision of goods and services, takes precedent over attempts to change values and attitudes or direct attempts to change the social and economic structure of the nation."[26] Nonetheless, there is a further need now for the NFPB's work—despite its central location in the all-important Prime Minister's Department—to be better coordinated with other agencies of government and orchestrated within the context of Malaysian development objectives.

A move toward this was effected in mid-1973 with the creation of a "Manpower and Population Division" within the Economic Planning Unit. This division is entrusted with the responsibility of looking at problems relating to population from a policy viewpoint and its activities are meant to be centralized for the purpose of better planning of current and future economic goals of the government. At the moment, its major purpose and function concern manpower planning; implementation of population policies are the responsibility of the NFPB.[e]

---

[d]The NFPB was placed directly under the Prime Minister's Department, underlining its importance. The chairman in charge was again Khir Johari, the former Minister of Education and chairman of the Cabinet subcommittee on family planning, whose early conviction in the need for a family planning program in Malaysia has earlier been discussed.

The program operation was planned to be carried out in four phases, beginning from large metropolitan areas at Phase I and expanding into the rural areas at Phases III and IV.

[e]We are thankful to Dr. Mohd. Nor Abdullah of the Malaysian Center for Development Studies for this piece of information.

Structural Aspects in Organizing for Population Change

Thus far we have been discussing Malaysian population policy in terms of fertility control. Population policies, however, as we have noted earlier, encompass a whole range of governmental policies. In the context of the Malaysian setting, such "other" policies have been regarded in various terms: explicit policies of migration, like the Malaysian Migration Fund Board's policy of promoting migration to Sabah and Sarawak,[27] are essentially economic actions. A whole range of other policies—promotion of "new growth centers," land development schemes, promotion of agro-based industries, delineation of the capital, Kuala Lumpur as Federal Territory,[28] establishment of industrial estates and free trade zones in Malacca, Penang, and elsewhere, while originating as political and economic policies, may be interpreted as distribution-of-population policies.

These policies have conflicting effects. There has been a considerable influx of rural migrants to the urban areas, but among Malay migrants this migration is associated with fertility.[29] Yet there is an overriding need to urbanize Malays in order to increase their level of socioeconomic standing so as to be on par with that of non-Malays.

As more Malays become educated and urbanized, their proclivity to migrate to urban centers increases. In turn, if employment and other economic opportunities are scarce, dissatisfaction will develop and inevitably become a source of political disaffection with the regime. Demands for new opportunities could affect governmental services if politicians decide to respect rising group expectations, to capitalize on the awareness of group differences, or to respond to potentially effective organizational activities on the part of emergent groups.[30] (See Chapter 3 in this volume.)

The issue that is raised here concerns how regimes can effectively act on the basis of societal trends and conditions to organize for population change. Population control in Malaysia via family planning may reduce an already declining birthrate so that the economic objectives of the regime may succeed. But other policies, especially those involving the "restructuring of society" and the eradication of poverty as enunciated in the New Economic Policy of the Second Malaysia Plan and the Perspective Plan which extends to the 1990s,[31] have contrary effects.

A variety of models can assist political and administrative decisionmakers in thinking and acting upon the problem of coping with (rapid) population change. Both the Lasswellian and Montgomery models may be utilized as intellectual tools and heuristic devices for problem solving in population policy appraisal. Lasswell's policy science approach should enhance policy appraisal via the interrelating of population changes with the intelligence component of public policy. "Explicit consideration of interacting elements in the demand structure is necessary if governments are to cope with rapid population change comprehensively" (see Chapter 3 in this volume; also see Chapter 4).

The setting up of the Population Unit (PU) in Malaysia signifies the integration of planning for population within development planning. In proposing its establishment, Saunders and Hardee envisioned the unit's concern with three sets of data: (1) population variables; (2) other social and economic variables of interest to planners; and (3) relationships among variables within and among these categories.[32] Centrally located within the Prime Minister's Department, the PU should also use various methodologies in carrying out its work.[33] Figure 12-1 indicates the ideal relationship of the PU to other planning agencies and data centers. In terms of preparing for administrative effects of rapid population change, the country profile analysis can become a starting point in the work of organizing the Population Unit (see Chapter 3 in this volume).[f]

The PU might conceivably be an enlarged version of the "Manpower and Population Division" of the Economic Planning Unit (EPU), although in terms of the Saunders-Hardee proposal, the unit might be formed as a separate body, taking on the "Manpower and Population Division" and broadening its terms of reference to cover all aspects of population policy. Figure 12-2 shows the present relationship of the Manpower and Population Division with other relevant policy instruments of government.

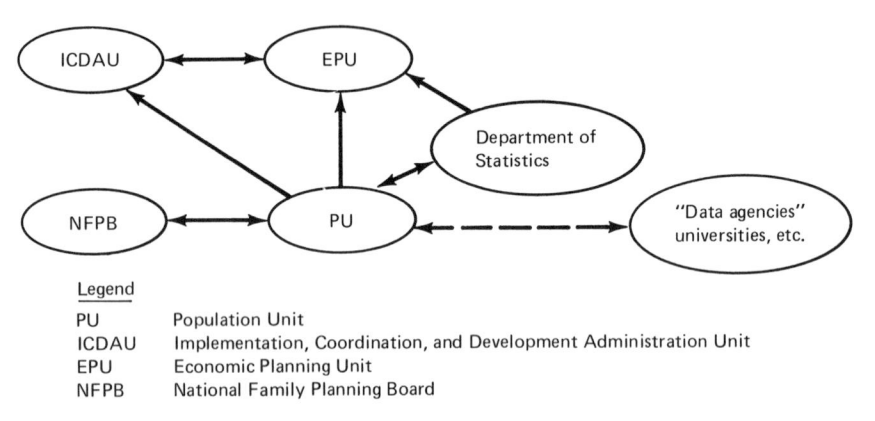

Legend
PU   Population Unit
ICDAU   Implementation, Coordination, and Development Administration Unit
EPU   Economic Planning Unit
NFPB   National Family Planning Board

The solid lines represent relationships we know to exist.
The broken lines represent probable relationships.

Figure 12-1. Structural Relationship of the Population Unit to Other Agencies

---

[f] Malaysia's current "population profile" is AHJMQ.

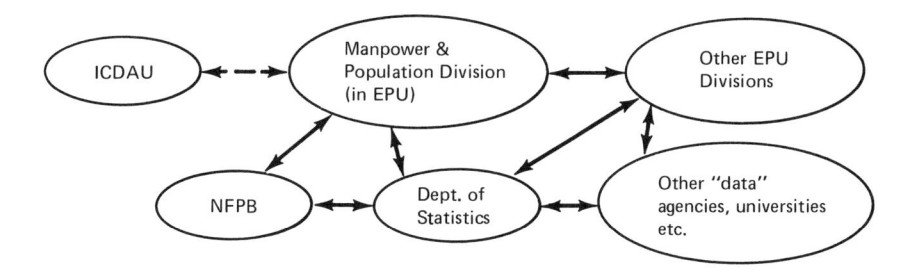

Figure 12-2. Present Structural Relationship of EPU and NFPB in Malaysian Population Planning

On the basis of data collected from the Department of Statistics, the NFPB and other sources, the PU will conduct inferential analyses and submit recommendations to the EPU and ICDAU (see Figure 12-1). Thus both the EPU and ICDAU will be able to prepare or alert administrative machinery to meet demands arising from rapid population change and improvise economic plans. Fortunately, these agencies are administratively located in the Prime Minister's Department, thus facilitating interagency coordination. In addition, we suggest an "outflow" of information to all agencies and their heads so as to "sensitize" the whole bureaucracy to the importance of the population planning element in overall development of the country.

Linkages between agencies and ministries, however, will not only occur on horizontal and vertical axes within the administrative context. In the history of family planning in Malaysia, linkages have occurred between private and public bodies and in international exchanges of technologies from bilateral and multilateral aid agencies.[3,4] We expect the "linkages" to continue, although the salience of each contact in terms of success or failure in population planning remains to be investigated.

While the success of the proposed PU as an important element in development planning remains to be seen, its establishment may serve as a model for other countries committed to population planning. Provided that the PU is given sufficient recognition and headed by the executive machinery of government, we do not envisage any problem beyond "normal" administrative or bureaucratic difficulties.[g] In the Malaysian bureaucratic context, this implies overlapping jurisdiction of agencies involved in population planning (and therefore probable interagency rivalry) and personality clashes between agency heads. These conflicts arise in spite of such agencies' location within the domain of the Prime Minister's Department, and the fact that they all report to the prime minister.

---

[g] We anticipate, above all, a shortage of personnel, such as demographers, statisticians, and other social scientists, at all levels. Research expertise, too, will be handicapped in the beginning.

In retrospect, a review of the evolution and development of population policy and the corresponding establishment of machinery to monitor population change demonstrates a high level of receptivity by Malaysia's policymakers to development administration.[35] This may not be so in the context of many other countries. In Malaysia's case, we may identify organizing for population change at the governmental level along the continuum shown in Figure 12-3.

Steps "5" and "6" are hypothetical, although parts of step "5" have occurred; nonetheless, they are expected to be ongoing soon or at about the time of this writing. The other "steps" in the continuum denote the "political and administrative conversions" in the process of organizing for population change (see Chapter 3 in this volume). The notion of "feedback" from intelligence-gathering and data analysis for population policy is of course implicit in our model.

Step 1—Recognition of need for population control: input from EPU, individual commitment and collective executive agreement, with advice from "foreign sources". KAP survey.

Step 2—Formulation of policy and corresponding legislation.

Step 3—Establishment of machinery for fertility control: the NFPB. Use of the Dept. of Statistics in intelligence-gathering, and training of personnel.

Step 4—Data collection and analysis: update of existing census data, vital registration, survey research (Family, Household, and Socioeconomic Surveys, and development of methodological competence.) Further, recommendation to set up the PU.

Step 5—Evaluation, inference, and recommendation. Review of performance by agencies, evaluated in terms of overall development performance of EPU: setting up "Manpower and Population Division"; analytical reports. Simultaneous with establishment of PU.

Step 6—More orchestrated population policy regarding migration and fertility for development.

Figure 12-3. Organizing for Population Change: Malaysia. Sources: G. Ness and H. Ando, "The Politics of Population Planning in Malaysia and the Philippines," *Journal of Comparative Administration* 3, 3 (November 1971); and L.J. Cho, J. Palmore, and L. Saunders, "Recent Fertility Trends in West Malaysia," *Demography* 5, 2 (1968).

Concluding Remarks

While organizing for population change has been regarded as important for development planning, the salience of the problem is less evident to political and administrative policymakers in terms of long-term planning and the effects of rapid population change. In the Malaysian case, even though a Population Unit has been proposed to monitor fertility and migration trends, its establishment, if realized, does not necessarily mean real gains in population and development planning. There is a likelihood that the Population Unit will be relegated to a status of just another agency of government, or that further structural changes will have to take place—either the incorporation of other bodies (say, the NFPB) within its span of authority, or its being subsumed as a major component of the EPU. Further, in a multi-ethnic country like Malaysia, population planning is rather a delicate task as any recommendation or analysis that the PU makes to the government, and the subsequent government policy, will be construed to favor one ethnic group and not the other. As stated by Montgomery, "organization is not a substitute for policy."[36] Nonetheless, the creation of the PU will mark another logical sequence in the path of organizing for population change in Malaysia.

Appendix A

Table 12A-1 shows the distribution of the population of West Malaysia by strata and race for the two censuses in 1957 and 1970.

Table 12A-1
Distribution of Population by Strata and Race, West Malaysia 1957 and 1970[a]

Strata	1957 Malay	1957 Chinese	1957 Indian	1970 Malay	1970 Chinese	1970 Indian	Avg. annual growth Malay	Chinese	Indian
Urban[b]	349,605	1,042,668	213,863	694,935	1,491,871	324,223	5.4	2.8	3.2
(percentage of urban)	21.0[c]	62.5	12.8	27.4	58.7	12.8			
Rural	2,775,869	1,291,088	482,323	3,976,939	1,639,449	612,118	2.8	1.9	1.9
(percentage of rural)	60.2	28.0	10.5	63.4	26.1	9.8			
Total	3,125,474	2,333,756	696,186	4,671,874	3,131,320	936,341	3.1	2.3	2.3

[a]1957 and 1970 census, unadjusted figures.
[b]Urban centers with more than 10,000 population.
[c]Figures do not add up because the "others" category has been left out of the table for the sake of simplicity.

Source: Adapted from Federation of Malaysia, *Mid-Term Review of the Second Malaysia Plan 1971-1975* (Kuala Lumpur: Government Printer, 1973), p. 25.

Notes

1. P.M. Blau, *The Dynamics of Bureaucracy*, 2nd edition (Chicago: The University of Chicago Press, 1965); H. Cohen, *The Demonics of Bureaucracy* (Ames, Iowa: Iowa State University Press, 1965).

2. A. Marzuki and J.Y. Peng, "Country Profile: Malaysia," The Population Council, July 1970, p. 2.

3. Federation of Malaysia, *Mid-Term Review of the Second Malaysia Plan 1971-75* (Kuala Lumpur: Government Printer, 1973), p. 209. Financed by a loan from the World Bank and a grant for technical support from UNFPA, the establishment of the population research unit (also referred to here as Population Unit) will combine with the integration of family planning and rural health services in overall population planning.

4. Information on Malaysian "New Villages" is still somewhat meager. However, its importance was emphasized with the appointment in 1972 of a Minister with Special Functions for New Villages. See also Section 16, *Mid-Term Review*, p. 7.

5. *Mid-Term Review*, pp. 23-24. These data were revised after the Post-Enumeration Survey of the 1970 Census. J. Palmore, R. Chander, and D. Fernandez had somewhat different figures in their paper, "The Demographic Situation in Malaysia," which was presented at the 1973 Population Association of America Conference.

6. K. Phang, "Economic Consequences of Population Growth," Proceedings of the Second National Seminar on the General Consequences of Population Growth (Kuala Lumpur, n.d.), pp. 50-54.

7. Palmer, et al., "Demographic Situation in Malaysia."

For treatments of demographic changes in the prewar and postwar periods, see *inter alia*: T.E. Smith, "Immigration and Permanent Settlement of Chinese and Indians in Malaya," in C.D. Cowan (ed.), *The Economic Development of Southeast Asia* (London: George Allen & Unwin, 1964); T.E. Smith, *The Background to Malaysia* (London: Oxford University Press, 1963); T. Shamsul, "Indonesian Labour in Malaya," *Kajian Ekonomi Malaya* 2 (June 1965); K.S. Sandhu, *Indians in Malaya–Immigration and Settlement–1786-1957* (Cambridge: Cambridge University Press, 1969); Y.L. Lee, *Population and Settlement in Sarawak* (Detroit: The Cellar Book Shop, 1970).

8. P. Tennant, "The Decline of Elective Local Government in Malaysia," *Asian Survey* 12 (April 1973); 347-365.

9. M.L. Rogers, "The Politicization of Malay Villages: National Integration or Disintegration?" *Comparative Politics* (January, 1975, forthcoming).

10. R.S. Milne, *Government and Politics in Malaysia* (Boston: Houghton Mifflin, 1967), p. 3. Distribution of population in Peninsular Malaysia has resulted in the formation of physical ethnic blocs. See K.J. Ratnam, *Communalism and the Political Process in Malaya* (Kuala Lumpur: University of Malaya Press, 1965), p. xii and Chapter I.

11. Federation of Malaysia, Mid-Term Review.

12. See V. Ponniah-Heussner, "An Appraisal of Population Policy to Affect Fertility in West Malaysia," paper prepared for Population Policy Seminar, Harvard University, 1974.

13. Federation of Malaysia, Mid-Term Review, p. 26. Youth dependency ratio here is defined as the ratio of the population below age 15 to the population in the working age group of 15 to 64.

14. Ibid., p. 27.

15. W. Hanna, *Family Planning in Malaysia: Program and Prospects*, American Universities Field Staff Report, 1971, p. 4. The objective of these activities was to improve the health conditions among mothers and children.

16. For example, the then Minister of Health and Social Welfare was quoted as saying: "the Alliance Government do not support family planning." E. Lee, M. Ong, and T.E. Smith, "Family Planning in West Malaysia: The Triumph of Economics and Health over Politics," in T.E. Smith (ed.), *The Politics of Family Planning in The Third World* (London: George Allen & Unwin, 1973), p. 266.

17. Ibid., p. 268.

18. Ibid., p. 268-9.

19. G. Ness and H. Ando, "The Politics of Population Planning in Malaysia and the Philippines," Journal of Comparative Administration Vol. 3:3, November 1971, p. 300.

20. E. Lee, et al., op. cit., p. 266.

21. Insomuch as Malaysia had a population policy at that time, it was a policy that, like so many other Southeast Asian countries in that period, was implicitly pro-natalist. This was the finding made by Dr. Lyle Saunders, a Ford Foundation adviser to the Economic Planning Unit in Malaysia. G. Ness and H. Ando, "The Politics of Population Planning in Malaysia and the Philippines," *Journal of Comparative Administration* 3,3 (November 1971): 300.

22. See E. Lee, M. Ong, and T.E. Smith, "Family Planning in West Malaysia: The Triumph of Economics and Health Over Politics," in T.E. Smith (ed.), *The Politics of Family Planning in the Third World* (London: George Allen & Unwin, 1973), pp. 256-290.

23. The KAP Survey involved a team of three American scholars from the University of Michigan in cooperation with local assistants and the government department of statistics. It included interviews with 3,850 married women, aged 15 to 45, in each of the three major regions: urban, small town, and rural.

Philip Hauser and John Cleland, among others, have cautioned against placing too much reliance on the results of KAP surveys as indicators of motivation. However, in the absence of other data, the KAP results in Malaysia provided the sole information available about the actual and potential clientele and the best way to reach them as a guide to policy development. See P. Hauser, "Family Planning and Population Programs: A Book Review Article," *Demography* 4,1 (1967); J. Cleland, "A Critique of KAP Studies and Some Suggestions for their Improvement," *Studies in Family Planning* 4,4 (1973).

24. Ness and Ando, "Politics of Population Planning," p. 275.

25. E. Lee, M. Ong, and T.E. Smith, "Family Planning in West Malaysia."

26. Ness and Ando, "Politics of Population Planning," p. 308.

27. Federation of Malaysia, *Second Malaysia Plan 1971-75* (Kuala Lumpur: Government Printer, 1971), p. 107: "The Board, since its inception in 1966, has arranged for the transfer of 5,000 workers, plus their dependents, mostly to meet the Sabah plantation industry's requirements." In the *Mid-Term Review of the Plan*, p. 108, the economic nature of migration is underscored by the statement: "The government will promote migration to areas with large economic potential."

28. D. Harner, "Kuala Lumpur," in D.C. Rowat (ed.), *The Government of Federal Capitals* (Toronto: University of Toronto Press, 1973).

29. S.E. Khoo, "Development Planning and Internal Migration, West Malaysia, 1957-1970," paper prepared for Population Policy Seminar, Harvard University, 1974.

30. J. Guyot, "Creeping Urbanism and Political Development in Malaysia," in R. Daland (ed.), *Comparative Urban Research* (Beverly Hills: Sage Publications, 1969); M.L. Rogers, "Patterns of Leadership in a Rural Malay Community," *Asian Survey*, forthcoming.

31. *Second Malaysia Plan*. See also H. Stockwin, "A Racial Balance Sheet," *Far Eastern Economic Review*, December 3, 1973, pp. 140-43.

Research is in progress to study the relationship between migration and its effects at the Center for Policy Research, Universiti Sains Malaysia and of the University of Malaya. At the Department of Statistics, Amos Hawley and Charles Hirschman are working on labor force characteristics and internal migration, while D. Fernandez is working on fertility. Manpower and household surveys are being carried out by the Economic Planning Unit. K.L. Chee and others at the University of Michigan are involved in similar research, not to mention the writers and collaborators of this chapter.

32. L. Saunders and J.G. Hardee, *Rationale and Suggestions for Establishing a Population Planning Unit: Malaysia* (paper prepared for the Government of Malaysia, 1972), p. 2. This is a rather comprehensive report and its coverage of the Planning Unit's mission is quite thorough.

33. A "gestalt" approach may be utilized in population planning. Zakaria Haji-Ahmad, "Demogenics in a Multi-ethnic Society: A Processual Policy Science Primer for Malaysia," paper prepared for Population Policy Seminar, Harvard University, 1974.

34. For an account of "linkages," see J. Montgomery, "Science Policy and Development Programs: Organizing Science for Government Action," *World Development* 2, 4 and 5 (April-May 1974): 65.

35. J. Montgomery and M. Esman, *Development Administration in Malaysia*, a report presented to the Government of Malaysia (Kuala Lumpur: Government Printer, 1966). See also M. Esman, *Administration and Development in Malaysia* (Ithaca: Cornell University Press, 1972).

36. Montgomery, "Science Policy and Development Programs," p. 69.

Index

Index

Abdullahi, Khalifah, 195
Abortion, and fertility, 19
Administrative decentralization, 83
Administrative infrastructure, 51, 271
Administrative knowledge, 16
Advantage, "rule of," 49
Africa, 82
Aggregation, 52
Agriculture/industry tradeoffs, 101
Ahmad, Zakaria Haji, 12
Ahmed, Mohammed, 195
Algeria, 100, 101
Alonson, William, 185
Andhra, India, 101
Ando, H., 285, 288
Appraisal, 130-131
Appraisal, India, 258-261
Area-based services, 7, 104, 105
Area/density relationships, 103
Argentina, 101, 103n, 106n
Attributes, as categories, 28

Balamoan, G.A., 10
Bangladesh, 100, 101
Barbour, K.M., 202
Barth, Heinrich, 174
Berelian, Bernard, 85
Bergman, Elihu, 264
"Big Push" hypothesis, 37
Bogota, 28
Bogue, Donald, 24, 79
Bolivia, 103n, 106n
Brasilia, 84
Brazil, 11, 67, 70, 84, 103n, 245-251
Bucharest, 145
Burma, 100, 101
Burundi, 103n

Canada, 102
Capacity, administrative, 106
CELADE, 27
Central African Republic, 106n
Ceylon. *See* Sri Lanka
Chad, 106n

Chin, Siew-Nyat, 12
China, 101, 103n, 106n, 110
"Choice budgets," 52
Christaller, Walter, 151
Civic order, 117
Civil servants, as interest group, 157
Civil subvention, in Sudan, 212
Claim. *See* demands
"Client-based" services, 7, 104, 105
Colombia, 101
Committee on Population Growth and Family Planning, India, 253
"Conceptual map," 120-122, 132
Congo (Brazz.), 103n, 158
Content analysis, 139
Correlations, of fertility, 25; policy relevance of, 16
Costa Rica, 108
Country profiles, 105-110
Crisis change, 95
Cross-sectional analysis, 55
Cyprus, 101

Dahomey, 106n
Davis, Kingsley, 24
Decision rules, 48-50, 271
Decision seminars, 133-135
Demand conversion, 106
Demand-supply relationship, 16; in fertility, 23; in migration, 81; in public services, 95
Demands, 124
Demographic transition, 23-25
Deprivations, 127
Deviant case analysis, 55
Differential fertility hypothesis, 27-36
Disaggregation, 54, 141
"Disequilibria," 73-75
Disequilibrium theory, 80
"Distant Early Warning" signals, 98, 111
Distributive justice hypothesis, of fertility decline, 36-37

301

Eastern European, 6
Economic Planning Unit, 286
Economic variables, in population change, 101
Education and fertility, 19, 29-36
Education, Nigerian, demands on, 182-183
Egypt, 103n
Egyptians, in Sudan, 209-210
El Salvador, 103n, 144
England, 100
Enke, S., 257
Equity, "rule of," 49
Ethnic composition and migration, 66
Ethnic demands, 102
Ethnic groups, Kenya, 156

Family allowances, 54
Family Planning Association, Malaysia, 285
Family planning clinics, 142
Family planning controversy, 140
Family planning program, stages, 144-146
Family Planning Services and Population Research Act, 269, 273
Federation of Employers, 158
Fertility, correlates of, 15
Fertility hypotheses, 22-36, 46, 239
Fertility, structural determinants, 247
Finkle, Jason L., 259
Food rationing, 85
Food and Agricultural Organization, 185
Ford Foundation, 287
France, 67n
Fulani, 172

Gabon, 106n
Gambia, 175
Germany, 84
Ghana, 106n, 175
Goodrich, Carter, 149
Grove, David, 151
Growth center policies, 85
Growth zones, Nigerian, 176-179
Guatemala, 106n

Gugler, J., 82
Guinea, 106n

Haiti, 101, 103n
Harris, John, 82
Hausa, 172
Heeren, H.J., 234
Hong Kong, 103n
Housing, 81
Huszar, Laszlo, 151

Ibadan, 186
Ibo, 172
Ilchman, Warren, 5, 13, 140, 274
Illegal immigrants, Sudan, 205-206
Incentive systems, decision rules for, 50
Incentives, 13, 26, 44-45, 127; in India, 253-265
Income policies, 82-83
Incremental change, 95-99
India, 12, 24, 39, 70, 84, 103n, 143, 253-265
Indonesia, 11, 70, 85, 106n, 108, 142, 143, 145, 217-239
Indulgences, 127
Industrial location, 84
Inputs, indicators of change in, 98
Intelligence structures and functions, 122-124
Interest groups, 158
Intermediate cities, 155
International Bank for Reconstruction and Development, 179
International Demographic Congress of 1878, 127
Internal migration and immigration policies, 87
Interventions, preferential, 86
Interventions, public, 38, 40-43, 123
Iran, 106n
Iraq, 100
Israel, 67, 101, 106n
Ivory Coast, 106n

Japan, 101
Java, 100, 218

Jos plateau, 174

Kachiragan, M., 262
Kaduna, 186
KANU, 158
KAP. *See* "Knowledge–Attitudes–Practices"
Kenya, 9, 70, 100, 103n, 108, 149-161
Keyfitz, Nathan, 21
Khanna project, 24
Khir Johari, 286-287, 288n
Knowledge–Attitudes–Practices surveys (KAP), 15, 28, 287
Korea, 100, 145
Korten, David C., 6, 7
Kothari, Davendra K., 13

Lagos, 186
Lasswell, Harold D., 3, 4, 12, 13, 80, 258, 270, 272, 289
Lead time, 142
Lebanon, 103n
Lebon, 201
Lee, Everett, 79
Lerda, Maria, 10
Levels of analysis, 53
Liberia, 103n
Liu, Korbin, 13
Local centers, 152
Local participation, 159
Longitudinal analysis, 55

Mabogunje, A.L., 174
Maffey, Sir John, 210
Mahdi, 195
Maintenance of service, 96
Makinwa, Paulina K., 9
Malaria control, 108
Malaysia, 12, 33, 67, 70, 102, 103n, 106n, 281-294
Malaysia Migration Fund Board, 289
Mali, 106n
"Malthusian Trap," 10
Maranhao, Brazil, 243
Marginal analysis, 55
Marginal utility, of children, 26

Marginalism, 54
Market centers, 152
Marketing Boards, Nigerian, 178-181
Marriage age, 238
Mata, Brazil, 244
Maternal and Child Health Services, 272, 276
Mauritius, 39, 103n
Meio-Norte, Brazil, 243
Mexico, 70, 100, 101, 108
Migrants, characteristics, 223, 230
Migration, 8
Migration/fertility relationship, 217-239
Migration, Indonesian, 20
Migration, internal, 65-90
Migration, Kenya, 156
Migration, Malaysia, 289
Migration policies, 65-66, 68
Migration, Sudan, 193-195
Migration theories, 79-81
Ministry of Population, 13
Modernization, and fertility, 38
Mombasa, 153
Montgomery, John D., 6, 7, 289
Moshavim, 184
Multiplier effects, of migration policies, 88

Nairobi, 153
National Center for Family Planning Services, U.S., 13, 269, 272, 276
National Family Planning Coordinating Board, Indonesia, 238
National Youth Corps, Nigeria, 185
Nehru, Pandet, 257
Nepal, 108, 111
Ness, G., 285, 288
New towns, 85
New villages, Malaysia, 282
Nicaragua, 103n, 144
Nigeria, 9, 70, 171-187
Northeast Brazil, 242-245
North Korea, 106n

Oey, Mayling, 10
Office of Economic Opportunity, 276

Omdurman, 197
"Optimal ignorance," 52-53

Pakistan, 101
Panama, 100, 103n
Pass laws, 85
Performance, indicators of change on, 98
Perlman, Janice, 149
Philippines, 143
Piaui, Brazil, 243
Planned Parenthood, 273
Planning, 96
Pohlman, E., 257
Policy analysis framework, 270
Policy instruments, for migration, 8
Policy knowledge, 16
Policy outcomes, 4, 122-132
Policy sciences, defined, 3, 119-120
Political economy model, 18
Political science, vs. policy science, 19
Population growth, consequences of, 96
Population planning unit, 7, 104, 111-113, 145, 281
Population policies, classification of, 40-43; defined, 117
Port Harcourt, 174
Prado, Caio, Jr., 241
Prediction of demand, 99-104
Prescription, 129
Primate cities, 152
"Primus," 72-73
Production function, analogy to policy, 48
Projections, 105-110
Promotion, 129
Public order, 117
Public services, 81

Quality of life. *See* values
Quota systems, 86

Raffles, Sir Thomas, 218
Razak, Tun Abdul, 286
Regional development, 84
REPECITA (Five-Year Plan, Indonesia), 218, 220

Repetto, R., 262
Resources, political, 27, 47, 128
Rhodesia, 102
Rio de Janeiro, 245
Rogers, Everett, 50, 257
"Routine" population policies, 39
Rumania, 106n
Rural growth centers, 9, 152, 154
Rural-rural migration, 173-175
Rural-urban migration, Nigeria, 171-173

Sao Paulo, 245
Sector resources, 271
Sertao, Brazil, 243
Simulation, population policy, 46-47
Singapore, 6, 39, 100, 106n
Slatin, Sir Rudolf von, 198-201
Social class, and migration, 66
Social context analysis, 126
Social experimentation, 14, 44, 45
Social interaction model, 124
Social process model, 14
Social science technologies, 55
Social Security Act, 276
Soja, E.W., 154
Sokoto, 173
South Africa, 67, 85, 103n
South Korea, 70
Sri Lanka, 39, 100, 101, 103n, 106n
Srinivasan, K., 262
Sterilization, India, 253, 262
Stouffer, S., 80
Sudan, 10, 103n, 106n, 193-214
SUDENE. *See* Brazil
Switzerland, 103n
Syria, 106n

Taiwan, 44, 100, 101, 103n
Tanzania, 103n, 108
"Target groups," 5, 15, 16, 51-52, 54
"Tasks," of policy making, 3-4
Terai, 108
Thailand, 70, 101
Thomas, Brinley, 87
Threshold hypothesis, of fertility decline, 25-27
Todaio, Michael, 82

Togo, 158
Town planning, 150
Tracer analysis, 55
Trade-off choices, 55
Transmigration policy, 11
Tunisia, 101
Turkey, 103n

United States, 13, 103n, 109
United States census, 123
United States, family planning in, 269-279
United States, population growth in, 96
Universal Declaration of Human Rights, 117
Urban centers, 152
Urban-rural flows, 100
Urban-rural ratio, Brazil, 246
Urban services, Nigerian, 185
Uruguay, 101
USSR, 103n

Vagabonds Ordinance (1905), Sudan, 204
Values, 80, 117-118, 125; used in appraisal, 131-132
Vasectomy, 13
Venezuela, 101, 106n
Vietnam, 67

Weiner, Myron, 8, 10
Wescott, Clay, 9
Wingate, Sir Reginald, 197-201
World Population Conference, 145

"Xenos," 70-72

Yoruba, 171, 172
Yugoslavia, 103n

Zaire, 103n, 106n
Zero population growth, 17
Zoning regulations, 67

About the Contributors

Zakaria Haji Ahmad is a candidate for the Ph.D. at the Massachusetts Institute of Technology on a National University of Malaysia fellowship. He has taught at the University of Science, Malaysia, and the University of Malaya and has also served in the Malaysian Prime Minister's Department and the Foreign Service.

George Balamoan is a senior lecturer in Zambia at the Evelyn Hane College and the National Institute of Public Administration; he is also a fellow at the Harvard Center for Population Studies.

Siew-Nyat Chin is a graduate student from Malaysia in the Department of Population Sciences, Harvard University.

David C. Korten is a visiting associate professor at the Harvard Graduate School of Business Administration. He has headed a research team studying family planning program management in Central America and serves as a consultant on population program management to the Ford Foundation, the International Committee on the Management of Population Programmes, and the Instituto Centroamericano de Administration de Empresas.

Devendra K. Kothari is a lecturer in the Department of Geography and an associate in the Centre for Population Studies, University of Udaipur, Udaipur (Raj.), India.

Maria Helen T. Henriques Lerda is a member of the Committee on the Comparative Fertility Analysis of the International Union for the Scientific Study of Population. She is a doctoral candidate in the Department of Population Sciences at Harvard University.

Korbin Liu is a doctoral candidate at the Harvard School of Public Health. He was formerly regional program director of the U.S. National Center for Family Planning Services.

Paulina Koroworola Makinwa is a doctoral candidate at the Harvard School of Public Health. She is the author of *A Modern Geography of Ghana* (London: Macmillan, 1971).

Mayling Oey received the M.S. from the Harvard School of Public Health in 1974. She is a research associate at the Institute for Economic and Social Research, Faculty of Economics, University of Indonesia.

Roger Revelle was science advisor to the Secretary of the Interior in 1962. In 1965 he was named the Richard Saltonstall Professor of Population Policy and Director of the Harvard Center for Population Studies. He was chairman of the National Academy of Sciences Panel, which produced *Rapid Population Growth: Consequences and Policy Implications* in 1971.

Clay Wescott is a candidate for the Ph.D. in the African Studies Program at Boston University.

About the Editors

Warren Ilchman, a former research associate at the Center for Population Studies at Harvard University, is now Dean of the College of Liberal Arts at Boston University. He is a coauthor of *The Political Economy of Change* (Berkeley: University of California Press, 1969).

Harold D. Lasswell is a research associate at the Center for Population Studies at Harvard. He is Ford Foundation Professor of Law and Political Science, Emeritus, Yale University. His most recent book is *A Preview of the Policy Sciences* (New York: American Elsevier, 1971).

John D. Montgomery is professor of public administration at Harvard University. He is the author of *Technology and Civic Life: Making and Implementing Development Decisions* (Cambridge: MIT Press, 1974).

Myron Weiner is professor and chairman of the Department of Political Science at the Massachusetts Institute of Technology. He is a coeditor of *Studies in Electoral Politics in the Indian States*, 4 vols. (Delhi: Manohar Book Service, 1974).